The Handbook of
Insurance-Linked Securities

For other titles in the Wiley Finance series
please see www.wiley.com/finance

The Handbook of
Insurance-Linked Securities

Edited by

Pauline Barrieu and Luca Albertini

A John Wiley and Sons, Ltd., Publication

This edition first published 2009
© 2009 John Wiley & Sons Ltd
Chapters 6, 7, 10, 11, 14, 16, 20, 23 and 25 – copyright details are given in the footnote on the chapter cover pages.

Registered office
John Wiley & Sons Ltd, The Atrium, Southern Gate, Chichester, West Sussex, PO19 8SQ, United Kingdom

For details of our global editorial offices, for customer services and for information about how to apply for permission to reuse the copyright material in this book please see our website at www.wiley.com.

Library of Congress Cataloging-in-Publication Data

The handbook of insurance-linked securities / edited by Pauline Barrieu, Luca
Albertini.
    p. cm. — (Wiley finance series)
  Includes bibliographical references and indexes.
  ISBN 978-0-470-74383-6 (cloth : alk. paper)   1. Risk (Insurance)
2. Securities. I. Albertini, Luca.   II. Barrieu, Pauline.
  HG8054.5.H363 2009
  332.63′2—dc22   2009019337

A catalogue record for this book is available from the British Library.

Typeset in 10/12pt Times by Aptara Inc., New Delhi, India
Printed in Great Britain by Antony Rowe Ltd, Chippenhan, Wiltshire

Contents

About the Contributors

Insa Adena heads the Advanced Risk Intermediation team at Allianz SE. This team was created in 2007 to develop innovative solutions for capital management and insurance risk transfer on behalf of Allianz SE and Group subsidiaries, with a focus on capital market-oriented structures. Prior to her current role, Insa was a senior member of the Group Treasury & Corporate Finance team at Allianz SE. Before joining Allianz in 2002, she worked for seven years in the Structured Finance and M&A departments of JPMorgan in London.

Luca Albertini is Chief Executive Officer of Leadenhall Capital Partners, an asset management company dedicated to insurance linked investments strategies. Luca has over 16 years of securitisation experience, having worked at Citibank, GE Capital, Credit Suisse First Boston and at Swiss Re, where he become responsible for the European Insurance Linked Securities team.

Pauline Barrieu is a Reader (Associate Professor) at the London School of Economics. She has two PhDs in Mathematics and Finance. Her research interests are mainly on the study of problems at the interface between finance and insurance, in particular ILS. She also works on quantitative methods for risk measurement and robust decision taking, with applications in finance and environmental economics.

Jean-Luc Besson is a Fellow of the French Institute of Actuaries, holds a PhD in Mathematics and is Chief Risk Officer of SCOR Group and a member of the Group Executive Committee. He has served as a Professor of Mathematics and as Senior Vice President of Research, Statistics and Information Systems at the FFSA (Fédération Française des Sociétés d'Assurance – the Federation of French Insurance Companies).

Adam Blakemore is a partner in the Tax department at Cadwalader, Wickersham and Taft LLP's London practice. He advises on the taxation aspects of a broad range of financing, restructuring and corporate transactions, including the taxation of credit and insurance-linked instruments, financial products and derivatives.

Shlomo Boehm is an associate at Cadwalader, Wickersham & Taft LLP. Shlomo's practice covers a broad range of federal income tax matters, including with respect to derivatives and financial product development, structured finance transactions, investment fund structuring, medium-term note programs, cross-border lending transactions and insurance-linked securities. Shlomo graduated from Ner Israel Rabbinical College in 1999 and from Columbia Law School, where he was a Harlan Fiske Stone Scholar, in 2003.

Ben Brookes originally joined RMS's Analytical Services team in 2004, having previously run a website design and development company, offering content management systems to educational establishments. Ben became manager of the Analytical Services group at RMS in the international region in 2005, providing consultative services to clients to assess their catastrophe risk exposure, and also supporting RMS's work on insurance-linked securities. As a part of this role, Ben managed RMS's graduate training programme in 2005 and 2006. In October 2006, Ben led the creation of RiskMarkets, a new practice within RMS Consulting, with the objective of aiding the rapid growth in the ILS market, as the sector grew following the events of 2004 and 2005 and demand for third party modelling services increased with more frequent cat bond issuance. In this role, Ben has led a significant number of ground-breaking cat bond projects and has worked on more than 20 insurance-linked security engagements, covering structural aspects, risk analysis, rating support, investor marketing and post-event calculation services. Ben has a first class Masters degree in Engineering Mathematics from the University of Bristol.

Sylvain Coriat is the head of Life Operations of AXA Cessions (i.e. the entity in charge of implementing the risk transfer decision for all AXA entities – be it through reinsurance or a capital market solution). As such, he manages the Life reinsurance flows of the AXA group, supports all AXA entities in the pricing of their products and supervises the underwriting and claims management processes of AXA at the group level. Sylvain holds an MSc in Engineering from Ecole Centrale Paris, an MSc in Finance and Economics from the London School of Economics and an MBA from INSEAD. He is a Fellow of the French Institute of Actuaries.

Guy Coughlan is Managing Director and Global Head of LifeMetrics and ALM Advisory within J.P. Morgan's Pension Solutions Group. As a specialist in ALM and risk, Guy has been involved in advising corporations, pension funds and insurers on strategic risk management, asset-liability management and capital structure. For the past three years he has been focusing on pension ALM as part of the Pension Solutions Team and led the development of LifeMetrics, an open-source platform for longevity risk management that includes longevity indices. Guy joined J.P. Morgan in 1994, initially within the Fixed Income Research department. Here he worked on projects involving optimal investment strategies, the development of RiskMetrics and built J.P. Morgan's FourFifteen risk analysis tool. In 1996 he moved to head the newly formed Risk Management Products group, which was later spun off from J.P. Morgan as The RiskMetrics Group. In 1998 he founded J.P. Morgan's ALM Advisory team. Prior to joining J.P. Morgan his previous experience includes working for a major oil company. Guy holds a BSc (Honors) degree from the University of Western Australia, a DPhil (PhD) in physics from Oxford University in the UK and an MBA. He is a member of the editorial board of the *Journal of Corporate Treasury Management*.

Nicola Dondi is an analyst in the Insurance Financing Group, Investment Banking Division, of Goldman Sachs International in London. Nicola holds a degree in Finance from Bocconi University, Milan, and a Masters in International Affairs from the Institut d'Etudes Politiques de Paris. Nicola has executed a number of insurance-related financing transactions, including the first ever sidecar by a Lloyds of London insurer, Panther Re for Hiscox plc, a $1bn catastrophe bond shelf programme for Glacier Re and a $400m Catastrophe Loan for Hannover Re. Nicola is also involved in asset– liability management transactions for European life insurers, particularly in the context of risk management and asset optimisation, and on M&A transactions involving insurance companies in Europe.

Jennifer Donohue is qualified as a barrister and as a solicitor. She is a partner and leads the transactional and regulatory insurance and reinsurance team of Simmons & Simmons, London. Her career has included advising, for a number of years, the UK Government on negotiation, drafting and implementing of the Insurance Single Market Directives. She advises on corporate and structuring aspects for insurance groups and solvency and forensic issues for life and non-life insurance companies. Jennifer advises regularly on insurance-linked securities and the dividing line between credit default swaps and other capital market instruments and insurance.

Emmanuel Durousseau is a fellow of the Institut des Actuaires. He began his insurance career in 1999 at MMA in Toronto, joining SCOR in 1994 as an underwriter and pricing actuary in the Alternative Risk Transfer department. In 1999, he became Managing Director at Commercial Risk Capital Markets, acting as an actuary/quantitative analyst in the Weather Derivative and Integrated Products division. Since 2005, he has been Retrocession Manager of SCOR.

Michael Eakins is an Executive Director in the Insurance Financing Group of Goldman Sachs and a Fellow of the Institute of Actuaries. Michael has executed a number of insurance-related financing transactions, including the first ever sidecar by a Lloyd's of London insurer – Panther Re for Hiscox plc, a $1bn cat bond shelf programme for Glacier Re and a €400m embedded value securitisation for Bank of Ireland. Michael is also involved in asset–liability management transactions for European life Insurers – particularly in the context of risk management and asset optimisation. Michael has previously spoken at industry conferences on the subject of insurance securitisation.

Matthew Feig is a senior associate in the New York office of the international law firm of Cadwalader, Wickersham & Taft LLP. His practice is concentrated in structured finance, corporate finance and corporate law. He has particular expertise in risk-linked securities and nontraditional structured finance products. He represents global investment banks, major reinsurance companies, large public and private companies and institutional investors in connection with securities, commercial and acquisition finance transactions. Mr Feig received a BFA from New York University and a JD from Columbia Law School, where he was a three-time Harlan Fiske Stone Scholar and a Michael Sovern Scholar.

James Frazier is a partner in the New York office of the international law firm of Cadwalader Wickersham & Taft LLP. He specialises in the area of ERISA and employee benefits, with a large part of his practice devoted to advising clients on the application of ERISA's fiduciary standards and prohibited transaction provisions to transactional and regulatory activities. This includes counseling financial services firms regarding the structure of investment vehicles and products offered to employee benefit plans, and the provision of investment management and brokerage services. He earned his BA from the University of North Carolina, his JD from the University of Arkansas School of Law, and an LLM in Taxation and Certificate in Employee Benefits Law, as well as an LLM in Labor Law, from the Georgetown University Law Center.

Harish Gohil is a senior director within the European insurance team of Fitch Ratings, based in London. He joined the agency in October 2002, and is responsible for overseeing a team of analysts covering a broad geographical range of life and non-life insurers within EMEA. He also heads up Fitch's EMEA Life Insurance analysis and ratings. One of Harish's key responsibilities is coordinating the analysis and ratings of European insurance-linked securities (ILS), liaising closely with colleagues in the US and in Structured Finance. Prior to joining Fitch, Harish was at Prudential plc, where he was one of a small central team of senior actuaries supporting the actuarial director. His actuarial experience in the industry includes product pricing and profitability, statutory valuation reporting, financial reporting, capital management and with-profits issues. Harish is a graduate of the London School of Economics. He is a qualified actuary, holding the professional designation Fellow of the Institute of Actuaries.

Guillaume Gorge works as AXA Property & Casualty Chief Risk Officer. He was previously Deputy CEO of AXA Cessions, the internal reinsurer of AXA. He graduated from ENSAE Paris Tech and is a member of the French Institute of Actuaries. He has written various papers on reinsurance, catastrophe risks, climate change and risk management. He lectures on reinsurance, securitisation and risk management at ENSAE.

Jay Green is a Vice President in the Capital Markets Insurance Solutions group of Swiss Re, specialising in the origination and structuring of insurance-linked securities, derivatives and related products. Jay joined Swiss Re in 2001 and has been structuring insurance-linked capital market products for six years. He holds a BBA in Finance from the University of Wisconsin.

Dominik Hagedorn holds an MSc in Financial Economics from Maastricht University. Dominik is an analyst with Munich Re's Risk Trading Unit, which he joined in May 2007. He is responsible for market research and company analysis.

Katharina Hartwig has worked, since 2002, in Group Legal Services of Allianz SE and advises, as senior legal counsel, on insurance-linked securitisation transactions of Allianz SE and subsidiaries. In 2007/2008 she was seconded for six months to the World Economic Forum where she was project manager for the Forum's project on the Convergence of Insurance and Capital Markets. Before joining Allianz, she was an associate in the M&A practice of Shearman & Sterling in Düsseldorf and Paris.

Cameron Heath is a Director of Standard & Poor's Insurance Ratings group in London. Cameron is the lead analyst of insurance-linked transactions in Europe, with particular emphasis on the non-life sector. He is also the Global Head of Non-Life Reserving for Insurance Ratings and a member of the Run-off Payment Assessment (RPA) team. Cameron is a Fellow of the Institute of Actuaries and holds a degree in Accountancy and Finance. He joined Standard & Poor's in June 2005, having spent ten years working in the UK insurance sector, largely in the London market.

Christian Heigl is a non-life actuary with Munich Re's Risk Trading unit. Amongst his duties is the modeling and pricing of ILS products as well as Munich Re's internal and external retrocession pricing. He joined Munich Re in 1999 as Casualty actuary performing different pricing, reserving and modeling tasks. Before starting in the Risk Trading unit he was working in the Corporate Underwriting department as project leader for the development of pricing and reserving tools as well as for Munich Re's central underwriting platform. Christian was born in 1971 near Munich and studied mathematics and computer science at the Technische Universität München. He holds a PhD in mathematics and has been a member of the German Actuarial Association (DAV) since 2003.

Oliver Iliffe is an associate in the Tax department at Cadwalader, Wickersham and Taft LLP's London practice. Oliver has advised on the UK taxation aspects of offshore catastrophe bond issuances. He also advises on the UK taxation aspects of debt securitisations, cross-border debt finance transactions, repo financing and corporate debt restructurings.

Douglas J. Lambert is a Vice President in the Insurance Products team within Morgan Stanley's Structured Solutions Group, focusing on bringing alternative capital sources to insurance risk concentrations. Specifically, he specialises in structuring catastrophe bonds, sidecars and other insurance-linked capital market products. He works with both life and non-life insurance risks and he has experience with captive insurer formation in domestic and foreign domiciles. Prior to joining Morgan Stanley in 2006, Mr Lambert worked at Citigroup in derivatives and structured products, concentrating on structured credit and interest rate and currency derivatives used in corporate risk management. He holds an AB in economics from Princeton University.

James Langston is an associate in the New York office of the international law firm of Cadwalader, Wickersham & Taft LLP. Mr Langston's practice is concentrated in the area of corporate law. Mr Langston represents large corporate entities, global investment banks, major reinsurance companies and private equity funds and their portfolio companies. He received a BA from the University of North Carolina and his JD from the University of North Carolina School of Law.

Kirsty Maclean is a lawyer, formerly practising in the transactional insurance and reinsurance team of international law firm Simmons & Simmons in London. She advises clients regularly on a wide range of transactions, in particular mergers and acquisitions, advisory work in respect of authorisations and prudential regulation, setting up insurance companies and offshore captives as well as corporate reorganisations and restructurings. Kirsty has a particular interest in the development of insurance-linked securities and has advised on a number of derivative structures and spoken on the point at conferences in London. Kirsty has also spent time in the capital markets team of Simmons & Simmons, advising on a range of debt and equity capital market issuances. Kirsty is a non-practising attorney of the High Court of Cape Town and was a lawyer with a top South African commercial firm before joining Simmons & Simmons. She graduated from the University of Cape Town with a Bachelor of Arts (psychology) and a Bachelor of Laws.

Chris Madsen is the Group Vice President of AEGON NV in The Hague, the Netherlands. A Danish and American citizen, he has over 18 years of experience in the re(insurance) and pension industry. He completed his Masters in Financial Engineering at Princeton University, USA, and he is an Associate of the Society of Actuaries and a Chartered Financial Analyst. He started his professional career in New York with PricewaterhouseCoopers, and subsequently worked in various roles as Consulting Actuary and Principal. He moved back to his native Denmark in 2003 with General Electric's Insurance Solutions group until joining AEGON NV in The Hague in April, 2007. At AEGON, Mr Madsen has responsibility for enhancing the AEGON Group's risk and capital profile through reinsurance and securitisation from a Group Risk perspective. He is a Member of AEGON's Treasury Risk and Capital Committee.

Alison McKie has been the Managing Director of the Global Life & Health Risk Transformation team at Swiss Re for the last 2.5 years, focusing on the transformation of Swiss Re's life and health business through selective risk transfer to the capital markets and through external retrocession. The role entails evaluation of internal and external risk appetites across the full spectrum of risks inherent in life and health contracts; determining appropriate transformation mechanisms for Swiss Re to achieve its strategic goals through active capital and risk management. Previously Alison was the Chief Financial Officer for Swiss Re Life & Health Limited. Alison joined Swiss Re in 2003 as the Finance Director for the Global Life & Health Business

Group having started her career at PricewaterhouseCoopers, where she focused on the insurance industry, working in both an audit and advisory capacity and on M&A transactions.

David S. Miller is a partner at Cadwalader, Wickersham & Taft, LLP. Mr Miller is a former chair of the New York State Bar Association's Tax Section. He is ranked the top tax lawyer in the United States by United States Lawyer Rankings, a ranking guide established by a consortium of US corporations. He is listed in Chambers Global's *The World's Leading Lawyers*, Chambers USA: *America's Leading Lawyer*, *The Best Lawyers in America*, and *The Legal 500*. Mr Miller is the author of a number of articles and book chapters and is a recipient of The Burton Award for Legal Achievement, which recognises exceptional legal writing. He is a member of the Tax Forum. A summa cum laude graduate of the University of Pennsylvania, Mr Miller graduated from Columbia University Law School, where he was a Notes and Comments Editor of the *Columbia Law Review* and a Harlan Fiske Stone Scholar. He was a clerk to the Honorable Mary M. Schroeder of the US Court of Appeals for the Ninth Circuit during the year following law school. He received his LLM. in Taxation from New York University School of Law.

Jean-Louis Monnier is head of European ILS in the Capital Markets Insurance Solutions group of Swiss Re, with responsibilities for distribution, origination and P&C structuring in Europe. Jean-Louis joined Swiss Re in 2002 and first developed ALM hedges for life insurance companies before specialising in the placement of insurance risk with capital market investors and the development of new risk transfer initiatives in bond or derivative form. Jean-Louis has 15 years' experience in marketing structured assets and risk transfer solutions to European financial institutions. Prior to joining Swiss Re, he worked in the derivatives solutions groups of Gen Re Securities, CIBC World Markets and Société Générale. He holds an MBA from ESSEC business school in France.

Andreas Müller is Head of Origination/Distribution/ILS Investments with Munich Re's Risk Trading Unit. Andreas joined Munich Re in 1998 in the Finite Reinsurance/Alternative Risk Transfer division. Before taking over the responsibilities of his current function at the Risk Trading Unit, he was in Munich Re's Group Transactions division working on the Mergers & Acquisitions and Corporate Finance side. He is the author of various publications on risk management, alternative risk transfer and life insurance and holds a PhD in economics.

Mark Nicolaides is a London-based partner with Latham & Watkins, an international law firm which specialises in structured finance with specific expertise in structuring and documenting investment vehicles and asset-backed securities backed by a wide variety of assets, including insurance receivables, IP royalty streams, European multi-country trade receivables and other loan and lease receivables. He is at the forefront in developing capital market-based longevity products. He also has broad experience in repurchase agreements and commodities and equities derivatives. In addition to his transactional practice, Mr Nicolaides is considered one of the leading experts on the Basel II Accord regarding regulatory capital requirements for banks, and represented the European Securitisation Forum in connection with its development and in connection with its implementation within the EU. As co-chair of the Legal, Regulatory and Capital Committee of the European Securitisation Forum, he is also active in developing a securitisation framework for the Solvency II Directive regarding regulatory capital requirements for insurance companies within the EU. Mr Nicolaides has been recognised by Chambers as a leading lawyer for capital markets securitisation (2008), and by *Legal 500* as a leading lawyer for securitisation (2008). His work developing longevity securities and longevity derivatives for Pensions First Limited was 'Highly Commended' by the *Financial Times* in its 2008 Innovative Lawyers Awards.

Norman Peard is Director of the Insurance and Pensions Solutions Group at Credit Suisse, London. Norman is an actuary with over 20 years' insurance and capital markets experience. His career has included roles with leading global actuarial consultants to the insurance and pensions industry, global reinsurers, investment banks and in financial regulation. He has worked to develop and implement nontraditional reinsurance and capital market-based solutions, including insurance-linked securitisation and has also contributed to the development of policy as to the regulatory treatment of insurance-linked securitisation in the UK as well as broader insurance regulatory policy. He has been closely involved with the Europe-wide Solvency II project and has represented the UK on the CEIOPS Pillar 1 Working Group. In his role at Credit Suisse, Norman combines his actuarial, insurance technical, commercial and regulatory experience to develop solutions for capital and risk management for insurance and pensions industry participants. Born in Dublin, Ireland, Norman is a graduate of Trinity College Dublin with an MA and Gold Medal in mathematics. Amongst the European actuarial bodies, he is a Fellow of the Institute of Actuaries and a Fellow of the Society of Actuaries in Ireland. Amongst the North American bodies, he is an Associate of the Society of Actuaries.

Kenneth R. Pierce is a partner with the law firm of Mayer Brown and is co-head of the US insurance and reinsurance practice. He has over 20 years' experience as a reinsurance professional, serving the industry as an attorney and as an investment banker. Mr Pierce has structured dozens of complex reinsurance-capital market convergence transactions, including several sidecar transactions, handling all aspects including financial structuring, legal, tax, accounting and the entire securitisation and capital markets distribution process. He has also developed innovative reinsurance products (patent pending on two products) and has structured captive and reinsurance transformer vehicles. He has equivalent experience in handling all facets of complex reinsurance disputes, arbitration and litigation, in connection with virtually every type of reinsurance product, including property, casualty, life, annuity, surety, financial guaranty and other lines. In addition, Mr Pierce has counseled clients on a wide array of insurance and reinsurance regulatory matters, including issues at the intersection of derivatives and reinsurance.

Georg Rindermann is Project Manager in the Reinsurance Department of Allianz SE and a member of the Advanced Risk Intermediation team. He is responsible for the origination, structuring and execution of insurance-linked securitisation transactions of Allianz SE and Group subsidiaries. Prior to his current role, he worked as assistant to the Board of Management of Allianz SE. Before joining Allianz in 2004, Georg worked as an assistant lecturer in International Business at the University of Münster. He holds a doctoral degree in Business Administration from the University of Münster and a double diploma in Business Administration from the universities of Frankfurt and Paris-Dauphine.

David Ross currently works as a Senior Actuary within the Risk Analytics division of Torus Insurance. His responsibilities at Torus include risk pricing, with a focus on energy and industrial property lines, and building and embedding the company's internal capital model. David joined Torus from the reinsurance broking firm Guy Carpenter, where he spent five years working as an actuary focussing on retrocession and capital markets products. He worked on the modelling and structuring of several ILS issues, including Bay Haven and Fremantle. David started his career at KPMG in 2000 and qualified as an actuary in 2003.

Simeon Rudin is a partner in, and head of, the structured finance team at Freshfields Bruckhaus Deringer LLP. He specialises in insurance-linked securities and other structured insurance transactions, structured products, derivatives and tax-based structured finance. He acted as lead legal adviser on the structuring and implementation of the four public listed embedded value transactions in the UK and Ireland – Mutual Securitisation (the first embedded value securitisation), Gracechurch Life Finance (the first whole business embedded value securitisation), Box Hill Life Finance (the first embedded value securitisation by a life assurer) and Avondale Securities (the first synthetic embedded value securitisation). In addition, he has advised on a variety of other transactions in the life sector (for example, financial reinsurance, structured pension buy-outs and longevity swaps) and non-life sector (including the FIFA Golden Goal transaction and a securitisation of a US P&C book for a European insurer). Simeon is co-chair of the European Securitisation Forum's Solvency II Working Group, which was established with a view to ensuring that securitisation and derivatives were accepted as risk mitigation techniques along with more standard reinsurance in the Solvency II Directive.

Steven Schreiber is a Principal and Consulting Actuary with Milliman, Inc. He co-manages the life and health consulting practice in Milliman's New York office and has been with Milliman for over 20 years. Much of Steve's time over the past several years has been spent advising insurance companies, banks and financial guarantors on capital market securitisations and private structured transactions relating to reserve redundancies, VIF transactions (including closed block transactions) and mortality catastrophe bonds. Steve has also been advising clients on longevity transactions in the UK. He also provides consulting services to his clients on merger and acquisition transactions, mutual merger transactions, Mutual Holding Company conversions and demutualisations. Steve spent three years in Milliman's Tokyo office in the late 1990s and continues to work with clients on projects in Japan and in other markets outside the US. He is a Fellow of the Society of Actuaries and a Member of the American Academy of Actuaries.

Gerold Seidler has more than 30 years' experience in the insurance industry, with more than 20 years at Munich Re (in underwriting and actuarial functions) and nearly ten years with different direct insurers. For the past two years, Gerold has been Chief Actuary in the Risk Trading Unit. Gerold has a university degree in mathematics.

Jonathan Spry is a Senior Vice President of GC Securities Ltd; the European Capital Markets affiliate of Guy Carpenter & Company Ltd. Jonathan has responsibility for capital markets advisory and the origination, structuring and execution of cat bonds and other innovative insurance-linked securities and the capital raising associated with reinsurance sidecars and start-ups. Jonathan was previously a Director and Head of the Insurance Linked Securities team in Standard & Poor's Insurance Ratings Group in London. At S&P Jonathan had primary analytical responsibility for rating life and non-life insurance securitisation and played an important role in the development of rating criteria for insurance securitisation, cat bonds and CDOs of insurance risk globally. Jonathan was also a member of Standard & Poor's Enterprise Risk Management team, with a particular focus on ALM, credit risk, catastrophe risks and economic risk models. Prior to joining Standard & Poor's in 2003, Jonathan held positions at Morgan Stanley, Nat West and Bank of Tokyo-Mitsubishi, where he was responsible for structuring and executing a number of corporate finance and structured finance transactions. Jonathan is a well-known speaker at conferences and has contributed to numerous articles on the topic of insurance-linked securities. He was *Insurance Day* magazine's London Market awards 'Young Broker of the Year' in 2008.

John Stroughair is the VP for Risk Markets at RMS; his responsibilities include ILS modeling and the development of parametric indices, and he is also responsible for Miu, RMS's ILS portfolio management tool. Prior to joining RMS, he was a Managing Director of Oliver Wyman. He was with Oliver Wyman from 1993 until the end of 2007 and has over 14 years' consulting experience in risk management. He has worked extensively on risk management issues for the corporate and investment banking areas of many of the leading banks in both the US and Europe. He has also worked with several leading energy firms in Europe on issues regarding trading risk management and on enterprise risk management. Before entering the Financial Services Industry, John worked for the UK Defence Ministry on issues relating to strategic planning. He holds a PhD in Theoretical Physics from Case Western Reserve University, Cleveland, Ohio, an MA in Physics from Cambridge University and an MBA with a major in Finance from the Wharton school of the University of Pennsylvania.

Rick Watson is Managing Director and head of the European Securitisation Forum, where he leads industry-wide efforts to promote education, understanding and development of cash and structured products business among its 160-strong member base. He is actively involved with a variety of industry initiatives to address the credit markets turmoil. Previously, Rick was Managing Director and Head of Structured Finance for FGIC UK Limited in London. Prior to joining FGIC, Rick was Head of ABS and CDOs at HSBC Bank plc, where he led a pan-European team of originators of consumer, CDOs and other products. He held a similar position at Bear Stearns in London, and was previously Executive Director at UBS Limited and at Morgan Stanley and Freddie Mac. Rick received an MBA from the Fuqua School of Business at Duke University. He was co-chair of the ESF's Legal and Regulatory Committee from 2000–2004. In January 2006, he co-edited the Euromoney Books publication *Asset Securitisation and Synthetic Structures: Innovation in the European Credit Markets.*

Malcom Wattman is a partner in the New York office of the international law firm of Cadwalader, Wickersham & Taft LLP. His practice is concentrated in structured finance, securities, corporate finance and corporate law. He has been instrumental in the development of new structured finance products for more than 25 years. For the past decade he has specialised in the structuring and documentation of risk-linked securities and nontraditional structured finance products. He represented sponsors, issuers or underwriters on a majority of the catastrophe bond transactions and has been instrumental in assisting clients with the development of new concepts in this evolving market. He represents investment banks, reinsurance companies, public and private companies and institutional and individual investors in connection with public offerings and private placements of debt, equity and structured securities, credit agreements, acquisitions and dispositions, contracts and general corporate and commercial matters. Mr Wattman received a BS from the University of Buffalo and his JD from Fordham University Law School. He held positions in engineering, finance and consulting prior to joining Cadwalader, Wickersham & Taft LLP. He has served as a director of several private corporations and presently serves as a trustee of not-for-profit organisations.

Jillian Williams has over 12 years' experience in catastrophe modelling, actuarial pricing and consulting in the insurance/reinsurance sector. Prior to joining Leadenhall Capital Partners she was Senior Vice President at Instrat, the modelling and actuarial department of Guy Carpenter, specialising in Capital Markets, Retro, Property and Marine classes. Among other things she has managed projects in ILS, Retro and overseen the analysis and development for new Property & Casualty business opportunities. Prior to Guy Carpenter, Jillian worked at Fidelity Investment as Performance Measurement Analyst.

Tibor Winkler is one of the veterans of the ILS space, with over 11 years of transaction and business development experience. Working as a senior model developer at EQECAT involved in consulting projects, he turned his focus to the space in the late 1990s. Initially he carried out trigger development, design and execution of risk analyses and marketing for cat bonds. At EQECAT he worked on the first modelled-loss transaction, Namazu Re in 1999. From 2000 to the end of 2008 he worked as Director of Risk Markets at RMS. Until 2006 he worked on cat bonds and private transactions in increasingly senior roles; his name is associated with the first parametric Europe Wind trigger, used in Prime Capital in 2000, the first Europe Wind securitisation for a corporate client, Pylon Ltd in 2003, the first parametric earthquake transaction to take account of ground motion uncertainty, GI Capital in 2004, and many others. After five years of designing and executing innovative solutions for transactions, he took up a client development function in 2006 and became one of the principal drivers behind Miu and Paradex at RMS. From 2006 to the end of 2008 he was the leader in charge of expanding RMS's core client base to the capital markets. He holds a PhD and an MSc in Earthquake Engineering from the University of Tokyo and an MSc in Structural Engineering from the Technical University of Budapest.

Acknowledgements

This project would not have been possible without the energy, time and effort of all the contributors, who have supported us in our initiative despite the difficult environment and busy schedules of year-end 2008. We would like to thank all of them for having completed their contributions, almost always within the tight timeframe we imposed on ourselves, and for the quality of the work done. We thank also those who believed in the project, but could not stay with us to see it finished due to events affecting their organisations, and are very grateful for the support of those who stepped in to complete the relevant chapters.

Special thanks are due to our editor, Caitlin Cornish, who has been extremely supportive, immediately and throughout this adventure. We are also very grateful to Andre, Anne-Marie and Annie, who have contributed to this project by working on the butterfly effect, and have been of constant and essential support; and to Claudia Ravanelli, for her patience and infallible support.

Editing this handbook required the editors to dedicate a considerable amount of time (which we found very exciting and professionally very rewarding) and we are very grateful to our colleagues for their patience, support and advice throughout the period.

Finally, a special thank you to Josie Green, who, without realising it, is at the origins of the whole project.

1

Introduction

Pauline Barrieu[a] and Luca Albertini[b]

There has been much said about the convergence of the insurance industry with the capital markets. Such convergence has taken many forms, and of the many attempts, some have been more successful than others. Insurance-linked securities, often referred to as ILS, have proven to be one of the most successful manifestations of this convergence, of how capital market technologies can find applications within the insurance industry, and how insurance-related risk can be transferred to capital market investors. As outlined in later contributions, there were approximately $13 billion of tradable non-life insurance-linked securities and $24 billion in tradable life insurance-linked securities as of the end of 2008. In addition, whilst traded insurance-linked securities are the most visible and headline-catching forms of risk transfer to the capital markets, there are a number of other forms of placement of insurance risk into the capital markets, including:

- Private placements of insurance-linked securities (also called 'club deals') which involve a small number of skilled investors, and which are estimated to be of significant size.
- Sidecars on non-life insurance risk, which reached an estimated $6 billion of capacity after Hurricane Katrina, and found new interest in 2008 with reduced retrocession capacity being available in the market.
- Insurance-linked derivatives, which are mostly over-the-counter contracts in life and non-life risk, transacted by financial institutions, brokers and regulated exchanges.
- Weather derivatives, also available via financial institutions, brokers and regulated exchanges.
- Traded life insurance policies – life settlements – which have been warehoused in significant size by financial institutions and are being distributed to capital markets as well as private investors.
- Collateralised reinsurance and industry loss warranties (ILW), which are typically reinsurance contracts but frequently backed by capital market investors (such as dedicated insurance-linked securities investors and hedge funds) which fund the collateral posting and assume the ultimate risk of the relevant insurance events.

The outstanding capacity deployed by capital market investors on the above mix of instruments was estimated to be well above $50 billion in 2008.

[a]London School of Economics
[b]Leadenhall Capital Partners

Moreover, the market has been enriched by a wider and deeper range of market participants over the last decade:

- Each year, new *originators* have approached the insurance-linked securitisation market, including a number of insurance and reinsurance companies, corporations and government institutions.
- Some of these originators who have tapped the insurance-linked securities market with a transaction have then sponsored *new transactions* covering new risks or *repeat transactions* on the same perils, thus capitalising on their positive experience with the technology, and in some cases have established *risk trading units* with the task of constantly monitoring opportunities for purchasing or ceding risk to the capital markets.
- A number of *modelling* and *actuarial firms* have the ability to perform risk analysis on different life and non-life risks with the rigour and methodology needed to describe them to capital market investors.
- A growing *number of risks* have been modelled for capital market transactions, thus enriching the potential for diversified exposures for investors.
- Diverse range *investors* have approached life and non-life insurance-linked securities across the risk spectrum. Investor types have ranged from money market managers, pension funds, banks, other institutional investors, insurance and reinsurance companies to a growing number of asset management companies dedicated to investing only in insurance-linked securities risk.
- There is a larger community of *arrangers*, *financial institutions* and *brokers* who have equipped themselves for origination and structuring of transactions, secondary trading of insurance-linked securities and in some cases providing secondary market pricing indications (although not yet at the level of market making).

After a decade of continuous growth, the insurance-linked securities market is now at a stage of consolidation of its past successes and further expansion, despite the recent turmoil in the capital markets, as discussed later in various chapters of the book. However, one could argue that the actual size of the market is still very small compared to its full potential. Supporting market participants with a transparent discussion on various aspects of this market and introducing insurance-linked securities to a wider class of originators and investors are essential in making this niche market more understandable, more transparent and more accessible. This is really what has motivated us in undertaking this project and what we would like to achieve with this handbook.

The main objective of this handbook is to present the state of the art in insurance-linked securitisation, by exploring the various roles for the different parties involved in the transactions, the motivation for the transaction sponsors, the potential inherent pitfalls, the latest developments and transaction structures and also the key challenges faced by the market.

To do so, we have decided to gather specialists with different backgrounds and experts with many years of experience in this field, representing the various perspectives and aspects of this market. Each chapter is therefore a contribution by one or several experts in insurance-linked securitisation. As a result, this book presents an independent view on the sector, with contributions from some of the key market players who have agreed to support our initiative. On the other hand, due to the healthy growth of the market and to the number of credible market players, it has not been possible to include all of those institutions that would have been able to provide valuable contributions within the targeted size of this handbook.

The handbook is organised into three parts, covering the various perspectives in insurance-linked securitisation, non-life and life.

The first part focuses on non-life insurance securitisation, and has been organised so as to focus on some key aspects of this market.

We start in Chapter 2 by offering an overview of the non-life insurance-linked securitisation market, its evolution and the key general structural features.

We have then asked three key originators, each of whom has sponsored a number of transactions, to offer, in Chapter 3, the cedant's perspective on this market and outline their motivations in approaching insurance-linked securities and the latter's impact on their overall risk transfer strategy.

Insurance-linked securities can be structured in a number of different ways. One of the most noticeable differences is the type of trigger which can be used to claim a payment from the securitisation structure. The various types of trigger are outlined in Chapter 4, and Chapter 5 guides you through an analysis for cedants in assessing the basis risk impact of the choice of a specific trigger for the transaction.

As rating agencies and modelling firms have been instrumental in supporting the development of the insurance-linked securities market, and have established and enriched their rating and modelling methodology to allow the placement of new types of transaction, we have then asked a leading rating agency to outline, in Chapter 6, its approach to rating non-life risk, and a leading modelling firm to outline its risk modelling methodology as well as the structure and the benefits of its newly established indexes related to catastrophic risk in Chapter 7.

Legal considerations are at the heart of the structuring of insurance-linked securities, and a number of transactions are affected by several legal aspects of federal and state legislation in the United States. Chapter 8 offers a perspective on such legal aspects, and on how structures have been affected.

Chapter 9 then offers the perspective of investors in non-life insurance-linked securities, including the key elements that drive investors' underwriting and pricing considerations and the key issues which are currently the focus of investors' attention. In addition, given the complexities related to the management and the monitoring of an investor exposure to the different risks in a portfolio of non-life insurance-linked securities, Chapter 10 outlines the characteristic of one of the leading tools available to investors to perform such analysis.

Having reviewed some of the key aspects of non-life insurance-linked securities, in Chapter 11 we offer an outline of sidecars, their role in cedants' risk management strategies and a comparison with insurance-linked securities.

To conclude the non-life insurance-linked securities section we offer two case studies with two different types of structures: a multi-peril first event excess of loss transaction (Atlas by SCOR) and a transaction triggered by a frequency of events (Vega by Swiss Re).

The second part focuses on life insurance-linked securitisation, which requires specific focus points due to its specific characteristics.

Chapter 14 offers an overview of the background of the general features of life insurance securitisation and offers the framework for the subsequent analysis.

The cedant's perspective for life securitisation is offered in Chapter 15, in which a leading life insurer and a leading life reinsurer, both active in a number of different types of securitisation transaction, outline their approach in assessing the use and the benefits of life insurance securitisation within their own organisations and provide some background on their own experiences in the field.

Rating and risk modelling of the transactions have also been highly developed to enable underwriting and risk assessment of various types of life insurance securitisation. A leading rating agency offers a perspective on its own methodology for life securitisation in Chapter 16, and a leading modelling firm outlines its modelling approach for various types of life risk in Chapter 17.

Legal issues have influenced a number of life insurance securitisation structures in each jurisdiction, each of which in turn has its own peculiarities. Chapter 18 offers a general overview of the most common legal issues facing life insurance securitisation structuring, with an emphasis on European markets.

Although a number of investors are active in both life and non-life securitisation, there are a number of key sensitivities and focus points which are peculiar to investments in life insurance securitisation; these are outlined in Chapter 19.

A number of market participants including originators, arrangers, law firms, rating agencies and investors have analysed at length ways to transfer longevity risk to the capital markets. This process has met with a number of difficulties, but there are also a number of success stories. Chapter 20 outlines what has been achieved in the specific field of insurance linked securitisation and the key challenges in using insurance-linked securities to transfer longevity risk. Chapter 21 outlines some of the solutions identified outside of the securitisation market, which have led to successful transactions in derivative form. The structures and indexes used could provide a basis for further evolution of this market in both securitised and derivative forms.

We then conclude the life insurance securitisation section by offering some case studies on catastrophic mortality securitisation (Chapter 22) as well as on securitisation of embedded value (or value in force) and of redundant reserves arising out of Regulation XXX (Chapter 23), for which the contributors have also offered some historical market statistics.

Part three focuses on tax and regulatory considerations affecting the insurance-linked securitisation sector. Whilst we acknowledge the specificities of each jurisdiction, this part touches on UK (Chapter 24) and US (Chapter 25) tax considerations, thus covering some of the largest markets with originators and investors in insurance-linked securities.

The handbook concludes with a perspective on the regulatory environment affecting the insurance and reinsurance industry in some key markets, the implications for the market players and the key future developments expected with the implementation of Solvency II.

In a nutshell, this handbook aims to give a general overview and expert insight on traded insurance-linked securities, this specific and relatively transparent market being considered by many as a benchmark for risk assessment and comparable pricing in other private capital market transactions involving insurance risk. Over the last decade, this market has been going through a process of constant innovation and drive to seek a balance between the needs of the protection buyers and those of the investors.

Note that, whenever we have felt it meaningful and helpful to better understand the insurance-linked securities market, we have included some references to other forms of successful insurance risk transfers. In particular, Chapter 11, dedicated to sidecars, underlines how capital markets have been fast reacting in providing significant additional capacity to a strained insurance and reinsurance industry (particularly in the aftermath of large insurance events) and outlines the differences between sidecar transactions and insurance-linked securities. On the life side, the handbook includes, in Chapter 21, a section on insurance-linked derivatives, as the risk transfer of some life risks (longevity in particular) to the capital markets has been, to date, more successful in derivative form than in insurance-linked form.

Finally, please note that the contributions have been delivered to the publisher in January 2009, and therefore any subsequent material event affecting the subject of one of more of the chapters is not reflected in this handbook. The insurance-linked securities market is an innovative and adaptive market, evolving fast. For this reason, the publisher has made available a website www.wiley.com/go/albertini_insurance on which the editors and contributors have the opportunity to provide updates to their chapters, although these are voluntary updates and no commitment is given on regular updates before the next edition is published.

We believe that the contributors have done an excellent job and put considerable effort into providing, in a pedagogical way, the reader with their perspective on the market. We hope you will find in this book the answers to your questions on insurance-linked securities and that you will benefit from it as much as we have enjoyed and learned from this experience.

Note that the editors have assembled an impressive panel of professionals who are all prime players in the insurance-linked securities arena and are considered to be experts in the field covered by their own contribution. The editors do not share the same specific expertise in all of the fields covered by the handbook and therefore the views expressed in each contribution – which the editors believe to have been produced in a professional and diligent manner – are the views of the relevant contributor and not necessarily of the editors.

Part I
Non-life Securitization

2

Non-life Insurance Securitization: Market Overview, Background and Evolution

Jonathan Spry[a]

2.1 MARKET OVERVIEW

The concept of securitizing insurance risks became established in the mid-1990s in the wake of significant pressure on capacity in the non-life reinsurance market and an increased focus on capital management across both the life and non-life insurance sectors. The most prominent form of insurance-linked securities (ILS) is the catastrophe bond, a structure that was borne out of a desire to broaden reinsurance capacity in the aftermath of Hurricane Andrew in 1992 and the impact this loss had on the availability and price of property reinsurance.

Catastrophe or 'cat' bonds were designed to facilitate the direct transfer of catastrophe insurance risk from insurers, reinsurers and corporations (referred to as the cat bonds' 'sponsors') to investors. They were designed to protect sponsoring companies from financial losses caused by large natural catastrophes by complementing traditional reinsurance for certain layers of risk. The first ever cat bond (or 'Act of God' bond as it was then termed) was completed in 1994 for the Nationwide Insurance Co. of Columbus, Ohio. The market for cat bonds has grown steadily since the early days of the market to $1–2 billion of issuance per year for the 1998–2001 period and then to over $2 billion per year following the attack on the World Trade Center in New York, which had an effect on available reinsurance capacity across perils. Issuance doubled again to a rate of approximately $4 billion on an annual basis in 2006 following Hurricane Katrina and then grew further to result in a record annual issuance of $7 billion in 2007, up 49% on the previous year. Issuance volumes in 2008 were down from the previous year, partly as a result of a softening reinsurance market but also as financial market contagion limited appetite from investors, but were still a fairly healthy $2.7 billion (Figure 2.1).

Cat bond risk capital outstanding was $13.2 billion at the end of 2008, slightly down on the figure of $13.8 billion reached at the end of the record-breaking 2007, a year which saw outstanding capital 63% higher than the $8.5 billion in 2006 and nearly three times the $4.9 billion outstanding at the end of 2005. Cat bond risk principal now composes an estimated 8% of the estimated property limits globally and 12% on a US-only basis. The capital markets' weight in reinsurance is even larger when adding investments in sidecars of natural catastrophe risk (see Chapter 11).

[a] Senior Vice President, Capital Markets, GC Securities

The Handbook of Insurance-Linked Securities   Edited by P. Barrieu and L. Albertini
© 2009 John Wiley & Sons, Ltd

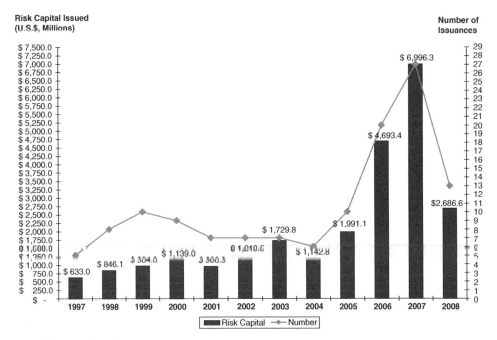

Figure 2.1 ILS market volume

Source: Guy Carpenter/GC Securities

Unlike traditional corporate bonds or other fixed-income instruments, the primary risk embedded in ILS is the occurrence of one or a number of adverse insurance-related events. The main risk to investors in cat bonds is that a natural disaster such as an earthquake or hurricane will 'trigger' the bond, wiping out some or the entire principal, which is used to pay claims. Cat bonds are often said to represent a form of a 'pure play' risk in as much as they offer investors the chance to be rewarded for gaining exposure to natural catastrophe risk without assuming risks such as investment risk or credit risk that are likely to be more heavily correlated with other investments in their portfolio.

Investors choose to invest in cat bonds because their return is largely uncorrelated with the return on other investments and they often pay higher interest rates than comparably rated corporate instruments.

Cat bond investors in general do not face the risk of default by the ceding insurance company because they are usually backed by cash collateral, although in some cases there is also some credit risk relating to the continuing payment of premiums; that said, risks other than pure insurance risk cannot be ignored when evaluating ILS. The risk of a 'credit cliff' in cat bonds is apparent when an investor can rapidly lose most or their entire principal and – in some cases – unpaid interest if a triggering event occurs. The art and science of computer modelling is crucial to assessing and managing the risk in cat bonds and also drives the pricing, yields and ratings. These models are, in turn, extremely sensitive to the data used (See Chapter 6 on modelling risk and rating methodology). The quality and quantity of data vary depending on the peril or other type of risk being securitized. Further potential risks for investors include liquidity risk due largely to the fact that most ILS are sold as unregistered investments, available only to large institutional investors and not subject to the SEC's full registration and disclosure requirements, although it should be noted that in 2008 for the first time, key trading houses have estimated that the volumes of secondary market trading have been larger than the volumes of primary issuance, and the mark-to-market losses in the most challenging months for the general markets have been, on average, below double-digit figures, thus showing a comparatively healthier market in the ILS sector. An additional risk that ILS investors need to consider is that of counterparty risk, ILS issuers commonly enter into swap or deposit arrangements with third parties that guarantee interest and principal payments to investors, as long as the triggering event does not occur; counterparty risk exists on these collateral arrangements and this risk along with the risks inherent in the underlying collateral itself is one that has been highlighted during the credit crunch of 2007/2008 and the demise of Lehman Brothers. For more on the investor's perspective, please refer to Chapter 9.

Cat bonds are usually issued by a special purpose vehicle (SPV) which typically invests the proceeds from the bond issuance in generally low-risk securities (the collateral). The earnings on these securities, as well as insurance premiums paid to the sponsor, are used to make periodic, variable-rate interest payments to investors. The interest rate is typically based on LIBOR plus a promised margin, or 'spread' above that.

As long as the natural disaster covered by the bond does not occur during the time investors own the bond, investors will receive their interest payments and, when the bond matures, their principal back from the collateral. Most cat bonds generally mature in three years, although life securitizations typically have longer tenors to reflect the nature of the risks being securitized.

The basic structure of the cat bond is shown in Figure 2.2, the transaction being very similar to a traditional reinsurance contract for the sponsor/cedant albeit it here engaging with an SPV reinsurer, which in turn then securitizes the contract by issuing notes to investors and collateralizing the proceeds.

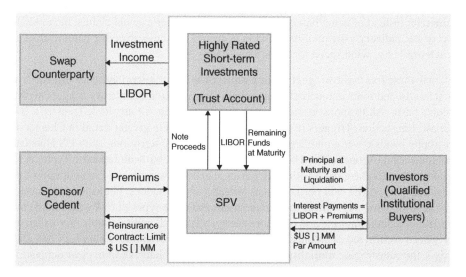

Figure 2.2   General non-life ILS structure

Source: Guy Carpenter/GC Securities

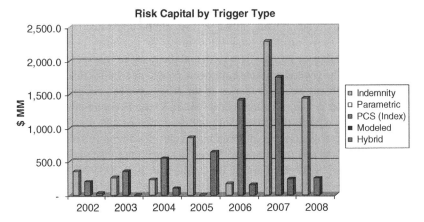

Figure 2.3   Evolution of triggers in ILS transactions
Source: Guy Carpenter/GC Securities

The sponsor of a cat bond must choose the type of trigger that will be used to signify that a 'catastrophe' has occurred. There are four basic trigger types (Figure 2.3):

- **Indemnity:** triggered by the issuer's actual losses, so the sponsor is indemnified in much the same way as if they had purchased traditional catastrophe reinsurance.
- **Modelled loss:** sponsor's expected loss is calculated by catastrophe models using objective data, the bond is triggered if the sponsor's modelled loss post an event is above a specified threshold.
- **Indexed to industry loss:** the bond is triggered when the amount of the overall industry loss from an event, usually determined by an independent third party such as PCS, exceeds a certain amount.
- **Parametric:** instead of being based on claim size (the insurer's actual claims, the modelled claims or the industry's claims), the bond is triggered by some objective parameter of the natural hazard (e.g. wind speed for a hurricane bond).

In addition to these four basic trigger types a number of hybrid triggers have been used in structuring cat bonds, and innovations such as granular disaggregation of industry triggers in order to minimize basis risk to sponsors can be seen, for instance, in Allianz Risk Transfer's 2008 'Blue Coast' transaction. Triggers in non-life ILS are covered in greater detail in Chapter 4.

Catastrophe bonds cover a number of perils and geographic territories, with US Hurricane and Earthquake and European Wind being the most prominent, but with Japanese Typhoon and Earthquake and earthquake risk in other territories also being securitized. Less common is the securitization of flood risk and perils such as volcano and tornadoes, but as models develop, investors have shown a willingness to evaluate more and more types of risk with future cover for terrorism or aviation/marine and off-shore energy risks all thought possible. Terrorism risk has rarely been securitized, with the exception of the Golden Goal transaction for FIFA and – indirectly – the catastrophic mortality programmes discussed later; despite clear demand for such cover following the attacks on the World Trade Center, the securitization of terror risk has been hampered by the lack of faith placed in terrorism models, although the acceptability of these models is increasing over time and it is likely therefore that cat bonds covering terrorism risk will become feasible in the future.

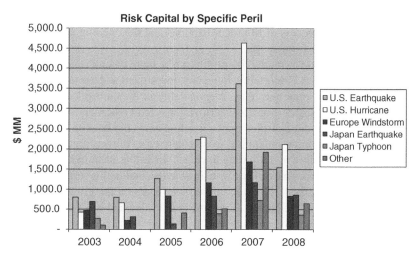

Figure 2.4 Geographical breakdown of exposures

Source: Guy Carpenter/GC Securities

Some cat bonds are straightforward in offering only one class of securities. Other issuances can offer several classes, or tranches, which vary in payment terms, coupon rates and credit ratings. Different tranches can also cover different perils or territories, as shown in Figure 2.4.

In the early years of the catastrophe bond market, bond terms varied dramatically from one year to as many as ten years. As the market has matured, one-year and long-term (five years or greater) tenors have become increasingly rare, with three-year deals becoming by the far the most common.

The market for non-life insurance securitization has moved beyond cat bonds and the transfer of 'peak-risk' in recent years with the arrival of a number of motor securitizations that are designed to transfer non-catastrophe risks to the capital markets with a view to optimizing risk-adjusted economic, rating agency and regulatory capital requirements.

The market for life insurance securitization has also developed considerably since the early 1990s and is now concentrated around a number of asset classes including embedded value (EV) or value in force (VIF) securitization, financing 'surplus' statutory reserve requirements (for example US statutory XXX reserve securitizations) and types of cat bond where the underlying risk relates to mortality spikes (so-called 'mortality (cat) bonds'). The area of much focus for the securitization market, but one where, to date, few transactions have been completed, is that of longevity risk, where insurers or pension funds secure hedging against increases in longevity (mortality improvements) on a pool of policyholders using securitization techniques.

The motivating factors for insurers in utilizing life securitization are numerous but generally fall into the following categories:

- the desire to find an efficient form of raising capital, often in the form of 'operational' rather than financial leverage;
- a tool for managing capital requirements;
- a form of illiquid asset monetization;
- a technique for managing 'peak risk' exposure.

The details and parties involved in life securitizations are outlined further in Chapter 14, where we will see that the process of life securitizations and the ongoing administration and dynamics of the deals are far from simple.

For investors in life securitizations the risk profile can be more complicated than for non-life ILS, and various combinations of mortality, longevity, investment and expense risks and even policyholder behaviour can come into play, most notably in the embedded value and XXX reserve securitization asset classes. For EV securitizations credit risk cannot be ignored either; the ability to continue to produce surplus to pay noteholders is likely to be contingent on the continued solvency of the sponsor and for this reason these types of securitization are generally rated below that of the sponsor by the rating agencies. Investors in mortality and longevity bonds do, however, benefit from pure play life insurance risk and in this respect they are more akin to, and sometimes classified as, a type of cat bond. Data on the growth of the life ILS market are presented in detail in Chapter 23 on embedded value and XXX transactions.

Insurance-linked securities have evolved significantly since the early days of the market. In the beginning, investors were scarce and required substantial education before making a commitment. Today, the ILS marketplace features a solid, expanding core of experienced investors, often with funds dedicated to the sector. Rating agencies and cat modelling firms have also played critical roles in increasing the confidence of market participants by working on and providing analysis of nearly all transactions. Issuers too have become far more comfortable with using ILS strategies and their use as hedging instruments has evolved from being somewhat experimental to an integrated part of the risk management toolkit, with benefits ranging from managing earnings volatility to capital management and the ability to monetize illiquid assets.

The role of ILS in the context of traditional reinsurance has evolved from one of a threatened substitute to that of a complementary product and an increasingly symbiotic relationship has developed. This dynamic has been fuelled not only by evolving structures and the convergence in capital markets and traditional reinsurance pricing but also by the evolution of the capital market players themselves, who, armed with increasing levels of sophistication and backed by state-of-the-art modelling, are able to play across the ILS, industry loss warranties (ILWs, or contracts triggered by a predefined level of industry loss) collateralized reinsurance and 'sidecar' space.

2.2   MARKET DYNAMICS

Since the 2005 losses of hurricanes Katrina, Rita and Wilma (also often denoted KRW) the ILS market and the market for cat bonds in particular has witnessed significant growth. The capital markets today represent core providers of risk transfer capacity to insurers and reinsurers alike and the number of large international (re)insurers that have utilized capital markets' capacity in the non-life sector now outnumbers the number that have not.

Cat bond market activity levels have ended the argument that these instruments are only a novelty purchased for prestige or used only in times of desperate shortages of traditional capacity. While the cat bond market has been in existence for well over a decade, development has not been smooth over this time span. In a manner consistent with other modern economic innovations such as the growth in derivatives or credit trading, market growth progressed slowly for several years before reaching a critical mass and then accelerating dramatically from 2005 before slowing again during the credit crunch of 2008.

The growth of life ILS has not been stellar although securitization has become a prominent form of financing for XXX statutory reserves in the US and the notion of mortality cat bonds has grown in importance with increasing focus on the risks for pandemics and, more generally, life securitization is seen by issuers as being a potentially useful source of financial flexibility in the future.

One of the key dynamics of the post-KRW environment was the increased visibility of nontraditional capacity sources, such as proprietary trading desks within banks, hedge funds, institutional asset managers including pension funds and other non-reinsurer capital providers. To a certain extent, it was clear that not all sponsors were comfortable with these new providers, in part because of a lack of process and personal familiarity among counterparties. Trust levels were lower, because relationships with traditional reinsurance providers often spanned several decades. Though significant amounts of work remain, great strides have been made to reduce these 'familiarity barriers'. The results of these efforts are clear. The increased velocity and flexibility of new capital entering the market of 2006 truncated what otherwise would have been an almost certainly more protracted hard market.

The dramatic growth of cat bond issuance post KRW was unsurprising. The losses sustained by the industry from 2004 and 2005 catastrophe activity created a capital shortfall with the underlying storm activity causing risk transfer prices to skyrocket. In an expected reaction to a perceived opportunity, high-velocity capital or 'hot money' entered the market to address some of this demand overhang. Because of an established investor following, marketing and issuance and documentation protocols, the cat bond market was particularly well-suited to address this need.

Figure 2.5 shows the impact that ILS issuance and increased capital markets capacity is having on reducing the amplitude and frequency of the reinsurance pricing cycle.

The record market activity of 2007 demonstrated a fundamental shift in the perception of the capital markets as a risk transfer solution. During the year, the paradigm shifted away from the idea that sponsors were seeking capital markets protection as a defensive, tactical measure taken only in the context of a dearth of traditional capacity. Rather, they took the view that the capital markets represent a valuable source of significant amounts of high-quality risk transfer

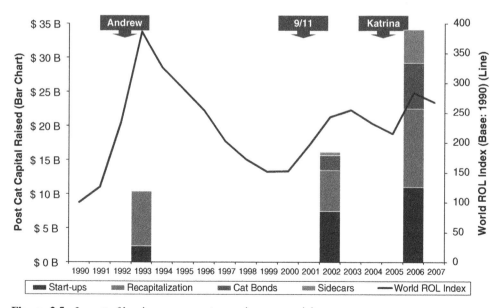

Figure 2.5 Impact of key insurance events on reinsurance pricing

Source: Guy Carpenter/GC Securities

capacity, causing them to invest in this area. In fact, several large sponsors that were unwilling to purchase expensive protection during the hard market of 2006 turned to cat bonds during 2007, even with additional traditional capacity available. With the market again hardening in late 2008 and into 2009, issuers are again turning to ILS solutions in order to best utilize available capacity.

A relatively recent phenomenon in the cat bond market is the introduction and continued use of shelf-programmes in which a sponsor acquires the option to issue additional bonds (often referred to as 'takedowns') as it sees fit over the course of a prescribed risk period. Among the advantages of this approach is that the sponsor incurs substantially lower issuance costs for each additional takedown than it does for the initial programme. Shelf offerings support both long-term planning and near-term manoeuvring. While they make it easy to access capital quickly in the event of emergency, shelf offerings also signal to capital markets and traditional capacity providers that a sponsor is interested in being a consistent, repeat issuer. Committed catastrophe risk investors tend to reward repeat issuers with progressively tighter execution pricing, provided that the issuer has a strong track record.

The capacity crunch of 2006 left most potential cat bond sponsors concerned that they could be vulnerable to an excessively volatile reinsurance risk transfer market. Companies throughout the industry re-evaluated their approaches to risk management. Most favoured an enterprise risk management (ERM) approach rather than focusing on risk at the operating unit or 'silo' level. The number of cat bond and shelf offering issuances in 2007 suggests that some potential sponsors were wary of relying on a single supplier (i.e., the traditional market) for such a critical component of their business models and that they increasingly saw value in the cycle management benefits of the multi-year protection afforded by ILS solutions.

A global environment in which catastrophe events appear to be increasing and insured values are expanding rapidly in catastrophe-exposed areas calls for diversification of risk capacity sources. For certain sponsors, there may be tangible benefits associated with being able to show public equity markets, rating agencies and regulators that, in the event of the next capacity crunch, a cat bond shelf programme provides an additional conduit to risk transfer capacity and financial flexibility. The advantages of product consistency (i.e., more reliable year-over-year capacity and pricing) can benefit both insurance and reinsurance companies directly, not to mention shareholders and policyholders. The ability to curtail post-event volatility through product consistency thus may be the most important attribute of the capital markets as a supplemental risk transfer solution.

Secondary market trading of ILS has often been described as attaining low volumes and is sometimes characterized by rather opaque pricing. As generally private ('144A') transactions are bought often with the intention to hold to maturity, and with demand for ILS often outstripping supply, the market has not been deemed to be particularly liquid in terms of two-way pricing, whilst sellers of ILS have traditionally met liquid demand within (if not better than) the indicative bid offers published by broker/dealers in ILS. Liquidity has been reduced in the darkest months of the 2008 credit crisis, but this still allowed transactions with mark-to-market losses which have been relatively small when compared with other types of fixed-income instruments.

2.3   THE QUESTION OF BASIS RISK REMAINS

Evidently basis risk could constrain the further rapid growth of the ILS market; however the industry has shown that the management of basis risk is changing quickly. Perceptions regarding indemnity triggers and basis risk continue to evolve. As the cat bond market has become mainstream, sponsors have spent considerable time and resources understanding their exposures to basis risk. While sponsors generally prefer indemnity protection to non-indemnity protection if all else is equal, the practical utility of this position is waning. With respect to indemnity versus non-indemnity transactions, all else is not equal, and the differences between each type of protection represent important cost–benefit decisions that sponsors are making in an increasingly sophisticated fashion.

Sponsors perceive indemnity transactions as reliable and familiar, largely because they resemble ultimate net loss (UNL) traditional cover and result in minimal basis risk. But they typically entail three disadvantages relative to non-indemnity triggers: risk spread premium, disclosure requirements and perceived legal exposure and the process, time and cost necessary to issue. In recent years sponsors have focused on the interplay of these factors, relative to the potential basis risk, pricing and execution achievable through non-indemnity transactions. There is a growing awareness that specific transaction objectives should trump the perceived superiority of one trigger type over another (refer to Chapter 5 on basis risk).

The cat bond investor community, particularly the core group of longstanding committed investors, is adjusting its perception of potential basis risk. The rejection of indemnity risk on the basis of moral hazard alone has become outdated. Now, many committed cat bond investors tend to recognize indemnity risk as simply another risk component in a transaction, provided that they have sufficiently reliable modelling and are comfortable with the ceding entities. Depending on sponsor-specific judgement, in conjunction with considerations such as the longer post-event loss adjustment and principal payout process, investors will adjust their required spreads or available capacity. As the understanding of sponsor-specific risk increases, investors are not uniformly changing their required spreads upward while reducing capacity allocations (though this is the norm). Judgement as well as understanding of traditional reinsurance is playing a more prominent role than ever before.

Savvy investors (including several reinsurers) are recognizing that basis risk typically cuts both ways. If one believes that catastrophe models provide reasonably accurate loss estimates on an industry-wide basis, it's reasonable to expect some insurers to outperform (pay less than expected) while others underperform (pay more than expected). Over a large enough portfolio of individual sponsors, basis risk should net out in the aggregate. For this theory to manifest itself in practice there must be a sufficiently sized pool of indemnity transactions to include in a diversified portfolio. The market's desire for a larger pool of indemnity transactions on this basis may also be contributing to an increased appetite for indemnity trigger deals, although dedicated ILS investors able to understand underwriting risk make an effort to focus on outperforming insurers and to stay clear of the underperforming ones.

Flexibility rather than the desire for a single trigger type appears to be the prevailing force in the cat bond market. The ability of all market participants to understand, evaluate, price and ultimately transact efficiently using various triggers indicates the cat bond market's continued maturation. Over time, the size of the risk spread premium (if any) should reflect the market's perception of a sponsor's internal processes, as long as there are no shocks. To the extent that a sponsor feels that the market misunderstands its true risk profile, it can elect to purchase non-indemnity cover. With the continued development of improved index and parametric tools (still an area of considerable focus for modelling firms and the industry in general), these types of cover should become more reliable and widely accepted by sponsors.

2.4   ILS AND THE CREDIT CRUNCH

The credit crisis of 2007/2008 has provided an opportunity to evaluate how ILS asset classes have performed in a tightening credit market. Since the inception of the ILS market, participants have believed the theoretical claim that ILS returns are not correlated with other asset classes. Because cat bond values are principally linked to the occurrence of physical phenomena, it was claimed, fluctuations in value should bear little relation to changes in general financial markets.

Evidence to support this theory has been limited but was supplied to some extent during the financial crisis of 1998 (the 'Russian Crisis'), the decline in stock markets in the years 2000 and 2001 driven by the collapse of the 'dot com' boom, the World Trade Center disaster and the demise of Enron and most importantly through the credit crisis of 2007 and 2008. Credit spreads in general widened by unprecedented amounts during the credit crisis whereas ILS spreads in general performed robustly in 2007. In 2008 the picture became more complicated with the performance of certain cat bonds being adversely affected by credit crisis contagion – notably the impact of the insolvency of Lehman Brothers (who acted as TRS counterparty to a number of transactions) and the impairment of the collateral behind some of the vehicles in the cat bond universe.

The impact of the credit crisis on the ILS market and the future prospects for both issuers and investors is mixed. The impact on investors is likely to be positive over the long run, as generally ILS have been validated as a diversifying non-correlated asset class and as investors have become increasingly sensitive to credit market risk, desire for the non-correlated, more stable returns will benefit the ILS sector. The short-term impact has been less positive and has caused a source of distraction for some of the non-dedicated 'multi-strategy' funds, increased volatility and attractive spreads in other asset classes have caused temporary outflows of funds to other strategies or to meet redemptions. Furthermore some apprehension over the security of TRS swap counterparties and collateral funds exists whilst structures adapt to the changing perceptions of investors to this risk and the likelihood that collateral arrangements for cat bonds and collateralized reinsurance in general will be tightened going forward.

The outlook for the life securitization market is also mixed, issuance has fallen significantly during the credit crisis and the demise of the 'monoline' bond insurers that were prevalent in many life securitizations has led to a number of downgrades and areas of the market becoming tainted (refer to Chapter 14 on the general features of life insurance securitization). The credit crunch has had a direct impact on life securitizations with assets backing a number of the transactions becoming impaired and with sponsors themselves suffering weakened solvency positions and ratings downgrades. Whilst the short-term impact has been negative for life securitization, the longer term need for capital and the desire to bolster balance sheets might once again cause issuers to turn to securitization techniques as an attractive alternative to expensive equity or debt capital raising.

For non-life and life insurance issuers alike the immediate impact of the credit crunch is to highlight the strategic imperative of sophisticated ERM and diversification of funding sources, particularly as traditional capital-raising sources are affected by credit market conditions. The longer term impact of the credit crunch on ILS issuance is also likely to be positive, with the collapse of a number of major financial institutions and the strain on reinsurers' balance sheets highlighting counterparty credit risk and the value of stable collateralized capacity.

The author would like to acknowledge the contribution of Ryan Clarke, Chi Hum and Cory Anger of GC Securities.

3
Cedants' Perspectives on Non-life Securitization

Understanding the key motivations of a cedant in an ILS transaction is essential for the development and growth of this market. In this chapter, three major players present and analyse their perspectives, the context, some concrete examples, the challenges and the opportunities of non-life securitisation as an advanced tool for risk mitigation, capital management and as a complement to traditional risk management solutions.

3A INSURANCE-LINKED SECURITIES AS PART OF ADVANCED RISK INTERMEDIATION

Insa Adena,[a] Katharina Hartwig[b] and Georg Rindermann[a]

This contribution outlines the perspective of Allianz as a cedant to access the insurance-linked securities (ILS) market. The analysis is structured as follows. Section 3A.1 starts with an analysis of the motivation for Allianz as a transaction sponsor to take part in advanced risk intermediation activities. In this context, the competitive changes in the insurance industry are explored as well as the strategic implications for Allianz as a global insurance group with a business focus on primary insurance. Taking up general considerations for transferring insurance risk to the capital markets, Section 3A.2 outlines the objectives pursued by the cedants in ILS transactions. Section 3A.3 discusses a cat bond transaction sponsored by Allianz by means of a case study of the first issuance under the Blue Fin Ltd Program. It outlines the motivation for securitizing European windstorm risk and highlights details related to the structuring and the distribution of the bond.

3A.1 Motivation for Allianz to take part in ILS activities

The strategic decision for an insurance group like Allianz to promote and get involved with advanced risk intermediation activities is principally motivated by the dynamics in the insurance industry setup. In the past, the competitive landscape was characterized by relatively benign conditions. Entry barriers were high, the threat of substitutes was low, competition was moderate, capital suppliers were patient and customers were loyal. Today, as barriers to entry are lowered, and disintermediation (e.g. via securitization) increasing, the relatively non-aggressive insurance industry has evolved into a highly competitive pool of very diverse participants. Capital suppliers focus on growth whilst optimizing capital efficiency and return on capital, and the bargaining power of customers is rising (see Ralph, 2008).

The transformation of the insurance industry has been driven by various factors. First, the traditional distribution of roles between primary insurance and reinsurance has changed over time with the borders getting blurred (for a detailed analysis see Booth and Fischer, 2007). Global insurance groups have emerged with the diversification potential of a large and geographically widespread insurance risk portfolio, and these continue to gain market share at the expense of small and medium-sized players. These large insurance companies are, to some extent, comparable to reinsurance companies in terms of their financial ratings and capital positions. Second, new players have entered the reinsurance market, such as the Bermudian insurers. Attracted to the insurance markets in the 80s and 90s, they often supply capacity opportunistically after large industry loss events. Third, capital markets perform an increasingly important function by offering an alternative channel for reinsurance and retrocession capacity via sidecars and catastrophe bonds. The multitude of ways to transfer insurance risk to the capital markets in the competitive landscape of the modern insurance industry is illustrated in Figure 3A.1.

---

[a] Allianz SE, Advanced Risk Intermediation
[b] Allianz SE, Group Legal Services

The Handbook of Insurance-Linked Securities   Edited by P. Barrieu and L. Albertini
© 2009 John Wiley & Sons, Ltd

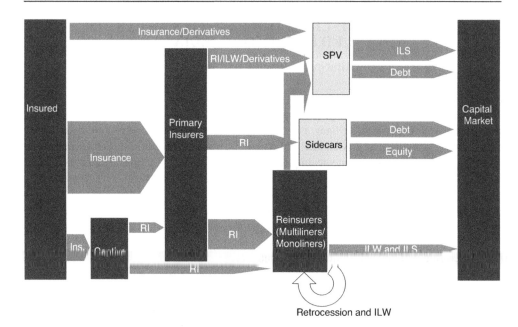

Figure 3A.1   Multitude of ways to transfer insurance risk to the capital markets. RI: reinsurance; ILW: industry loss warranties (contracts triggered by a given industry loss in a defined territory); sidecars are explained in Chapter 11; captives are insurance companies owned normally by a corporate group and providing cover within the group

Source: World Economic Forum Research and Analysis, reproduced with permission

With the traditional roles of insurance and reinsurance companies being challenged, Allianz has increasingly internalized value-adding activities previously assumed by reinsurers. For example, by ceding peak insurance risk of international subsidiaries to Allianz Re, a dedicated in-house reinsurer, the insurance group is taking advantage of diversification and pooling effects, and deploys the financial rating and capital position of the holding company. Moreover, a rising portion of risk is retained in the group, partly by keeping costly lower layers in the books. This approach is supported by enhanced reinsurance know-how and sophisticated risk management tools. The outplacement to external reinsurers is increasingly shifting from traditional quota share agreements to less costly higher excess of loss layers, or to peak risks with detrimental characteristics to overall portfolio diversification. As a consequence, external reinsurers are being offered a higher relative participation in natural catastrophe risks versus lower volatility risks.

In addition to traditional reinsurance solutions, Allianz is considering advanced risk intermediation techniques, such as ILS and other nontraditional risk transfer instruments for risk management purposes. As illustrated in Figure 3A.1, securitization creates a possibility to outplace parts of insurance risk portfolios directly to professional investors via special purpose vehicles. The following reasons cause cedants to transfer insurance risk to the capital market:

• The capital market provides additional capacity for insurance risk. Capacity has become increasingly important with respect to perils where the traditional reinsurance and retrocession markets have tightened after large loss events, such as with respect to hurricane cover in the US after Hurricane Katrina.

- The capital market is an additional source of capital. Although there is no financing element in cat bonds, the transfer of insurance risk by way of ILS should release risk and – ideally – regulatory capital, which can then be deployed for other purposes.
- Cat bonds offer multi-year cover whereas reinsurance and retrocession treaties usually have a one-year term. The longer term of cat bonds allows the pricing cycles of the reinsurance market to be smoothened.
- Capital market transactions decrease the credit risk of the cedant vis-à-vis reinsurers and retrocessionaires, as the proceeds of the transaction remain with the special purpose vehicle and are invested as collateral for the cedants' contingent claim against the special purpose vehicle.
- Trading of insurance risk on the secondary market creates price transparency.

From the perspective of Allianz, the transfer of insurance risk to the capital markets provides a supplement rather than an alternative to traditional reinsurance given the existing limitations in terms of available perils and triggers. Moreover, the dependency on the conditions in the financial markets and the related placement risk complicate a full integration of ILS solutions into the retrocession program of an insurance group like Allianz. In order to better understand the limitations and potential obstacles related to the use of ILS transactions, the following section takes a closer look at the objectives of insurance companies.

3A.2 Objectives of insurance companies

Assuming an ILS transaction can be undertaken at competitive economic terms, the cedants generally will pursue the following objectives. First, the instrument should provide cover that is tailored to the underlying insurance portfolio and exposes the sponsors to a minimum of basis risk (for more details, please refer to Chapter 5 on basis risk and see Figure 3A.2 for instruments with and without basis risk). With respect to cat bonds, the degree of realization of this objective depends on the trigger chosen. Indemnity-based cat bonds are structured similarly to excess-of-loss reinsurance, as investors assume the specific loss exposure of the sponsor's underlying portfolio within the limits of the respective instrument. Accordingly, the

	Instruments with basis risk	Instruments without or with limited basis risk
Non Life	• Cat bonds with modeled loss, industry loss or parametric triggers • Cat swaps • ILW	• Sidecars • Cat bonds with indemnity based trigger
Life	• Extreme mortality bonds • Longevity ILS	• Embedded value securitization • XXX and AXXX bonds

Figure 3A.2 Instruments with and without basis risk

Source: World Economic Forum (2008), reproduced with permission

sponsor does not retain any basis risk. Instruments with a modeled loss trigger, an industry loss trigger or a parametric trigger, on the other hand, leave more or less basis risk with the sponsor because the underlying portfolio and the protection provided by the risk transfer instrument are not fully correlated. The basis risk will vary according to the granularity of the trigger chosen, the relevant peril, the quality of the risk model used and the insurance portfolio for which protection is sought. Retaining basis risk not only leaves the sponsor with an imperfect hedge, but may also have negative impacts for the sponsor on the accounting, regulatory and rating treatment of the instrument. Having said that, indemnity-based transactions are less transparent and objective for the investors and raise moral hazard and adverse selection issues, which may be expressed in an increased risk premium. The choice of the trigger type and the structuring of the transaction will have to take into account these aspects (for further discussion, please refer to Chapter 4 on choice of triggers).

Second, the instrument should expose the sponsor to a minimum of counterparty risk. In cat bond transactions, the proceeds of the bond issuance remain with the special purpose vehicle and fully collateralize the investors' repayment claim and the sponsor's payment claim, the latter being contingent upon the occurrence of a triggering event. Typically, the proceeds are invested in an asset portfolio, the returns of which are swapped in a total return swap against LIBOR- or EURIBOR-based quarterly payments and payment of the principal amount upon termination of the total return swap. Investors and sponsor are exposed to the counterparty risk of the total return swap provider and, upon the latter's default, to the market risk of the portfolio assets. Recent developments in the financial markets have led to a review and a discussion of these collateral structures in terms of transparency of the underlying asset portfolio, the eligible asset classes, top-up obligations of the swap counterparty and the overall collateral structure.

Third, the instrument should receive favorable treatment with respect to risk capital, regulatory capital and credit ratings. Whereas risk capital models take an economic view on the risk transfer and the risk capital that is being released thereby, release of regulatory capital is, in most jurisdictions, still governed by a more rigid view which favors indemnity-based transactions (for more details, refer to Chapter 26 on regulatory issues and solvency capital requirements). The objective of the sponsors with respect to rating – other than the rating of the ILS itself – is to obtain credit for the risk transfer instrument in its financial strength rating and to thereby achieve a positive impact on its capital adequacy ratio. Methods to evaluate basis risk and to allocate capital to it, rather than applying a 'haircut', are being developed to ensure a consistent treatment of risk transfer instruments.

3A.3   Case study: Blue Fin Ltd

In the past few years, Allianz has adopted a revised approach to reinsurance which has entailed a shift towards more active and group-wide risk portfolio optimization and has led to greater centralization of reinsurance purchases. Internally, this has implied an increased participation of Allianz Re, the group's in-house reinsurer, in local reinsurance programs operated by group subsidiaries; externally, it has resulted in the creation and placement of several large global reinsurance programs. While these centrally managed programs allow for the crystallization and partial retention of diversification benefits that come with a large and geographically widespread risk portfolio, they also spotlight risk concentrations and potential current or future capacity shortages for such peak risks.

Uncomfortable with the risk of being faced with globally increasing demand for (catastrophe) cover as a result of mega trends such as climate change (see Allianz, 2008 and Mills, 2006), increasing urbanization and greater connectivity of people through technology and modern communication on the one hand, and a limited amount of risk capacity being available from a concentrated group of providers on the other hand, Allianz took the strategic decision to start using nontraditional retrocession capacity offered by the capital markets as a supplement to its global reinsurance programs. Since then, Allianz has sponsored two cat bond transactions, its first issuance under the Blue Wings program set up for the benefit of Allianz Global Corporate & Specialty in April 2007 and its first issuance under the Blue Fin program created for the benefit of Allianz Re in November 2007. Both of these securitized risks originated from the group's insurance operations. A third transaction issued through Blue Coast Ltd was targeted at third party client business originated by Allianz Risk Transfer. The following paragraphs will take a closer look at the motivation for and structural features of the Blue Fin Ltd (Series 1) issuance.

Through the Blue Fin Ltd (Series 1) transaction, Allianz Re was able to cover a peak natural catastrophe scenario, the risk of significant windstorm-related losses in seven European countries at a stable premium for a multi-year period, and without carrying the contingent credit risk of a reinsurer. In addition, the transaction reduces the general dependency on the traditional reinsurance market. Issued through Blue Fin Ltd, a Cayman Islands based special purpose entity, the two-tranche deal with an aggregate volume of approximately €200 million constitutes the first series under a program with an initial maximum size of €1 billion. The cat bond transfers to investors the risks of windstorms in Austria, Belgium, France, Germany, Ireland, the Netherlands and the UK.

Payouts from the cat bond are contingent on the triggering of a parametric index based on wind speeds at various locations measured directly from anemometers managed by the meteorological offices of the countries in the covered territory. The trigger relies on the RMS Europe Windstorm Model *RiskLink* version 7.0 that is also applied by Allianz for internal modeling purposes. In order to minimize the basis risk, the index was tailored to the insurance exposure of Allianz by calibrating the weights assigned to each location.

As shown in Figure 3A.3, the securities issued by Blue Fin Ltd (Series 1) are denominated in US dollars and euros and offer investors a coupon of 4.40% and 4.55% over the applicable reference rates LIBOR and EURIBOR, respectively. Both tranches are scheduled to be redeemed in 2012 and hold a rating of BB+ by Standard & Poor's.

When structuring the transaction, several key decisions had to be taken:

1. Whether to choose an indemnity, a modeled loss or a parametric trigger.
2. Whether to target the cover at higher or lower return periods.
3. Whether to denominate the bonds in US dollars or euros.
4. Whether to go for a longer or a shorter maturity.

In each of these areas sponsor and investor preferences had to be assessed and balanced, which led to the choices outlined below.

While an indemnity or modeled loss trigger would have allowed the virtual elimination of basis risk, or at least the restriction of it to unmodeled risks, the parametric index ultimately chosen was meant to respond to investor preferences at the time by offering maximum objectivity and transparency combined with timely information and settlement mechanics following a potential triggering event. As the density of anemometers operated by various national weather

Sponsor	Allianz SE (Reinsurance Division)
Issuer	Blue Fin Ltd (Cayman Islands exempted SPV)
Issuance volumes	Class A: EUR 155m
	Class B: USD 65m
	Class A: EURIBOR + 455 bps
	Class B: LIBOR + 440 bps
Scheduled Redemption Date	April 10, 2012
1st Call Date	April 8, 2010
Peril	European windstorm
Covered area	Austria, Belgium, France, Germany, Ireland, Netherlands, UK
Trigger mechanism	Parametric index
Risk level	Annualized attachment probability: 1.38%
	Annualized expected loss: 1.20%
	Annualized exhaustion probability: 1.04%
Rating	BB+ (S&P)

Figure 3A.3   Blue Fin Ltd (Series 1) summary terms of the Class A and B notes
Source: Allianz

agencies throughout Europe is relatively high, Allianz felt comfortable that a parametric index could be designed at acceptable levels of basis risk.

The choice of a suitable return period for the bond was, on the one hand, driven by a specific coverage need in the 75–100 year return period area. On the other hand, Allianz felt that the collateralized nature of bond cover was particularly valuable for higher return periods and thus larger, more remote events.

The inclusion of the US dollar tranche was meant to offer the traditionally US dollar oriented cat bond investor base a currency alternative, although Allianz pursued the objective to place as much of the capacity as possible in euros to minimize the currency exposure.

With a scheduled redemption after approximately 4.5 years, Allianz went for a slightly longer maturity than is customary in the cat bond market. This choice was principally motivated by the expectation that, given the strength of Allianz's primary insurance business in Europe, European windstorm risk will continue to be a peak peril for the Group in the foreseeable future.

With 25 investors on board, the cat bond was placed with a significantly broader group of investors than is usual for this asset class (see International Financing Review, 2007). The final investor allocation by region on the left-hand side in Figure 3A.4 shows that the majority of the paper was sold to European investors. As concerns the breakdown by investor outlined on the right-hand side, specialty fund managers and hedge funds took more than half of the securities, with 22% and 34%, respectively. Overall, the deal was 1.5 times oversubscribed.

The deal was the first to come to market in the 2007 European windstorm season. The target volume of the transaction could be easily achieved due to both the market timing and the strong investor reception, particularly in Europe. The successful placement of the bond showed that the demand for these types of securities continued to be strong and that this

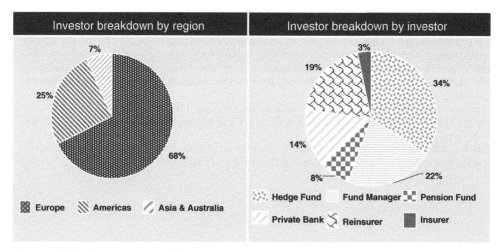

Figure 3A.4   Final allocation and investor breakdown of Blue Fin Ltd (Series 1)
Source: Allianz

market segment had been virtually unaffected by the brewing turmoil in the financial markets at that time.

Overall, Blue Fin Ltd was set up to offer Allianz a flexible multi-peril risk transfer platform aimed at alleviating potential capacity constraints for certain peak catastrophe exposures and to release risk capital. The shelf program supports the company's risk management strategy and provides – within a reduced transaction implementation timeline – access to alternative, nontraditional retrocession capacity, and thus an option for better diversification of reinsurance capacity.

The short- and medium-term viability of this strategy is currently being challenged, however, through the effects of the 2008 financial crisis. While cat bond prices have held up comparatively well relative to other asset classes, the cat bond investor base has not been spared the increasing pressure resulting from the crisis. The failure of Lehman Brothers in September 2008 led to the collapse of total return swaps in those transactions where Lehman Brothers acted as swap counterparty and highlighted deficiencies of the underlying collateral structures. While Lehman Brothers' involvement as swap counterparty concerned only four transactions, the experience there demonstrated that many cat bond structures are not as isolated from financial market risks as both investors and sponsors would like. The result was greater uncertainty on secondary market valuations of outstanding bonds and increased price volatility in particular for those transactions with swap counterparties perceived to be under financial stress. In addition, the persisting shortage of liquidity and the massively increased cost of fresh capital have forced some investors, hedge funds in particular, to stop new investments, liquidate positions and in some cases even wind down altogether. Since the Lehman Brothers bankruptcy, no new cat bond transactions have come to market in 2008 and it remains to be seen what capacity capital markets can provide in the short and medium term and how quickly risk premiums demanded by investors return to levels broadly in line with reinsurance premiums for comparable risks.

REFERENCES

Allianz (2008) *Hedging climate change – How insurers can manage the risk of increasing natural catastrophes.*

Booth, C. and Fischer, M. (2007) The insurer/reinsurer view of the changing, in: Britton, N. *Managing the changing landscape of catastrophe risk*, 10th Aon Re Australia Biannual Hazard Conference, pp. 1–19.

International Financing Review (2007) *Allianz broadens cat-bond*, 17th November.

Mills, E. (2006) *From Risk to Opportunity: How Insurers Can Proactively and Profitably Manage Climate Change*, Ceres Report, August.

Ralph, J. (2008) The changing risk landscape for (re)insurers in Asia, *Asian Insurance Review*, June.

World Economic Forum (2008) *Convergence of Insurance and Capital Markets.*

3B REINSURANCE VS SECURITISATION

Guillaume Gorge[a]

For any company, managing risk consists mainly of removing risk sources except if it has unique expertise in them or if these risks are not sufficiently tradable (see for instance Froot, 2007). Compared to other industries, an insurer has the choice to outsource its risks through risk securitisation, a risk transfer available to any industry, but also through the more specific mechanism of reinsurance. Therefore, in its risk management decision, an insurer must decide whether it wants to keep the risk internally, buy reinsurance or securitise risk.

I propose here to expose how an insurer such as AXA decides between these alternatives in practice, looking especially at the role of information in modern risk management. We will then study which solution is currently the most appropriate for the main risks of a Property and Casualty insurer. Following this, we discuss two ILS transactions sponsored by AXA before concluding on the key success factors for the development of insurance-linked securities.

3B.1 Keeping risk vs transferring it

An insurer has first to choose between keeping risks internally (and exposing its earnings and capital) or transferring risk. For each risk, insurers will have to decide the level of retention on this risk (equivalent to equity tranche) and up to what level to transfer risk (capacity). In practice, most insurers try to keep their risk retention low compared to the risks taken in financial assets for instance. Risk retention may even be defined as being as minimal as possible, until it's not economically sustainable. The main reason for such low relative retention is not risk aversion but the better steering of business it brings: for complex organisations, knowledge – especially on risk – is key, and therefore, we may be ready to pay for it. Indeed, can you imagine assessing the performance of a risky company or one of its lines of business without knowing its level of risk?

In practice, an efficient way of creating information on its risk is to use risk markets and to transfer risk.[1] The extra information provided by the ILS market compared to the more illiquid reinsurance market mainly explains why an insurer may decide sometimes to use securitisation instead of reinsurance despite the lack of a compelling cost advantage.

If you invest in information and the understanding of tail risks, you can increase retention, but this investment is costly and practically limited to the biggest cedants. Even for them, modeling rare events on the basis of their own claims and experience is still challenging.

Regarding the capacity they buy, insurers often tend to show much more heterogeneity, international insurers being generally more covered than their local peers. This apparent

---

[a]Group P&C Chief Risk officer, Group Risk Management, AXA
[1] Hayek (1945) has defended the efficiency of markets compared to scientific 'plan' in his role of 'communicating information'.

---

paradox can be explained by the fact that reinsurance is often designed more to protect the volatility of the insurers' profit and loss accounts than their balance sheets.

3B.2 Reinsurance vs securitisation

When an insurer has decided to cover its risk, it can then choose between reinsurance and securitisation. Reinsurance is traditionally the main risk management tool of an insurer. The links between an insurer and a reinsurer are complex but based on a long relationship: for the most complex risks (such as Directors' & Officers' liability insurance, or Engineering), the reinsurer has an excellent knowledge of the portfolio and can be considered an insider of the company. Traditionally, the cedant applies the same terms and conditions to the reinsurers of a program (under the favorite reinsurer's clause). The recent and still marginal use of differentiated terms and conditions applied to reinsurers has reinforced the need for the reinsurer to have excellent underwriting and risk management skills, as a reinsurer can be offered conditions that leading reinsurers would refuse.

Securitisation is close to reinsurance, even if the sophisticated mechanism to transform a risk into a note may hide this proximity. However, the main difference doesn't come from the structure but from the creation of a tradable asset: this latter means a weakened link between the risk taker and the cedant. Thanks to this new secondary market in traded insurance risk, an investor can decide to step out of the transaction by selling his bond into the secondary market, an option that is not available for the reinsurer.

The existence of a secondary market offers outsiders the possibility to invest in the risk, without entering into a formal relationship with the insurer. In addition, if the market is sufficiently liquid, outsiders may invest in this market without being experts on the risk, as there is an explicit price for all players. For instance, when a cat bond risk is reassessed by the market (by comparison with other cat bonds for instance), its price reflects this new view of the risk.

If we sum up the main respective features of reinsurance and securitisation, we obtain Table 3B.1.

This 'insider/outsider' difference has probably been reaffirmed by the subprime crisis, as investors will (hopefully at any rate) no longer disregard the level of knowledge necessary to take risk.

Also, the structural differences between reinsurance and ILS imply they will also be appropriate for different types or levels of risk: securitisation should not be seen as an alternative to reinsurance but more as a complement.

Table 3B.1 Reinsurance and ILS main features

	Reinsurance	ILS
Structuring	Risk as a liability	Risk as an asset
Secondary market	No, illiquid position	Yes, possibility to get out of the risk
Structuring cost	Low	High
Investor's relation with the issuer	insider	outsider
Counterparty risk	Reinsurer	Collateral structure
Term	Normally one year	Normally three to five years
Reinstatements	Normally agreed	Not available

Source: AXA

3B.3   Application to main P&C risks

In this section I propose to explore instances when ILS may be a good complement to reinsurance, specifically in a European environment with the development of Solvency II. Even if the framework of Solvency II is still under development, it's already sufficiently established to detect some future trends for P&C ILS issuers.

Securitisation is currently mainly concentrated on catastrophe risks, a category set to develop as regulatory capital in Europe will be risk-based capital measured through a one-year, 200-year Value-at-Risk. This means that European insurers, some of whom are currently protected against a storm with a recurrence period that can be as low as 50 years (probability of occurrence of 2%), will have to increase their protection up to 200 years (0.5% probability) if they want to obtain the maximum capital relief.

However, Solvency II epitomises the major changes the insurance industry is facing, with a demand by its stakeholders for more transparency in the risk and also the protection it takes. In this respect, we can foresee that some risks that are currently retained within each company may be transferred in the future in order to increase this transparency.

Which risks may therefore be suitable for securitisation? Good risk candidates will be those that are significant at the level of the insurer, with low insider information needed.

The main risks in Property and Casualty insurance are catastrophes, reserve adequacy and market cycle. Only the first is traditionally reinsured[2] and, as mentioned, securitised, through cat bonds. Nevertheless, there is no reason to limit ILS transactions to cat bonds, as has been seen with the successful securitisation of motor risk or counterparty risk of reinsurers. Reserve risk and market cycle may be good candidates for ILS: for decades, reserve and market cycle risks have been mitigated by prudent reserving strategies. However, Solvency II and IFRS will request insurers to give a more economic view of reserve and therefore, insurers will be increasingly on the lookout for appropriate protection for these risks. Obviously reinsurance (through adverse development cover for instance) may bring solutions, especially on the junior layers with potentially more adverse selection, but as the amounts at stake are huge, ILS may potentially be an alternative to capital for insurers.

Obviously, there is a significant information gap for an investor vis-à-vis a reinsurer on such transactions, and therefore for all indemnity-based transactions we can imagine a risk transfer with the lower, more volatile layers placed as reinsurance and the higher, low-frequency and high-severity layers placed as ILS transactions.

A last risk category, *underwriting of a single risk*, is heavily reinsured even if it does not appear as one of the major systemic risks of an insurer, due to its good diversification properties. Even if the impact of such reinsurance on capital is limited, we don't expect significant decrease in reinsurance buying of such cover as it provides insurers with vital information on the quality and price of their risks. In practice, in addition to the price of the risk provided by the transaction, the audit of risk performed by the reinsurers before underwriting the risk may be useful to reassure the company on the quality of its under-writing and claims process. Reinsurance is really well adapted for all these risks that are so different between each portfolio and transaction. In contrast, we don't think there is much

---

[2] Albeit it can be argued that large quota shares have a significant impact on reserve and cycle risk because quota share is generally a long-term reinsurance.

future for securitisation underwriting risk due to the specific information needed on each transaction.[3]

3B.4   Case studies: AURA RE and SPARC

AXA has been a pioneer in the ILS market. In addition to WINCAT, the first European cat bond in 1997 issued by Winterthur (now AXA), AXA has launched AURA RE (2005 – European Windstorm), SPARC (2005, the first securitisation of a motor insurance portfolio), OSIRIS (2006, the first extreme-mortality risk coverage program from an insurance company) and SPARC EUROPE (2007, the first securitisation of a multi-jurisdiction motor insurance portfolio).

Through the AURA RE transaction, AXA has bought protection against low-frequency, high-severity European Windstorm events. Several features are worth mentioning with regard to the structure of this transaction.

First, we chose an indemnity structure. After a first experience of a cat index in 2001 showing a lower correlation than expected with our final cost, we analyzed basis risk linked to wind speed as inappropriate for AXA, as cat windstorm risk is one of our major risks, our role as risk manager is to ensure that our protection from extreme events will work when we need it. An indemnity structure has no more risk than an index structure from the investor's point of view and theoretically should not cost more. However, we reckon it's difficult to place any indemnity transaction because in such cases, investors (and rating agencies) can't rely only on external information (models for instance) but must analyze additional information specific to the issuer (potentially *insider* information). We solved this issue with AURA RE by giving full transparency to investors on our reinsurance program: investors were protected against any potential arbitrage due to their inferior knowledge of the specific AXA risk. Nevertheless, the long-term solution for investors and issuers probably relies on the development of indexes with lower basis risk, such as a market loss index, as this would allow more investors to participate in such a transaction and reduce the issuance costs due to the standardisation of the transaction.

Second, AURA RE was really structured as a complement to our reinsurance program. In order to ensure a perfect adherence between the two, we requested a euro-denominated structure and, more innovative, the yearly reset clause (to adapt the structure to any change in underlying exposure) was applied to the spread instead of the attachment point.

The second transaction I would like to mention is SPARC, which transfers the risk of deviation of the loss ratio of a motor insurance book (above a certain threshold). SPARC FRANCE was launched in 2005 for an amount of €200m on the French motor portfolio only. SPARC EUROPE was launched two years later, extending the principle of SPARC to a diversified portfolio of motor books in Germany, Belgium, Spain and Italy and for a volume of issuance of €450m. This latter transaction is particularly interesting as we were able to materialise diversification between all our books.

Thanks to SPARC, we were able to explore transactions on risks with high frequency and low probability. By generally keeping these risks internally, insurers act as risk warehouses.[4] The alternative model, risk intermediation, tested with SPARC and used by banks for years, is based on the transfer of all risks and not only the extreme or catastrophic ones. It's too early

---

[3] We have nevertheless contemplated at least one occasion where an ILS transaction may be useful: the insurance of a nuclear plant, due to the high amount at stake.

[4] See Cummins (2004) for illustrations of both models of risk warehouses and risk intermediation.

to know which model will emerge as the most appropriate for insurers but at least SPARC has proved that investors are ready to support the extension of the risk intermediation model to insurance risks.

3B.5   Limits and success factors to securitisation

Insurers face many challenges when entering into an ILS transaction, and these challenges mainly concern information: as investors have less inside knowledge than reinsurers, insurers have to disclose a high degree of information on the risk, especially if the transaction is directly based on the risk of the insurer (indemnity-based transaction). The alternative for the insurer is to base the transaction on an objective index (market loss, modeled loss or index loss) but the remaining risk within the insurer (basis risk) may be huge if the index is not sufficiently well correlated to the real cost of the insurer, as mentioned for AURA RE. For an in-depth discussion on basis risk, please refer to Chapter 5.

With all the characteristics described above, we can predict that ILS will develop:

- For the highest layers of reinsurance, which are capital-intensive but with a remote transferred risk, the cedant will value the counterparty risk in the economic equation and therefore ILS, being cash collateralised, may appear more appealing than traditional reinsurance (in a way, newly created cat monoline reinsurers can be considered 'managed CDO of cat reinsurance', but with a high default option for the cedant as the capital of this reinsurance is less than their nominal exposure).
- When the basis risk is limited, either because this is an indemnity-based transaction or because the chosen index for the transaction is highly correlated to the real loss of the insurer. A key success factor is the development of indexes that are really correlated with insurance losses, which explains why major European insurers support the creation of a market loss index for Europe, indexes based on wind speed being inappropriate in terms of basis risk. In addition, indexes allow standardising conditions and therefore reduce the time required to structure a transaction as well as the transactional costs (and provide an additional example of the creation of knowledge created by the development of a market).
- When there is a real benefit for the insurer to signal to his stakeholders that he is well protected, especially compared to his peers. As the ILS market is accessible to many more stakeholders than reinsurance, the signal is stronger. If the value brought to this signal becomes higher and is higher than the cost of securitising risk, it may even transform the model of insurers from risk warehouses to risk intermediators.
- Where knowledge is key (for instance, rapid changes in the environment) but not (too) specific to a risk or portfolio (catastrophe risk, longevity, liability inflation trend, etc.).

With the development of risk management in insurance companies, information and transparency will be more and more valued and, as a consequence, so will ILS as a key tool for transferring risks. However, due to the specificity of each insurance risk and their consequential high illiquidity, reinsurance is here to stay as the main transference tool for insurers, especially on underwriting risks. In the long term, reinsurance and securitisation will probably be complementary risk-transfer tools: reinsurance for specific and information-intensive transactions or layers and ILS for capital-intensive ones.

REFERENCES

Cummins, J. D. (2004) *Securitisation of Life Insurance Assets and Liabilities*, Financial Institutions Center.

Froot, K. A. (2007) Risk management, capital budgeting, and capital structure policy for insurers and reinsurers. *The Journal of Risk and Insurance*, **74**, 273–299.

Gorge, G. (2007) Titrisation et Réassurance, *Risques*, **69**, March.

Gorge, G. (2008) La Crise des Subprimes signifie-t-elle la fin des Titrisations d'assurance?, *Revue d'Economie Financière*, hors-série, July.

Hayek, F. A. (1945) The Use of Knowledge in Society, *American Economic Review*, **XXXV** (4), 519–530.

Menioux, J.-C. (2008) Securitisation as a complement to reinsurance, *An illustration on AXA strategy*, *Conference Rendez-Vous Monte Carlo*, September.

Plantin, G. (2006) Does Reinsurance needs reinsurers? *Journal of Risk and Insurance*, **73** (1), 153–168.

3C SECURITIZATION AS A DIVERSIFICATION FROM TRADITIONAL RETROCESSION

Jean-Luc Besson[a]

SCOR, as an international reinsurer, aims to optimize its capital allocation by line of business and geographical zone. The main aim of purchasing capacity in the retrocession market[5] is to meet its capital needs, particularly in relation to peak risks due to natural catastrophe exposure. In addition to this optimization of required capital, the purpose of retrocession of peak risks is to:

- limit the volatility of annual results;
- satisfy the risk appetite requirements and risk tolerance constraints defined by the Board;
- satisfy the requirements of local regulators;
- reduce the capital charge imposed by the rating agencies.

The purchase of retrocession capacities has focused, and continues to focus, on the following areas of risk:

- catastrophe risks in life portfolios (pandemic) and non-life portfolios (natural catastrophes);
- industrial and commercial large risks (facultatives).

For several years (namely since 2000) SCOR has accessed the capital markets for its retrocession needs, with the issue of various cat bonds (Atlas I to IV) and in 2008, the signature of a mortality swap with JP Morgan to reduce the mortality risk connected with a pandemic. There are four main reasons for this development:

1. The international retrocession market is not always able to cover the risk or cannot offer the required security at an economically viable price. It should be noted that from a risk management point of view it is necessary to pay particular attention to retrocessionaires' credit risk, which naturally leads to a diversification of suppliers to limit the impact of the bankruptcy of a provider of retrocession capacity on the losses on reinsurance recoverables (i.e. claims made post event) as well as on the available retrocession capacity.

   In particular, the traditional retrocession market has not been able to provide capacity for pandemic risk for significant amounts of exposure. As a result, capital market solutions have been considered. SCOR studied a mortality bond solution with banks but because of the high related costs, decided to abandon the project and finally entered into a mortality swap.

   The situation is similar for non-life natural catastrophe risk. For several years the traditional natural catastrophe retrocession market has been characterized by uncertainty relating to the level of available capacity and price level, and particularly following a major event.

   The planning and optimization of reinsurance underwriting for the main renewal dates (1st January mainly for treaties) requires a precise knowledge of the available capacities,

---

[a] Jean-Luc Besson SCOR

[5] With the exception of some Lloyds syndicates, almost all the significant players in the retrocession market are Bermudian or American. They are also operating as reinsurers, especially in the US cat market.

security level (credit risk) and price in the retrocession market. It should be noted that the balance of risks underwritten and retrocession purchased, as well as the profile of the book of business, cannot be changed significantly without Board approval.

Over the last few years the requirements of enterprise risk management (ERM) governance and practices have demanded we take into account the uncertainty of available capacity and higher prices in the retrocession market. The available retrocession capacity and prices are determined by the US natural catastrophe market (both direct insurance and reinsurance) and this holds true whether we consider the situation after the series of hurricanes Katrina, Rita Wilma or the 2008 financial crisis. For retrocessionaires, who are mainly focused on the US market, the European and Asian markets should provide diversification. But currently the price of natural catastrophe cover is considerably higher in the US. As a consequence, this market price factor overrides the advantage of diversification. This economically rational attitude increases the uncertainty of the availability of capacity in Europe and Asia, covering mainly European Windstorm and Asian Earthquake.

2. ILS-type solutions offer multi-year, annually adjustable cover
3. Cat bonds give additional capacity from the capital markets for events with a low probability in Europe and Asia.[6] The market price of such capacity is currently different from the price of traditional retrocession and hence may be closer to the technical price (linked to the probability of the event and expected loss).
4. Finally, ILS allows an additional diversification of players and a reduction of counterparty risk.

However, these solutions have certain characteristics, which could be considered drawbacks:

- The basis risk in the case of a non-indemnity solution (model loss or individual solution). This is often difficult to evaluate precisely but to reduce it requires more onerous solutions, which include overlaps (please refer to Chapter 5).
- Legal risks, especially in the case of indemnity solutions. Claims could be contested if it is established that certain information was not revealed to investors.
- Counterparty risk on the assets following a default of the financial institution guaranteeing the total return swap.

In conclusion, SCOR uses capital market solutions to transfer natural catastrophe risks in order to provide diversification from the traditional retrocession market.

With such solutions, particular attention should be paid to the risks associated with the collateral assets in the transaction (total return swap), basis risk and legal risk.

These ILS solutions also give additional capacity and flexibility alongside the more traditional retrocession market, which remains the key player for the mitigation of SCOR's natural catastrophe risks.

---

[6] For many investors, European and Asian cat bonds provide interesting diversification.

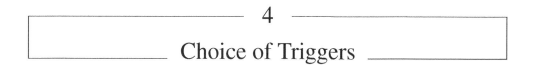

4

Choice of Triggers

Dominik Hagedorn,[a] Christian Heigl,[a] Andreas Müller[a] and Gerold Seidler[a]

This chapter provides insight into payout triggers used within cat bond transactions. First, we provide an introduction to the topic. Then, we describe indemnity as well as the range of non-indemnity triggers. Lastly, we discuss the choice of trigger, highlighting the fact that the ideal trigger may be different for every cat bond sponsor and that reinsurers can add significant value in the context of cat bond transactions.

4.1 GENERAL ASPECTS

Trigger selection is a central component in a non-life insurance securitisation because it determines the scope of indemnification of the cat bond sponsor.

In a cat bond transaction, a payment to the protection buyer is contingent on the occurrence of a predefined event. From a sponsor's perspective, such payment ideally equals the incurred ultimate net loss, because this provides a perfect hedge for the payable claims to the policyholders. Transactions that provide such a perfect hedge incorporate a so-called 'indemnity trigger', which covers the protection buyer for the agreed attachment and for the agreed limit for its certified ultimate net loss. Sponsors can incorporate indemnity-based capital markets cover well into their traditional programme at the inception of the cover, as the cat bond can attach to a traditional reinsurance layer without any gaps in between.

Investors, the ultimate risk bearers, have mixed views about indemnity transactions. A large group of investors prefers non-indemnity to indemnity cat bonds mainly because of the latter's inherent reduced transparency, the lengthy loss verification and payout process and the complexity of an insurance portfolio in general. This often leads to investors requiring higher risk spreads for indemnity transactions. Yet, an indemnity transaction from a well-known sponsor with the willingness to disclose information on loss history, internal underwriting processes, exposures and claims handling can be attractive to a smaller group of investors. Other investors do not have a preference for a specific trigger at all and seek to develop a well-balanced portfolio containing cat bonds with all existing triggers.

For cat bond sponsors, there is thus the trade-off between higher effectiveness of coverage of indemnity bonds versus better price and placement certainty of non-indemnity transactions. But it may not always be necessary to transfer a risk on an indemnity basis to the capital markets. For some (re)insurance companies, it might be sufficient to issue the cat bond on an

---

[a]Munich Re

industry loss or parametric trigger basis and keep the basis risk, which is the risk of incurring a loss but not being adequately indemnified by the bond (for an in-depth discussion, please refer to Chapter 5 on basis risk). For others, it may be more efficient to engage in a traditional reinsurance contract with a reinsurer, which then transfers the risk on a non-indemnity basis to the capital markets and thus keeps the basis risk on its balance sheet. In such a case, the reinsurer acts as a so-called 'transformer'. Apart from assuming basis risk, reinsurance companies can use their balance sheets to provide price and capacity guarantees, bridge covers, a third defense line, reinstatements and liquidity support when managing a cat bond transaction for a primary insurer.

Figure 4.1 shows that trigger distribution has been volatile in recent years. This can partly be traced back to changes within the investor community. One important cat bond investor class is the insurance industry, which has been a key investor group in the early phase of insurance risk securitisation. Generally the motivation for (re)insurance companies to invest in insurance products is to make use of available risk capital not fully used through core (re)insurance activities. Because of the fact that (re)insurance companies are familiar with the risk modelling processes, know other insurance companies in the market and adhere to an internal pricing system, sponsors were able to place transactions on an indemnity basis in the early phase of the market. However, the idea of insurance risk securitisation was not to find a different way of transferring risks to the same risk takers, namely the (re)insurance companies. Instead, it was to open the market to players that are not bound to the reinsurance cycle and can provide capacity when reinsurance companies are unable to do so. This led to a situation in which insurers were looking for risk takers outside of the reinsurance world, but these could not understand indemnity-based risks as well as the (re)insurance companies and were therefore reluctant to assume these risks at a reasonable price. Sponsors therefore started to engage in more transparent non-indemnity cat bonds and thereby enlarged the investor base immensely. This reduced the relative market share of indemnity triggers used within cat bond transactions and non-indemnity triggers became more predominant. Over the years, this changed again.

The relatively large proportion of indemnity transactions in recent years, as shown in Figure 4.1, demonstrates that investors have become increasingly familiar with insurance risks and can assume these if insurance companies are willing to disclose sensitive information on their insurance practices and pay the adequate price. However, sponsors should be careful about adding too many innovative features to a cat bond transaction. As was seen in some transactions at the beginning of 2008, placement success can be put at risk if investors are unable to entirely grasp the risk they are engaging in.

This chapter will introduce different types of triggers applied in cat bond transactions, describe the process of optimal trigger choice and analyse how reinsurers can optimise transaction value.

4.2 INDEMNITY TRIGGERS

Insurance companies sponsoring cat bonds incorporate such covers into their traditional reinsurance programme. The securitised amount and attachment point are aligned with their traditional covers to optimise reinsurance protection. The alignment with traditional covers works best with indemnity triggers because traditional protection is usually also based on the incurred ultimate net losses. Moreover, such a trigger does not entail any basis risk. It

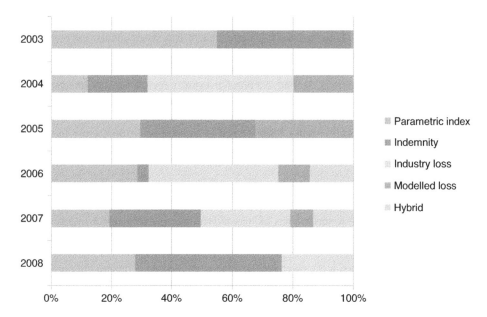

Figure 4.1 Distribution of triggers over the last six years (2003–2008) in terms of volume
Source: Munich Re

is, however, important to note that an indemnity-based cat bond does not exactly provide the same coverage as a traditional reinsurance contract.

4.2.1 Scope of coverage

Cat bonds usually provide cover for specific perils. A sponsor thus knows explicitly for which losses it will be indemnified by the bond. A California Earthquake bond on an indemnity basis, for example, cannot be triggered by a loss incurred due to strike, riot or civil commotion (SRCC). The reason for investors exclusively accepting specific peril risks is the fact that they are only willing to assume insurance risks that were modelled by independent agencies. Since risks such as SRCC or wildfire are barely modelled by the accepted modelling firms, investors are reluctant to assume these risks. Traditional catastrophe excess of loss covers are not limited to modellable perils. For top layers of large insurance programmes this is not so relevant because, besides terrorism, there is only a very remote chance that perils other than a modellable natural catastrophe could cause such a significant loss. For aggregate covers, however, this plays a significant role because smaller losses with a higher probability of occurrence are covered.

4.2.2 Payout timing

Besides scope of coverage, sponsors must be aware that payout timing works differently in a cat bond transaction than in traditional reinsurance contracts. There are two main reasons for this. First, reinsurance companies typically have a good understanding of the claims-handling process of their cedants, are very experienced in loss assessments, have a highly qualified claims staff and are therefore better prepared to react to loss events. Consequently, the indemnification of the reinsured in a traditional reinsurance contract takes place shortly after the losses have been reported. Second, cat bond investors generally are not interested in a long-term relationship with a specific primary insurance company. Investors first and foremost purchase cat bonds that are available and have the required risk and return profile. In case of non-indemnity triggers, there is usually little interest in the ceding insurer. Only in case of indemnity triggers one can observe a closer relationship between sponsor and investors.

4.2.3   Loss verification

Cat bond investors insist on a verification of losses done by an independent loss reviewer, which results in a longer time to payout than in traditional reinsurance contracts. This has several implications.

Once a relevant loss occurs, a reviewer verifies claims and losses to ensure the correctness of the claims payments of the sponsor. Since a severe event creates a very large number of claims, it is impossible for an external institution to verify if all claims are rightfully paid. The loss verification agents can only verify the correctness of the claims payment mechanism and test the correctness of payments randomly. This leaves some room for uncertainty on the part of the indemnity cat bond investors.

The indemnification of the sponsor only takes place when the independent loss reviewer has made a final decision about the amount of the ultimate net loss figure. This process can be very time-consuming, as this ultimate figure can only be announced once all claims are handled and possibly settled. If the review process overruns the maturity date, investors earn a significantly lower spread but cannot withdraw their funds. For these reasons, investors usually require a spread pick-up to non-indemnity triggered cat bonds.

4.2.4   Transparency

One of the aspects of indemnity triggers seen most critically by investors is the reduced transparency. While non-indemnity triggers are based on an independent set of transparent parameters, which are easier to understand, payout in an indemnity-triggered transaction ultimately depends on the claims payments of the sponsor. From an investor's perspective this is more challenging because the investor must understand the client's business processes, underwriting policies and claims-handling practices.

This section has described different views on indemnity triggers in cat bond transactions. On the one hand, indemnity triggers are most attractive for the sponsors because the ultimate net loss is what a sponsor needs protection for. On the other hand, it is important to note that indemnity cat bonds are not identical to traditional reinsurance contracts. Except for the disclosure requirements and the potential lengthy time to payout, an indemnity trigger cat bond has the most favourable characteristics for the sponsor. Investors, however, do not like some of the indemnity trigger aspects. They are not willing to agree to a principal reduction based on the loss indication given by the sponsor but require a third-party assessment. The resulting longer time to payout is disadvantageous for both parties involved. Alternative trigger solutions with shorter times to payout will be explained in the next section.

4.3 NON-INDEMNITY TRIGGERS

A sponsor may opt to use a more transparent non-indemnity trigger for its transaction. In such a case, the principal reduction of the cat bond does not depend on the sponsor's ultimately incurred losses but on the parameters of a natural catastrophe resulting in an index value or industry loss figures. The following section describes different types of non-indemnity triggers, while hybrid triggers are a combination of those.

4.3.1 Parametric triggers (pure and index)

The simplest case of a non-indemnity trigger is a purely parametric trigger. When using such a trigger, the sponsor defines a minimum event parameter, such as the moment magnitude of the earthquake, and a geographic area for which it requires protection. An example of a geographic area could be a federal state or a defined circle or box around insured objects. Independent of the incurred losses of the sponsor, payout of the bond takes place if an event with the defined minimum magnitude occurs within the covered area.

Typically, no exposure weights are applied in a purely parametric trigger, which consequently leads to an increased basis risk. In order to reduce this basis risk, a parametric index trigger can be used. In such a trigger structure, the measuring takes place on a much more granular level. To define the trigger, the sponsor chooses measuring stations in the geographical area where the cat bond is required. These measuring stations are assigned a weight, which corresponds to the exposure vulnerability of the (re)insurance company. In the case of an event, the weights are multiplied by the physical parameter measured in this event. These products are aggregated and if this sum exceeds a predefined attachment point, the cat bond is triggered.

An index formula could be constructed along the lines of the example below:

$$I = f \times \sum_{i=1}^{n} \left[w_i \times (v_i - v_0)^m \right]$$

where

I = index value
f = scaling factor
n = number of measuring stations (e.g. wind speed measuring stations)
w_i = weight assigned to measuring station i
v_i = observed physical parameter at measuring station i
v_0 = threshold
m = exponent

With $(v_i - v_0)$ used only when it is a positive value.

The basis of the index function is formed by the observed physical parameters v_i. These values are, for instance, peak ground accelerations or recorded wind speeds. Low v_i parameters typically do not cause relevant damage to insurance companies. Therefore, a specific level v_0 is used as a threshold for the observed values v_i. This way, it is assured that only those v_i parameters with a meaningful loss potential are considered for the trigger. In order to account for the individual exposure of the sponsor of the cat bond, the measuring stations are weighted according to the underlying exposure. The dominant influencing factors for the weights are local value concentration and vulnerability of the insured risks.

Weights can, for example, be based on sums insured or probable maximum loss per geographic location. Moreover, the weights can be set in such a way that the higher loss probability of vulnerable, more loss-prone insured objects is taken into account by overweighting areas with accumulations of such objects. The accuracy of the output, however, strongly depends on the density of measuring stations. Insurance companies know their exposure, for example, on a postcode or street address level. Measuring stations usually do not have the same granularity. Therefore, mathematical methods are used to best match the weights with the underlying exposure.

Lastly, the sum of the index contributions of the used measuring stations is multiplied by a scaling factor. This is mainly done to represent the numbers in a simpler form. The output of the model is an index value. If this value exceeds the index value that corresponds to the attachment point of the bond, the sponsor is indemnified.

The connection between the measured parameters and the resulting losses varies as a consequence of several aspects. The ultimate net loss to an insurance company caused by a natural catastrophe depends on the time of occurrence, the physical parameter and the duration. However, in the case of an earthquake cat bond, the earthquake magnitude measuring stations only account, for example, for the ground acceleration. The timing and duration of the earthquake are only estimated, which increases the basis risk.

While the model considers exposure distribution and loss vulnerability of the sponsor, the difficult part of the modelling process is to analyse what loss amounts a natural catastrophe with given parameters causes. This issue is addressed by developing an index function to best match traditional modelling. In doing so, it is possible to see how the underlying portfolio reacts to different natural catastrophe parameters. This function is used to determine the index level at which the sponsor of the bond wants to receive payout and to assign a probability to such a level.

Example of a parametric index trigger: Queen Street Ltd

Queen Street Ltd protects Munich Re, which acted as the sponsor and lead manager of a transaction against losses arising from European windstorms in the area shown in Figure 4.2. The bond was issued in March 2008 and has a term of three years. It is divided into two classes:

- Class A, which has the structure of an annual aggregate excess of loss cover. This protects Munich Re against an accumulation of windstorm events during one year. This class has an expected loss of 1.24% and an issuance volume of €70 million.
- Class B is a standard per occurrence cover. It protects Munich Re against a 28-year event and has an issuance volume of €100 million.

Munich Re used 216 wind speed recording stations in the United Kingdom, France, Germany, Belgium, The Netherlands, Ireland and Denmark. The wind speed threshold was set at 29 km/h.

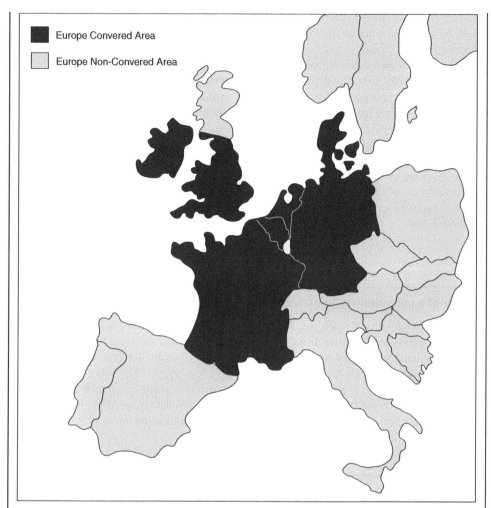

Figure 4.2   Covered area for the transaction Queen Street Ltd.

Source: Munich Re and EQECAT, reproduced with permission

4.3.2   Industry loss triggers

The payout of a cat bond with an industry loss trigger depends on the announced industry loss for a specific area (normally a state or a country or an aggregation of states and
countries) which is surveyed by an independent institution. Since this industry loss verification is only well established in the United States, US Hurricane and Earthquake bonds
are the dominant perils for this type of trigger. Currently, European and Japanese industry losses are not available from independent and systematic sources to provide such data

for trading purposes. In the future, European Wind cat bonds with an industry loss trigger will also be marketed since an external market loss determination concept is currently under development.

As is the case for parametric triggers, industry loss triggers exist in both pure and modified forms. The latter takes portfolio exposure on a more granular level into consideration. In the context of industry loss triggers, an unweighted version of the trigger causes principal reduction if the industry loss figure for a catastrophic event released by the responsible institution exceeds a certain amount, for instance, $35 billion. Unless the sponsor's losses are perfectly correlated with the industry loss, a significant risk in differences is assumed, namely the basis risk. The correlation depends on the market share of the sponsor. Since most insurers do not have the same exposure as the industry average, it is possible to apply weights to the geographic locations up to county level granularity. Similar to the parametric index trigger, the weights are set on a geographic level. This allows the sponsor to adjust for its individual exposure and loss vulnerability.

Example of a pure industry loss trigger: Carillon II Ltd

Carillon II Ltd protects Munich Re, which acted as the sponsor and lead manager of a transaction against losses arising from US hurricanes in the area shown in Figure 4.3. The $150 million bond was issued in May 2007 and provides coverage for four wind seasons. In this transaction, Munich Re chose a pure industry loss trigger. The event attachment amount (see Figure 4.4) is at $35 billion and the respective event exhaustion amount is at $45 billion. The bond has an expected loss of 4.59% (modelled by AIR). The payout function is linear between the event attachment and event exhaustion amounts.

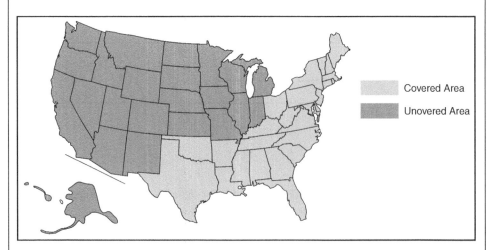

Figure 4.3   Covered area for the transaction Carillon II Ltd.
Source: Munich Re and AIR, reproduced with permission

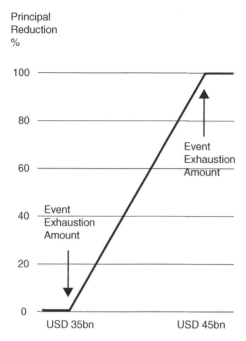

Figure 4.4 Payout function of the transaction Carillon II Ltd.

Source: Munich Re and AIR, reproduced with permission

4.3.3   Modelled loss triggers

A modelled loss trigger uses a synthetic exposure portfolio in combination with catastrophe modelling software. The synthetic portfolio is matched with the sponsor's portfolio to reduce basis risk. In the case of a large event, the event parameters such as wind speeds or ground acceleration are run against the exposure database in the cat model. If the modelled losses are above a specified threshold, the bond is triggered. As seen earlier in Figure 4.1, the number of transactions with a modelled loss trigger is quite small. This is mainly due to the fact that other non-indemnity triggers are often more appealing to cat bond sponsors and investors, due to their simplicity and transparency.

The following section will elaborate further on the optimal choice of trigger.

4.4   CHOOSING THE OPTIMAL TRIGGER

All of the triggers outlined in the previous subsections have their advantages and disadvantages. In this section, the triggers are compared on several important features that are relevant to sponsors and investors.

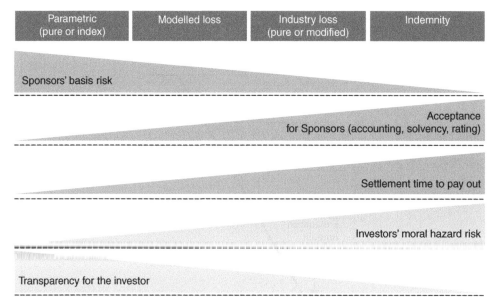

Figure 4.5   Characteristics of triggers used in cat bond transactions
Source: Munich Re

4.4.1   Comparison of trigger types

Figure 4.5 compares the four types of triggers described above using five important aspects in the decision-making process of a cat bond sponsor. These are discussed below.

Since indemnity bond payouts are based on the incurred ultimate net losses, a sponsor of an indemnity cat bond does not run basis risk except the commutation risk for those claims not settled before the bond's legal final maturity and/or before the commutation date. This is a very important aspect since, with such a trigger, the sponsor cannot be challenged by its stakeholders for buying inadequate protection. Industry loss triggers have reduced basis risk because the incurred ultimate net losses influence the industry loss to some degree and all effects of a natural catastrophe are reflected in the industry loss. This is not the case with parametric and modelled loss triggers, as only the physical parameters are measured. Duration and timing are only estimated. Basis risk is therefore highest for these trigger types. Non-indemnity covers bear the inherent risk for a sponsor that such structures are not, or not correspondingly, triggered in case of an event resulting in losses to the sponsor. The sponsor would then have to justify to its stakeholders why an insurance premium was paid in vain.

The acceptance of non-indemnity triggers by regulators, rating agencies and auditors is negatively correlated to basis risk: since indemnity triggers have a quasi-reinsurance status, they are treated in that way by the aforementioned bodies. A sponsor can, for example, apply reinsurance accounting to an indemnity transaction. The higher the basis risk, the higher the uncertainty about indemnification in case of a loss and the lower the acceptance and thus capital relief.

Time to payout is longest with indemnity transactions as the incurred losses must be verified. It also takes time to obtain information on industry losses following an event, and parametric and modelled loss triggers are fastest in that respect, because the observed physical parameters can be processed quickly. From a liquidity perspective, this is most beneficial to both sponsors and investors.

The investors' moral hazard risk is lowest with parametric and modelled loss triggers, because the payout is solely dependent on observed physical parameters which cannot be influenced by the sponsor. It is highest with indemnity transactions, because claims payments cannot be monitored individually, but are only checked randomly. Therefore, there is room for sponsors to be more lenient in claims payments.

Trigger transparency is highest with parametric structures because it is ultimately an independent set of observed physical parameters that decides on payout. Industry loss and indemnity triggers are less transparent because, for example, underwriting practices, contractual conditions and quality of risks play an important role and are more difficult to understand than an observed physical parameter.

4.4.2 Choice of trigger and alternative solutions

The choice of trigger is a crucial component in the structuring process of a cat bond transaction. This is not only because the trigger is the decisive factor pertaining to indemnification of a sponsor but also because the trigger is an essential factor for the pricing of a cat bond. The sponsor of an indemnity cat bond is typically required to pay a higher risk spread to the investors because they engage in a more opaque risk with possibly longer time to payout. There is thus a conflict of interest between sponsor and investor.

A sponsor must hence weigh off the described advantages and disadvantages of each trigger and make a choice about which solution is most efficient. Of course, this choice may be different for each sponsor. For example, for an insurance company with high market penetration in a given area, an industry loss trigger could be an effective cover. By creating more transparency, the sponsor would therefore have a higher chance of getting a more favourable risk transfer premium at the cost of assuming basis risk. With large industry exposure, however, this risk might not be as high as for smaller insurance companies with a more concentrated exposure.

However, it is not always necessary to decide on one type of trigger. There are two practicable ways to reconcile the interests of sponsors and investors. A first solution involves a double trigger structure: an indemnity trigger is used to fulfil the sponsor's requirement for an indemnity cover and a parametric trigger is installed to satisfy the investors' demand for a non-indemnity cover. For a payout to occur, both triggers have to be met. An efficient way to structure such a double trigger setup is by setting the probability of the more transparent trigger a little higher than the indemnity trigger probability. If this is done, the investors regard the transaction as a non-indemnity cat bond and will price it by disregarding the indemnity trigger and assume a total loss already when the parametric trigger is reached and the index exhausted. The indemnity component of the trigger usually allows the sponsor to apply reinsurance accounting.

A second solution involves a reinsurer acting as fronter and transformer. This solution combines all positive effects of traditional reinsurance with the benefits a capital market solution provides. Figure 4.6 illustrates such a structure. Instead of engaging in a direct relationship with the special purpose vehicle (SPV), the risk seller signs a traditional indemnity-based reinsurance contract with a reinsurance company. Time to indemnification and accounting and regulatory treatment of the protection are thus as in traditional reinsurance contracts. The

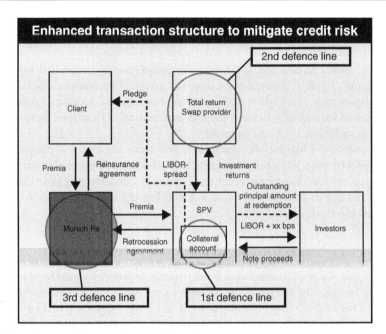

Figure 4.6 Reinsurer acting as a fronter and transformer

Source: Munich Re

underlying risk can then be transferred on a parametric or industry loss basis from the rein-surer's book to the capital markets. This provides the investors with the desired transparency, which can lead to a lower required risk premium. In such a scenario, basis risk is assumed by the reinsurer. The collateral of the SPV is assigned to the risk seller of the transaction. There is thus triple security in place: First, the reinsurance contract with the reinsurer is in place to indemnify the risk seller. In the case of the reinsurer's default, the collateral pool of the SPV is assigned to indemnify the risk seller. In the case where the assets within the collateral pool lose value, the total return swap provider or the swap bank must cover for the difference. This reduces the risk seller's exposure to the total return swap counterparty and quality of the collateral assets. Apart from that, the legal risks to the sponsor are minimised since the reinsurer acts as the legal sponsor of the transaction. These benefits come in addition to the reinsurers' ability to provide price and capacity guarantees to their clients.

5

Basis Risk from the Cedant's Perspective

David Ross[a] and Jillian Williams[b]

With the prevalence of index-based triggers in insurance-linked securities (ILS) design, it is paramount to understand the implications of these triggers and the basis risk to which they give rise. By defining basis risk appropriately and developing methods and measures by which to quantify it, basis risk can and should be viewed like any other risk, then analysed and managed accordingly. In this chapter we examine, in turn, the main types of index triggers used in the construction of ILS. After a recap on the basic tenets of catastrophe modelling software, we discern between the different sources of basis risk and establish the degree to which these sources arise through the use of alternative trigger types. We then proceed to a more detailed definition of basis risk and provide key mathematical measures that practitioners may use in the assessment of such risk. We conclude with a discussion of how basis risk may be minimized via important structural and data-related considerations.

5.1 INTRODUCTION

Historically, the term 'basis risk' has been most widely used in financial risk management circles. Within this context, we need an observable market price for two investments or financial instruments held by an investor, the second investment having been purchased as a financial hedge against the first. Basis risk denotes the risk that the price of the second investment does not move to offset perfectly the price movements of the first, hence leaving the holder of these investments with a residual risk. Mathematically, basis risk will exist whenever there is not perfect negative correlation[1] between the price movements of these two assets. In finance, the second investment is often a derivative purchased to hedge the spot price of the first.

Moving now to the insurance/reinsurance arena, the term 'basis risk' is adopted within a slightly different context. Here, it is not the difference in price movements of investments to which practitioners refer; rather the difference in the payouts between a sponsor's own losses and a risk transfer mechanism structured to hedge against those losses. To preclude basis risk, we now need perfect correlation between the sponsor's losses and the recoveries, for the stretch of insured losses over which the hedge is deemed to apply.

---

[a] Torus Insurance

[b] Leadenhall Capital Partners

[1] Pearson correlation.

The Handbook of Insurance-Linked Securities   Edited by P. Barrieu and L. Albertini
© 2009 John Wiley & Sons, Ltd

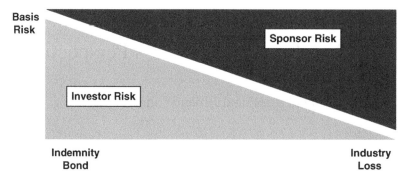

Figure 5.1 Investor risk and sponsor risk by trigger
Source: Standard & Poor's 2008, reproduced with permission

Traditional plain vanilla reinsurance contracts know nothing of basis risk,[2] the sponsor understands the risks for which he is buying protection and the reinsurance contract will pay losses to protect the insured in accordance with contract terms and conditions. A broker/insurer/reinsurer would label this 'UNL' cover (ultimate net loss) – indemnity in the purest sense of the word. Alternative risk transfer mechanisms, including ILS, do not always indemnify in the same way and it is this feature which gives rise to basis risk.

5.2   INVESTOR VS SPONSOR RISK

Figure 5.1 outlines the balance between investor risk and sponsor risk.

Investors will always be more comfortable with financial instruments whose inherent risks they understand. The potential for 'surprise' losses – either those arising through definition risk or those that may be otherwise unforeseen or underestimated – will be retained by the investor in basis risk free ILS products. If investors *do* take positions in such assets, they may find that they are more illiquid, thus making it harder to transfer the risk out of their portfolios quickly if needed. Collectively, these risks may be defined as 'investor risk'.

For these reasons, structures incorporating indemnity protection are seen as the highest risk to investors, and the supply of this capacity is more costly. More often than not, the sponsor will accept some basis risk in the product design to encourage market capacity and reduce price. Establishing the balance of this risk will be a critical part of the construction of an ILS issuance – the residual basis risk may be defined as 'sponsor risk'.

5.3   TRIGGER TYPES

While we need not confine ourselves to ILS in the examination of non-indemnity hedges, this chapter is, after all, a digest on catastrophe insurance-linked securities, so we have these products in mind as we develop our train of thought. There are several types of hedge, invariably referred to as 'trigger types' that permeate the world of ILS. The nomenclature may differ

---

[2] For the purposes of this argument, we ignore counterparty credit risk, which one could argue is a source of basis risk.

between authors, but our convention is detailed below and will be used for the remainder of this chapter.

- **Industry loss index triggers.** The ILS payout is a function of a measure of industry-insured loss. In practice, the industry loss measure will be a figure published by an acknowledged third party, which is perceived to have the expertise and ability to calculate industry loss to within an acceptable degree of accuracy. In the United States, the third party is usually PCS (Property Claims Services) and they are often contracted to the ILS issue and receive a fee for this service. Outside the US, other sources of industry loss can be used and others are under development. (See Chapter 4 on the various types of triggers).
- **Modelled loss index triggers.** The ILS payout is a function of catastrophe model output. The methodology prescribed to calculate the index is defined through extensive contract language setting out an unambiguous procedure to be followed post loss. Subjective interpretation of data is not permissible, and the process may therefore differ somewhat from the methodology cat modelling firms employ to issue standard industry loss bulletins after an event. A footprint of the catastrophe event is created by the modelling firm contracted to the issuance. The footprint is a systematic recording of physical data representing the nature of the loss that is compatible as input into the hazard module of the catastrophe model. Once within the model framework, the event can be run through a set of predefined exposures to calculate the modelled loss experienced by these exposures for the event in question. The exposures could relate to the industry or could be bespoke for the ILS deal, representing an exposure set closely mirroring the sponsor's own exposure data. The latter is frequently called a 'notional portfolio modelled loss index.'
- **Parametric index triggers.** The ILS payout is a function of some observable and recordable meteorological data or other physical parameters of an event. In the case of windstorm, the function may be a formula whose inputs are interpolations of wind speed readings across an expansive predefined network of weather stations. The function will likely weight each input to reflect changing geographical exposures and will give more weight to weather stations in the vicinity of larger loss potential, whether this exists through larger volumes of insured locations, more exposed occupancy types, different coverage types or any other feature with a bearing on loss potential. While a catastrophe model is not required post loss, catastrophe models are paramount in calibrating the functional form and parameters of the index to reduce basis risk.

In practice, there is nothing to stop a product containing more than one of these trigger types, or even a combination of both an indemnity and a non-indemnity trigger type. Beyond the world of ILS issuance, this mechanism is already evident in catastrophe excess of loss indemnity treaties (nonproportional treaties) with embedded industry loss warranties.

The choice of index will have a bearing on the level of basis risk. *All other things being equal,* a risk-averse sponsor will always choose to minimize basis risk to protect his downside. The unfortunate reality is that these 'other things' are *rarely* equal, primary among them price. Due to lack of transparency and moral hazard, capital market investors will command a risk premium for indemnity investments, thus presenting a trade-off for the sponsor wishing to purchase a hedge: basis risk versus price.[3] If the sponsor chooses the former, he must accept

---

[3] This assumes that indemnity protection capacity exists at a price. This will depend on several factors, primary among these being the market's perception of the sponsor, the perils covered, contract terms and conditions and the state of the ILS market in general.

one of the basis risk-prone non-indemnity hedges previously described. (For an in-depth discussion on triggers, please refer to Chapter 4).

5.4   CATASTROPHE MODELS

When defining trigger types in the previous section, we drew reference to catastrophe models several times. Later, we will describe how these models are needed to quantify basis risk. Therefore, whether for index definition, index calibration or basis risk analysis, they are integral to the understanding of ILS, and it will serve our purpose to recap on the basic tenets of catastrophe modelling below.

5.4.1   Key components of catastrophe models

Hazard module

The hazard module (Figure 5.2) contains a set of possible losses known as an 'event set'. While finite in size, one should think of the event set as a discrete, finite representation of an infinite number of catastrophe events that could occur in reality. Here, the whereabouts and sizes of the events are determined along with the frequencies with which they occur. The physical parameters of each event are also recorded here.

The hazard is the peril which has caused the loss. The severity of each peril at a site is defined in terms of intensity, based upon which the catastrophe model quantifies damage, via vulnerability functions. Let's now examine these site intensities for the four main natural perils: earthquake, hurricane/extra-tropical cyclone, tornado/hail and flood.

- **Earthquake:** the primary characteristic that determines the event severity at a site is ground motion, which may be measured on scales including Modified Mercalli Intensity (MMI), peak ground velocity (PGV) and peak ground acceleration (PGA). Some of the main actors that determine the severity of the ground motion include the epicentre's geographic location and depth, the earthquake magnitude and the attenuation of the seismic waves as they travel through the ground, which is in turn dependent on geology and the local soil conditions at the site under consideration.

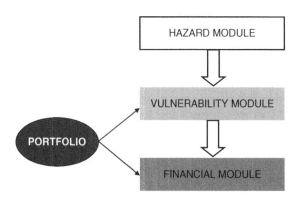

Figure 5.2   Catastrophe model components
Source: Guy Carpenter 2000, reproduced with permission

- **Hurricane/extra-tropical cyclone:** the severity of a hurricane or windstorm at a site is typically quantified in terms of wind speed, with storm duration being a further factor that may be considered for extra-tropical cyclones. Several factors determine the wind speed. For a hurricane these include landfall location, central pressure, radius of maximum winds and distance from the eye, forward speed, track angle, terrain roughness and filling rate (rate of decay) after landfall. Extra-tropical storms are somewhat less organized, but the wind speed may vary according to the depth of the low with which the storm is associated, distance from the centre of the storm, gust density, air pressure, topography and ground roughness.
- **Tornado and hail:** as for hurricanes and windstorms, the site intensity measure for a tornado is wind speed and the factors which govern the intensity are the same as for hurricanes. The site intensity measure for hail damage can be quantified using a number of parameters, including hailstone size and the kinetic energy per unit area of ground imparted by the falling hailstones.
- **Flood:** a wide variety of factors combine to determine flood intensity at a site. Depth is the most commonly used parameter, but velocity and duration are also significant, as are the type of water (sweet water, salt water, polluted water, etc.), sediment and debris loads. The various factors may have different degrees of importance depending on the type of flooding; for example, in flash flooding, velocity is a larger component of the severity than in river floodplain events, in which depth typically predominates.

Within the context of catastrophe models, there is a series of 'secondary' or 'collateral' perils that may augment the losses generated by the 'primary' perils discussed above. Secondary perils do not occur in the absence of primary perils. These secondary perils include sprinkler damage and fire following earthquake, and sea surge for hurricane and extra-tropical cyclones. Loss amplification, which is the estimated increase in the cost of goods and services after a large event, is often considered a secondary peril as well. Sponsors and investors should always seek to understand subtleties in coverage definitions, as the presence or absence of secondary perils in index construction and index calibration may have a material impact on the level of coverage provided.

Portfolio

When portfolio modelling, we are concerned with the location and exposure of the risk. The locations can be recorded at fine levels of resolution (e.g. latitude and longitude) or at aggregated levels (US county, Caribbean island, European cresta, etc). For property damage, the exposure is the replacement value of the risk in monetary terms, whereas business interruption exposures record the maximum loss potential from subsequent outage/downtime (consequential loss).

Vulnerability (engineering) module

In the vulnerability module of a catastrophe model, we focus on details relating to the type of exposures. Typically, catastrophe models have an expansive list of field inputs, describing the exposures in granular detail. Occupancy types, construction type, year of construction, etc. can all form part of the field inputs to describe the exposure set. These fields, in turn, determine the damage the exposures will suffer in response to catastrophe parameters from the hazard module. The damage will be a function of the previous field inputs and the catastrophe parameters. The function itself is usually referred to as a 'vulnerability function.'

Financial (actuarial) module

This module is often called the 'actuarial module' of catastrophe models and focuses on how the policies work and interact with the physical risk. The physical damage to the exposure set will bring about contractual liabilities for the insurers, but only in accordance with the insurance policies protecting those exposures. How the insurance structures apply, the size of the limits and deductibles and other such contract features are determined in the financial module.

5.4.2   Uncertainty

Uncertainty in natural catastrophe modelling can be broadly categorized into two distinct types: 'aleatory uncertainty' and 'epistemic uncertainty'.[4]

Aleatory uncertainty

> 'This uncertainty arises because of natural unpredictable variation in the performance of the system under study.'
>
> (Daneshkhah, 2004)

This uncertainty represents the very heart of what cat models endeavour to achieve from the specification of their event sets. Within a stochastic simulation approach, different 'years' may be simulated from the event set, each year containing random draws from the event set. Each year will have a number of losses occurring (which may be zero), and each loss pertains to a specific event in the event set to which a loss value may be attributed. While we used the word 'random' to describe these draws, they are weighted in accordance to how likely each event is deemed to occur, as specified in the hazard module. When we assimilate a vast number of these simulated years together, we have a spread of possible outcomes and a representation of the inherent uncertainty in the modelled system.

Epistemic uncertainty

> 'This type of uncertainty is due to a lack of knowledge about the behaviour of the system that is conceptually resolvable.'
>
> (Daneshkhah, 2004)

This type of uncertainty is far-reaching in its implications. Some catastrophe models do not capture it at all, and those that do can only claim to partially. Once an event draw has been made from the event set, the corresponding loss amount may be taken as an 'average' value and a distribution of possible outcomes around the average may be permitted.

Epistemic uncertainty may arise within all four modules of a catastrophe model. Some of the key manifestations of such uncertainty are listed below.

- **Hazard module**
  - limitations of historical data;
  - unreliable data quality from old records;
  - lack of understanding and relationship of physical chaotic phenomena underlying hazard behaviour (e.g. El Niño and La Niña for hurricanes).

---

[4] Aleatory and epistemic uncertainty are perhaps better known to actuaries as process risk and model risk, respectively.

- **Portfolio**
  - ○ measuring replacement value for physical exposures;
  - ○ assessing monetary values for nonphysical exposures (e.g. business interruption);
  - ○ detailed location vs aggregated location information (e.g. postcode level data might place floating casinos at the postcode centroid, which may be on dry land).
- **Vulnerability module**
  - ○ claims data used to calibrate vulnerability functions may be limited and not describe the extent of damage;
  - ○ unreliable data quality from old records;
  - ○ new types of loss (e.g. new technology);
  - ○ lack of understanding of the structural behaviour under severe loads.
- **Financial module**
  - ○ insurance/reinsurance policy dynamics;
  - ○ interaction of different insurance and reinsurance policies;
  - ○ the relationship between exposure and insurance/reinsurance structures.

An understanding of these areas of uncertainty is required to interpret the cat model output appropriately within the context of a basis risk analysis.

5.5   SOURCES OF BASIS RISK

Understanding the sources of basis risk in an ILS transaction is absolutely critical to comprehending the downside in any deal. It is a challenge to separate these clearly, and the approach adopted in the following paragraphs may differ between authors.

5.5.1   Source 1: Catastrophe model error/shortcomings

This source of basis risk can only be present in a transaction to the extent that catastrophe models are used to calibrate the index (i.e. parametric/modelled loss indices) or to calculate the index post loss (i.e. modelled loss indices). This is a subtle point, yet important. One may argue that a catastrophe model is used in all transactions; even for industry loss indices, a catastrophe model would be used to structure the transaction via iterations around key metrics such as probability of attachment and expected loss (indeed, around any metric which could have ramifications on the price and capacity available for the ILS issuance). This is undoubtedly true. The key point to understand here is that the catastrophe model does not always calibrate or define the index (e.g. for our industry loss index example) and 'Source 1' basis risk is absent in these cases.

Imagine a *modelled loss* index embedded within a plain vanilla cat bond protecting US Hurricane. We can use the notorious 'Katrina' event to demonstrate perfectly Source 1 basis risk. Suppose a footprint of Katrina is taken in line with the cat bond contract language and yields a modelled loss of $20 billion. The actual industry loss, according to the most recent PCS estimate,[5] was in the region of $41 billion. The difference is model error. We must do the cat modelling fraternity justice here by pointing out that the majority of the difference is down to flood losses that, through the concept of proximate cause, would be collectible under many insurance policies despite not being attributable to wind damage directly. No catastrophe

---

[5] PCS Bulletin Estimate No 49-17, 8th August, 2007.

model yet exists to cover the risk of the damaged New Orleans levees so the models were not even *claiming* to capture this source of loss.[6] For the purposes of our example though, this is irrelevant. The shortcoming has produced a manifestation of basis risk, and a severe one at that. If our US Hurricane bond attached at a level in excess of $20 billion, investors would escape unscathed to the detriment of the sponsor.

Source 1 basis risk includes instances where sponsor exposures are not faithfully represented, either due to data miscodings or missing exposures.

5.5.2   Source 2: Discrepancy between the modelled index loss and the modelled company loss

Imagine a world with no model error – the models are perfect and all-encompassing (and, by definition therefore, all equivalent). Strictly speaking, we need not be so restrictive here; we need only insist that the vulnerability and financial modules are error free so that once we know a loss has occurred with specific physical parameters, the insured loss emanating from the model is always precisely equal to the actual loss experienced in reality. This really is an abstract argument, but we need it to segment Source 2 basis risk from Source 1. In this ideal world, we will still rarely have perfect positive correlation between the sponsor's loss and the hedge – the difference between the two is driven by the extent to which the sponsor's underwriting is unrepresentative of the index.

5.5.3   Source 3: Dynamic basis risk

You could regard this as a special case of Source 2, but we split it out here to drive home an important point. Both the structuring of cat ILS and calibration of indices are typically processes carried out in reference to in-force exposures – i.e. a data dump at a given point in time. Anyone involved in insurance risk management will know that exposures are far from constant. Depending on the sponsor's business plan, the insurance market within which it competes, availability and price of reinsurance and the general market environment, net exposures may change over time, occasionally markedly so. This should be one of the most serious considerations for any purchaser of ILS, more so when one digests the implications of a multi-year tenor (present in most ILS covers). Will the cover purchased today be valid and useful for exposures going forward? If exposures change, payouts under ILS protection may not mirror sponsor losses as accurately as they did at the commencement of the transaction, and this itself may be regarded as a distinct source of basis risk.

5.6   DEFINING BASIS RISK

A one-line synopsis of basis risk was given earlier:

> 'The difference in the payouts between a sponsor's own losses and a risk transfer mechanism structured to hedge against those losses.'

---

[6] Unmodellable losses are generally a serious concern for counterparties of an indemnity transaction, and there are numerous recent examples of such losses comprising a significant portion of the whole. Hurricane Ike (September 2008) has in the region of $1 billion of insured loss emanating from such sources (RMS, 2008b).

While this cursory definition might be acceptable in passing, our considerations of basis risk must run much deeper before we move on to an appraisal of measures to quantify basis risk.

First, a sponsor may only be seeking protection over a specific stretch of loss; a price constraint is likely to feature somewhere among the sponsor's risk management objectives, so it is unlikely that this stretch will operate from the ground up. Otherwise put, for an excess of loss protection, price constraints would impose a non-zero retention, leaving the sponsor on risk for the smaller catastrophe losses and attritional (small non catastrophe) claims.[7] The sponsor should care little how the index responds below this retention – he is not seeking protection here. He wants to know, and will be focusing his attention on, how the index responds over the vertical stretch where the hedge is sought. For a non-indemnity hedge, the vertical stretch does not exist other than in the sponsor's mind – we will refer to this stretch as the 'notional layer.'

A second consideration presents itself as we probe the word 'risk' itself. The manifestation of risk can be favourable or unfavourable to the sponsor. The ILS cover may pay out *more* than was expected or modelled under certain loss scenarios, but this will not be a major consideration in product design for the risk-averse sponsor. He is interested in his downside, so it is intuitive to define basis risk along similar lines.

We must deliberate further over the structure of the hedge. Thus far, we have pondered over a very specific sort of hedge. As the sponsor's loss increases by x dollars, we want the risk transfer mechanism to yield a further x dollars to offset this hedge. We will call this a 'pro rata' hedge. Plain vanilla cat bonds have traditionally employed this mechanism, but there is another category that we cannot sweep under the carpet in our more detailed look at basis risk. These are 'digital' or 'binary' hedges. Analogous to the world of vanilla industry loss warranties (ILWs), these types of protection pay nothing until a given threshold is breached, whereupon a fixed limit is paid out. This is an 'all or nothing' payment that is not designed to be a dollar for dollar loss. The sponsor purchases this cover under the requirement that, when losses get sufficiently bad, he wants a P&L credit. He is less concerned about the precision of the offset, but is relying on it when the wind blows or the ground shakes. Several public transactions have incorporated this feature, including Bay Haven and Fremantle, having met with widespread investor interest due to the transparent nature of the trigger.

To recapitulate the main ideas of this section, we sacrifice a succinct synopsis for a cumbrous one:

'For pro rata hedges, basis risk is the risk that a sponsor's own losses exceed the payments under a risk transfer mechanism structured to hedge against those losses over a predefined stretch of cover. For digital hedges, basis risk is the risk that a sponsor's losses exceed a threshold at which the risk transfer mechanism is expected to pay, without this payment occurring.'

In the interest of completeness, we should appreciate that there is nothing to prevent a risk transfer mechanism incorporating both of these hedge types, for which a definition of basis risk can be manipulated from the above. An example would be a cat bond which 'kicks in' digitally at a given threshold and whose payment then increases pro rata up to a defined exit point.

---

[7] The retention may be large if the ILS is sought to dovetail with the sponsor's existing or future planned reinsurance purchase sitting below. This is often how reinsurance brokers structure cat bonds in today's market.

5.7   QUANTIFYING BASIS RISK

Source 1 basis risk (catastrophe model error/shortcomings) is real and cannot be ignored. The unfortunate reality is that quantification of this risk using catastrophe models is impossible by definition. The extent to which model error exists can be gauged via consideration of soft factors such as the way the index would have responded historically to losses (think back to the Katrina example earlier) but, even then, we would likely have a relatively small set of losses to work with and the final call will always remain a judgemental one. As catastrophe models and academic research improve over time, one could expect the degree of model error to diminish, but putting a number on the residual risk will be a challenging, if not impossible, task.

Contrarily, Source 2 basis risk (discrepancy between the modelled index loss and modelled company loss) *can* be readily quantified using catastrophe models. There are a variety of basis risk measures one could use for this purpose. The suitability of the measures will depend on the structure of the ILS issue. All measures presented below restrict attention to the concept of downside risk as described in the previous section and are not suited to a two-tailed definition of basis risk (i.e. downside and upside). The measures shown are a subset from hundreds of potential candidates, but are among the most intuitive and easiest to communicate.

Let Y be the modelled loss to notional layer and X be the modelled recoveries under ILS.

Y and X are random variables as defined by the stochastic event set in the catastrophe models. We can consider Y and X to be aggregate losses drawn from the frequency-severity model over the tenor of the bond. Alternatively, we can regard both variables as single-event draws from the event set listing, weighted for frequency means,[8] which is easier to implement within a spreadsheet.

5.7.1   Measures for pro rata hedges

- Probability of positive shortfall given non-zero loss
  1) $P(Y - X > 0 | X > 0)$
     i.e. of the cases where there is a modelled recovery under the ILS, what is the likelihood that this modelled recovery fails to provide adequate protection?
  2) $P(Y - X > 0 | Y > 0)$
     i.e. of the cases where there is a modelled loss to the notional layer, what is the likelihood that the ILS modelled recovery fails to provide adequate protection?
- Expected shortfall given positive shortfall
  3) $E(Y - X | Y - X > 0)$
     i.e. of the cases where the modelled loss to the notional layer exceeds modelled recoveries under the ILS, what is the expected (average) amount of this recovery shortfall?
- Expected non-negative shortfall given loss
  4) $E(\max(Y - X, 0) | X > 0)$
     i.e. of the cases where there is a modelled recovery under the ILS, what is the expected (average) amount by which the modelled loss to the notional layer exceeds the modelled recovery under the ILS (giving no weight to instances where the recovery exceeds the loss)?

---

[8] i.e. conditional severity draws (losses conditional on event frequency = 1).

5) $E(\max(Y - X, \, 0) \,|\, Y > 0 \,)$

   i.e. of the cases where there is a modelled loss to the notional layer, what is the expected (average) amount by which this modelled loss exceeds the modelled recovery under the ILS (giving no weight to instances where the recovery exceeds the loss)?

- Probability of shortfall in excess of a non-negative threshold given non-zero loss

   6) $P(Y - X > r \,|\, X > 0)$ for $r \geq 0$

   i.e. of the cases where there is a modelled recovery under the ILS, what is the likelihood that this modelled recovery falls short of the modelled losses to the notional layer by r (a dollar amount) or greater?

   7) $P(Y - X > r \,|\, Y > 0)$ for $r \geq 0$

   i.e. of the cases where there is a modelled loss to the notional layer, what is the likelihood that the modelled recovery falls short of the modelled losses by r (a dollar amount) or greater?

Measures 6) and 7) are extensions of 1) and 2) and are functions of r (i.e. a threshold) rather than single values. Measures 6) and 7) could be considered among the most informative quantifications of basis risk for pro rata hedges. Depending on the catastrophe model in question, these measures can be calculated via stochastic simulation methodologies or in spreadsheets.

5.7.2   Measures for digital hedges

Assume the ILS pays out a single limit upon the index breaching a single threshold.

1) $P(X = 0 \,|\, Y > r)$ for $r \geq 0$

   i.e. of the cases where there is a modelled loss to the notional layer in excess of r (a dollar amount), what is the likelihood that the digital trigger is not activated?

Measures 6) and 7) from the previous section could be used to determine whether or not enough limit is being bought, but this single measure is probably the most intuitive measure for a digitally triggered cat bond.

5.7.3   Measuring positive basis risk

The calculations and discussion above have deliberately focused on measures of basis risk that quantify shortfalls for the sponsor (negative basis risk). For completeness, we should remark that sponsors can gain from these transactions (a recovery from the ILS that is greater than the sponsor's actual loss over the notional layer) and each of the formulas can be inverted to provide a measure of positive basis risk if required.

Both manifestations of positive and negative basis risk may be encompassed via examination of correlation coefficients.[9] According to Zeng (2000) 'The basis risk associated with index-based instruments has been traditionally measured by the hedges' effectiveness. It is generally defined as the square of the linear correlation coefficient (R^2) between the insured's loss ratio and the catastrophic loss ratio related to the underlying index. The higher the R^2, the lower the basis risk is, and vice versa.' (reproduced with permission of Emerald Group Publishing Limited).

---

[9] As for one-sided measures of basis risk, there are many more two-sided measures that could be used beyond those shown in this chapter.

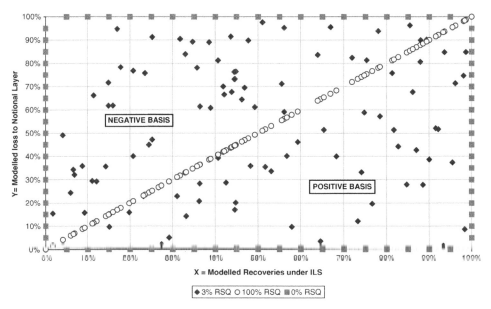

Figure 5.3   Correlation of ILS recoveries and notional portfolio by event

Pearson's Correlation measures the degree to which modelled losses move in tandem with the modelled ILS recoveries (Figure 5.3). The coefficient can assume values from −100% to +100%. R^2 (the square of the Pearson Correlation coefficient) can be used as an alternative. It ranges from 0 to +100%. In each case, the closer the coefficient's value is to 100%, the lower the basis risk.

5.8   MINIMIZING BASIS RISK

While developing the arguments that follow, we will have pro rata hedging mechanisms in mind. Similar approaches can be used for digital hedging mechanisms.

5.8.1   Over-hedging

Two-tailed measures of basis risk have been glossed over in this chapter as we focus solely on downside risk. Despite this, many two-tailed measures exist and, once defined, can be minimized via various mathematical routines and algorithms in pursuit of the optimal hedge. For the one-tailed measures we discussed previously, we must change our mindset. There is nothing preventing us from decreasing the basis risk measure without bound by simply increasing the limit of the risk transfer mechanism or decreasing the attachment point (or both). The problem essentially reverts to minimization subject to a constraint, and the constraint is once again price. For a predefined index and a predefined notional layer attachment and exit point, the sponsors will seek to minimize basis risk subject to price and the optimal solution will flow from the sponsor's perceived risk–return preference. We demonstrate this concept through an example involving Company ABC.

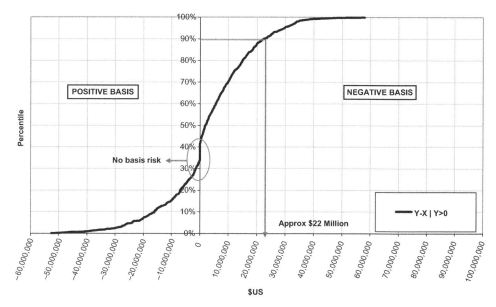

Figure 5.4 Exceeding probability of ILS recoveries compared to notional portfolio

Example

Company ABC is seeking a pro rata industry loss index cat bond as a hedge against a notional layer with limit $100 million. We define the ILS payout such that it yields $100 million in the event of a total loss, hence providing an exact hedge in these instances. We choose basis risk measure 7) from the previous section, $P(Y - X > r \,|\, Y > 0)$.

Figure 5.4 shows the probability of a shortfall or gain from the ILS in those instances when Company ABC takes a loss. The example shows that there is a 9% chance of a perfect hedge. There is approximately a 10% chance of a recovery shortfall exceeding $22 million.

We can make the following observations:

1. The distribution is continuous with a 'mass point' at zero. The mass point represents all those scenarios where there is a modelled limit loss to the notional layer and to the cat bond – hence a perfect hedge over the stretch. As indicated, we have deliberately not 'over-hedged' in terms of limit, so this mass point occurs at zero. If we bought more limit, the mass point would occur somewhere else, to the left of zero.
2. Buying more limit whilst keeping the attachment point and exit point of the index constant is equivalent to translating the graph to the left along the horizontal axis.
3. All points not situated on the mass point will be instances of partial loss, either to the notional layer or to the cat bond, where the likelihood of perfect hedge is infinitesimally small.
4. The metric used is biased, in the sense that it only looks at recovery shortfalls conditional on there actually being a loss to the notional layer. There will be many scenarios for which the notional layer takes no loss even though the cat bond does, yet these instances do not contribute to the risk measure. This explains why the mass point is centred on a percentile below 50%.

By increasing the maximum limit payable from the cat bond, we can translate the graph to the left, scaling the price up proportionally (as the capacity scales up[10]) until the residual basis risk and price is commensurate with the risk tolerance of the sponsor.

Similar approaches, more steeped in mathematics, could be used if we kept the limit constant and reduced the attachment point of the hedge.

5.8.2   Choice of index

We remarked earlier how industry loss index triggers can remove Source 1 basis risk (catastrophe model error/shortcomings). While not readily quantifiable, many practitioners feel that it is overshadowed by the prevalence of Source 2 risk (discrepancy between the modelled index loss and modelled company loss).

Index formulations that mirror the sponsor's underlying exposures more closely will reduce Source 2 basis risk. Parametric indices or notional portfolio modelled loss indices calibrated to the sponsor's book of business will do this. Industry loss indices are not necessarily cast asunder, as bespoke indices can be developed which weight industry losses by geography. An example might be an index consisting of PCS reported losses weighted by US state and/or line of business. Combined with an appropriate scale factor, this example would seek to mimic the losses emanating from the sponsor's actual exposures to minimize basis risk.

As we intimated earlier, the choice of index cannot be made in isolation of other soft factors which have a bearing on price. This includes the level of transparency in the index, which may be important to some investors less acquainted with the asset type. Even more importantly, we must ensure that our choice of index is supported by the catastrophe modelling firm contracted to the issuance. Ascertaining this fact early on will remove one potential obstacle in bringing a deal to market.

5.8.3   Reset clauses

Most reset clauses are triggered upon the confirmation of a new cat model release. Cat model vendors will continually strive to improve their models. Sometimes this involves merely updating the industry exposure databases underlying them as their interpretation of industry exposure evolves over time. It is possible to segregate the impacts of model changes into two categories: changes in the industry exposure database and changes in model mechanics.

Changes in industry exposure database

Even if the model mechanics (including the vulnerability curves and hazard module) do not change, some indices will be impacted by changing exposures upon release of a new cat model version. Industry loss index triggers are an example of this; a new model version may have a bearing on the modelled probability of attachment and expected loss, both key metrics in the market's determination of price. The contract language may provide the facility to reassess attachment points and exit points in line with new model releases. This usually affords more protection to the investors, rather than the sponsor, since exposures usually inflate over time. The presence of a reset clause is unlikely to be a prerequisite for sponsors who would welcome the natural migration towards over-hedging as industry exposures increase over time.

---

[10] This assumes the marginal cost of capacity holds constant.

Other types of index are impervious to changes in industry exposure since the model and methodologies for the deal are put into escrow upon finalization of the contract terms and conditions and are not superseded by new model releases.

Changes in model mechanics

Even if exposures are constant through time, changes in model mechanics can also change the modelled probability of attachment and expected loss. Model resets can work to the advantage of either the investors or the sponsor, depending on the nature of the change. Who knows for certain if the new model release is actually better or worse than the preceding version? Under the assumption that it is better, a model reset clause would allow the sponsor to reduce perceived Source 1 basis risk (catastrophe model error/shortcomings) when new model releases move against them.

While not a reset clause arising through model changes, it is possible to integrate a reset clause for changing sponsor exposures. This would be the clause of interest to reduce Source 3 basis risk (dynamic). This is not a common feature in catastrophe insurance-linked securities at present. Nevertheless, for a sponsor concerned about changing exposures over time and one willing to pay the additional structuring costs involved, this feature could be a valuable addition to any product design.

5.8.4   Cat model input

Catastrophe models are complex and require copious quantities of granular level detail to work as they were intended. Errors in data coding (whether they are present within the portfolio, vulnerability or financial modules), and altogether missing exposures can contribute significantly to discrepancies in output. During the structuring phase, Source 1 basis risk can be reduced by experienced catastrophe modellers and rigorous data collection processes embedded in the aggregate management function of the sponsor.

5.9   CONCLUSION

Insurance literature abounds with talk of catastrophe ILS and their increasing role in the risk and capital management repertoire of (re)insurance carriers. While some sources of basis risk will remain challenging to quantify, others can be readily addressed via analytic techniques and should be integrated into the design of an optimal non-indemnity ILS issuance. By understanding how catastrophe models work, defining basis risk, applying analytical techniques and understanding a sponsor's portfolio, a sponsor can minimize basis risk to design a structure which meets its reinsurance needs.

ACKNOWLEDGEMENTS

The authors would like to thank John Major, Guy Carpenter and Jane Toothill, JBA consultants for their contributions in reviewing and very helpful suggestions.

REFERENCES

AIR Corporation (2008) Hurricane Ike Advisory: Latest Observation, October 2008, www.air-worldwide.com

American Academy of Actuaries Index Securitisation Task Force (1999) *Evaluating the Effectiveness of Index-Based Insurance Derivatives in Hedging Property/Casualty Insurance Transactions*, American Academy of Actuaries, October 4.

Daneshkhah, A.E. (2004) *Uncertainty in Probabilistic Risk Assessment: A Review*, The University of Sheffield, August 9.

Gatzert, N., Schmeiser, H. and Toplek, D. (2007) *An Analysis of Pricing and Basis Risk for Industry Loss Warranties*, University of St Gallen, June.

Major, J. A. (1998) The Impact of Basis Risk on Insurance-Linked Exchange-Traded Products, *Financing Risk & Reinsurance*, International Risk Management Institute, September.

Major, J. A. (1999) Basis Risk: Less Than Meets The Eye, *Financing Risk & Reinsurance*, International Risk Management Institute, August.

Modu, E. (2006) *Gauging the Basis Risk of Catastrophe Bonds*, A.M. Best, September 25.

RMS (2008a) *RMS Modelling and Industry Loss Estimates for Hurricane Ike*, RMS, 23 September, www.rms.com.

RMS (2008b) *Hurricane Ike: Final Summary*, 6 November, www.rms.com.

Securitisation of Non-Life Insurance Working Party (2008) Basis Risk, *GIRO 2008*.

Standard & Poor's (2008) *Insurance-Linked Securities-Capital Treatment and Basis Risk Analysis*, Standard & Poor's, September 12.

Zeng, L. (2000) On the Basis Risk of Industry Loss Warranties, *The Journal of Risk Finance*, Summer, 27–32.

6

Rating Methodology

Cameron Heath[a]

This chapter will explain how Standard & Poor's rates non-life ILS transactions. It will include a description of the methodology and criteria currently employed to analyze the risks; to review the accompanying documentation; and to determine the amount of credit that might be given to a rated entity for the protection offered by ILS issuances. A brief walk through the process Standard & Poor's uses when rating an ILS transaction will serve as an introduction to the methodology involved in generating that rating. Figure 6.1 shows a typical timeline for the rating of an ILS transaction.

6.1 STANDARD & POOR'S RATINGS SERVICES' RATING PROCESS

6.1.1 Initial interaction

The ceding (re)insurer initiates the process by requesting a rating on a transaction. At this stage, Standard & Poor's typically will identify any features that might require new criteria to be established. The analyst will prepare a recommendation for consideration by the criteria committee, the outcome of which will form part of the overall analysis of the transaction.

Standard & Poor's will inform the cedant on how the transaction is likely to be analyzed under our criteria, how various elements factor into our opinion and whether or not we believe, at this early stage, that we can rate the transaction as proposed. However, we are not engaged in the creation, design or structuring of any transaction. Standard & Poor's may ask for further information if we feel we need it in order to have a clear understanding of the proposed transaction.

6.1.2 Risk analysis

Standard & Poor's will typically review the preliminary offering circular outlining the terms of the transactions as represented to investors (the OC) and the pricing supplement outlining the term of the tranche being issued, if in a program structure (the PS), to assess any changes to the information the cedant provided in the initial pitch presentation made to the rating analysts. However, Standard & Poor's assigns its ratings based on legal documentation and not on offering materials.

---

[a] Standard & Poor's

The Handbook of Insurance-Linked Securities   Edited by P. Barrieu and L. Albertini
Chapter 6 kindly contributed by Cameron Heath for Standard & Poor's® – © McGraw-Hill International (UK) Limited (2008) – All rights reserved

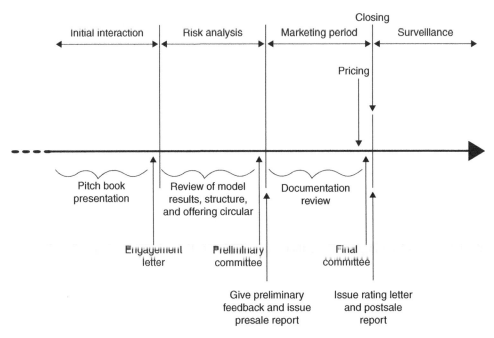

Figure 6.1 Stages in the rating process

Source: Standard & Poor's

Standard & Poor's methodology emphasizes evaluating the results of the model to analyze the probability of loss of the transaction. We analyze the reasonableness of the model and stress test the results it gives. The stress testing will vary according to the type of structure, the modeling assumptions and the individual characteristics of the transaction under review.

Based on the information in the preliminary OC (and PS, if applicable), the analysis of the model results and information from other sources available to us, the transaction's primary rating analyst will prepare a recommendation for the preliminary rating committee. The rating voted on by this initial committee is only preliminary, since the cedant will not have provided transaction documents, including legal opinions, at this stage. Final ratings will depend on receipt and review of all final documentation and legal opinions. The analyst may have questions on various aspects of the documentation, and the documents may go through several versions, each of which will typically be reviewed by the analyst.

Based on the committee's rating decision, Standard & Poor's will provide the cedant with preliminary feedback.

Once the cedant launches the transaction, Standard & Poor's may publish a presale report disclosing the preliminary rating on the transaction. The presale report will reflect information known and believed by Standard & Poor's at the time to be relevant to the preliminary rating, and serves to inform potential investors on the primary market about the preliminary rating and the underlying structure and the risk analysis we undertook.

6.1.3   Documentation review

The final rating on the notes will depend on receipt and review of all final transaction documentation, including legal opinions by Standard & Poor's. The receipt of additional information after the assignment of a preliminary rating may result in a final rating that differs from the preliminary ratings.

If we do not receive final documentation within a reasonable timeframe, or if final documentation departs from material reviewed at an earlier stage in the process, Standard & Poor's reserves the right to withdraw or revise its preliminary rating on the transaction.

Since ILS are usually hybrid instruments, rating analysts from the insurance and the structured finance areas may review the documents. Further, internal general counsel would typically review legal opinions and a swap analyst the total return swap documentation.

The final rating is usually issued after all documents have been reviewed by rating staff in these areas.

6.1.4   Transaction closing

During the documentation review process, the primary rating analyst typically updates the documentation he/she will provide to the rating committee with any supplemental information relevant to the committee's vote on the final rating.

Standard & Poor's will notify the cedant of the committee's final rating decision.

Formally, Standard & Poor's will release the final rating by transmitting a rating letter to the cedant. We typically issue the rating letter a short time prior to the closure of the transaction.

Once the transaction has closed, we may publish a post-sale report. This report typically follows the form used for the presale report and serves to inform the market about the assigned rating and the underlying structure and the risk analysis we undertook.

6.1.5   Surveillance

After the transaction closes, Standard & Poor's will re-examine it as part of our scheduled surveillance, and whenever any event occurs that in our view might trigger the transaction notes.

Depending on the structure of the transaction, Standard & Poor's typically will review quarterly and annual performance reports. We usually also review transactions in which attachment and exhaustion points (i.e., respectively, the level after which investors start losing their principal and the point at which all principal is completely lost) reset annually to assess whether, in our view, the probability of attachment has increased and whether other terms and conditions have changed.

If a potential covered event occurs, Standard & Poor's will revisit all outstanding notes that might be affected, and reassess the likelihood of the notes being triggered.

For a per-occurrence deal, Standard & Poor's may flag the potentially affected notes for closer surveillance until the effects of the event are known by placing the notes on Credit-Watch.[1] The direction in which we expect the rating to move will be indicated by stating

---

[1] CreditWatch highlights the potential direction of a short- or long-term rating. It focuses on identifiable events and short-term trends that cause ratings to be placed under special surveillance by Standard & Poor's analytical staff. These

whether the implications of the CreditWatch placement are positive, negative or developing (used when the rating may go either way). We will resolve the CreditWatch placement as soon as possible. For an aggregate-loss transaction, Standard & Poor's will usually discuss the transaction with the calculation agent before deciding on any rating action.

6.2 RISK ANALYSIS

6.2.1 Trigger options

Natural catastrophe (nat-cat) bonds provide protection to the ceding company for insurance-linked risks. The coverage can be determined according to four possible basic trigger options: parametric, industry loss, modeled loss or indemnity transactions (as detailed in Chapter 4). Additionally, sidecars, which will be discussed in Chapter 11, and hybrid structures – the latter utilize features from more than one of the basic options – also offer insurance-linked cover options to cedants. The type of trigger selected by the cedant for the transaction will affect Standard & Poor's analysis of the transaction.

6.2.2 Indemnity vs non-indemnity triggers

Why Standard & Poor's views indemnity bonds differently

Indemnity nat-cat bonds are much more closely related to the practices of the ceding company than non-indemnity structures. The risks borne by holders of indemnity bonds are directly affected by how the cedant underwrites its book of business, its loss estimation and claims settlement processes and the completeness and quality of the policy data provided by the cedant and used to populate the model and generate the modeled results.

As a result, Standard & Poor's may request more information, in scope, type and amount, when presented with an indemnity bond than we request when rating non-indemnity bonds. We generally will also request information regarding the data used to generate modeled results (in terms of both quality and completeness) and the underlying modeled loss calculations that we will be reviewing as part of the rating process.

Information on the cedant

To rate an indemnity nat-cat bond, Standard & Poor's will first seek to become familiar with and understand the ceding company's operations (underwriting, risk appetite, enterprise risk management, etc.). Furthermore, to maintain the ratings, this information will have to be refreshed and updated periodically, and augmented by a dialogue with the ceding company as long as the rated securities remain outstanding.

When the ceding company is rated by Standard & Poor's, this data exchange will usually occur via an interactive process in conjunction with maintaining a public rating on the ceding

---

may include mergers, recapitalizations, voter referendums, regulatory action or anticipated operating developments. Ratings appear on CreditWatch when such an event or a deviation from an expected trend occurs and additional information is necessary to evaluate the current rating. A listing, however, does not mean a rating change is inevitable, and whenever possible, a range of alternative ratings will be shown. CreditWatch is not intended to include all ratings under review, and rating changes may occur without the ratings having first appeared on CreditWatch. A 'positive' designation means that a rating may be raised; 'negative' means a rating may be lowered; and 'developing' means that a rating may be raised, lowered or affirmed.

company. While Standard & Poor's will consider rating nat-cat bonds issued by a ceding company we do not rate, we typically will only do so after understanding and being able to assess the ceding company's operations and processes.

Data requirements

Indemnity structures depend heavily on the quality and completeness of the cedant's under-writing data, which is used to populate the model. These models are complex and the results are highly reliant on the data input into them.

Therefore the quality of the input data can have a significant impact on modeled results. Standard & Poor's places great emphasis on the quality of the data used to generate probabilities of attachment, loss and exhaustion estimates and will usually make qualitative adjustments to the calculated results based on the perceived quality of the underlying data. Standard & Poor's will ask for information on the extent to which the ceding company audits and verifies the data, as well as the frequency of data analysis and reviews. Specific examples of the kind of information we would request include the level of geocoding, exposure measure, occupancy type, year built, number of stories and type of construction.

In a similar fashion, Standard & Poor's expects that the ceding company will also be prepared to provide information on, and discuss the completeness of, the data used in the modeling process. We may enquire about the level of unknown or incomplete information and the validation process used to check the completeness of the data, for example the level of geocoding provided. We may ask whether issuers perform heuristic checks on the data to ensure there is no bias or evidence of miscoding, to avoid a situation where data fields are block-coded or incorrectly coded to improve the data completeness score.

Standard & Poor's understands that perfect data is an unattainable goal for catastrophe modeling. Where data are incomplete, we may look for the use of sensitivity analysis to identify the potential impact of those missing data on the modeled results.

Standard & Poor's likely will view data from an issuer that has a rigorous data-checking process and has considered the impact of incomplete and erroneous data as more reliable than that of an issuer that appears to have complete data but has not or cannot perform checks on those data.

We view bonds where the subject portfolio has better quality and more complete data underlying the modeled results more positively. In our experience this is more often the case with personal lines, rather than commercial lines. Furthermore, a smaller number of larger commercial risks are statistically more risky than a larger number of smaller personal line risks.

Similarly, we will typically view bonds issued by primary insurers more positively than those issued by reinsurers, as the latter are one step further removed from the original policy data and consequently have less control of the quality and completeness of the input data.

Standard & Poor's usually views the participation of a third party in the review of the data used to generate the modeled probabilities of attachment as an indication of a better data review process. We believe that the participation of a third party in the data review process may significantly mitigate the risk of any moral hazard related to selective information disclosure that might skew modeled results.

In the case of third party involvement in the data input, we generally request copies of both the scope of the review and the work product generated in this process. We expect that the third-party reviewer typically would choose any representative sample analyzed. Furthermore, we expect the third party's analysis to include a discussion of the sample size used and an assessment of the potential sampling error and statistical significance of the results.

Standard & Poor's usually also requests information on historical events that may have caused losses to the rated obligations under consideration, as well as more granular loss information.

Alignment of interests

Standard & Poor's will review the bond structure and analyze the extent to which the ceding company's interests and those of the investors are aligned. Standard & Poor's considers this alignment of interests, both at closing as well as during the tenor of the bond, as a significant qualitative ratings issue. Our analysis would include a review of the bond documents to ensure that the ceding company had a contractual obligation to maintain a defined percentage (net of any reinsurance that does not inure to the benefit of both the cedant and bond) of the coverage layer addressed by the nat-cat bond. We would likely view an absence of a contractual commitment to maintain a meaningful alignment of interest for the tenor of the bond as indicative of greater uncertainty and it could have a negative impact on the rating.

6.2.3   Risk factors

Each nat-cat bond transaction rated by Standard & Poor's is unique and is rated on its individual merits. However, a number of risks are common to transactions of the same type and we consider each of these when assigning the rating.

The sponsor's initial estimate of the risk of a natural event occurring is based on one or more catastrophe models; however, it is important to note that the output of these models is only an estimate and is not definitive. Therefore, we usually adjust the probability of attachment based on the risk factors detailed in this section. The size of that adjustment is subject to quantitative and qualitative factors, and we may make different adjustments to different indemnity transactions, based on transaction-specific features.

Model risk

To date, Standard & Poor's has not rated a nat-cat transaction in which the ceding company used a model other than one provided by Risk Management Solutions Inc., EQECAT Inc. or AIR Worldwide Corp., although some sidecars included certain risks (e.g., crop insurance) that were not modeled by these companies. These particular risks, however, correspond to an insignificant level of losses relative to the trigger point of the sidecar debt. We do not anticipate altering our current policy at this time, and currently we do not, and do not expect to, rate nat-cat bonds that rely solely on the output of a company-generated model.

Modeling risk captures the possibility of the catastrophe model misestimating the frequency and/or severity of catastrophic events. All models, by definition, are simplifications of reality and their ability to accurately predict future events depends on many factors. We believe that the three modeling agencies mentioned above have the experience and skill needed for nat-cat risk modeling. Standard & Poor's inclusion of modeling risk when assigning a rating should not be taken as an indictment of the models. Rather, it reflects our belief that a certain level of uncertainty must occur when modeling tail events, and other inputs are subject to significant volatility (e.g., demand surge). Similarly, the complexity of each hazard varies. Factors are often difficult to allow for, either because of a lack of data or because their impact is difficult to quantify, e.g., the impact of the North Atlantic Oscillation.

Model risk includes a number of components, some or all of which may be present in a particular transaction structure. While industry loss triggers require the use of all modules from the model, parametric and modeled loss triggers use fewer modules, only up to the estimation of the hazard value. In other words, investors in industry loss transactions face additional model risk compared to investors in parametric or modeled loss transactions. The loss estimates as modeled for industry loss transactions incorporate assumptions about the severity of damage to insured buildings and the financial cost of this damage if a natural disaster occurs. If these assumptions underestimate the severity of damage, the true probability of attachment will be greater than the modeled probability of attachment for these types of trigger.

Data risk

Indemnity structures not only use the full output from the model but also depend heavily on the quality and completeness of the cedant's underwriting data, which is used to populate the model.

When applied to a complex model, we believe data risk can form a significant portion of an investor's total risk in this type of transaction. Furthermore, indemnity structures rely on the claims handling and actuarial estimating skill of the issuer and its agents, which adds a moral hazard component to the analysis.

A related risk arises because the probability of attachment is based on a portfolio as of a certain cut-off date. When the sponsor determines the probability of attachment, exhaustion and expected loss, either at issuance or reset, it bases them on the portfolio at that time. The actual ceded portfolio will be different, albeit slightly, which introduces another level of uncertainty.

Another lesson, learned from Hurricane Katrina, was that the total sum insured for many commercial properties was significantly understated. This meant that the modeled losses were also significantly understated for both primary and, more particularly, excess lines.

Other risks

A number of other factors will affect the level of stress applied to an individual transaction. The list below is not exhaustive and, like the type of trigger chosen for the transaction by the ceding company, each of these factors may have a different impact on different transactions and, consequently, will suggest a different level of stress test.

When compared to per event or single-year structures, or those in which losses incurred by the transaction are reset annually, multi-year aggregate structures are more prone to model error. Any imperfections in the underlying model will be compounded over the term of the transaction. However, we believe this may be offset to an extent if these structures are triggered by less severe events. The skill of the modeler running the catastrophe model is important, as this is not a mechanical process. Ensuring that codes in the underlying data (e.g., geographic, construction type, roof material) are correctly mapped to those used in the model requires skill and experience, as does interpreting and checking the model output. It is essential that these processes be performed correctly – there is little benefit in having complete, good-quality data if they are not used correctly.

The annualized probability of attachment is important beyond a pure assessment of the likelihood of a nat-cat bond defaulting. All models contain errors and the further into the tail the results, the more the assumptions underlying any model tend to break down. For the most remote risks, there may be no recent events against which to compare models. Consequently, the more remote the risk, the greater the potential for model error is.

Although sidecars are basically indemnity structures, they are also subject to business risks. The quota share agreement places restrictions on the type of business that the sidecar will reinsure, but the cedant has some latitude in defining the portfolio of risks. The modeled probability of attachment for debt issued by a sidecar is based on the expected portfolio, but changes in strategy by the cedant and conditions in the market could cause the actual portfolio of risks to differ from expectations. The modeled probability of attachment also requires assumptions for premium and expenses. An unfavorable variance in these assumptions will increase the probability of attachment – all else being equal.

Additionally, sidecars sometimes contain potential losses from perils that are not modeled. Sidecars usually follow the fortune of the cedants on the covered business, which sometimes includes policies that cover losses from perils or events that are not simulated in a model that will be used by Standard & Poor's as part of the rating process. For these unmodeled risks, we typically examine the cedant's historical losses and industry experience of the volatility of these types of losses. Then, we increase the estimate for modeled losses by the amount of expected losses that would not be included in that estimate.

6.2.4   Adjusted probability of default

Standard & Poor's assigns ratings to nat-cat bonds based on the revised probability of attachment, which represents the potential of a missed principal or interest payment. The revised probability of attachment equals the modeled probability of attachment plus an adjustment to address the possibility of error in the modeling process.

Standard & Poor's makes an allowance for the above risks in its ratings by applying stress tests to the aggregate exceedance probability (AEP) or occurrence exceedance probability (OEP) curves (which put into relation a level of monetary loss or index value – in aggregate or per occurrence – with its probability), as appropriate, before assigning a rating. The adjustments will vary according to the type of structure and the individual characteristics of the transaction under review. The test gets more rigorous as the number and magnitude of risks present in a particular transaction increase. While it is rare for transactions to be directly comparable, the paragraphs below are intended to give an indication of the relative magnitude of the risk inherent in different types of trigger mechanism on a like-for-like basis.

Parametric and modeled loss-based transactions, which use the output from a catastrophe model only up to the hazard-generation stage, typically receive a less onerous test than industry loss or indemnity loss transactions, each of which use all of the modules in the catastrophe model to generate the probability of attachment and related exceedance probability curves.

An industry-loss-based transaction normally receives a less onerous test than an indemnity-based transaction, which uses the full output from a catastrophe model and relies on the quality of the cedant's underwriting data to populate the model.

An indemnity-based transaction usually receives a less onerous test than a sidecar-style transaction, which uses the full output from a catastrophe model up to the financial-loss-generation stage, relies on the quality of the cedant's underwriting data and contains other non-modeled risks.

Table 6.1   Indicative stress test level

Type of structure	(%)
Parametric	5
Modeled loss	5
Industry loss	10
Indemnity	20

Source: Standard & Poor's

To provide the market with some guidance, Table 6.1 gives indicative stress levels that we would apply to the AEP or OEP curve of a nat-cat bond. Please note these levels are indicative only. We tailor the actual adjustment applied when rating each nat-cat transaction to reflect the transaction's individual characteristics and adjustments may exceed or, more typically, fall short of this figure.

6.2.5   Application of methodology

The following example illustrates how we typically apply the adjustment for a nat-cat bond linked to industry losses on a per-occurrence basis with an annual reset, an attachment level of $600 million and a modeled probability of attachment of 1.33%, which equates to a one-in-75-year event.

We may apply an adjustment of, for example, 9%, which will decrease the attachment level to $546 million. The AEP curve supplied by the modeling agency indicates that the new probability of attachment is 1.79%, which equates to a one-in-56-year event (illustrated by the flat AEP curve in Figure 6.2). We compare this revised probability of attachment to the default table used to rate insurance-linked securitizations (ILS). If this were the sole metric used to assign a rating, the bonds would be assigned a rating of 'BB'.

Had the AEP curve generated a probability of 1.41%, then the rating outcome for this metric would have been 'BB+' by applying the rating implications of the cumulative default

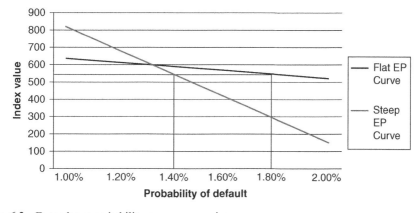

Figure 6.2   Exceedance probability curves comparison
Source: Standard & Poor's

Table 6.2 Cumulative default probabilities

Default table for insurance-linked securitizations

Maturity (years)	AAA	AA+	AA	AA−	A+	A	A−	BBB+	BBB
1	0.003	0.010	0.015	0.025	0.040	0.060	0.085	0.234	0.353
2	0.027	0.048	0.074	0.106	0.150	0.200	0.264	0.514	0.825
3	0.052	0.085	0.133	0.188	0.260	0.340	0.443	0.850	1.405
4	0.076	0.123	0.191	0.269	0.370	0.480	0.621	1.246	2.073
5	0.100	0.160	0.250	0.350	0.480	0.620	0.800	1.704	2.812
	BBB−	BB+	BB	BB−	B+	B	B−	CCC+	
1	0.547	1.632	2.525	3.518	4.510	5.824	8.138	23.582	
2	1.279	3.211	4.946	6.915	8.885	11.751	16.674	38.104	
3	2.177	4.758	7.230	10.095	12.960	17.152	24.004	46.752	
4	3.213	6.270	9.380	13.037	16.691	21.921	30.023	52.288	
5	4.339	7.703	11.403	15.743	20.087	26.089	34.943	56.138	

Source: Standard & Poor's

probabilities table (see Table 6.2 and Standard & Poor's, 2008a). If one were to plot an AEP curve with probability of default along the X axis and index/loss value along the Y axis, clearly a steep curve would be expected to minimize ratings volatility and a flat curve would likely intensify it (see Figure 6.2).

6.2.6 Default table

We assign a rating to each note by comparing two rows of the cumulative default table (a portion of which is shown in Table 6.2). The first row corresponds to the maturity of the note (or, in the case of a resetting note, the reset term); the second is a surrogate for the instantaneous probability of attachment. Standard & Poor's compares the note's lifetime and annual probabilities of attachment with the appropriate maturities and locates in each row the first rating category for which the likelihood of default exceeds the corresponding probability of attachment. The lesser of these ratings will be the maximum possible rating on the note.

6.2.7 Multi-event criteria

Under Standard & Poor's criteria, single-event catastrophe bonds are generally subject to a maximum rating of 'BB+'. However, if the one-year probability of attachment is no more than 40 basis points (bps) or 20 bps, the notes could be rated as high as 'BBB−' or 'BBB+', respectively. Otherwise, second-event notes are capped at 'BBB+'. A third-event catastrophe bond may be rated as high as 'A+' and a fifth-event catastrophe bond may be rated 'AA'. For a note to be rated 'AA', Standard & Poor's would expect there to be limited correlation among the modeled perils. In addition, the occurrence of any trigger event cannot result in a downgrade, based on the probability of attachment, of more than one rating category. Standard & Poor's will have discussions with the modeling agency to verify the methodology and results.

6.3   LEGAL AND SWAP DOCUMENTATION REVIEW PROCESS

As mentioned in Section 6.1, Standard & Poor's – including analysts from insurance, structured finance, swaps and legal – will review the documentation that will govern the bonds. Standard & Poor's will review the documents and assess whether any particular terms (or absence thereof) may bring, in our view, additional risks to the bonds. We usually inform the cedant or arranger, or their counsel, of any such opinion. Any subsequent changes to the documents will also be reviewed by Standard & Poor's until the final version is issued.

Below we list two groups of major areas where Standard & Poor's documentation review process will typically concentrate.

6.3.1   Insurance focus points

- event definition;
- reporting procedures;
- event verification;
- post-event loss calculation;
- replacement of critical service providers, such as the calculation agent and, if applicable, the reporting agency; and
- receipt by Standard & Poor's of any expected reports, such as event reports and reset reports that are issued during the life of the transaction.

6.3.2   Legal and structural focus points

- review of the structure of corporate and partnership entities involved including bankruptcy remoteness, grant of security interests to the cedant and noteholders and sufficiency of collateral to support obligations;
- priority of funds/flow of funds (to ensure cash flows to the issuer are sufficient to meet payments due on rated notes), including what happens after events of default;
- swaps: no termination for non-credit-related events;
- legal opinions on enforceability of agreements, insurance regulation, security interest and taxation;
- ratings on cedants, swap counterparties and guarantors; and
- review of service providers.

Before issuing the rating letter, Standard & Poor's may obtain confirmation from the transaction counsel that we have all documents in final form and that all documents have been executed.

6.4   IMPACT ON SPONSOR

6.4.1   Capital model treatment of ILS

Until now, Standard & Poor's has considered capital credit for ILS case by case (other than for catastrophe bonds), based on our analysis of the instrument involved. We expect that we will continue to do this, but the rapidly maturing ILS market may lead us to establish some globally consistent principles for recognizing capital credit in our capital model.

For natural catastrophe (nat-cat) bonds, the most mature ILS class, we include the net effect that catastrophe bonds have on the capital requirement for a (re)insurer's one-in-250-year property catastrophe modeled loss. This may arise from being a sponsor of, or investor in, catastrophe bonds. However, for sponsors, this credit is subject to a review of basis risk. Basis risk will chiefly arise on non-indemnity catastrophe bonds, but it may also arise, to a lesser extent, on indemnity bonds. If the basis risk is material, we may reduce or exclude the credit for the catastrophe bond in question when calculating the modeled loss. These practices are expected to continue.

For other types of ILS, we typically place the onus on the sponsor of the ILS issue to demonstrate its economic benefits. Sponsors normally achieve this by providing us with the incremental impact of the instrument on the insurer's capital requirements according to its economic capital model. We would normally give capital credit of no more than this incremental benefit in our own model.

Insurers may represent to us that our capital model treats certain risks or lines of business (e.g., motor) too conservatively for their own risk profiles. We understand that this may well be true, but the reverse also may be true. Our model is intended to be most relevant for insurers with a reasonably diverse risk profile. We tend to tailor our model for monoline insurers, rather than use the generic capital requirements. Our concern is to avoid 'cherry picking' individual risks or lines of business for capital relief. Hence, we usually focus on the economic benefits for the insurer as a whole.

Some securitizations envisage scenarios that far exceed the capital requirements we examine in our capital model. For instance, the events that trigger extreme mortality catastrophe bonds may only occur in the aftermath of extreme scenarios, which are not contemplated in our model. Accordingly, we may allow little or no credit for such securitizations.

For insurers for which our capital analysis is influenced by both our capital model and the insurer's economic capital model, the capital benefit of any ILS captured by the internal model may directly influence our assessment of capital adequacy. However, our analysis of the insurer's economic capital model may identify components (including those that refer to the impact of ILS) where we may increase the insurer's economic capital calculations for our own analytical purposes.

The remainder of this chapter focuses on the key analytical issue of quantifying and adjusting for basis risk in our capital model.

6.4.2 Summary of basis risk analysis

Quantifying basis risk is not straightforward. It can be defined in different ways. Standard & Poor's has adopted the definition below, which is intended to cover the key risks associated with ILS transactions and should not be used in any other context.

> *Basis risk is the risk that the quantum, timing or currency of the receipts from a particular mitigation strategy fail to at least cover the indemnified losses of the sponsor, for the protected perils and territories.*

In analyzing basis risk, we have sought to identify its key components. Some parts of basis risk can be modeled and some cannot. Table 6.3 shows a breakdown of the different subrisks we have identified and how we have categorized them (see Section 6.4.3 on the sources of basis risk).

Table 6.3 Basis risk

Sub-Risks By Category

	Quantifiable			Chargeable	
	Trigger	Timing	Currency	Model	Data
Parametric	Potentially significant	Minimal for all trigger types	Minimal for all trigger types	Significant	Potentially significant
Modeled loss	Limited			Significant	Potentially significant
Industry loss	Potentially significant			Potentially significant	Modest
Indemnity	Minimal			Minimal	Minimal

Source: Standard & Poor's

Where the risk can be modeled, we would expect the sponsor to perform this analysis and present its results for us to review. Where the risk cannot be modeled, we establish charges to reduce the credit given in the capital model that reflects the part of the risk inherent in the structure.

Here, we focus on the four generic types of trigger, but numerous forms of hybrid triggers can be created (e.g., that used in the transaction issued by Blue Coast Ltd). We assess these individually, using the criteria outlined here.

6.4.3 Sources of basis risk

The component parts allow a sponsor to more easily quantify the aggregate risk associated with a particular bond. Some of these risks can be quantified with reasonable certainty and others cannot. Where it is possible to quantify the risk we would expect to rely on the results of the sponsor's assessment, whilst retaining the option to review and adjust the results of that modeling. Where it is not possible to quantify the risk, Standard & Poor's will establish the set of charges that reflects the typical risk for different ILS structures. A key factor in determining the charge is the structural feature that may trigger the instrument.

Trigger options range from parametric notes, which are triggered by a mathematical formula related to the quantifying characteristics of an event (e.g., earthquake magnitude and depth, or maximum wind speed) rather than by a sponsor's exposures, to indemnity triggers, which mirror the actual losses of the sponsor. Non-indemnity (e.g., parametric) triggers generally embed a significantly greater level of basis risk for the issuer than indemnity triggers (see Standard & Poor's, 2008c).

Trigger risk

This addresses the possibility that the modeled recovery from the bond is less than the modeled portfolio losses; in other words, the risk – as captured by the model – that the bond does not trigger in the quantum it was intended to. Figure 6.3 illustrates the distinction between trigger risk and model risk. It can be measured as the adverse semi-deviation between the modeled losses and the modeled recovery under the bond. We have selected the semi-deviation rather than the standard deviation because only adverse outcomes are relevant.

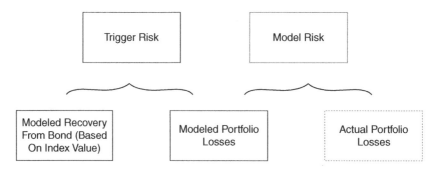

Figure 6.3   Trigger risk in insurance-linked securities
Source: Standard & Poor's

Figure 6.4 illustrates the recovery from a particular cat bond as compared to the losses on the portfolio it is intended to protect. The diagonal line represents perfect indemnity cover, where losses on the portfolio exactly match recoveries from the catastrophe bond. The portion above this line represents scenarios where recoveries from the bond exceed losses on the portfolio. The section below the line represents trigger risk: where the recoveries from the bond are less than losses on the portfolio.

If we were asked to rate the bond in question, we would expect to see the results of this basis risk analysis as part of the bond-rating process. It should also be made available to the sponsor's primary rating analyst as part of the sponsor's financial strength rating review process.

Although each transaction is unique, the following cat bond structures are listed in typical ascending order of basis risk arising from the trigger mechanism. However, using a hybrid

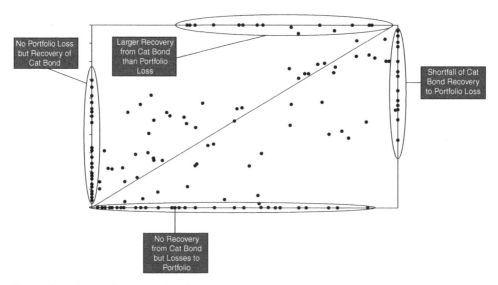

Figure 6.4   Recoveries on a cat bond
Source: Guy Carpenter, reproduced with permission

trigger may reduce the trigger (basis) risk for industry loss and parametric structures. In this situation, the order may change.

- **Indemnity:** this trigger is typically likened to nonproportional catastrophe reinsurance with a commutation at the end of the extension period, that is, an artificial cut-off to allow the bond to have a legal final maturity. Here, the risk centers on the possibility that total claim payments could ultimately exceed the amount estimated at the end of the extension period (where the bond has only produced a partial recovery). However, we expect this risk to be minimal.
- **Modeled loss:** the trigger established in this structure is based on a notional portfolio normally designed to reflect as closely as possible the actual underlying portfolio that the insurer intends to underwrite. The degree of trigger risk is therefore largely a function of how accurately the notional portfolio matches that of the actual business written. Assuming the notional portfolio of risks is a good proxy of the expected portfolio during the period of cover, we believe there is limited risk.
- **Parametric:** the size of trigger risk depends on the granularity and appropriateness of the weights in the index, and the accuracy and availability of the related sources (e.g., wind stations) that measure the event, compared to the sponsor's modeled exposure. We usually expect bonds covering windstorm events (e.g., Green Valley Ltd) to have lower trigger risk because there are numerous recording stations, which more accurately reflect the exposure in the portfolio. Bonds covering earthquake risk (e.g., MIDORI Ltd) will typically contain higher trigger risk because they use fewer measurement stations.
- **Industry loss** (currently only used in the US)**:** unless the issuer is a well-diversified national insurer, covering all major lines of business, we believe there is a significant risk that the recovery from the bond may not match indemnified losses.

In all these situations, our view is that it should be possible to model the expected shortfall between portfolio losses and recoveries.

Timing risk

Timing risk covers the likelihood that the delay between the issuer paying claims on the underlying portfolio and receiving payment under the ILS transaction is longer than that typically seen in traditional reinsurance contracts. This can be quantified using a stochastic cash flow model; however, we would expect it to be minimal for all trigger types.

Currency risk

Currency risk will occur where claims are paid in a different currency to that of the recovery under the bond and the exchange rate has moved since the date of issue of the bond. This can be quantified using financial models; however, we would expect this to be minimal for all trigger types.

Model risk

It is possible to perform sensitivity and scenario tests to give an indication of the quantum of model and data risk (below) but the results and/or scenarios are open to judgment and, as such, are not definitive. It is relatively easy to adjust the modeled results for a specified

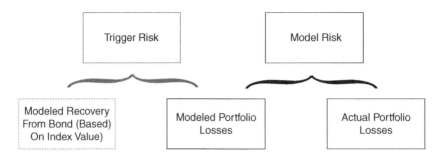

Figure 6.5 Model risk in insurance-linked securities
Source: Standard & Poor's

increase in frequency, for example, a 15% or 25% increase. However, it is more onerous to adjust for severity; a simple percentage increase will often overstate the impact for primary writers and understate the impact for excess lines writers and reinsurers. It is possible to create scenarios by synthetically increasing the underlying exposure, e.g., by increasing sums insured or altering building codes, which requires a full rerunning of the model for each scenario.

As Standard & Poor's has not identified a robust method to quantify the following risks, we typically establish a set of charges to apply to the different types of structure (see Section 6.4.2 earlier in this chapter).

Model risk captures the possibility that the catastrophe model could misestimate the impact of catastrophic events. Figure 6.5 illustrates the distinction between trigger risk and model risk. All models, by definition, are simplifications of reality and their ability to accurately predict future events depends on many factors. The impact of model risk depends on the type of trigger employed within a particular bond. At one extreme are indemnity bonds, where the effect on the sponsor is minimal, and at the other are parametric and modeled loss triggers, where the effect is significant.

The severity of catastrophic events could be incorrect in the catastrophe model. As a result, portfolio losses could be greater than the recovery under the bond. If the modeled severity does not trigger the bond, under modeled loss and potentially parametric trigger mechanisms, there may be losses to the portfolio but no recovery at all. Apart from the absolute severity of the event, three other factors may affect the loss to the portfolio relative to the recovery under the bond:

- **Location:** the risk that the location or track of catastrophic events could be misestimated such that the results of the catastrophe model understate the effect on claims relative to the recovery under the bond.
- **Financial loss for a given event:** the risk that the loss from a particular event is greater than expected, as a result of the model underestimating damage to individual properties.
- **Definition of an event (under the bond):** the risk that the measurement of the parameter values gives different results than those estimated by the catastrophe model for a given event, such that the issuer incurs losses that were expected but are not covered by the bond.

The frequency of catastrophic events could be incorrect in the catastrophe model, allowing the sponsor to suffer losses that are not covered by the bond. This is most prevalent in an aggregate transaction where the deductible would often be expected to be eroded by a number

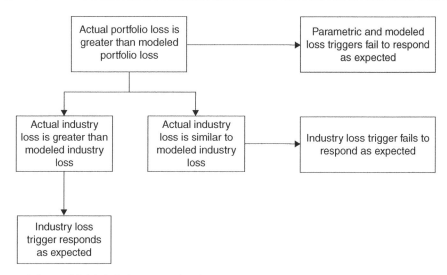

Figure 6.6 Model risk in industry loss bonds
Source: Standard & Poor's

of events. Strictly speaking, this is more a 'hedging strategy' risk than a basis risk to the sponsor; however, we may take it into consideration.

While the distinction between indemnity and non-indemnity structures is relatively obvious, the distinction between industry loss and parametric/modeled loss is less so. Mechanisms in the latter two leave the issuer with the risk that the actual loss to their portfolio could be greater than the modeled loss/parametric index. Even if the industry loss is greater than the modeled industry loss, a bond with an industry loss trigger will still respond approximately as expected. It is only where portfolio loss is greater and where the modeled and actual industry losses are similar to each other that this mechanism would not respond as intended. Figure 6.6 shows how model risk for an industry loss bond is, in effect, a subsection of model risk for parametric/modeled loss bonds.

Data risk

Data risk will arise where the sponsor's portfolio data, used to populate the model, is either incomplete or inaccurate. As a result, the sponsor may suffer greater losses to its portfolio than estimated for a given level of index value.

For indemnity cat bonds, data risk is minimal for the sponsor because it is passed to the noteholder in this type of structure. However, the risk of lawsuit/cancellation exists, if data quality led to the risk being materially misrepresented to potential investors.

For industry loss bonds it is less relevant, since the sponsor's portfolio is modeled only to select the appropriate industry loss attachment and exhaustion points. In this structure, the data risk is that the estimated share of industry loss could be inaccurate.

For modeled loss and parametric triggers, this risk can be significant because of the challenge presented in matching the generic trigger to the actual insurer's portfolio.

These models are highly complex and rely on the quality of data input into them. Data risk can form a significant portion of a sponsor's total basis risk in these types of transaction.

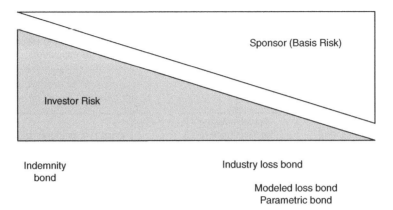

Figure 6.7   Model risk
Source: Standard & Poor's

However, the risks remain essentially the same, though different triggers cause different participants in a transaction to bear those risks.

6.4.4   Link to ILS revised probability of attachment

The methodology to assess basis risk supported the development of the stress tests applied in arriving at the revised probability of attachment used when we rate ILS transactions.

When rating an ILS transaction, we will consider the risks from the perspective of the investor; for the capital model, we will review the risks from the perspective of the sponsor. These risks are broadly similar, but how investors and sponsors share them will depend on the trigger type and the structural features of the specific transaction. For example, model risk is a permanent feature of any structure. Figure 6.7 illustrates how the sponsor and investor share risk for the different trigger types. Please note that the diagram is for illustration purposes only, it is not to scale and the specific characteristics of the individual transaction will ultimately determine how much risk passes to the investor and how much the sponsor retains.

REFERENCES

GIRO (2008) Working Party on Basis Risk (a subgroup of the Securitization of Non-Life Insurance Working Party).

Standard & Poor's (2007) *Framework for Rating Natural Peril Catastrophe Bonds*, July 5.

Standard & Poor's (2008a) *Default Table Used To Rate Insurance-Linked Securitisations, Updated*, May 8.

Standard & Poor's (2008b) *Guide to Rating Process for Insurance-Linked Securities*, September 5.

Standard & Poor's (2008c) *Methodology and Assumptions Used for Rating Natural Catastrophe Insurance-Linked Securities*, September 11.

Standard & Poor's (2008d) Approach To Rating Indemnified Natural Catastrophe Insurance-Linked Securities, September 15.

7

Risk Modelling and the Role and Benefits of Cat Indices

Ben Brookes[a]

The first commercial catastrophe (or 'cat') models were developed in the late 1980s, and usage grew rapidly following Hurricane Andrew in 1992. Making landfall in Southern Florida, Andrew caused unprecedented losses and pushed many insurers to the limits of their solvency. With this shock to the insurance industry, a probabilistic approach to catastrophe risk analysis was necessitated by the relative paucity of historical data; given the infrequent nature of large loss-causing catastrophic events, actuarial and statistical methods do not provide the full picture – it was no longer acceptable to rely solely on past experience to predict the future.

The cat modelling industry has grown rapidly with scientific advances in the understanding of natural hazards, and technological developments in information systems that now allow stakeholders to capture exposure information in great detail. At the time of writing, in 2008, cat models are used widely throughout the insurance industry for the measurement, pricing and management of risk, and are a key input to insurance-linked securities.

The science of catastrophe risk modelling essentially calls on two fundamental principles – managing exposure and understanding hazard. At its heart, a catastrophe model combines these two areas of expertise, overlaying scientific studies of natural hazards on a representation of the properties at risk.

Catastrophes, by their very nature, are complex physical phenomena. To quantify catastrophe risk requires the compilation of detailed inventories of insurance risk, estimating physical damage to many varied structures and their contents, quantification of time-element losses, translating physical damage to financial loss, and aggregating this across portfolios of risk. The modellers' task is to simulate, realistically and representatively, the principal aspects of this complex natural dynamical system. Model users must familiarize themselves with the underlying modelling assumptions, and thereby understand the implications and limitations of the model output when informing risk management decisions.

Catastrophe models are data hungry, requiring vast amounts of information for model construction and validation, as well as for model usage. Further, a model's validity and reliability depends on the scientific understanding of the principal mechanisms controlling the occurrence and behaviour of catastrophe events. With increasingly sophisticated hazard measurement technology, computing capabilities and ever-increasing market demand for better exposure data, cat models now represent the accumulation of vast amounts of information and knowledge about

---

[a]Risk Management Solutions, Inc

the underlying physical phenomena. By leveraging this knowledge, these complex phenomena can be simulated in an increasingly detailed manner using a probabilistic approach.

7.1 COMPONENTS OF A CAT MODEL

The four main components of a cat model represent hazard, inventory, vulnerability and loss.

The 'hazard' component consists of a stochastic event set – a large number of catastrophe event scenarios that together provide a representation of possible loss-causing events, and an associated modelled rate of occurrence for each. For each event scenario, the physical parameters of the event are represented, including the hazard – the measure of the event's potential to cause damage, for example the wind speeds, ground shaking or flood depths across the event extent.

The 'inventory' component represents the exposure. It is made up of the properties and their contents, or more broadly the portfolio of locations that is subject to catastrophe risk. The process of 'geocoding' translates address information into geo-spatial references, and also calls on underlying data sets representing a location's susceptibility to natural hazards – for example, surface roughness for hurricane modelling or soil type for earthquake analysis. Similarly, the items in the inventory are categorized in terms of aspects that affect the amount of damage to a structure for a given level of hazard (vulnerability). These typically comprise construction materials, occupancy and building age and dimensions, and are continually increasing in detail as catastrophe modelling technology develops. In order to estimate financial impacts, the values and associated insurance structures are also captured.

The 'vulnerability' component quantifies the expected damage that will result to a portion of the inventory as a result of the occurrence of varying levels of hazard, as well as an associated uncertainty. This is achieved through a set of damage curves for each element of the inventory, relating hazard severity to a damage ratio.

Once the aforementioned modules have determined the mean damage ratio for each component of the inventory, the financial impact is quantified by the 'loss' module. For each element, this calculates the distribution of loss, and applies any insurance structures such as policy and treaty terms to determine the outputs for different financial perspectives. This output is typically an exceedance probability representing the likelihood of exceeding given loss thresholds in a fixed timeframe – and is essentially a measure of value at risk (VaR).

Typical metrics used for the assessment of catastrophe risk associated with an ILS structure are attachment probability, exhaustion probability and expected loss. These represent, respectively, the modelled annual likelihood of a first dollar of loss, full loss and mean loss.

7.2 INSURANCE-LINKED SECURITIES

7.2.1 General overview

The last decade has seen a dramatic increase in the volumes of insurance-related risk transferred to the capital markets. The majority of this risk transfer has been accomplished through the use of insurance-linked bonds and reinsurance sidecars, and recently there has been increasing interest in the use of derivatives to transfer risk into the capital markets. The evolution in the insurance-linked market represents an opportunity for analytics firms like RMS to provide solutions to business needs: the Paradex suite of indices is one of the tools intended to reduce the cost and complexity of issuing a cat bond and the Miu portfolio analysis tool is another intended to demystify cat bonds for mainstream investors.

7.2.2   Insurance-linked security triggers

Insurance-linked securities, and particularly catastrophe bonds, differ from many other forms of financial instrument, in that the offering materials will usually contain a risk analysis quantifying the probability of default in the expert view of a third party modelling agency. As such, there are a number of important criteria for ensuring the appropriate modelling and trigger structuring of insurance-linked securities:

- **Objectivity and transparency:** rigorous event definitions must allow the objective deter-mination of event occurrence, and a third party measurement of the event parameters for triggering must be available. These event definitions must cover such considerations as:
  - *When and where an event occurs:* the precise time and location of an event is necessary to determine the occurrence within the risk period and covered area, and put into motion the sequence of actions that determine any payment made under the notes.
  - *Trigger parameters:* given the occurrence of an event, the parameters that constitute the event must be defined. This may mean detailing the process by which claims will be handled and verified in an indemnity structure, or it might determine the objective selection of hazard values to be used in a parametric index (see the section below entitled 'Parametric').
  - *Multiplicity of events:* the definitions must determine whether a specific set of circum-stances constitutes one or more events, and in the case of multiple events, how these are separated in space and time.
- **Quantification of risk:** any structure must be analysed to determine the likelihood of default, on the basis of the trigger parameters above, preferably with a commercially available model. As such, the modelling method must be consistent with the trigger mechanism.
- **Basis risk:** ILS structures must have manageable basis risk – the structure is first and foremost an insurance risk hedge, and as such, payments must correlate well to insurance losses (see Section 7.3).
- **Verification of past performance:** the risk analysis for an ILS will typically contain an analysis of any significant historical events to have occurred over a particular time horizon. This may be performed on the basis of modelled event representation or actual measured values – or both. It is therefore important that past historical data can be obtained in order to provide this information in the risk analysis.

An ILS may be triggered by several different mechanisms, each with their own benefits and disadvantages. Typically, the ILS market may be described in terms of four different types of trigger, as described below with emphasis on the modelling challenges associated with each.

Risk transfer mechanisms triggered by direct insurance and reinsurance losses are often referred to as 'indemnity-based' structures. These have a clear benefit to the sponsor of the transaction – the precise loss experience is used as the trigger, and thereby the structure matches the underlying claims as closely as possible. From the investor standpoint, these types of transactions include not only natural catastrophe risk, but also insurance risk – that is, exposure to the underwriting, claims handling, portfolio management and associated risks of the sponsoring insurance or reinsurance company. As a consequence, the pricing of indemnity risk is usually higher than equivalent parametric risk.

Due to the nature of the risk, indemnity transactions will usually require a significant lead time for settlement following an event under the structure. As a consequence, indemnity transactions will include significant extension periods at additional cost to the sponsor.

Indemnity modelling challenges   Indemnity transactions are the closest form of ILS to insurance and reinsurance contracts – as such, the modelling is based on the insurance loss itself. These transactions therefore use the full catastrophe modelling framework.

Data quality   The biggest modelling challenge is the accurate inventory of all insurance risks, and the ensuring of high data quality associated with these. This is a particular challenge for reinsurance-based deals; often the data quality becomes less granular as it flows through the insurance chain.

Data quality comprises two aspects: accuracy and completeness. The latter is often easier to determine – using, for example, a key set of metrics such as the number of locations in a portfolio that contain unknown attributes. Data accuracy is a deeper challenge: the issue of the verification of data against the underlying exposures is significant, and data sets can often contain indications of bias; issues such as bulk coding, unknown attributes in high-hazard areas or inaccuracies caused by data capture practices can all lead to significant indicators of material data risk. Recently, indemnity transactions have included specific data quality assessments as a way to ensure investors are able to understand their exposure as best as possible.

In order to ensure consistency and repeatability of analysis, data quality should be assessed within a standardized framework, with questions asked along various dimensions to ensure a holistic and constructive perspective, covering the following topics:

- **Data completeness:** an assessment of the resolution and granularity of the data elements, as well as the number and importance of unknown data elements. A second and difficult to measure aspect of this is where risks have been excluded entirely from the exposure dataset.
- **Data accuracy:** data may be complete, but they must also be accurate. Data accuracy should be assessed using portfolio level checks and also detailed account and location level checks, which can also be aggregated to investigate any systemic data quality issues.
- **Sensitivity testing:** sensitivity testing of model outputs should be carried out to understand the potential variation in estimated losses due to the above data quality issues.
- **Process for improving data over time:** not only should there be appropriate metrics and processes for assessing data completeness, data accuracy and calculating their impact on model results, there should also be associated processes for addressing any highlighted issues and improving data quality over time.

Non-modelled risk   Catastrophe models are generally used to establish a 'technical rate,' which is often then loaded by insurance companies who themselves take a view on the true cost of risk inherent to a particular contract. For example, for an account particularly exposed to tree damage that is quoted for hurricane cover, it may be appropriate for the insurer to consider the comprehensiveness of the commercially available model for this particular case. To deal with these types of differences between the technical rates as quantified by catastrophe models, and the true cost of doing business for the insurance company, adjustments to modelled losses are often determined by the sponsoring insurance or reinsurance company, and included in the modelling results by the modelling agency.

Resets   Since the direct loss experience of the sponsoring insurance or reinsurance company is used to trigger an indemnity transaction, it is necessary to perform regular resets to ensure that portfolio growth does not materially alter the probability of default. In general, these resets are included at least on an annual basis, and in some recent transactions have been included on the basis of event occurrence – once an event is known to have occurred, the most recent portfolio representation is used to reset the attachment and exhaustion points that are required at the time of the event to maintain the probability of attachment and expected loss. As a consequence of these reset requirements, the maintenance of an indemnity transaction would also require management time and costs beyond other forms of ILS, though it can be argued that such efforts would be in line with the work to be performed in connection with traditional reinsurance renewals.

Industry loss

In some regions, especially the US, the availability of industry-wide insured loss surveys allows the structuring of industry loss-based transactions. The simplest of these are industry loss warranties (ILWs), whereby the total industry loss in a particular region is the trigger.

Industry loss-based structures are essentially a 'pooled indemnity' solution – the indemnity loss experiences of many companies are used to determine the industry loss estimate through surveys. As such, these industry loss structures have many of the same properties as indemnity transactions. For an insurer or reinsurer with a profile much like the industry as a whole, they present a good mechanism for hedging insurance risk, whilst not linking directly to its own portfolio and indemnity loss experience. Industry loss transactions tend to require similarly long extension periods – it can take up to two years for a final loss estimate of large catastrophic events to be published in some cases.

Industry loss modelling challenges

Modelling the industry   In order to quantify the magnitude of insured industry losses, it is first necessary to quantify the total insurance industry exposure. Estimates of total insured values are typically obtained by sampling company premium information, census demographics, building square footage data and representative policy terms and conditions. Detailed population and business statistics are used to distribute any aggregate information to more granular levels, such as the postal code.

Non-modelled risk   As with indemnity structures, it is necessary to quantify any 'non-modelled' risk, or eliminate this through the appropriate structuring of trigger definitions. For example, the RMS US Hurricane Model includes 23 states, and does not cover Midwest states. The recent initial PCS (Property Claims Services) bulletins for Hurricane Ike have indicated significant loss (around $1.1 billion at the time of writing) for the state of Ohio due to Ike's large wind field, and a significant component of broad, low-level loss in the Midwest as a result. Therefore, transactions that include the Midwest states would accumulate losses, yet the risk of these losses would not be included in the transaction risk analysis.

Basis risk   As with any non-indemnity structure, an industry loss-based trigger will contain a material probability that the payment under the structure does not match the loss experience perfectly. This risk increases as the subject portfolio exposure deviates from the industry exposure. As such, these solutions are often 'indexed' – losses by region may be weighted via the application of market share factors, in order to tailor the industry loss estimates to a particular portfolio.

Resets   As with an indemnity transaction, it is usually considered necessary to include resets in an industry loss-based transaction. There are exceptions, but broadly the industry insurance exposure growth is considered large enough year on year that resets are required on at least an annual basis, updating the modelling agent's view of industry exposure as this is available.

Parametric

A parametric transaction uses measured physical properties of a catastrophe event as a trigger. These are typically an event's wind speeds, ground motions or flood depths – the direct drivers of physical damage. A parametric transaction is typically based on an index of the event hazard, with the index designed to correlate to modelled portfolio losses.

The event parameters are measured as the event occurs, and are generally published within a matter of days. These types of transactions are therefore much more rapidly settled, and as such can lead to greater liquidity in the marketplace.

Parametric structures remove insurance risk from the transaction structure, with these risks becoming basis risk for the sponsoring re/insurer. As such, parametric structures are considerably easier to understand from the investor standpoint, leading to considerable pricing advantages, and the potential to open the market to non-insurance specialists.

Parametric modelling challenges

Independent model calibration   Parametric transactions are not dependent on the financial loss of an insurance or reinsurance company, or of the industry. Hence, parametric structures only require certain components of the catastrophe model, which results in a greater requirement for independent calibration of the separate components of the model. The event and hazard representation must characterize the distribution of potential event occurrence independently of any financial loss experience.

Model differences   Often, the definitions used to describe a parametric solution are heavily dependent on the catastrophe model used to assess the structure – for example, the choice of event parameters will be made in consideration of the consistency with the model used to assess the risk inherent in the transaction. As a consequence, there can be many subtle differences between structures modelled by different modelling agencies, which must be accounted for when reassessing a structure with an alternative model. For example, different models may be based on different interpretations of European Windstorm risk, including the manner in which wind speeds are modelled and treated following event occurrence.

Basis risk   As with any non-indemnity structure, a parametric index will contain a material probability that the payment under the structure does not match the loss experience perfectly. A parametric index must therefore be 'tuned' to correlate to the underlying portfolio and expected loss experience as closely as possible. Without careful structuring, this can often lead to highly customized structures, which are often difficult to compare on a like-for-like basis. To counter this challenge, RMS has developed the Paradex suite of parametric indices – please see Section 7.3.5 for more detail.

Modelled loss

A modelled loss transaction uses a modelled representation of a catastrophe event, applied to a notional portfolio – the representation of the underlying insurance risk – in order to determine a modelled loss estimate, which is then used as a trigger. In essence, a modelled loss transaction is a more complex and less transparent parametric structure – the event parameters form the representation of the event that is then fed into a catastrophe model rather than an index function.

Modelled loss modelling challenges   Being essentially parametric, a modelled loss trans-action contains many of the same challenges as a parametric transaction. In many instances, modelled loss transactions require simpler representations of events (e.g. hurricane central pressure and forward velocity, rather than measured wind speeds) and rely on the model to 'fill in' the structure of the event.

Basis risk and volatility   It is often assumed that because the model is used to perform the risk analysis as well as the triggering, the modelled basis risk is zero. This is only true if one assumes the trigger to be entirely consistent with the model design; often the parameters used (such as the radius to maximum winds, R_{max}, for hurricanes in the US) may not definitively be available following an event, leading to a degree of subjectivity in the post-event process.

   Further, the non-modelled basis risk of a modelled loss transaction may be significantly higher than a parametric transaction, due to increased volatility. Many modelled loss transac-tions are based on a few parameters, such as the central pressure, forward velocity and radius to maximum winds. Small variations in these key parameters can lead to large variation in the potential modelled loss outcomes.

Summary

Each type of transaction has its own associated advantages and disadvantages. Broadly, these can be simplified into complexity, basis risk and settlement time (Figure 7.1). Each has its own

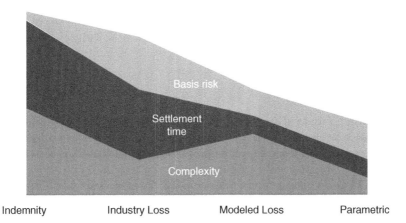

Figure 7.1   ILS trigger comparison
Source: RMS

varying levels of importance dependent on the application – for example, a structure designed to provide contingent capital may consider the 'basis risk' to be less important.

At the simplest level, a sponsor's choice of the optimum solution for the creation of an ILS then comes down to a question of price versus basis risk. Further description of the important considerations a potential sponsor must make in choosing the appropriate trigger can be found in Chapter 4.

7.2.3 Basis risk

Basis risk has many different interpretations within the insurance-linked securities sector, and has even broader interpretations in the reinsurance arena. For the purposes of this discussion, we will define basis risk as:

The degree to which the indemnity loss experienced as a consequence of an event or set of events does not match the payment received under a related contract designed to cover these losses.

Non-modelled basis risk

Importantly, from a risk analysis standpoint, there are several components to this. The non-modelled basis risk has two components, and is the net consequence of:

1. The degree to which the peril model's estimate of the indemnity loss is not consistent with that of the actual coverage required; and
2. The degree to which the peril model's estimate of the trigger payment is not consistent with that of the actual payment.

There are many factors at play contributing to the difference between the cost of doing business and the 'technical rate' one should charge for a specific insurance product. As a consequence, many re/insurance companies will make adjustments to catastrophe modelling output to account for the specific properties of accounts or contracts where the exposure is known to have certain properties. Perhaps one of the largest drivers of the first component is the data quality, in terms of both accuracy and completeness of the underlying portfolio.

In essence, this definition of non-modelled basis risk is really a reformation of the question 'does stochastic modelling, as applied to indemnity contracts or ILS triggers, give an accurate account of the risk inherent therein?'.

Modelled basis risk

A catastrophe model consists of a set of modelled events, as a collection representing the space of possible catastrophe events. If an ILS is considered to be a hedge for an insurance portfolio, then there will also be an equivalent layer on the portfolio which the ILS is designed to cover (Figure 7.2).

To assess the basis risk in a non-indemnity structure, the modelled loss and payment under the transaction structure for each event are examined. For example, under an industry loss structure, the portfolio loss is compared with the modelled industry index loss. Similarly, for a parametric transaction, the parametric index value is calculated for each modelled event and compared with the modelled portfolio loss.

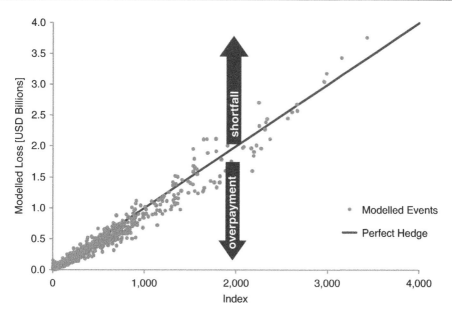

Figure 7.2   Modelled basis risk
Source: RMS

Where the payment under the structure is less than the modelled loss experience, a 'shortfall' results, and the amount received is not sufficient to cover loss. Where the opposite occurs, and the payment is greater than the loss experience (sometimes referred to as 'basis chance') then an overpayment occurs. Whilst at first glance not necessarily a significant problem, a significant risk of overpayment will lead to an inefficient transaction, since the contribution to the probability of default resulting from these overpaying event scenarios must be paid for in the transaction spread.

We can then define the modelled basis risk more formally, as a shortfall:

Conditional expected shortfall: *The expected magnitude of deviation of the modelled indemnity loss from the modelled trigger payment, conditional on the modelled trigger payment falling short of the modelled indemnity loss.*

Defining the 'Payment' as the actual payment arising from the hedging strategy, and the 'Loss' as the would-be payment from a perfect hedge, we have:

$$\text{Conditional expected shortfall} = \text{Expectation (Payment} \mid \text{Payment} < \text{Loss)}$$

In a modelling and ratings context, this is often also thought about in terms of the likelihood of certain levels of shortfall:

$$P(x\% \text{ shortfall}) = P(x\% \text{ shortfall} \mid \text{Payment} < \text{Loss})^*P(\text{Payment} < \text{Loss})$$

Given that each modelled event has a quantification of the expected portfolio loss, and the payment under the transaction structure, it is also possible to represent the 'benefit' to the sponsoring re/insurer.

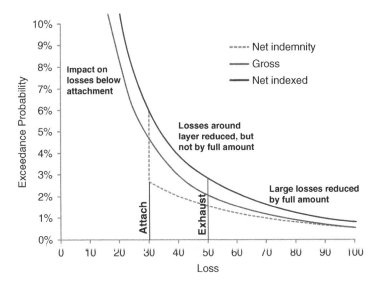

Figure 7.3   Impacts on an exceedance probability curve
Source: RMS

The underlying insurance portfolio will have a 'gross' exceedance probability curve – that is, a representation of the likelihood of exceeding various levels of loss, before the application of the ILS linked to the portfolio. Since there is a material probability of both an overpayment and a shortfall as a result of the basis risk inherent in the transaction, there is a resultant probability that a payment will be received from the transaction before the loss to the underlying portfolio reaches the equivalent level. Similarly, there is potential for losses within the covered portfolio layer that may not be reimbursed fully by the ILS payment. As such, the 'net' exceedance probability curve – that is, the portfolio exceedance probability curve accounting for the modelled ILS payment – shows a reduction before the portfolio attachment level, and a less than 100% reduction beyond the portfolio layer (Figure 7.3).

Now, with these exceedance probability curves quantified, one can assess the 'efficiency' of the transaction; if, for example, the 100 and 250 year return period losses for a given peril are known before and after the application of the modelled ILS, the resultant reduction in the PML can be used to determine efficiency, assessing the PML reduction against the volume of the ILS offering.

Key drivers of basis risk

The key drivers of basis risk determine the ability to characterize the modelled loss distribution, as well as the uncertainties that exist between the parameters that trigger the payment and that modelled loss distribution.

In the case of industry loss triggers, the highest contribution to basis risk stems from the incongruence of the industry exposure profile to the company exposure profile. This is alleviated somewhat by 'industry loss index' triggers, which allow macro-scale weightings to adjust the loss contributions of predefined subregions to the event index value. Increasing the granularity of the subregions improves the flexibility of a tailored index which, provided these subregions are appropriately weighted, will reduce the basis risk. However, given the relatively low resolution of most industry loss surveys, this incongruence can be material. See Section 7.3.5 for a discussion of an alternative industry loss estimating index, which may be used on a more granular level.

In the case of parametric triggers, the key component of the basis risk is the vulnerability uncertainty: that is, given a complete set of parameters that fully describe the physical nature of an event, the amount of loss caused by that event remains uncertain. Additionally, it is not feasible to obtain a fully continuous physical description of an event, so there is parameter uncertainty; the risk that the chosen parameters do not fully characterize the event's severity.

For any non-indemnity structure, a significant driver of basis risk is the data quality of the underlying portfolio representation. In the case of an indemnity structure, this data quality remains a significant risk – though here the majority of the risk may well be passed to the investor as part of the overall insurance risk transferred.

For a more detailed analysis of basis risk, its quantification and its implications for a ceding company, please refer to Chapter 5.

7.3   CAT INDICES

There are several existing indices providing sponsors access to the capital markets through somewhat standardized means.

7.3.1   Property Claims Service (PCS)

The majority of industry loss-based catastrophe index instruments in the market currently are based around PCS industry loss estimates. PCS is a subsidiary of the Insurance Service Office (ISO). After an event, PCS uses data gathered from the polling of insurance companies and trending to form a view of the potential industry level losses from a US event. These are aggregated from expectations of the individual surveyed companies' losses. While this has been a tried and tested way to approximate losses from various catastrophes, the challenges in using this methodology for capital market deals are mainly two-fold:

- There is a long lead time until PCS is able to provide a final estimate of the losses. The process often takes up to 18 months and, for very large events, can take even longer; this can be an issue in terms of liquidity as the value of an instrument is not ultimately known until this final report is provided.
- The process used might be considered subjective and can vary considerably from the initial report to the final loss result. This perceived lack of transparency is unfavourable to some investors.

7.3.2   Re-Ex – NYMEX

The Re-Ex index is based upon the Property Claims Service (PCS) catastrophe loss estimates aggregated for the calendar year to date. The index covers the perils of hurricane, tropical storm, wind and thunderstorm, water damage, winter storm, riot, volcano, utility service disruption and wild fire, but does not at the time of writing cover losses from earthquake. The index is defined as the sum of the PCS US dollar losses, in units of $10 million.

Since it is based on the PCS index, the Re-Ex index is subject to similar limitations. In addition, the index is built around only three aggregated areas:

• all US;
• Florida;
• Eastern Seaboard (excluding Florida).

This makes it difficult to build an intelligent portfolio hedging instrument due to the lack of granularity, unless the issuer has exposures similar in distribution to that of the industry.

7.3.3   Insurance Futures Exchange Service (IFEX)

The IFEX index is published on the Chicago Climate Futures Exchange and is another example of an industry loss based index which feeds directly from the PCS loss figures.

The traded instruments driven by IFEX are event-linked futures (ELFs) which aim to mimic the mechanics of an industry loss warranty (ILW), where there is a binary payout from the ELF once the industry strike price as defined by PCS is reached.

There are a series of first- and second-event futures which are triggered at a series of predefined industry loss levels ($10 billion, $20 billion, $30 billion, $40 billion and $50 billion), much like ILWs.

7.3.4   Carvill Hurricane Index (CHI) – Chicago Mercantile Exchange (CME)

The CHI is a parametric hurricane index created by the broker Carvill and traded on the Chicago Mercantile Exchange. It is based on the macro parameters of hurricane events impacting the East Coast of the United States and not purely upon industry loss estimates.

The CHI value depends upon three parameters of an event to estimate the potential losses caused. These are:

• maximum wind velocity;
• radius to maximum winds;
• region of impact.

The regional parameter is the portion of the East Coast where landfall occurs. The coastline is divided into six different zones, defined as:

• Northern Atlantic Coast;
• Southern Atlantic Coast;
• Florida;
• Gulf Coast;
• Eastern US (aggregation of all other zones);
• CHI 'cat in a box' offshore region.

Although this methodology removes any subjectivity in the index, the regions remain large. As such, an insurer using this index to provide cover will have a wide range of potential losses which yield the same index value.

The index is based upon macro parameters and not loss-causing effects on the ground and thus it is a challenge to achieve a strong correlation between the loss experience and the index recovery, even on an industry level. As such, while this form of index is interesting from an investor point of view, it is of limited use for providing protection to insurers.

7.3.5   Paradex

What is Paradex?

Paradex is a suite of indices, designed and built by RMS to estimate industry loss levels on a parametric basis. This means that the physical properties of an event – the hazard values – are used to determine event severity, and thereby infer index values, which represent estimates of industry insured loss levels.

Crucially, Paradex is designed to offer numerous advantages over alternative trigger types, addressing both sponsor and investor concerns.

Advantages of use

Paradex presents various advantages. Among them are:

- **Simplicity and transparency:** Paradex provides the simplest and purest form of catastrophe risk transfer – the cession of parametric hazard risk. As such, trigger mechanisms are simple and transparent, and easily quantified by both sponsors and investors. It is not necessary to understand or quantify detailed insurance risk – making the solution considerably more accessible to the broader ILS investor market. Because Paradex uses estimates of insured industry loss as the basis of each index, multiple Paradex transactions can be directly compared with each other in an intuitive fashion. Where a custom parametric index will usually contain a nondimensional index function, or arbitrary units, Paradex indices are designed to estimate industry loss levels. Two such indices may therefore be compared – if Miami-Dade has a weighting of 2% in one index and 5% in another, it is simple and intuitive to understand the difference in exposure between these two indices.
- **Objectivity:** Paradex is designed to offer complete disclosure of the methodologies and process used for the purposes of an event calculation. Using the information publicly available via the Paradex website, it is possible to recreate the event calculations, providing complete documentation of the processes. These are executed without human judgement, and therefore cannot be exposed to the subjectivity and moral hazard associated with other forms of trigger mechanism.
- **Liquidity:** whereas indemnity or industry loss triggers may take years to settle, Paradex triggers are guaranteed to present final index values within 40 business days of the identification of an event.
- **Efficiency:** Paradex allows parametric transactions to be structured without significant documentation requirements for each deal. Since the methodologies, event definitions and calculation processes are all documented and made publicly available on the Paradex website, these do not need to be included in the deal documents directly. Whereas the definitions for a custom parametric index may span tens of pages in an offering circular, Paradex condenses the required definitions to a few pages at most.

Paradex provides an all-in-one triggering solution – RMS contracts directly with data providers for the provision of index values. As such, it is not necessary for sponsors or arrangers to form these contracts as part of the offering; the Paradex licence provides all aspects of the service needed to structure and trigger a parametric transaction.

In the subsection below, we examine Paradex US Hurricane as an example of a Paradex index. Whilst this example is specific to US Hurricane, the considerations, criteria and structure are representative of all Paradex indices.

Case study: Paradex US Hurricane

Measuring hurricane wind speeds   Until recently, pure parametric hurricane risk transfer has not been possible, due to the lack of a reliable network for the measurement of hurricane wind speeds. Many existing wind stations are either switched off as a hurricane approaches, or fail during very high wind speeds. This leads to a 'survival bias' – that is, only those stations that do not experience the most severe winds are likely to survive.

To meet this challenge, RMS has partnered with WeatherFlow Inc., which owns and operates a network of hurricane-hardened weather stations (Figure 7.4) along the US coast that can accurately measure and record hurricane-strength wind speeds.

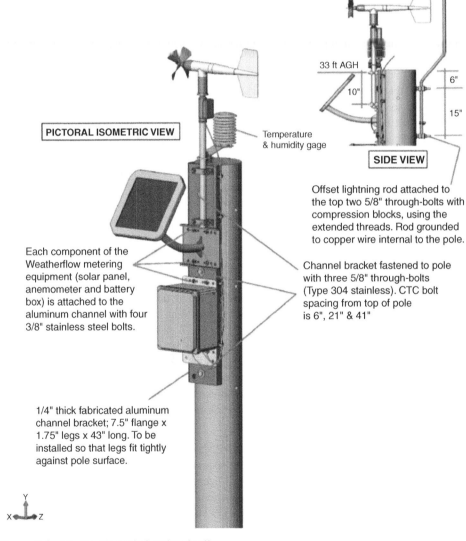

Figure 7.4   WeatherFlow wind station detail
Source: WeatherFlow, reproduced with permission

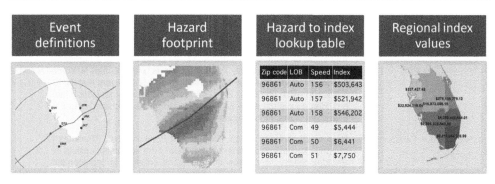

Figure 7.5   Anatomy of a Paradex index
Source: RMS

The stations in the network have been specifically sited to capture concentrations of hurricane risk. The network currently covers all of Florida and Houston, Texas and the surrounding areas, with an extension to the entire Gulf Coast and Eastern Seaboard planned.

Stations provide multiple redundancies to ensure the accuracy and reliability of data capture. Each contains an anemometer, rated to 220 mph and powered by a photo-voltaic cell, with battery backup. This allows stations to function if the power supply grid fails during a storm. Wind speed data is transmitted in real time via the cellular network, and also captured and stored on a flash device. Each measurement device is mounted on a commercial tower or a specially constructed concrete pole.

All parties involved in transactions that use the WeatherFlow network have access to individual specifications for all stations, as well as visual details about terrain surrounding the stations.

Creating the Paradex US Hurricane index   Using the WeatherFlow hurricane network, it is now possible to measure accurately the wind speeds experienced during damaging hurricanes. The Paradex US Hurricane index takes these wind speeds and uses them to infer the estimated industry loss levels for each zip code within a covered area.

This follows a framework similar to the broader catastrophe modelling framework, whereby modules representing stochastic event scenarios, hazard experience, vulnerability of exposures and financial structures apply. For Paradex, we also apply four similar modules (Figure 7.5).

Event definitions   These definitions (Figure 7.6) determine, in an objective fashion, the occurrence (or nonoccurrence) of a covered event. The definitions, published publicly, are developed using RMS's experience over many catastrophe bond transactions to determine with rigour the event occurrence time and location, and to identify and potentially separate events in space and time.

This set of rigorous definitions is fundamental to the structuring and potential settlement of any ILS transaction. These will, for example, determine exactly which hazard values, measurement locations and measurement times should be included in a calculation process.

The event definitions are designed to give consistency between the analysis of risk using catastrophe models and the triggering process should an event occur. Since they are publicly

U.S. Hurricane

Hurricane .... Any storm or storm system that has been declared to be a hurricane by the National Hurricane Center, which is part of the National Oceanic and Atmospheric Administration, and in the event that NHC ceases to exist and there is no successor, another organization that provides equivalent data, and for which the Index Provider issues a Hurricane Bulletin ("**Hurricane**").

Index Provider; Paradex .... Paradex, a division of Risk Management Solutions, Inc. ("**Paradex**") or any successor-in-interest thereto, or if no successor exists or Paradex ceases to provide the Hurricane Bulletins, a replacement named by the Issuer ("**Index Provider**").

Hurricane Bulletin .... Any publication or report originated and disseminated by the Index Provider in any medium including, without limitation, one titled "Hurricane Bulletin" which identifies and assigns a name or number to a Hurricane, and/or gives preliminary calculation or, subsequently, revisions of the Hurricane Index Value arising from such Hurricane.

A Hurricane Bulletin specifies Hurricane Index Values by region and by line of business ("**Hurricane Bulletin**").

Hurricane Covered Area .... The state of Florida and the metropolitan area of Houston, Texas ("**Hurricane Covered Area**").

Hurricane Occurrence Date ...... In respect of any Hurricane, the first date specified in the "Date" data field of a Hurricane Bulletin or the comparable data field if the Hurricane Bulletin reporting format changes ("**Hurricane Occurrence Date**").

Hurricane Index Value .... On any date of determination for each Hurricane, the total of the Hurricane Index Values reported by the Index Provider, using [Version [7.0] / the most recently updated version] of the Paradex wind speed-index value lookup tables, for each CRESTA of the Hurricane Covered Area and all lines of business as a result of the Hurricane, from the most recent Hurricane Bulletin ("**Hurricane Index Value**").

Hurricane Payout Factors .... The percentages by line of business and region specified below (each, a "**Hurricane Payout Factor**", and collectively, "**Hurricane Payout Factors**")

[Factors inserted here – by region and LOB]

Hurricane Index Value .... On any date of determination for each Hurricane, the Hurricane Index Value is determined by the following formula ("**Hurricane Index Value**"):

Hurricane Index Value = $\Sigma_{R,L}(P_{R,L} \times I_{R,L})$

Where $P_{R,L}$ is the Hurricane Payout Factor for region R and line of business L and $I_{R,L}$ is the hurricane index value for region R and line of business L reported by the Index Provider, using Version 8.0 of the Paradex U.S Hurricane lookup tables, from the most recent Hurricane Bulletin ("**Hurricane Index Value**").

Figure 7.6   Sample Paradex definitions

Source: RMS

available as a core constituent of the Paradex offering, it is not necessary to include these definitions in the deal documents – they are simply referenced therein.

Hazard footprint   Following the event definitions, the hazard footprint is determined in order to calculate an estimated hazard value at each area of interest. For Paradex indices, these are typically the zip code centroids in the covered area.

To achieve this, an interpolation process is used, such that the hazard values as measured at the individual stations can be translated to the required points – the zip code centroids.

Hazard to index lookup table   For each Paradex index, RMS has developed a set of relationships between the hazard values experienced in each geographic region (in the case of US Hurricane, zip code) and the expected industry loss level that would result from this hazard value. For example, according to RMS models, a wind speed of 100mph in zip code 33140 (Miami Beach) is expected to cause an estimated industry residential lines wind loss of $56 m.

In this manner, index lookup tables relate expected industry insured losses by line of business and zip code to the hazard value experienced, estimated for each zip code.

Once the index values by zip code have been established, given the hazard footprint and the index lookup tables, the index values may be determined by region as a simple summation of the relevant zip code index values.

While the parametric index value gives a good approximation of the industry's total insured losses, it will clearly not match an individual insurance company's loss experience. However, the postcode-level resolution of the subindices allows re/insurers to tune the overall index to their portfolio exposures. This is achieved through the selection of 'market share' factors – for each zip code (or set of zip codes) a factor is applied to the index values to tailor these to a specific portfolio.

For US Hurricane, RMS has also developed nine regions within the state of Florida that are designed to disaggregate accumulations of risk, allowing the reduction of basis risk through the application of granular market share factors, but retaining simplicity by reducing the number of share factors required; in many cases a share factor for each zip code or county is not necessary to meaningfully reduce basis risk. However, at the option of the cedant, the index may be tailored at a zip code level.

7.4   SUMMARY

The catastrophe risk insurance market is highly concentrated – one need only look at Florida, which, according to RMS models, accounts for 80% of extreme hurricane risk in the US. This poses a significant challenge for re/insurers who must attempt to diversify this risk to balance their portfolios. Although many insurers have significant exposure in Florida, very few have a profile that closely matches the average industry exposure to the state.

This means that a solution based on state-level industry losses can leave many potential cat bond issuers exposed to significant levels of basis risk. Yet a parametric approach is easier for most potential investors to intuit: it is much easier to understand the chance of 100mph wind speeds than the probability of a particular insurer incurring $1 billion of losses; understanding the constituents of the portfolio is hard enough, let alone the probability of losses to these.

Whilst there will certainly remain a strong demand for indemnity-linked structures, the potential cost savings of parametric structures, particularly during tougher parts of the reinsurance cycle, will make these liquid, simple indices particularly attractive as the market evolves. Insurers and reinsurers are uniquely positioned to understand the relative risks and exposures associated with particular insurance portfolios, as well as the relative pricing requirements in order that such a portfolio may be profitable. However, re/insurers may be less advantaged in determining the likelihood of occurrence of the physical phenomena causing damage – the catastrophic hazard. As such, parametric risk transfer provides a simple and efficient mechanism for significantly reducing the volatility of returns on an insurance portfolio.

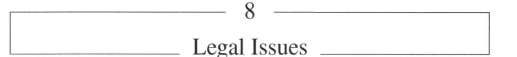

8

Legal Issues

Malcolm Wattman,[a] Matthew Feig,[a] James Langston,[a] and James Frazier[a]

Non-life catastrophe bond insurance-linked securities (ILS) transactions involve an insurer, reinsurer or other party obtaining collateralized cover for one or more specified insurance events in a specified covered area from the capital markets. ILS are issued as notes governed by an indenture specifying the obligations of the issuer and the rights of the noteholders. The notes are issued by a special purpose entity (the 'issuer') organized for each catastrophe bond program. The issuer has no obligations other than its obligations under the ILS program. The issuer sells the notes to initial purchasers (acting as underwriters) pursuant to a purchase agreement. The initial purchasers resell the notes to capital market investors pursuant to terms described in an offering circular distributed to potential investors.

The issuer will use the proceeds of the note issuance as collateral for its obligations under a risk-transfer contract with the risk transfer counterparty (the sponsor of the transaction or a transformer insurer), to whom it provides risk protection for the specified catastrophic event or events (the 'risk transfer contract'). Depending on the type of transaction, the risk transfer contract may take several different forms. This chapter covers certain legal issues relating to the issuance of ILS, starting with the Securities Act of 1933 (the 'Securities Act'), which is a key piece of legislation, as failure to adhere to its provisions would prevent the placement of the notes within the United States, a major component of the overall ILS investor base.

8.1 THE NOTE OFFERING – FEDERAL SECURITIES LAW IMPLICATIONS

8.1.1 The distribution of the notes

Assuming the offering of ILS involves the offer or sale of securities within the United States,[1] the Securities Act's registration requirements apply absent an exemption.[2] Because of the

---

[a]Cadwalader, Wickersham & Taft LLP

[1] An offering of securities outside the United States will not implicate the Act's registration requirements. Regulation S provides a safe harbor from registration for certain offshore securities offerings. See 17 C.F.R. §§ 230.901-.903. Regulation S is not an exemption from Section 5, but rather represents the Commission's refusal to exercise jurisdiction over securities offerings that satisfy the terms of Regulation S. Although the issuance of ILS could be structured as a Regulation S offering, this safe harbor has not been widely adopted in this space due to suitability concerns and the potential for flow back to retail investors in the United States after the expiration of the distribution compliance period.

[2] 15 U.S.C.A. § 77e(c). Absent an exemption from Section 5's registration requirements, it is unlawful to offer to sale a security or engage in any selling efforts until the issuer of the securities has filed a registration statement with the Securities and Exchange Commission. *Id.*

The Handbook of Insurance-Linked Securities   Edited by P. Barrieu and L. Albertini
© 2009 John Wiley & Sons, Ltd

difficulty, expense and delay inherent in registering complex securities, all offerings of ILS have been structured to avoid the registration requirements of the Securities Act.

The issuer will offer and sell the ILS to one or a group of investment banks (the 'initial purchasers') in a so-called private placement. Section 4(2) of the Securities Act exempts 'transactions not involving any public offering' from the Securities Act's registration requirements.[3] So long as the initial offer and sale of the ILS is limited to the initial purchasers[4] and none of the issuer, the sponsor or any of their representatives engages in any actions that could be considered general solicitation,[5] it will fall within the private placement exemption.

After the private placement to the initial purchasers, resales of the ILS, including by an initial purchaser, are made in reliance on exemption provided by Rule 144A.[6] Under the terms of Rule 144A, certain offers and sales of securities to 'qualified institutional buyers' or 'QIBs'[7] are considered not to involve a distribution and, accordingly, persons participating in such offers and sales are not 'underwriters' for purposes of the Securities Act. Application of the Rule 144A exemption is also conditioned on prospective investors' receipt of a brief statement of the nature of the issuer's business and most recent balance sheet and financial statements.[8] Moreover, securities acquired pursuant to the Rule 144A exemption are 'restricted securities' and are thus subject to the transfer restrictions set forth in Rule 144.[9] Notwithstanding that the Rule 144 restrictions lapse after certain periods, the ownership of ILS has typically been restricted to qualified institutional buyers for suitability and other purposes.

The transaction documents provide for the enforcement of this regime in several ways. First, ILS may only be transferred to an investor who the transferor has a reasonable belief is a QIB. For these purposes, the dealers generally require certification from the purchasers to that effect. The transaction documents include related representations described in the offering circular, which are deemed to be made by investors. Second, the offering circular will clearly disclose that the ILS have not been, and will not be, registered under the Securities Act and can only be transferred to QIBs. Third, if, despite these restrictions, an investor that is not a QIB acquires a catastrophe bond, the issuer is required to force the prohibited investor to transfer the catastrophe bond to a qualified institutional buyer.

8.1.2 Application of the anti-fraud provisions of the federal securities laws

Although offerings of ILS are exempt from the registration requirements of Section 5 of the Securities Act, the antifraud proscriptions found in Section 10(b)[10] and Rule 10b-5[11] under the Securities Exchange Act of 1934 (the 'Exchange Act'), which prohibit fraudulent conduct

---

[3] 15 U.S.C.A. § 77d(2). Only an issuer of securities can rely on the private placement exemption.

[4] See Securities and Exchange Commission v. Ralston Purina Co., 346 U.S. 119 (1953) (interpreting application of the private placement exemption to turn on (i) access of offerees to information that would be contained in a registration statement and (ii) sophistication or ability of offerees to fend for themselves).

[5] See, e.g., Nonpublic Offering Exemption, Exchange Act Release No. 33, 4552 27 Fed. Reg. 1136 (Nov. 6, 1962).

[6] 17 C.F.R. § 230.144A.

[7] Rule 144A defines a 'qualified institutional buyer' as, among other things, an institution that owns more than $100,000,000 in securities of unaffiliated issuers. 17 C.F.R. § 230.144A(a)(1)(i).

[8] See 17 C.F.R. § 230.144A(d)(4)(i).

[9] 17 C.F.R. § 230.144.

[10] 15 U.S.C.A. § 78j(b).

[11] 17 C.F.R. § 240.10b-5.

in connection with the purchase or sale of a security, will apply. As a result, if the purchaser of a catastrophe bond can establish the other elements of a Rule 10b-5 claim (including scienter and reliance), the issuer and the seller may be liable for material misstatements or omissions contained in the related offering documents. One defense may be available to the extent that the material misstatement or omission is made on the authority of an expert, such as the risk analysis included in the offering circular on the authority of an expert modeling firm (as discussed below), if the issuer did not have a reasonable ground to believe and did not believe that the risk analysis contained a material misstatement or omission. Although due diligence is a statutory defense only to a claim of strict liability under the Securities Act for registered securities, the initial purchasers in Rule 144A transactions customarily conduct due diligence both out of professional responsibility to their clients and to mitigate the ability of a plaintiff to establish the necessary element of intent for a successful claim under Rule 10b-5. In most transactions, because the sponsor realizes the benefits of the transaction, the sponsor agrees to indemnify the initial purchasers for any potential liability it may incur as a consequence of any material misstatement or omission in the offering materials except for very limited statements provided by the initial purchasers.

While the information in the offering circular is intended to satisfy Rule 144A by providing sufficient information for certain sophisticated investors to make an informed investment decision, it is also intended to provide such investors with all of the material information necessary to make an informed investment decision, thereby limiting exposure to liability under the antifraud provisions of the Exchange Act for material omissions.

8.1.3   Securities offering reform

Pursuant to the Offering Reform Act of 2005,[12] securities law liability for misleading statements and omissions under the Securities Act with respect to registered securities is assessed according to the information conveyed to the investor at the 'time of sale'.[13] Since the investor is typically bound at the time of pricing, that is considered to be the time of sale. While no mention is made in the Offering Reform Act of 2005 of exempt offerings, the securities industry has generally adopted the same practice for Rule 144A transactions and for registered offerings. Any material changes or corrections to pricing information, including the preliminary offering circular, should be made before pricing, and may be provided in various forms, from an email to a completely revised preliminary offering circular, depending on the amount of changes or corrections involved. Material changes or corrections made after pricing will require an offer of rescission to the investors and a reaffirmation of the pricing or a repricing.

8.1.4   Provision of information

Rule 144A(d)(4) requires the provision of specified information to noteholders[14] and investors generally require additional information, such as notices of losses, extensions and terminations, among others. The availability of the information required by Rule 144A and information requested by investors is described in the offering circular and provided for in the corresponding

---

[12] Securities Act Release No. § 591, 70 Fed. Reg. 44, 772 (July 19, 2005).

[13] See 17 C.F.R. § 230.159.

[14] 17 C.F.R. § 230.144A.

transaction documents. In addition, a practical mechanism must be implemented for furnishing such information.

8.1.5 The Investment Company Act of 1940

Section 3(a)(1)(C) of the Investment Company Act of 1940 (the 'Investment Company Act') defines an 'investment company' to include a company engaged in the business of holding securities which owns investment securities having a value exceeding 40% of the company's total assets.[15] Since the catastrophe bond issuer typically invests the proceeds of the offering in investment securities, the issuer, pursuant to the Investment Company Act, would be required to register as an investment company unless there was an applicable exemption. Registration entails a serious regulatory regime with which the issuer is unlikely to be able to comply. Consequently, the issuers rely on the exemption provided in Section 3(c)(7) for any issuer, the outstanding securities of which are owned exclusively by 'qualified purchasers' and meet the other qualifications provided in that section.[16] In an effort to limit the extraterritoriality of the Investment Company Act, the SEC limits the need to meet the Section (3)(c)(7) exemption for issuers located outside the United States to the United States securities holders of such issuers. The transaction documents require, and the offering materials clearly provide, that United States persons owning the ILS must be qualified purchasers. As a general matter, any investor that is a QIB for Securities Act purposes will be a qualified purchaser for purposes of the Investment Company Act, although the definitions are not the same.

8.2 THE NOTE OFFERING – THE OFFERING CIRCULAR

8.2.1 Important terms

The offering circular will include a detailed description of the transaction including a summary of the transaction documents, a description of the issuer, the program structure and the terms of the note issuance. Important terms to note include:

- **The original principal amount of each class of notes.** The original principal amount is reduced by payments made to the risk transfer counterparty upon the occurrence of the specified loss event or losses. Some programs provide for funds to be repaid by the risk transfer counterparty to the issuer under certain circumstances, resulting in principal increases (though never resulting in the principal amount being in excess of the principal amount as of the note issuance date). This requirement injects a potential reliance on the credit standing of the risk transfer counterparty and also requires that provision be made for reinvestment of the amount of any principal increase in permitted collateral.
- **The scheduled and extended redemption date for each class of notes**. Typically, the scheduled redemption date is close to, but is later than, the expiration of the period during which the notes are at risk of loss from the specified events. The scheduled redemption date is later than the expiration of the risk period to allow for a risk transfer counterparty to determine whether or not to extend the maturity of the notes in respect of a specified event that occurs or is in progress at the termination of the risk period. While each class of notes is scheduled to mature on the fixed date, that date is subject to extension for a

---

[15] 15 U.S.C.A. § 80a-3(a)(1)(c).
[16] 15 U.S.C.A. § 80a-3(c)(7).

limited period of time at either the option of the risk transfer counterparty without any conditions, or upon the satisfaction of certain conditions (such as losses reaching a high percentage of an applicable attachment point). Typically, an extension would be elected if the risk transfer counterparty believed it was likely to receive a loss payment when its losses were fully developed or determined pursuant to the risk transfer contract (and was willing to pay investors at the specified rate for such extension). However, such losses must relate to an event which commenced prior to the expiration of the applicable risk period. If the transaction provides for a potential increase in the outstanding principal amount and a payment has been made to the risk transfer counterparty, the risk transfer counterparty may be required to extend the redemption date of the notes to determine the amount of any required refund. The term of the notes must match the term of the risk transfer contract, and the risk transfer contract must provide for appropriate funding of interest during such period.

- **Early redemption events provide for the catastrophe bond transaction to be redeemed on the next payment date upon the occurrence of certain specified events.** These may include a default in payment by the risk transfer counterparty under the risk transfer contract, the loss of an essential service provider (and the unavailability of replacements), among others. The notes may also be subject to early redemption at the option of the risk transfer counterparty, typically subject to payment of a prepayment premium.

- **The catastrophe bond may only be sold to investors who will purchase and hold the notes in a permitted US or non-US jurisdiction listed in the offering circular.** The permitted jurisdictions are generally those where the transaction counsel has a basis for a reasonable belief that the local laws do not subject the holder of a catastrophe bond to regulation as a provider of insurance or reinsurance in relation to the holding of the catastrophe bond. If a holder of a note is not a resident of such a jurisdiction, it is required to either sell its note to a holder in a permitted jurisdiction or obtain an opinion from local counsel providing that the holder of the note will not be treated as a provider of insurance or reinsurance in the applicable jurisdiction. The designation of a jurisdiction as a permitted jurisdiction relates solely to the characterization of the notes for certain insurance law purposes. The engagement of local counsel or consultation with the local insurance regulator is required to permit the inclusion of a particular jurisdiction for a prospective purchaser if that jurisdiction has not previously been vetted.

- **The calculation and payment of interest may also create legal concerns.** Typically, interest is paid to investors on the outstanding principal amount of the relevant class based on the sum of (a) premiums paid by the risk transfer counterparty under the risk-transfer contract[17] and (b) the investment return on the collateral, usually a LIBOR-based interest rate. If interest is payable based on LIBOR or a similar floating rate, the question arises as to whether or not the proceeds of the note issuance can be invested in a way which will reliably achieve such a floating rate. Often, the issuer will enter into a total return swap with a swap counterparty under which the income and gains on the collateral are exchanged for the payment by swap counterparty of a LIBOR-based interest rate and an amount equal to any losses on the collateral. The total return swap provides a smooth source of funds for the payment of interest. The flexibility of the investment of the collateral is

---

[17] The portion of interest relating to the risk transfer contract may be calculated on the original principal amount for a period time, effectively guaranteeing investors a minimum return, even in the case of the occurrence of a catastrophic loss event early in the life of the transaction.

limited, however, by certain ERISA restrictions, as discussed further below. Because of these restrictions, catastrophe bond transactions generally do not permit the active management of the proceeds of the note issuance, and require that the proceeds be invested under specified investment guidelines with no one exercising discretion. Investment guidelines are set at the issuance of the cat bond transaction and identify the specific collateral and the order of acquisition and disposition, within the acceptable characteristics of the collateral, such as rating, type and maturity.

8.2.2   ERISA considerations

One section of the offering circular which discusses an issue with significance for the structuring of the catastrophe bond transaction is 'Certain ERISA Considerations'. If it is contemplated that plans or entities subject to the US Employee Retirement Income Security Act of 1974, as amended ('ERISA') and/or Section 4975 of the Internal Revenue Code of 1986, as amended (the 'Code') may invest in a catastrophe bond transaction, the application of ERISA and Section 4975 of the Code can impact certain aspects of such a transaction, including, but not limited to, the choice and management of the collateral.[18]

Background

ERISA is a federal law that regulates US private-sector employee benefit plans.[19] ERISA and the regulations and rules promulgated thereunder address, among other things, the rights of plan participants and beneficiaries, funding standards and reporting and disclosure requirements. More relevant to catastrophe bond transactions, ERISA also provides general fiduciary standards for conduct relating to the handling of plan assets, and ERISA and Section 4975 of the Code impose certain restrictions on plans and on persons who have certain specified relationships to plans ('parties in interest' under ERISA and 'disqualified persons' under the Code). The offering circular generally contains a brief discussion of the fiduciary considerations and the applicable prohibited transaction rules.

General fiduciary considerations and prohibited transactions

Regarding general fiduciary considerations, a fiduciary of an ERISA plan considering an investment in a catastrophe bond transaction should determine whether, under ERISA's fiduciary standards of investment prudence and diversification, an investment in notes issued in a catastrophe bond transaction is appropriate for the plan. In so doing, the fiduciary must take into account, among other things, the overall investment policy of the plan and the composition of the plan's investment portfolio.

With respect to the prohibited transaction provisions of ERISA and Section 4975 of the Code, because of their own activities and the activities of their respective affiliates, the parties

---

[18] Unless otherwise noted, references to ERISA will be deemed to include references to the corresponding provisions of Section 4975 of the Code.

[19] The provisions of ERISA described herein do not apply to governmental plans (as defined in Section 3(32) of ERISA), church plans (as defined in Section 3(33) of ERISA) with respect to which no election has been made under Section 410(d) of the Code, or a plan maintained outside the United States primarily for the benefit of persons substantially all of whom are nonresident aliens. See Section 4 of ERISA.

associated with a catastrophe bond transaction (e.g., the issuer, any initial purchaser and/or any swap counterparty) may be or become a party in interest or disqualified person with respect to one or more plans. Accordingly, the acquisition and holding of notes by a plan could be deemed to constitute a transaction prohibited under Title I of ERISA or Section 4975 of the Code. Certain statutory or administrative exemptions, however, may apply. The US Department of Labor (the 'DOL') has issued five prohibited transaction class exemptions ('PTCEs') that may provide exemptive relief, if required, for direct or indirect prohibited transactions relating to an investment in notes issued in a catastrophe bond transaction. These exemptions include PTCE 84-14 (exempts certain transactions entered into on behalf of a plan by a 'qualified professional asset manager'), PTCE 90-1 (exempts certain transactions involving insurance company pooled separate accounts), PTCE 91-38 (exempts certain transactions involving bank collective investment funds), PTCE 95-60 (exempts certain transactions involving insurance company general accounts), and PTCE 96-23 (exempts certain transactions entered into by or on behalf of a plan by an 'in-house' asset manager). In addition to the foregoing, Section 408(b)(17) of ERISA and Section 4975(d)(2) of the Code, which exemptions provide relief when the party in interest or disqualified person is only such by reason of providing services to a plan or its relationship to a service provider, may be available. It should be noted, however, that even if one or more of the foregoing exemptions is generally applicable, it is possible that none would apply to all of the transactions that could be deemed prohibited transactions in connection with a plan's investment in a catastrophe bond transaction. As described below, plan investors will be deemed to represent that the acquisition and holding of notes in a catastrophe bond transaction will not result in a non-exempt prohibited transaction.

Plan asset consideration/internal activities of the issuer

There is another dimension of these deals addressed in the offering circulars that must be considered in connection with the application of ERISA. Many deals are structured in a manner such that the underlying assets of an issuer could potentially be considered 'plan assets' of investing plans under the applicable provisions of ERISA and DOL regulations. If such is the case, care must be taken to avoid the application of the ERISA fiduciary provisions to the activities of the issuer, including the investment of the collateral.

The DOL has issued a regulation[20] concerning the definition of what constitutes the assets of a plan subject to ERISA and/or Section 4975 of the Code ('Plan Asset Regulation'). Certain aspects of the regulation have been modified by Section 3(42) of ERISA. As a general rule, the underlying assets and properties of corporations, partnerships, trusts and certain other entities in which a plan subject to ERISA purchases an 'equity interest' will be deemed to be assets of the investing plan for purposes of the application of ERISA unless certain exceptions apply. In this regard, when a plan acquires an 'equity interest' in an entity that is neither (a) a 'publicly offered security,' nor (b) a security issued by an investment company registered under the Investment Advisers Act of 1940, the plan's assets include both the equity interest and an undivided interest in each of the underlying assets of the entity, unless it is established either that the entity is an operating company or that participation by 'benefit plan investors' is not 'significant'. For these purposes, participation by 'benefit plan investors' (defined in Section 3(42) of ERISA to mean (i) any employee benefit plan subject to Title I of ERISA; (ii) a plan to which Section 4975(e)(1) of the Code applies; or (iii) any entity whose underlying

---

[20] 29 C.F.R. Section 2510.3-101.

assets include plan assets by reason of a plan's investment in the entity) is 'significant' if such investors hold in the aggregate 25% or more of the value of any class of equity in an entity. The Plan Asset Regulation defines an 'equity interest' as any interest in an entity other than an instrument that is treated as indebtedness under applicable local law, and which has no substantial equity features. Although the notes issued in a catastrophe bond transaction are denominated as debt, the notes are commonly assumed to be 'equity interests' for purposes of the Plan Asset Regulation.

If an issuer in a catastrophe bond transaction were deemed to hold 'plan assets' by reason of an ERISA plan's investment in notes, such 'plan assets' would include an undivided interest in the assets held by the issuer, including the issuer's interest in the risk transfer contract, the total return swap and, potentially, the proceeds of the note issuance and any collateral in which the proceeds are invested. In such an event, persons that have discretionary authority with respect to such assets may be subject to the fiduciary responsibility provisions of Title I of ERISA and the prohibited transaction provisions of ERISA and Section 4975 of the Code with respect to transactions involving such assets. As such, certain actions taken with respect to such assets could be deemed to constitute prohibited transactions under ERISA and/or Section 4975 of the Code. Since it rarely can be established that benefit plan investor participation is less than significant, to avoid the application of these rules discretion with respect to the investment of note proceeds or the amount of any principal increase in the collateral is eliminated by the use of strict investment guidelines that require all such proceeds or amounts to be invested in specified ways at specified times. These investment guidelines must contemplate extensions of the catastrophe bond transaction as well as reinvestments and partial liquidations. Assuming the discretion has been removed, the guidelines act to protect any parties in a catastrophe bond transaction that might otherwise be regarded as exercising discretion with respect to the assets of an ERISA plan investor in the catastrophe bond transaction.

It is important to note that in catastrophe bond transactions where a total return swap is entered into, it can strongly be argued that the collateral does not constitute plan assets. This is because the investment performance of the collateral has no bearing on return of the notes issued in a catastrophe bond transaction; the swap counterparty bears the risk of loss and enjoys the benefit of any gain with respect to the investment of collateral.[21]

Notwithstanding the foregoing, other structures may be possible that provide for the floating interest rate portion with or without investment guidelines, although the satisfaction of ERISA requirements will require a fact-specific analysis in each case. In any event, the investment of the proceeds of the catastrophe bond issuance and the source of funds for the provision of the floating portion of interest must be subjected to a rigorous ERISA analysis.

Deemed representations

In order to minimize the potential for the violations described above, the offering circular provides that each investing plan subject to ERISA and/or Section 4975 of the Code, when purchasing notes in a catastrophe bond transaction, is deemed to have (i) directed that the assets be invested in the collateral specified by the investment guidelines and directed the issuer to enter into the risk transfer contract, the indenture and the respective total return swap, if any, and (ii) represented and warranted that one or more statutory or administrative exemptions from the prohibited transaction rules of ERISA and Section 4975 of the Code

---

[21] See 29 CFR 2510.3-101(g).

applies such that the acquisition and holding of the notes will not constitute a non-exempt prohibited transaction. Further, when relevant, often each investing plan, by purchasing the notes in a catastrophe bond transaction, will be deemed to have agreed with the respective swap counterparty that neither considers the swap counterparty a fiduciary for purposes of ERISA or Section 4975 of the Code with respect to any assets of investing plans.

Other ERISA considerations for insurance companies

The offering circular also briefly addresses insurance company investors, providing that an insurance company considering an investment in a catastrophe bond transaction with its general account or a wholly owned subsidiary thereof should consider whether its general account may be deemed to include assets of plans subject to ERISA investing in the general account, for example, through the purchase of an annuity contract. In *John Hancock Mutual Life Insurance Co. v. Harris Trust and Savings Bank*, 510 U.S. 86 (1993), the United States Supreme Court held that assets held in an insurance company's general account may be deemed to be 'plan assets' under certain circumstances. However, PTCE 95-60 (described above) may exempt some or all of the transactions that could occur as the result of the acquisition and holding of notes in a catastrophe bond transaction by an insurance company general account as a wholly owned subsidiary thereof. Therefore, insurance company investors should analyze whether the John Hancock decision and PTCE 95-60 or any other exemption may have an impact with respect to their purchase of notes issued in a catastrophe bond transaction.

Non-ERISA plan considerations

Finally, as noted previously, employee benefit plans that are governmental plans (as defined in Section 3(32) of ERISA), as modified by Section 3(42) of ERISA, certain church plans (as defined in Section 3(33) of ERISA) and non-US plans (as described in Section 4(b)(4) of ERISA) are not subject to the requirements of ERISA or Section 4975 of the Code; however, such plans may be subject to non-US, federal, state or local laws or regulations which affect their ability to invest in the notes. Any fiduciary of such a governmental, church or foreign plan considering an investment in a catastrophe bond transaction should determine the need for, and, if necessary, the availability of, any exemptive relief under such laws or regulations.

8.2.3   Other considerations regarding the proceeds and payment of interest

However the floating rate of interest is financed, care must be taken to provide that the collateral can be liquidated as required to make payments under the risk transfer contract. This means the structure must be capable of accommodating a total liquidation on the first payment date, a series of partial liquidations ending up to two years after the scheduled redemption date of the notes or an early redemption of the notes. Whatever form the proceeds of the issuance are invested in, the resulting collateral is normally deposited in a security account in the United Kingdom subject to a deed of charge except for certain transactions undertaken by US-based insurers or reinsurers described below. The deed of charge provides that the issuer's interest in the collateral account, the underlying collateral and its rights under the various transaction documents is assigned to the indenture trustee on behalf of the noteholders as security for the issuer's obligation to repay the principal on the notes, subject to its obligations to the risk transfer counterparty and any amounts payable to the swap counterparty, if any. A note payment account set up for the payment of interest is subject to the same deed of charge but is pledged solely to satisfy obligations to the noteholders. For a transaction with a United States sponsor, the underlying collateral and collateral arrangements may have to satisfy the requirements for insurance trusts under relevant state laws and regulations, and the collateral will be maintained in a qualifying trust account as discussed below.

8.2.4   The risk analysis

The offering circular for each transaction will normally contain a risk analysis prepared by an expert risk modeling company. This section describes the natural catastrophic events to which the notes are subject and the probability and magnitude of expected losses associated with notes based on proprietary simulation models. Typically, the modeling agent will be engaged by the sponsor pursuant to an agent agreement. The modeling agent may also be engaged by the issuer to perform certain calculations or resets during the life of the transaction. The modeling agent will expect to be indemnified by the sponsor of the transaction

The modelling agent will normally act as expert in the risk analysis section. This provides a potential defense against securities law liability to the parties to the transaction other than the expert for misstatements or omissions made on the authority of the expert. The modeling agent must consent to being named as such in the offering circular.

8.2.5   Opinions

It is standard practice in ILS transactions for the transaction counsel to give an opinion to the effect that the material transaction documents (e.g., the indenture, the notes, the risk transfer contract and the swap, if any) conform in all material respects to the description thereof in the offering circular. The opinion also addresses the summaries of legal considerations, including US federal income tax and ERISA concerns and the enforceability of certain transaction documents. The opinion is not addressed to, and may not be relied upon by, the investors in the notes. Counsel will also be asked by the initial purchasers, as part of their due diligence, to write a letter stating, in effect, that, subject to certain qualifications, nothing has come to their attention to cause them to believe that the offering circular at the time of pricing or closing contains a material misstatement or omission. This letter will exclude any numerical information and any 'expertized' material such as the risk analysis and other financial and numerical information.

8.3   TYPES OF TRANSACTIONS

While ILS may cover any variety of events in any number of places, there are specific, and quite different, mechanisms for determining if the specified event has occurred and a payment is due to the risk transfer counterparty (a 'trigger') under the risk transfer contract, and a number of legal considerations for each.

A number of mechanisms work on the basis of objective data, usually produced by independent third parties. This may be as simple as the magnitude and location of an earthquake as reported by a government agency (a simple parametric trigger), the report of a third party of estimated industry losses caused by an event (an index trigger) or the application of a fixed mathematical simulation model to the physical parameters of an event (a modeled loss transaction). Other transactions may be based on indemnity to the sponsor for losses resulting from specified events. The selection of the triggers for each transaction will be driven by the sponsor's needs, tolerance for basis risk, market conditions and investor appetite (for more details on the choice of triggers, please refer to Chapter 4).

8.3.1   Parametric, index and modeled loss transactions

General

The risk transfer between the issuer and the risk transfer counterparty for the types of transactions described above (other than indemnity) is typically documented in an ISDA swap form consisting of a standard master agreement, a schedule and a confirmation containing terms specific to each transaction.

The risk transfer contract will provide for the payment by the issuer of loss payments only if the applicable trigger is met. Depending on the trigger, a full or partial payment of the principal amount of the bonds may be due to the risk transfer counterparty. In return, the risk transfer counterparty agrees to make periodic payments equal to a portion of the interest spread or extension spread. In certain circumstances it may also provide for repayments of amounts received as loss payments but owed back to the issuer if the trigger is no longer satisfied; for example, if an index value is subsequently lowered after it has exceeded the applicable trigger point in a previous period. Typically, by separate agreement, the sponsor will also agree to pay the expenses incurred in establishing and maintaining the program.

Legal issues

For index transactions, a license to use the relevant index must usually be obtained unless the index is derived from published government statistics. Often a service provider must be engaged to perform verification of the occurrence of an event or of calculations, or to perform resets or to run models and the transaction parties and their counsel will negotiate appropriate engagement and indemnity arrangements with these providers. If a model is to be run for resets or to determine modeled losses, an escrow arrangement may be required to make certain that there are no material changes to the model and to provide access to the model if the modeling company cannot, or fails to, perform its responsibilities.

When documented on standard ISDA forms, the legal status of the risk transfer contract is well understood. However, risk transfer contracts for the triggers described above are not, by definition, reinsurance – they do not indemnify for losses actually sustained – and do not provide reinsurance credit for the risk transfer counterparty.

8.3.2   Indemnity transactions

While the preference for entering into an indemnity-based cat bond may vary from risk management to regulatory accounting, the nature of the transaction requires additional disclosure and different forms of documentation. For US-based risk transfer counterparties to obtain reinsurance credit for the transformer, certain additional requirements must be met.

The disclosure

Indemnity transactions require disclosure of the risk transfer counterparty's (or the 'reinsured') business to be covered in the offering circular. This disclosure is important to investors because unlike in a non-indemnity transaction, where losses are based on some objective criteria, losses in indemnity-based transactions are whatever the reinsured reports them to be, typically subject to verification. Accordingly, it becomes important to understand the business of the reinsured; for instance, how they write policies, how they control risk, what their claims review procedures are, their staffing and resources, their loss and loss development experience, but also detailed information about their current book of business and likely renewals. To that end, a description of the reinsured and the subject business is typically included in all indemnity transactions, and requires substantial attention from the reinsured as to its form and content.

This can lead to a number of issues. While it is clear why investors need to know about the risks they are agreeing to become liable for, the detailed disclosure involved can create confidentiality concerns for sponsors of these transactions, who may be reluctant to publish market-sensitive or confidential information. Substantial negotiation may be required over the scope and substance of the description. Moreover, sponsors which are not reporting companies may not be familiar with the securities markets, and the form and process of producing such a description may be unfamiliar and challenging. Sponsors which are publicly traded may have concerns about disclosing information in the offering circular which has not been disclosed to their public shareholders or bondholders. In non-indemnity transactions, a detailed description of the underlying policies and exposures is not considered to be relevant information because the information does not affect the noteholder's potential losses under the catastrophe bond. Only the relevant trigger can cause losses, and the reinsured accepts any basis risk between their actual losses and the cover provided under the ILS.

Diligence

Since substantial disclosure of the reinsured and the subject business is incorporated into the disclosure of an indemnity-based cat bond transaction, such disclosure requires diligence on the part of the initial purchasers and counsel involved in the transaction. This in-depth diligence process, although typical for most other capital markets transactions, is of a type not required in non-indemnity based transactions simply because such disclosure does not exist. Initial purchasers and transaction counsel will have to provide diligence for the factual statements and descriptions made in the disclosure. This may involve the review of policies, handbooks, manuals and other information which the reinsured will need to produce. This review may be conducted on site or remotely, delivered in physical or electronic form. The decision as to how to best conduct this diligence is a matter of balancing cost, convenience and confidentiality concerns of the reinsured, with electronic delivery for a remote review normally being the least expensive, while on-site diligence with original files may provide the highest degree of confidentiality. Successful management of the diligence process is important to keeping to a tight deadline.

Accountants

As part of the due diligence by the initial purchasers, an accounting firm (generally the sponsor's outside audit firm) is normally retained to conduct agreed-upon procedures on all financial and numerical information included in disclosure of the reinsured and the subject business and to produce an agreed-upon procedures letter prior to pricing. The agreed-upon procedures are negotiated between the accountants and the initial purchasers and are tailored to the specific details of the transaction. To the extent practicable, data should be traced back to accounting records. Data which are not part of the accounting records can be traced back to source information or work sheets of the reinsured. The purpose of the agreed-upon procedures letter is to give comfort to the initial purchasers of the validity of the information and to provide a potential defense to a securities law claim.

SPV status

If the issuer is writing a reinsurance contract (rather than a risk-transfer contract in the form of a derivative contract), it is writing insurance. The nexus of insurance is indemnity. A company cannot write insurance unless it is appropriately licensed in the jurisdictions in which it conducts its business. If the issuer is a Cayman Islands entity it must be licensed as a Class B Insurer (subject to special thin capitalization rules) in the Cayman Islands. Bermuda and other jurisdictions have their own insurance licensing regimes, whilst a number of European jurisdictions have set up or are setting up the legal and regulatory framework for insurance SPVs in application of the Reinsurance Directive (for more details on the Reinsurance Directive, please see Chapter 24). Experienced local insurance counsel is required to obtain the necessary licensing, a process which varies as to time and complexity from one jurisdiction to another.

Other documentation

Indemnity deals typically have somewhat more complex or additional documentation than non-indemnity transactions. The risk transfer from the issuer to the reinsured is documented as a reinsurance or retrocession agreement, each of which is longer and more complex than an ISDA-based risk transfer contract. Indemnity transactions typically require an agreement with a claims reviewer to establish procedures to verify that the reinsured's losses were actually paid, and paid in conformity with the requirements of the underlying policies. Similarly, a loss reserve specialist is engaged to determine that any loss reserves relevant to the transaction are established by the reinsured in accordance with appropriate actuarial practices. Legal issues can arise regarding the provision of data to these service providers, as the confidentiality of detailed claims information and reserves may be a sensitive issue for the reinsured. However, without data in sufficient detail, the service providers cannot perform the necessary procedures to permit payments of losses to the reinsured.

Another issue can arise as to the timing of these services. Reinsured parties are eager to be paid promptly; however, service providers have practical limitations on how quickly claims can be reviewed or reserves assessed. Moreover, such claims and reserves may develop over a substantial period of time. Typically, 'final' reports are delivered by the service providers and a commutation (with a payment of loss reserves) is provided for in the reinsurance agreement at the end of the extension period. As with all service providers, a claims reviewer or loss reserve specialist will expect to be indemnified for their participation in the transaction, which may involve negotiations about standards of care. As in other transactions, reset and calculation agents may also need to be retained in certain indemnity transactions.

Insolvency considerations

Where the primary sponsor is reluctant to engage in the bond transaction directly, a reinsurance company may act as a transformer by writing an indemnity policy and sponsoring a back-to-back indemnity catastrophe bond transaction. As the indemnity transaction requires the provision of data concerning paid losses, expenses and reserves, transactions involving a transformer require additional attention to the functioning of the documents in the event of an insolvency of the ultimate reinsured. The transformer should avoid finding itself in the circumstance where it is liable to pay losses but is unable to provide the data necessary to qualify for payment under the catastrophe bond. This may be accomplished by providing for indemnity from the issuer based on a look through to the ultimate reinsured's losses until such time as it becomes insolvent, after which losses would be based on indemnity for losses paid by the transformer. Similarly, provision should be made for commutation of the risk transfer contract under the catastrophe bond if there is a still-ongoing insolvency and receivership of the ultimate reinsured upon the final redemption date of the catastrophe bond.

Special considerations for indemnity transactions for a US-based reinsured

For a US-based risk transfer counterparty, obtaining reinsurance credit for the cover provided by the issuer will require that specific requirements be met. Because the issuer is always a foreign-domiciled entity not licensed or admitted in the jurisdiction of the sponsor's primary regulator, if the sponsor is to get credit for reinsurance the issuer will be required to post qualifying collateral in a trust satisfying the requirements of the applicable regulatory regime. While the regulations vary from state to state, because New York is the primary regulator for many insurance companies, the rest of this chapter will focus on the trust provisions of New York law.

Regulation 114 trust

An unlicensed, unaccredited insurer such as the issuer may become the grantor of a trust under N.Y. Comp. Codes R. & Regs. tit. 11, § 1269 ('Regulation 114'). The Regulation 114 trust is documented with a reinsurance trust agreement between the issuer (as grantor), the reinsured (as beneficiary) and a bank (as trustee). The trust must be 'clean and unconditional.' The proceeds of the catastrophe bond issuance are deposited in the related US-based trust account and may only be invested in the types of collateral permitted by N.Y. Ins. Law § 1404(a) paragraphs (1), (2), (3), (8) and (10), which are generally the debt obligations of US government, states and agencies or American institutions with at least an 'A' rating. These requirements may limit the potential options for the investment of the proceeds of the catastrophe bond offering more than in transactions which do not need to meet the requirements of Regulation 114.

Another significant feature of the Regulation 114 trust is that the reinsured must be able to withdraw the posted collateral at any time. The ability of the reinsured to withdraw assets from the reinsurance trust account creates several issues. Although the reinsured is legally able to withdraw such amounts, apart from under specified conditions, such as a loss payment being owed to it under the risk transfer contract, it is not entitled to do so. Such a withdrawal would mean that the assets were not available to repay the holders of the notes upon maturity if not returned, and once withdrawn, the investment income of such assets in the Regulation

114 trust would not be available to finance the floating rate portion of interest for payment on the notes. The holders of notes in the catastrophe bond transaction typically accept this risk because the reinsured is generally a creditworthy institution with a long history of honoring its obligations under these and other arrangements and because there would be legal recourse for unwarranted withdrawals. The reinsured typically agrees to pay the applicable floating rate on the portion withdrawn as well as an additional sum (often 2%).

The assets in a Regulation 114 trust account may be subject to a total return swap, provided that the requirements of the regulation are met. This means that the total return swap counterparty will have to accept the risk of the withdrawals described above, and the total return swap should be documented in a way which reflects a potential mismatch between the principal balance of the notes outstanding and the amount in the Regulation 114 trust account. Regulation 114 also requires that withdrawals and substitutions be done with the consent of, or at the direction of, the reinsured, although certain substitutions may be agreed upon by the reinsured in advance. The reinsured can consent to the necessary withdrawals in respect of investment income on the collateral for payment to the swap counterparty. The Regulation 114 trust agreement must be carefully drafted to provide a workable mechanism for the total return swap, given the need for substitutions and reinvestment from time to time.

8.4 CONCLUSION

The legal issues involved in catastrophe bond transactions may have significant impact on the ultimate form and terms of the deal, and should be resolved as early as practicable in the transaction process. Fortunately, experienced counsel will be well attuned to identifying these issues and developing workable solutions for even the most complex structure. Continuing attempts at improving the documentation will further reduce legal and execution risk, and enable the transactions to adapt to the continually evolving market for these securities.

9
The Investor Perspective (Non-Life)

Luca Albertini[a]

The objective of this chapter is to offer the perspective of an investor in non-life insurance-linked securities. It may be useful for the reader to know that my background is one of originator and arranger of insurance-linked securities (having led Swiss Re's European Insurance-Linked Securities team from 2003 until 2008) and that I am currently managing a dedicated insurance-linked asset management company (also defined in the market as a 'dedicated ILS fund'). Dedicated ILS funds represent a very large portion of the investor base for non-life insurance-linked securities and are estimated to have in their portfolios over 50% of the outstanding cat bonds in 2008. This is because for investors with a targeted portfolio exposure below triple-digit million dollars, the costs associated with qualified staff and infrastructure necessary to properly invest in the sector are too high, thus creating a barrier to entry. In addition, given the relatively recent growth of the sector, skilled resources able to operate direct investments in insurance-linked products are not widely available.

The first section of this chapter outlines the development of a sustainable insurance-linked investor base; the second section offers a summary of the key elements investors look at when investing in insurance-linked securities; and the last section covers the evolution of the instruments and the key focus points from an investor perspective.

9.1 THE CREATION OF A SUSTAINABLE AND LIQUID MARKET

The insurance industry has been looking to the capital markets for equity or debt capital for a long time, but the repackaging of non-life insurance risk into securitised or derivative form has reached a significant size after the shortage of reinsurance capacity which followed Hurricane Katrina in 2005. In the early days of this market prior to Hurricane Katrina, the general investor community, which was comfortable taking insurance risk blended with other risks in the stock market or in debt instruments, was less comfortable underwriting 'pure' insurance risk repackaged in securitised or derivative form.

On the product side, a number of structures have been designed and some level of customisation to the needs and the business profile of the protection buyers have helped bankers to attract a large number of first-time sponsors to market. At the same time, a level of standardisation of structures and documentation has been achieved, thus helping the investor community in its analysis of each investment.

---

[a]Leadenhall Capital Partners

The Handbook of Insurance-Linked Securities   Edited by P. Barrieu and L. Albertini

Bankers and modelling firms have been putting a lot of effort into educating the investor community on insurance-linked products, as they understand the paramount importance of each and every investor being fully aware and understanding exactly what they are buying. Surprising institutional investors with unexpected losses could create a crisis of confidence in the bank syndicate as well as in the whole sector, with the consequences we have seen in the securitisation and other fixed-income markets in 2007–2008.

This investor education process has focused on a number of areas, which include:

- creation of common terminology;
- risk analysis;
- correlation with other investments in an investor portfolio;
- relative value;
- valuation and liquidity.

9.1.1   Creation of common terminology

The insurance industry and the capital markets use very different technical language, where the same or similar terms can mean different things. The creation of a minimum level of common terminology to be used in insurance-linked securities has been helpful in bridging such gaps, but a continued process of 'translation' has been and still is key to developing the knowledge base on insurance risks within the capital market community. When insurance terms are adopted in the prospectus and in the marketing material, arrangers make an effort to carefully define and explain such terms to investors. There is no right and wrong terminology to be used, but eventually, to maintain the current growth of the insurance-linked market, both protection buyers and investors will need to agree on a common set of terms, or at least familiarise themselves with the terminology of the other side.

One example: the 'expected loss' of a catastrophe bond is normally expressed in percentage terms, and an investor would be told that the annual probability of losing its capital as a consequence of an earthquake is – say – 1% per annum. The rating agencies would add that a 1% annual expected loss for a three-year earthquake transaction is – subject to acceptable documentation and other structural elements – in the BB/Ba rating range. The expected loss percentage and the ratings are clearly useful to a non-specialised investor to give some common basis to the risk profile of a transaction and that of other investments in its portfolio. In the property insurance industry, the same concept would be defined as the 'return period' and the 1% probability would be defined as a 'one in a hundred years event' (a 2% expected loss would be defined as a one in fifty years event, and so on).

Also, different types of insurance lines have different terminology and a different analytical approach. Life risk (which will be covered in later chapters) and casualty risk are not normally expressed in terms of years of return period and have quite different features from natural catastrophe risks. Nuclear, terrorism, marine and aviation risks are each analysed and underwritten with their own specific methodology.

To date the majority of non-life insurance-linked securities are 'cat bonds' or sidecar investments covering natural catastrophe risk. A small amount of marine, aviation, satellite and casualty risk has been sold to the capital markets, mostly in sidecar form, due to modelling constraints and to lower capacity constraints in the traditional markets. High frequency and low severity non-life risks (such as motor insurance risk) have been securitised in only two transactions and by the same protection buyer (with more transactions expected once market conditions for senior securitised paper improve).

Given investor appetite for a more diversified offering of insurance risk to place in their insurance-linked portfolios, the incentives are all there for the market to continue this 'translation' effort and to make more 'pure' insurance risks available to capital market investors. This would include more risks and perils being modelled for capital markets, and explained to investors.

9.1.2   Risk analysis

The risk analysis of non-insurance fixed-income instruments normally relies on the credit or on the structured portfolio descriptions in the prospectuses as drafted by the arranging bankers and by the originators (with the due oversight of the transaction counsels) and is in some cases backed by a further analysis by one or more rating agencies. Furthermore, investors are often able to get access to generally available information and analysis about their investment.

Prospectuses of traded catastrophe bonds include a 'Risk Analysis' section in which a modelling agency (independent from the arranging banks and the protection buyers) describes in great detail the peril/hazard. For example, this section would describe an earthquake, the way it is measured and the process used by the modelling agency to determine their opinion of the probability of loss and other risk parameters of the transaction. The risk analysis section then concludes with a summary of the risk profile of the transaction and a comparison of the impact of some material historical events on the portfolio covered by the securitisation.

The risk analysis section of prospectuses and the roadshow presentations for new issuance are important in educating investors to understand the specific insurance risks taken.

Sophisticated investors now are able to compare and contrast the risk analysis from different modelling agencies on the same peril, and to understand which modelling agency is more or less conservative in its assessment of a given peril/hazard. Such sophisticated investors may also now invest in transactions without a risk analysis thanks to the experience developed in reviewing the work done on insurance-linked securities in the past as well as by hiring skilled resources from the insurance and reinsurance industry. The lack of a proper risk analysis is, however, normally associated with illiquid private placements, which would command a liquidity premium, as it cannot be safely assumed that other investors are ready to perform their own analysis in a secondary offering or reach similar conclusions.

9.1.3   Correlation with other investments in the portfolio

Insurance-linked securities are normally presented to new investors as instruments having 'very little' or 'low' correlation with other investments in their portfolio, thus improving its diversification and therefore its efficient frontier (relating the expected return and the risk of the portfolio).

A correlation analysis is beyond the scope of this chapter. Also, given the relatively recent history of cat bonds and the long-tail nature of the insurance risks which have been securitised, any analysis performed on the actual data series would necessarily embed assumptions and approximations.

However, when focusing on the underlying risks and looking at a macro level, it can be validly argued that natural catastrophe events have not caused financial turmoil and clearly financial turmoil does not cause natural catastrophes. Of course a very large Tokyo earthquake could correlate with losses on Japanese stocks and securities; a hurricane can badly damage oil rigs, causing an increase in oil prices and affecting refineries; and an earthquake in the Silicon Valley may have a negative impact on technology stock. On the other hand, such impacts are mostly at a localised level and a portfolio of investments diversified by instruments, industries and geography should see a low impact from an insurance event on the rest of the equity and fixed-income assets within it. This diversification feature of insurance-linked investments in the portfolio of a general investor should reduce the volatility of the portfolio performance and, as a consequence, increase the portfolio's efficient frontier (i.e. the maximisation of the expected return for a given amount of risk, typically measured by the volatility).

The impact of the turmoil in the financial markets on the insurance-linked securities sector is more complex, with three trends observed in 2008:

- **Resilient primary and secondary market:** the insurance-linked securities market has been one of the very few capital market sectors to see a functioning primary market with a number of transactions being oversubscribed, as well as a very large volume of trades in the secondary market which occurred at non distressed level. The most testing month in 2008 was October, when some investors sold large volumes of insurance-linked securities to cover their own redemptions and for deleveraging. These portfolio liquidations caused some level of secondary spread widening, but mark-to-market losses from issuance prices have been on average within the single-digit percentage range. This compares extraordinarily well with most other structured fixed-income and credit products.

- **The impact of Lehman's bankruptcy:** the bankruptcy of Lehman Brothers in September 2008 affected a very small number of transactions where Lehman was providing a total return swap to guarantee, among other things, the market value of the investments of the securitisation vehicle (which must invest the proceeds of the issuance of the insurance-linked securities in high quality collateral following predefined criteria). Whilst details of the individual transactions are confidential, the Lehman bankruptcy has further highlighted the issue of collateral selection criteria, mark to market and margining by the total return swap counterparties. The market had spotted these structural weaknesses in autumn 2007, and required transactions to perform more frequent mark to market of the collateral and margining calls for any shortfall. As of the time of this contribution (December 2008) and in the next few months, the debate is still, and is expected to remain, open on what form these structures can take to further reduce the risk of contagion. In my opinion, structural enhancements tested against 2008 market conditions are likely to contribute to further reducing the contagion of credit default risk in the insurance-linked securities market.

- **The impact of the crisis on reinsurance and insurance pricing:** insurance, reinsurance and retrocession pricing had been gradually falling since Hurricane Katrina, following the pattern of a reinsurance pricing cycle (which sees an increase in premium in the aftermath of a large insurance event, followed by a gradual reduction until a floor is reached or another event affects the industry). The financial turmoil in 2008 has affected insurance capacity in various forms. First of all, some large hedge funds were important providers of retrocession capacity. The losses and the outflow of funds from the hedge fund industry have affected retrocession capacity and, as a consequence, have increased the pricing of related capital market placements such as insurance-linked securities, collateralised reinsurance, catastrophe swaps and industry loss warranties (ILWs). In addition, insurers and reinsurers have suffered losses both in their liabilities and in their assets side, thus reducing available capital and creating the basis for possible increases in pricing, particularly for peak catastrophe perils. Hurricanes Ike and Gustav (not sufficient to affect any known insurance-linked securities) contributed to make 2008 likely to be one of the costliest years in history in terms of insurance losses. And lastly, the collapse of AIG in September 2008 has caused a migration of business which has been taken up by competitors with their available capital. In summary, the market conditions in 2008 have underpinned an increase in insurance pricing for some lines of business, which normally translates into an increase in returns for insurance-linked securities investors as well, without having seen any event causing a principal loss to traded insurance-linked securities.

It has therefore been possible to observe the resilience of the non-life insurance-linked securities sector during 2007 and 2008 relative to the rest of the structured fixed-income market. This, together with the limited correlation between a natural catastrophe event and a financial crisis, does support the arguments of those stating that a portion of non-life insurance-linked securities in an investor portfolio normally represents a source of diversification from other equity and fixed-income instruments.

9.1.4 Relative value

Insurance-linked securities historically attracted a novelty premium when compared with other investments of similar rating. Whilst the novelty premium gradually reduced, in normal market conditions investors have been provided with a return which is competitive with that of investments with comparable rating available in the other fixed-income sectors, whilst at the same time improving portfolio diversification and efficient frontiers. These features made the asset class very attractive to those available to do the analysis, particularly when coupling superior returns with low correlation as well as diversification benefits. Such relative value can be observed by comparing the available BB-rated catastrophe bond total return indexes with other indexes tracking the total return of BB fixed-income investments.

By the close of 2008, in the wake of the volatility in the financial markets, there were traditional fixed-income products where pricing had fallen to below the long-term economic value of the securities. This has moved the attention of some investors to such asset classes, in some cases to the detriment of insurance-linked securities. On the other hand, whilst such opportunistic trades are the result of a short-term market arbitrage (also embedding a strong mark-to-market volatility risk) and cumulate credit and/or structured credit risk in an investor portfolio, insurance-linked securities are likely to deliver value as well as diversification over the medium to long term.

9.1.5 Valuation and liquidity

The ability to monitor the secondary market value of a portfolio of insurance-linked securities, and the creation of a secondary market, have also been very important in the development of investor appetite in the sector.

Some of the key broker-dealers provide regular indicative bid and offer spreads on all traded catastrophe bonds. Whilst we are still far from market making in insurance-linked securities, as deals are normally done on a matched trade basis, such indicative bids have been invaluable for portfolio valuation purposes and in supporting the secondary market pricing analysis for trading purposes, and investors hope that more market participants will equip themselves to provide regular indicative bids.

In terms of market liquidity, up to the second half of 2007 it was normally much easier to sell rather than to buy insurance-linked securities in the secondary market, as the demand for bonds was larger than the supply, primary issuance was oversubscribed and investors were holding on to their bonds in the fear of not being able to find the same exposures in the secondary market. Trading was, in many cases, occurring on a 'switching' basis, where investors were exchanging one security for another. At the same time, net buyers had been frequently paying above indicative offer levels to be able to put money to work.

In 2008, the exit of some investors from the sector provided a sustained supply of insurance-linked securities in the secondary market. Healthy secondary market trading ensured pricing levels for most traded non-life insurance-linked securities remained above 90 cents, comparing very well with the rest of the structured fixed-income market. 'Forced sellers' needing to liquidate large portfolios quickly due to deleveraging and redemption constraints may have seen some distressed pricing, but what was considered 'distressed' pricing in insurance-linked securities would not have been considered such in many fixed-income markets.

In general terms, the insurance-linked securities sector demonstrated its maturity in 2008, with a functioning secondary market – thus proving its liquidity relative to similar instruments – and with a number of traditional as well as new players (including securities inter-dealer brokers) being active in supporting the market with intermediation as well as indicative securities pricing.

9.2   KEY TRANSACTION FEATURES FROM THE INVESTOR PERSPECTIVE

The insurance-linked securities landscape is one of constant innovation and enrichment of structural alternatives, products, instruments and underlying risks being proposed to the capital markets.

In this context, and conscious of the fact that a full and exhaustive analysis would require a book in itself, this section summarises some basic features that have been observed to be the key focus of insurance-linked securities investors:

- assessment of the underlying risks being securitised;
- risk assessment of the instrument;
- pricing and risk/reward profile.

9.2.1   Assessment of the underlying risks being securitised

The key analysis for an insurance-linked securities investor is on the actual risk being securitised. The information memorandum for modelled catastrophe bonds offers an outline of such risks in the 'Risk Analysis' section, whilst for high frequency/low severity non-life securitisations (such as motor insurance securitisation), the best reference for such analysis is in the rating agencies' reports. Of course, whilst extremely useful, professional investors do not limit their analysis to these reports, but disaggregate the risk into its underlying components and form their own view to compare with that of the modelling firm or of the rating agencies. In addition, there are known differences between the approaches and risk assessment of similar risks by different reputable modelling agencies, thus reinforcing the need for supplemental analysis.

The analysis of the risk is very different in nature according to the type of peril as well as the type of trigger used in the transaction (for detailed analyses of types of triggers, please refer to Chapter 4).

For natural catastrophe risks the starting point for all of the notes is the probability of occurrence of a certain event with various degrees of intensity (such as a range of windstorms with different wind speeds or a range of earthquakes with different magnitudes). Having reached a view on the likelihood of an event occurrence, the investor should assess the impact of such an event on the portfolio of risks being securitised. In non-indemnity transactions, the impact of an event for the affected insurance-linked securities is easier to understand and estimate, as the key parameters to determine the extent of the loss as a consequence of a given event are defined at the inception of the transaction. For indemnity transactions, the loss severity of each event depends on the actual losses suffered by an insurance or reinsurance portfolio. The underwriting of such loss severity will take into account, among other things, the property insured, its use, its locations and the underwriting standards as well as the claims management of the ceding company sponsoring the transaction. In general terms, the more granular the exposure (such as for personal insurance lines), the easier it is to estimate the loss severity, whilst in the presence of large concentrations of insurable value or of collateral losses, such as, for example, business interruption (included in commercial lines), it is harder to predict loss severity and hence the likely results are more volatile. For this reason some investors are unwilling to take on any indemnity risk, other investors will assume indemnity risk only for personal lines (or in portfolios with the majority of the risk being in personal lines) while some other investors will be prepared to take the full spectrum of risk at a premium to the pricing of other structures of comparable modelled expected losses. The premium is likely to be even higher if the transaction is retrocession (i.e. reinsurance for reinsurers) rather than reinsurance.

For high frequency and low severity portfolios (such as motor insurance securitisation) the structures normally base their trigger definition on a given loss ratio (expressed as insurance losses over premium income) for a sponsor's block of business. Investors in these structures need to analyse all risk components of a loss ratio and its dynamics in order to make a considered investment decision. These transactions have also 'structured around' some risk elements of the loss ratio, by, for example, putting a floor to the possible decline of premium income, or putting a cap on a single claim. In any case these structures require an even higher degree of sponsor analysis, as the investor exposure to the sponsor's pricing and claims management performance is continuous throughout the life of the investment, and not subject to a single major event as would be the case in per-event catastrophe securitisation. Claims inflation is monitored because it is partly affected by the sponsor of the transaction (who should also actively fight insurance fraud and inflated claims) but can also be affected by slow or sudden adverse changes in the size of claims awarded by the courts in different jurisdictions, as well as by general inflation affecting the replacement or repair cost of affected property. Also, as these structures are exposed to an element of pricing risk (albeit normally subject to a pricing floor), investors need to familiarise themselves with the dynamics affecting the pricing of the underlying policies and the timing profile of the renewal of the policies being securitised. Pricing can be influenced by the sponsor of the transaction, but in markets with the risk of a pricing war, the premium decline could affect all competitors, thus adversely affecting the industry loss ratios for the affected business lines. Key for such analysis is a sufficiently long data series on the markets as well as on the protection buyer's performance, in addition to a qualitative analysis of what could drive performance going forward.

Having analysed the risk profile of each instrument, investors should then look at how the investment and its risk profile might impact on the risk profile of their total portfolio. Some investors like to maintain a level of diversification in their exposure and monitor the maximum loss impact of any event to their portfolio. Given the availability of sufficient data, the investor should study the correlation between investments in their insurance-linked securities portfolio before finalising the investment decision.

9.2.2   Risk assessment of the instrument

Insurance-linked securities are structured products with a number of parties involved, all of whom are tied up in the transaction via a web of legal documentation. Investors in most securitisation structures can only have sight of the prospectus prior to their investment decision and most other documents are made available only to those who have already invested in the transaction. A proper review of the prospectus is important to understand the workings of the transactions, the terms to which each party is committed and the mechanism allowing each party to terminate their participation (or be replaced).

Early termination features

A key focus for insurance-linked securities are the early termination provisions, which, in most cases, are activated for reasons outside the control of the protection buyer, in which case the notes are normally called at par. In some transactions sponsors are given the option to terminate them before their expected maturity. Some investors are totally opposed to these optional 'call features' on insurance-linked securities, whilst others require a call option premium which covers in full or in part the loss of margin for the investor. For those investors accepting callable bonds, pricing normally needs to be at a premium compared to structures without such a call feature. The principal reason is that an investor provides the protection buyer with a three-to five-year cover at a fixed price irrespective of changes in reinsurance pricing, and does not want in return the protection buyer to call the bonds in the first year in which traditional reinsurance is marginally more attractive, leaving investors with reinvestment risk. An additional very important point is that any call or early termination provision should not allow the protection buyer of a seasonal peril (such as wind perils or floods) to terminate the transaction at the end of the risk season without paying the equivalent of a full year of premium. For example, the European wind season is considered to be over in April. If a bond is callable at the end of March, the bond holders have run half of the wind season for the relevant year, but would only get a quarter of the premium over what a traditional reinsurer would have received. Insurers generally are committed to paying a full year of premium to their reinsurers irrespective of the occurrence of an event. Call option premiums can be used to equalise such imbalance and therefore are higher than those of non-seasonal perils.

Extension periods

Having analysed what can cause the transaction to unwind before its expected maturity, another element to carefully consider is what happens if an event occurs shortly before the expected maturity. Most structures allow for the transaction to be extended and the extra period (called the 'extension period') is used to allow the calculation agent in the transaction to assess whether the event has caused a loss to the investor before returning the cash. When analysing the extension period in a structure, investors carefully look at its duration, the possibility of conducting accurate measurements and reporting the results within the given timeframe, the spread payable during the extension period to investors, the information flow and (for indemnity transactions) the claims certification, the probability of a commutation and the process and presence of independent verification of any commutation. For investors it is important that the structure has sufficient time to properly assess the right amount to claim, but at the same time investors do not look favourably at locking in their collateral for more than necessary in addition to patchy information flow during this period in which the relevant bond is expected to trade at distressed levels.

Total return swap

A key structural feature which is closely analysed is the total return swap structure (or any alternative structures), which is covered at length elsewhere in this chapter. The analysis not only looks at the collateral, but the structural features in the total return swap document are also crucial to the full analysis of the instrument.

Measurement systems

For non-indemnity transactions, an important part of the structural analysis focuses on the way data is collected to input in the model or in the formula to determine whether a transaction has been triggered. The accuracy of the instruments performing the measurement (also assuming a catastrophic event), the ability of the measurement agent to collect such data on time and any possible data manipulation by any party are all elements being considered by insurance-linked securities investors.

Features of indemnity transactions

For indemnity transactions, the focus is on the alignment of interests of the protection buyer with those of the investor (normally achieved with a vertical retention of at least 10% in the risk of the securitised layer and in some cases with junior and senior retention as well), on loss reporting and on the commutation structure. On top of structural considerations, indemnity transactions require a full underwriting of the protection buyer to include his own underwriting criteria, portfolio characteristics, data accuracy and claims management. All of the above-mentioned characteristics could have a different impact on the loss severity post event as well as on the timing required to crystallise the loss on the insurance-linked securities affected by an event. These are some of the reasons why some investors limit their activity to non-indemnity transactions and a premium is charged for investments in indemnity transactions over other non-indemnity structures (which protection buyers justify due to a better cover from the transaction, i.e. the absence of basis risk).

9.2.3 Pricing and risk-return profile

Investors are naturally very focused on pricing and on the risk-return profile of their portfolios, as their value proposition is to maximise the returns for an agreed risk profile.

As in other fixed-income investments in the capital markets, the analysis of comparable investments is a key element in validating pricing. On top of this, some investors include a comparison of the traditional insurance and reinsurance pricing in their analysis, and make an assessment of its direction.

Given the multi-year nature of insurance-linked securities, investors commit to a given price over a period of time. Should the traditional pricing increase, new issuance of insurance-linked securities is also likely to be at a higher spread over the floating rate for the life of the transaction, thus posing a mark-to-market risk to the investors in existing issuance. Conversely, in a declining pricing environment, investors may expect mark-to-market gains in the future for the existing portfolio. In making these considerations one needs to take into account the fact that sudden large events could materially affect traditional pricing, and so any maturities strategy from an investor is directional, but should not disregard the possibility of an event.

At the risk of oversimplification, pricing for natural catastrophe investments is often calculated as a multiple to the expected loss. Like other investments in the capital markets, those perils (such as Florida Hurricane) which are in high demand (defined in the industry as 'peak perils') command a higher multiple to expected loss than other perils more rarely available in the capital markets (such as, for example, Mexico Earthquake). Clearly the driver is that the non-peak perils are very much sought after by those investors seeking diversification in their portfolios, and therefore such investors are happy to receive a lower return in exchange for a higher level of diversification.

In addition, in most cases the higher the expected loss, the higher the absolute value of the premium, but the lower the multiple to expected loss. In particular, there seems to be a pricing floor in insurance-linked securities driven by the cost of capital of specialised investors so that very remote risks command a very high multiple in terms of pricing, unless the transaction can command an investment-grade rating and be placed with traditional structured fixed-income investors, when such markets are open to innovative ideas.

Multiples to expected loss are therefore an interesting tool to monitor pricing developments in the market but are not the sole driver; outlined throughout this chapter are some of the various other elements being assessed by investors in making their investment and pricing decisions. To pick some of the elements outlined (without reducing the importance of the other elements) when comparing investments for pricing consideration, I would stress:

- Structural details which could command a different pricing for what appears to be similar risk. For example, a different collateral and total return swap structure could – among other details outlined in the structuring considerations in this chapter – have a material impact on pricing decisions.
- The modelling agency performing the analysis. In some cases there are known differences among the agencies in their risk assessment of a given peril, therefore the insurance-linked securities modelled by the more conservative modelling agency are expected to price and trade tighter than those modelled by the more aggressive modelling agency for the same peril and at the same expected loss.
- The investors' own view of the risk (which may differ from that of the modelling agencies).
- The trigger type of the investments. Non-indemnity triggers are perceived as being less risky and more liquid than indemnity triggers and therefore indemnity transactions tend to price at a premium over comparable non-indemnity bonds.
- The perceived liquidity of the investment, which is itself a factor involving various elements including:
  ○ the structural characteristics of the transaction;
  ○ the size of the issuance;

○ the perceived acceptance of the modelling performed and the perceived understanding of the securitised risk by the investor community;
○ the ability of indicative secondary marks from the key broker-dealers on the instrument;
○ the availability of sufficient information during the life of the transaction to allow an investor to offer sufficient detail to a prospective investor in the secondary market;
○ the general success of the transaction with investors;
○ the market capacity for the risks embedded in the investment.

This last element of market capacity is a very important one to stress further. As outlined above, each investor has limits on how much it can take for each peril. Peak perils command premium pricing to attract further capacity, but in some cases capacity has dried up temporarily for a given peak peril. Issuance of insurance-linked securities has been quite seasonal and concentrated around the 'renewal season' for such peril, which is the period in which the traditional reinsurance market renews existing contracts (defined as treaties) for a one-year period. Those transactions reaching the primary market at the end of the renewal season have often required a higher price because most of the investors have used up their capacity for such peril. To date this capacity volatility has been greater for US perils and in particular for US Hurricane.

In summary, the comparables analysis and multiples to expected loss are key analytical tools for investors, but the analysis should also take into account a wide array of other factors influencing pricing, both those which are part of the insurance-linked securities business sector and those involving the wider insurance and reinsurance industry dynamics.

9.3   MARKET EVOLUTION: THE INVESTOR PERSPECTIVE

Despite the significant advances achieved by the insurance-linked securities market participants in creating a sustainable sector, the market is still in an evolutionary stage. New products are regularly introduced and investor demand supports innovation and improvements whilst at the same time requiring certain minimum standards. Currently, the key elements of investor focus are:

• collateral arrangements;
• data transparency;
• exposure monitoring;
• modelling rigour.

9.3.1   Collateral arrangements

As explained earlier, the risks underlying insurance-linked securities can provide diversification in a general portfolio of investments. At the same time, protection buyers look to this sector to minimise the credit risk of their reinsurance receivables and recoverables. For this reason, very tight collateralisation requirements that minimise the risk of contamination of the structure by turbulence in the financial markets are very important as they back a fundamental motivation of both the investors and the protection buyers: the management of credit risk.

Market consensus has been that the best structure to deliver collateral security at an acceptable return has been the total return swap structure (TRS). In a TRS structure, high quality collateral is selected in compliance with investment criteria indicated in the prospectus and agreed with the rating agencies. The market value of such collateral is then guaranteed by a highly rated swap counterparty. The original structures included very broad collateral eligibility criteria, under the assumption that it was against the interest of the swap counterparties to select illiquid collateral (this would have ultimately absorbed any mark-to-market loss as the collateral frequently has a term which exceeds the expected term of the insurance-linked securities structure).

Even by the second half of 2007 (i.e. before the full severity of the credit crisis was obvious to market participants and well before any impact on the ILS community), investors started to run stress scenarios in which a severe worsening of the financial markets could have caused issues to the collateral as well as to the swap counterparty, thus exposing protection buyers and investors. These scenarios were run as the early stages of the credit crunch was starting to affect the market value of very senior structured paper, thus making this scenario more likely. The structural innovation led to the requirement for regular marking to market of the collateral in the structure, with the swap counterparty posting additional collateral in case of a shortfall in the market valuation beyond a threshold.

The Lehman bankruptcy affected 'old style' total return swap structures. The resolution by market participants to further reduce the probability of losses arising from non insurance events has fuelled a debate on what further enhancements are necessary.

By the end of 2008, no final consensus had been reached on the appropriate collateralisation structure, but two main approaches were discussed:

- Some key dedicated ILS funds indicated their preference for truly 'risk-free' collateral (such as rolling short-term government securities) even if this meant structuring notes as a margin over risk-free rates instead of over LIBOR. This solution would go make the most headway in resolving the issue, and would be good for protection buyers as they would reduce the cost of the total return swap structure; however, on the other hand, it would reduce the absolute return, abandon a standard benchmark for fixed-income investors and could discourage non-specialised investors from entering this market, thus affecting the liquidity of the overall sector.
- Other dedicated ILS funds and generalist investors would still like to purchase a LIBOR-based product (exchanging the extra return for a slightly higher level of possible cross contamination) and bankers are trying to deliver a LIBOR-based structure which sees more detailed portfolio guidelines and very frequent mark to market and margining with additional collateral posting in cases of shortfall (the best structures in my view having highly rated TRS counterparties, daily margining calls with the marks on the collateral being provided by a party independent of the total return swap counterparty).

Other ideas have been circulated, but we note that the general effort is toward the creation of collateral structures which can withstand very severe stress cases. Such a trend is likely to further consolidate insurance-linked securities as a diversifying asset for general investors and a safe reinsurance credit for protection buyers.

9.3.2 Data transparency

With the growth in indemnity trigger transactions being offered to the capital markets, the question of data on the underlying exposure is very topical. There is a difference between the data that a broker or a protection buyer makes available to a traditional underwriter and the data available in indemnity insurance securitisation structures to investors. Often the securitisation sits in the same reinsurance tower alongside traditional reinsurance or retrocession, and this can cause an asymmetry of data between the reinsurance world and the capital markets.

Given the different language and the different sensitivities between the insurance industry and the capital markets, and given the space reasonably available on prospectuses, data is expected to be aggregated in different forms or even explained in a different way. Some of the arguments used to support less granular information to insurance-linked securities investors are linked to securities law considerations, but we note that the information is, in any case, provided to reinsurers and reinsurance brokers. Continued improvements to bring about more disclosure on the underlying insurance risk are always the focus of insurance investors.

Another element of data transparency regards the collateral initially purchased by the securitisation vehicle. To date, information about the collateral is only available to actual, rather than prospective, investors, and even when investors own a bond, the process of obtaining collateral information is not always straightforward. Given the current focus on the collateral quality and on transparency, investors are pushing arrangers to publish the list of the initial collateral investments in the prospectus, so that they can gain greater transparency on the overall collateral structure backing their prospective investment, before making their investment decision.

9.3.3 Exposure monitoring

As most insurance-linked securities are multi-year, the underlying exposure can change over the life of the transaction. Some parametric transactions and all properly structured indemnity transactions have a reset feature, which modifies the attachment point on a regular basis (normally yearly) to make sure that the risk profile of the note is unaltered for the investor. Whilst this is an important feature for investors in indemnity non-life insurance-linked securities, a professional investor would also need to constantly monitor its total exposure for each insurance risk and in each relevant area (with the ability to perform a granular territorial analysis), in order to build and manage risk accumulation and estimated losses due to simulated or actual events.

Indemnity insurance-linked securities should therefore include a large part of the data provided to investors in the prospectus in regular investor reporting. Again, this would put investors more in line with reinsurers, who receive the full data set in the yearly reinsurance renewal submissions.

Also, given investor focus on collateral and the possibility of mark-to-market movements and changes to the posted collateral, regular investor reporting should proactively inform of any movement in the collateral securities backing the notes (both in terms of substitutions, downgrades, margining, additional collateral, etc.).

9.3.4 Modelling rigour

A key investor consideration for the perceived liquidity of insurance-linked securities has been the independence of the modelling agency from both the protection buyer and the arranger. This is important in the insurance-linked securities sector as the rating agencies, whilst having played an important role in ensuring a level of consistency in documentation standards, have not yet fully developed a reputation for proper assessment of pure insurance risk without the backing of modelling agencies. The independence of the modelling agency is therefore an extra level of comfort (as well as a common denominator) in the risk assessment of the transaction.

To date a limiting factor for the market's development has been that not all risks being placed or considered for placement into the capital markets have been modelled by independent agencies, or not to the standards needed for use in capital market transactions. At the same time, the growing appetite for diversifying risks could lead to the launch of transactions which include elements of non-modelled perils or new modelling approaches.

Investors considering investing in such new diversifying transactions in the early stages of their development need to gain comfort from the state-of-the-art modelling approach and accept the potential for model evolution and an element of illiquidity, but they should generally gain risk diversification in return. At the same time, investors have shown less comfort with transactions which could have been modelled based on available technology but for which a protection buyer has opted not to use an independent model, or to simply make their own model subject to an independent modelling review.

In conclusion, whilst the refrain of this chapter is the observation of constant evolution as well as innovation in the non life insurance-linked securities sector, and whilst the investor community has an open dialogue on further improvements, we can confidently say that this small niche sector of the capital markets has performed very well when tested by one of the most severe financial crises in history, and has also responded well to natural catastrophe events such as Hurricane Katrina. The insurance-linked securities sector has equipped itself with all the infrastructure needed to make it a sustainable market into which investors can confidently invest and build a strategy for the medium to the long term.

10

ILS Portfolio Monitoring Systems

Tibor Winkler[a] and John Stroughair[b]

Risk Management Solutions (RMS) brings to the converging insurance and capital markets a new software platform for quantifying the risk of portfolios of insurance-linked securities (ILS) and other standard types of contracts of insurance-risk. The platform is called 'Miu' and it comes with a library of risk-profiles for live cat bonds called 'Characterisations'. These profiles represent RMS's view of the risk in each cat bond and have been built based on the information in the offering circulars. Miu is one of the software packages available to ILS investors, with the other main providers being AIR and EQECAT, each with their own distinct characteristics. Software such as Miu can be used by investors, market-markers, intermediaries and arrangers, and it supports:

- the risk analysis of each potential or existing investment; and
- the risk analysis of a portfolio of ILS investments.

This chapter is dedicated to describing ILS portfolio management software. Given the authors' background, the focus is necessarily on Miu and its characterisations, but this provides a framework to understanding and comparing other products.

10.1 INTRODUCTION

10.1.1 Completing the circle

After nearly a decade of sustained but modest growth, the ILS market took a leap forward in the wake of the hurricane seasons of 2004 and 2005. As the insurance industry was looking to shore up capital to strengthen balance sheets and sustain ratings, issuance of ILS intensified to a level hitherto unseen. In a hard insurance market with company ratings under increased scrutiny, choosing to sponsor an ILS issue now made both economic and strategic sense. As market conditions looked to be sustained for years to come, the time was right to develop new tools to support the ILS market.

With the increase in the number of ILS and growth of the market it was clear to RMS that the ILS market would need a portfolio management platform that was customised to its needs. It was also clear that, in the climate of the insurance and the capital markets converging, the new platform would need to be able to handle all forms of insurance risk, regardless of the form in which it was 'packaged'. Developing such a platform from a clean sheet of paper

---

[a]Formerly of Risk Management Solutions, Inc
[b]Risk Management Solutions, Inc

with clear objectives became a new initiative that wore the name 'Miu', the Egyptian word for 'cat'. Miu supports the analysis of portfolios of natural catastrophe ILS (cat bonds) and other natural catastrophe risk transfer instruments. This chapter is focussed on introducing Miu's structure, its features and its importance for the ILS market.

10.1.2 'Square peg in a round hole?'

The task facing risk managers when attempting to represent the structure of a complex cat bond in a regular cat model could be likened to that facing the astronauts of Apollo 13, when they had to fabricate a round air-filter using only a square cartridge, duck tape and plastic foil; an essential task to carry out but a very difficult one. Since the ILS market has grown sufficiently to lead to concentrations of correlated risk on the balance sheets of buyers of risk large enough to warrant rigorous quantification of portfolio risk by accounting for correlation, buyers of ILS products have employed various methods to produce portfolio metrics. Depending on their size, investment strategy, level of conservatism and degree of risk aversion, holders of ILS either develop their own, bespoke 'models', try to 'shoehorn' ILS into a regular cat model by omission or simplification of certain payout features, or simply make very conservative assumptions on correlation and give up entirely trying to 'code' the deals accurately.

Before we move on to discuss how Miu simplifies the above 'task', let us describe in some detail the main constituents of such a task. In the abstract, one could define it as having to apply a rule or a series of rules in order to determine the response of the transaction to any covered event, as defined in the term sheet. In plain English, in order to determine whether a certain covered event would cause a principal reduction or not, one may need to refer to the outcomes for the bond for previous events during the term according to a set of rules. It is this – the conditional evaluation of how or whether loss to the principal is to be calculated given an event – that is not supported by regular cat models. Let us introduce a few of the most common rules and structures used to date:

- **kth event:** a transaction is designed to cover not the first but, let us say, the 3rd or 4th or kth event occurring over the term. More elaborate variants of this could use additional rules, like covering two events in Year 2 or 3 of a multi-year deal but only as long as there was no 'first' event in the preceding years, for example. Thus, the calculation will need to keep track of previous event losses when proceeding to determine the outcome for a new event.
- **Drop-down:** there are deals in which the issuer wishes the trigger level for a second event to 'drop-down' to a level lower than that for the first event, in order to gain additional liquidity for smaller events once there has been a first event. Thus, in order to determine the payout for any subsequent event, we will need to 'remember' whether there has been a first event triggering a drop-down.
- **Seniority:** many transactions in the market have multiple tranches, or layers, responding to different events and representing different levels of risk to an investor. For example, one may have a transaction with two tranches, A and B, where B is the junior to A, meaning that the capacity of tranche B must be exhausted by events before tranche A can take a loss. Thus, in order to be able to allocate event losses to those tranches correctly, one needs to keep track of which losses have been caused by which events and to which tranche during the term.

Having reviewed the examples of these features, it will be clear to the reader that a cat model using an automated rather than a rules-based approach to calculate portfolio loss cannot capture non-trivial event logic for a transaction. In order to do that, we need an application designed specifically for that purpose.

10.2 MIU – AN ILS PLATFORM IN A CONVERGENT SPACE

10.2.1 Overview

Miu was designed to make possible, in a simple manner, analysis of portfolios of insurance risk, regardless of the form in which such risk was packaged. That is, to allow the user to represent with ease any mix of cat bonds, industry loss warranties (ILWs), insurance, reinsurance or retrocession contracts or derivatives and to enable the running of portfolio analysis and the obtaining of results with great flexibility.

Achieving these aims in Miu is subject only to feeding in a stochastic representation of risk underlying each contract. In RMS's parlance, that would be an event loss table (ELT); for example, in order to be able to include in a portfolio a US Hurricane cat bond with a PCS trigger, one must first enter the ELT of a stochastic run of a hurricane model on a US industry portfolio. Then, the only task remaining is to enter the transaction rules such as the term, attachment and exhaustion levels, single or multi-event cover, any drop-downs, seniority, and so on. Miu was designed to afford the user virtually boundless freedom in representing transactions of nearly unlimited complexity without any simplification of the terms. In addition, the platform enables the setting up of rules between transactions in a simple and flexible manner. This feature makes possible the coding of inuring relationships in the broadest sense and is used to programme rules of interaction between tranches of transactions.

In Section 10.1, we spoke of the need to lower the knowledge barrier to entry into the space as being a key component of market growth. In addition to the software, the other key piece of RMS's offering to achieve that is a library of risk profiles for live cat bonds, made available inside Miu. The RMS technical term for each of these profiles is 'characterisation', as the profile characterises the risk represented by each cat bond. A characterisation for a cat bond is developed on the basis of the offering circular for the transaction by a dedicated team. RMS uses the same methodology for all transactions, regardless of which company carried out the risk analysis for the offering. It is important to note here that all characterisations represent an RMS view of the risk in a transaction and that those may be materially different to those in the offering circular. Section 10.3 describes the RMS library of characterisations in more detail.

10.2.2 Nuts and bolts – how the platform works

Miu calculates all results by simulation. The simulation-set for each unique event loss table (ELT) is called year loss table (YLT) – actually a misnomer since it covers an entire holding period up to five years – and it is precompiled for each ELT. The ELT represents the loss experience by a cat bond for each of the RiskLink stochastic events. The YLT is a simulated representation of the risk and it takes the form of a catalogue of which stochastic event occurred on what date and what its severity was. The YLT refers to the same stochastic events as the ELT, only each event severity is sampled from the distribution defined by the mean and the standard deviation in the ELT.

The beauty of this approach is that all representations of risk in Miu are fully consistent with RiskLink (the RMS cat model) and that Miu leverages the quality, completeness and robustness of stochastic event sets used in RiskLink. Above all, it is this trait that enables one to take account of correlation between each contract and all other contracts properly and implicitly, without the need for any assumptions to be made by the user. It is significant to note that Miu's ability to use the full stochastic sets from RiskLink is important for the stability of results.

What does Miu's architecture mean for run time? It is very efficient, as all simulation sets are precompiled. Furthermore, the outcome of any simulation set for a given contract is calculated only once. Consequently, when a user performs repeated analyses on a portfolio with only some of the portfolio's constituents changing only some of the time, only the newly added contracts are run while the ones remaining unchanged have their results reused from the first run. This allows, for example, iterations in the course of a portfolio development exercise to be run very rapidly, thereby allowing the user to determine, on the basis of reviewing combined portfolio metrics in a matter of minutes, whether it 'makes sense' to add a certain transaction to its portfolio or not.

10.2.3 Step by step – entering a contract

As we mentioned above, the process of entering a new piece of risk, or contract, begins with uploading an ELT representing the underlying risk. Once the ELT is 'in', it can be used to create a YLT using standard functionality. Then, the final step is to associate the desired YLT with a set of rules specific to the contract. This step creates what Miu calls a 'class'. Once a class has been created, it can be added to form part of a portfolio and run.

The process of creating a class is as simple in practice as it appears in the description here. Once the YLT has been created by the engine, the user may proceed to assemble a class. This is done by clicking to select a YLT and specifying the mechanics of the contract. As we recall from the Introduction, this process consists of selecting the type of trigger required, attachment and exhaustion levels, the type of the payout function and so on. There are drop-down menus from which the user may select any of the most common trigger-types, such as single or multi event, per occurrence or aggregate, drop-down and so on. Then, the user proceeds to selecting the shape of the payout function, which can be binary or tapered, and then linear or nonlinear.

For classes requiring a bespoke logic for event processing and payout there is a 'custom' option, which allows the user to set up a trigger with virtually unlimited complexity. This is done by setting up a template in Microsoft Excel of how loss to the class can be calculated given an event. Miu will pipe through this 'prescription' each simulated event and use the rules set up in the Excel spreadsheet to determine the outcome of that event for the class. If the rules for determining the outcome of an event can be set up in a spreadsheet, the transaction can be modelled in Miu. It is notable that the RMS team responsible for creating characterisations for live cat bonds has built classes for all cat bonds live in the market with less than a handful of exceptions and it is yet to come across a structure Miu would be unable to accommodate. The exceptions, in which the team did not create a characterisation, had unique reasons to do with the restricted availability of information in the offering circular rather than Miu's functionality.

10.2.4 Portfolio analysis

Portfolio construction and analysis

A portfolio can be constructed by selecting classes from the library of classes set up as described in Section 10.2.3. The user will tick to select a class and enter the amount invested in that class. As was explained above, each class has a YLT associated with it as standard, describing stochastically the risk underlying the contract. At the step of selecting a class for inclusion in a portfolio the user has the option to have either the preassigned YLT selected automatically, or to select another YLT to be associated with that class in order to represent another view of risk for that class. More on this may be found in the section entitled 'Sensitivity analyses' below. Although it might be intuitive, let us note at this point that a YLT may be built not only to represent a stochastic analysis but for a single historical event or a series of historical events as well. Thus, the user may select a YLT to rerun a large earthquake from the past, or an entire hurricane season for a 'what if' type analysis.

Once a class and a YLT have been selected and the size assigned, the contract or contracts are ready for analysis. In order to run an analysis the user will enter a time period over which the analysis will be run. This means a period of real time, starting on a certain date and ending on another. Currently Miu supports analysis time periods of any length between one day and five calendar years. The current limit of five years is set by the size of the underlying simulation sets created to be appropriate for that period; RMS's choice of five years as an upper bound was guided by the lengths of terms of cat bonds seen in the market over the past years and deemed appropriately long. Should it be found desirable, larger simulation sets may be produced to enable terms longer than five years – it is only a question of space on one's hard disk.

Before we are ready to hit run, there is one last parameter to choose – the number of simulations to be run. As the reader will now have guessed, this step determines the level of simulation error in the results and runtime. A smaller number of simulations may be run for a 'quick and dirty' set of results or a greater number for a greater degree of convergence to the theoretically correct result. Please note that running a larger number of simulations will reduce the error in the simulation itself but will not improve the absolute correctness of results. Hence, it may be perceived that there is little sense in calculating very accurately portfolio results for risk that has a significant amount of inherent uncertainty. Thus, the user will need to determine the appropriate number of simulations for getting a satisfactory degree of convergence while keeping the runtime acceptable; the error term shown in the portfolio summary report, discussed below, will be a useful guide for this.

Results and reports

Our latest analysis of a portfolio has now run and we are ready to view the results. How does that all work? It is very simple and intuitive. Miu uses Microsoft Excel as its interface for processing and viewing results. All simulation results are piped into spreadsheets and Miu enables the user to select from a drop-down menu various types of report in which those results may be displayed. The user may design any custom template for processing and viewing results and add those to the library of templates in the drop-down menu, which has in it a few basic types set up as standard. These include:

- portfolio summary report;
- expected loss by peril region;
- class correlation report; and
- CDO report.

The portfolio summary report contains the headlines such as probability of attachment, exhaustion, expected loss and simulation error for each contract (class) in the portfolio as well as for the portfolio as a whole. In addition, the user gets a loss-exceedance curve for the portfolio as well as a chart showing the accumulation of expected loss over the time period of the analysis. This chart always makes for interesting viewing as the user may trace the temporal variation of the risk profile in response to seasonality of windstorm or flood risk in the portfolio.

Another basic view of portfolio risk is the breakdown of expected loss by peril. Most readers will be familiar with the requirements for this from their reviews of offering circulars over the years. This view of the risk helps the user to assess concentrations of risk by peril, thus enabling them to verify and design the risk profile required. Of course, a similar view of the results may be set up by the user to show contribution to attachment, exhaustion or any other metric. As stated above, these templates may then be added to the drop-down under 'Reports' and reused time and time again.

The class correlation report is one for those curious about the degree of correlation between classes in the portfolio as borne out by the simulation results. This report lists the correlation coefficients calculated for each class and each other class.

Finally, the CDO report is yet another example of what sort of exercises might be interesting to run on a set of results. In this case, the developers set up a set of tranches into which the portfolio could be sliced, with each tranche having to meet a requirement for a certain level of attachment probability and expected loss, which could be seen as similar to the iterative work undertaken on multi-tranche, CDO-type cat bonds like Bay-Haven or Fremantle.

Sensitivity analyses

'Sensitivity analysis' is a term used in the context of ILS usually to refer to a calculation to determine the extent of change in an outcome as a result of changing one or several of the assumptions impacting the value of that outcome. For instance, a rating agency may wish to examine the sensitivity of the attachment probability for a transaction, or a portfolio of transactions, to changes in the annual event rates used in the underlying model or models. Or, reviewing a multi-peril transaction with an earthquake component, it might ask: 'If we shift by half of a standard deviation the damage functions used in the earthquake model, what will that do to the combined expected loss?'

Similarly, an investor with strong views on the likelihood of occurrence of certain cat events might say: 'I prefer my own view on the annual rate of CAT 5 hurricanes, so that is what I will use to run my portfolio of cat bonds.' Or, a chief underwriter tasked with giving input into reserving strategy might say: 'How would our capital charge change if we took a 5% less conservative view on these flood severities?'.

Answering any of the above questions used to require much manual exercise, designed from the beginning for every transaction and rebuilt and executed again every time a different degree of change to the same parameter was made. As a result, for complex transactions with multiple perils, tranches and years, the analyst was forced to be quite frugal and make do with perhaps just one or two analyses and infer the results for others from the outcomes of those.

With software like Miu available, this is no longer the case. To see how this may be done, let us look back at what we learned in the earlier section on 'Portfolio construction and analysis' about assigning to each class a YLT before running the portfolio. We learned that the user may select any of the YLTs and link it with a class for analysis. In practice this means that the user may prepare a number of YLTs representing a series of different assumptions on frequency or severity of the underlying risk. Once the YLTs have been prepared, the user simply ticks and selects to link them with a class or a set of classes and then hits run. This means the user may run a range of sensitivity analyses with alternative views of risk without having to touch the structure of the transaction, represented by a class or a set of classes, by simply linking the classes with a different YLT for each run.

10.3   RMS LIBRARY OF CAT BOND CHARACTERISATIONS

Up to this point the user has been introduced to the motivation for building Miu and its functionality on a macroscopic level. It is now time to describe the library of risk profiles developed by RMS for all live cat bonds and made available as classes inside Miu. These profiles are called 'characterisations'.

10.3.1   Motivation and objectives

Construction of a risk-profile for a cat bond has at least the following non-trivial prerequisites:

- material familiarity with cat bonds;
- access to a stochastic or statistical model;
- a degree of familiarity with that model's components and fundamental assumptions;
- solid knowledge of catastrophe risk and the issues involved in its modelling;
- advanced analytic capability; and
- a significant investment of time and effort.

While a number of potential sponsors, arrangers and investors possess several of these, very few indeed have all of them. Then there is the matter of efficiency and an effective use of resources. For a fund, for example, does it make business sense to employ one or several quants who would construct and maintain representations of cat bonds but, by not being true experts, perhaps make only an acceptable job of it?

As a result of confirmation by the market of the value and usefulness of software like Miu, a number of new dynamics began to develop in a short period of time. Perhaps the most interesting of those is one in which Miu clients wish to receive a characterisation for a new transaction before making an investment decision; that is, as soon as a client is presented the offering material, RMS is forwarded it and asked to develop and deliver the characterisation as a matter of urgency. This not only gives an investor the ability to view its portfolio risk profile with the new transaction included, but also provides a second opinion on the risk analysis in the offering circular. Now, most readers will appreciate the level of uncertainty associated with cat bonds represented by the uncertainty in catastrophic event occurrence and its stochastic modelling. There is an additional component of volatility depending on the appropriateness of the transaction structure and the quality of the risk-analysis. Hence, having another view of risk for such an instrument will be of great value not only to investors but all participants in the ILS space – in our view it will be valuable to sponsors, arrangers and modelling firms, too – as it will drive the standard of solutions.

10.3.2   How is it done? A bird's eye view

In order to provide a characterisation to a client RMS requires the client to forward a copy of the offering circular, pricing supplement and any other related documentation. RMS then produces the characterisation and uploads it to the client's installation of Miu into the library of classes. The client is then able to add the 'transaction' to a portfolio simply by ticking to select it by its name, as described in the earlier section 'Portfolio construction and analysis'.

What exactly is a characterisation? It is an RMS view of the risk represented by a cat bond, and it is developed on the basis of the standard documentation accompanying each transaction.

So, how are characterisations made? The first and most important point to make is that RMS performs their construction on the basis of information in the offering documents, its own proprietary cat models, industry exposure databases (IEDs) and its proprietary trigger solutions. There is strictly no use of any confidential information proprietary to any third party. The only trivial exception to this is the use of geocoding and mapping information licensed by RMS as part of its regular operation. Secondly, RMS employs the same set of approaches to all cat bonds, regardless of the identity of the company that produced the risk analysis for an offering circular. And thirdly, there is a Chinese wall between the team building and maintaining the characterisations and the team that carries out all work on new transactions supported by RMS; this is to ensure there is no influence in any direction between those teams. This is pivotal as it ensures consistency and impartiality of approach for the product, which is seen by RMS as vital to the market's ability to appreciate and use the characterisations with confidence.

Perhaps the reader already has concluded, on the basis of the above, that the transaction metrics in a characterisation, such as the attachment or exhaustion probability, expected loss, breakdown of those by peril or geography may be different to those in the offering circular. As a matter of course and as part of the provision of characterisations, the user gets a document with each one, describing the RMS results and going into a level of detail commensurate with the degree of difference in the results.

10.3.3 Apples to apples – a leap for the market

Now that we have reviewed the offering that is Miu, let us take a minute to ponder what widespread use of the platform and the characterisations could mean for the ILS market's future. We are certain that the ability to represent cat bonds in a portfolio of risk in a clean, transparent and consistent manner, designed and executed by specialist professionals, is a significant step forward for the growing market of ILS. In addition to the central matter of capturing correlation between the various instruments in a portfolio on the basis of perhaps the most complete event sets available today, there are the gains associated with advanced level, but easy, learning of the ropes for newcomers into the space.

In addition to hard, quantitative gains we may imagine feedback created between the process of developing characterisations and the structure and level of content included in offering circulars created for future transactions. Almost all participants in the ILS market would gain through an increase in clarity and disclosure. In our view such developments would lead to a broadening of the sphere of investors as well as sponsors, and bring about a significant increase in market size.

10.4 CONCLUSION

By the end of 2006, ILS market activity increased to a new level with the number of new cat bonds up and the volume of total outstanding ILS at a record high. In this climate RMS took the strategic decision to add ILS portfolio modelling software to its long-standing activity of advising on and executing ILS. The new software platform is called Miu and it supports not only analyses of ILS but insurance-risk contracts of any type. It is based on simulation and enables all complex transaction features to be represented simply and efficiently. In addition, Miu contains a library of risk profiles for all live cat bonds, called characterisations. Those profiles are developed by RMS using information in offering circulars and represent an independent view of the risk in each transaction. The characterisations may be added to any portfolio by a click of a mouse. With Miu and the characterisations, RMS brings to the converging insurance and capital markets a new level of clarity and transparency in support of significant growth.

11

The Evolution and Future of Reinsurance Sidecars

Douglas J. Lambert[a] and Kenneth R. Pierce[b]

In addition to more commonly cited insurance-linked securities (ILS), sidecars are an important vehicle for capital market investors to gain exposure to insurance risk. In general terms, while insurance-linked securities have been used by insurers and reinsurers to complement traditional reinsurance by providing excess of loss (XL) coverage, sidecars are aimed at providing extra capital, typically in the form of quota share (Q/S) participations.

A 'sidecar' is a special purpose reinsurer that provides flexible capacity to a sponsoring insurer or reinsurer, and focused 'line of business' exposure to investors. Sidecars are typically limited life vehicles that seek to capitalize on temporary dislocations in the insurance marketplace. It is difficult to develop an all-encompassing definition of a sidecar because of the structure's flexibility and continuous evolution in response to changing market conditions and opportunities. Most, but not all, of the sidecars that have been successfully created to date have the following shared characteristics:

- special purpose, limited life company, created to take advantage of short-term opportunity and thereafter to dissolve;
- capitalized either to the probable maximum loss level of the covered events or fully to the coverage limits; possibly with leverage; either pre-funded or funded over time as the reinsured portfolio ramps up;
- minimal to no active management, dependent on sponsor or validator for underwriting, pricing and servicing;[1]
- single treaty with sponsor, typically quota share for a line of business with a meaningful retention by the sponsor for alignment of interests with the investors; and
- ceding commission to compensate sponsoring cedant for expenses, plus profit commission based on underwriting profits (sometimes blended in a sliding scale).

There are exceptions to, and variations upon, each of these characteristics. While sidecars are mostly known for their application in the property catastrophe space after Hurricanes Katrina, Rita and Wilma, sidecars are already being applied to different lines of business.

---

[a]Morgan Stanley & Co. Incorporated

[b]Mayer Brown LLP

[1] Thus, the reason for the 'sidecar' moniker – the sponsor or validator drives the motorcycle while the special purpose reinsurer is a passive vehicle that is bolted alongside for the ride.

This chapter traces the evolution of sidecars, discusses their possible applications along with some challenges and addresses the potential for sidecars to evolve into convenient and critical components of the broader, and inevitable, convergence of insurance and capital markets.

11.1   A BRIEF HISTORY OF THE BRIEF HISTORY OF SIDECARS

Sidecar structures have been used in other contexts for many years. Although it may be argued that Hannover Re's 'K' program, dating back to the mid-1990s, represents a type of sidecar, awareness of reinsurance sidecars was limited until the 2005 US hurricane season and Hurricanes Katrina, Rita and Wilma ('KRW'). These events, combined with several hurricanes in 2004, were a wake-up call for the industry. They depleted capital and revealed the undercapitalization of catastrophe risk to regulators, risk managers and rating agencies. The result was a dramatic hardening of the property cat market by late 2005, focused in the US but felt worldwide, as insurers raced to raise premiums and capital. Many insurers scaled back their underwriting in cat-exposed areas to preserve their capital bases and limit the possibility of a single event causing significant loss. For example, a few insurers ceased writing new homeowner policies in Florida and other coastal regions, including parts of the US Northeast.

The P&C insurance and reinsurance marketplace has always been prone to pricing and capacity cycles. When capital is consumed by underwriting losses such as disasters (both natural and 'man-made') or investment losses, capacity decreases and, therefore, insurance premiums increase. With some cycles there is a time lag between capital erosion and premium increases, while in other cycles the impact is immediate. Premiums may remain elevated until insurers and reinsurers are able to replenish their depleted capital base, at which point competitive supply pressures force premiums down again. Underwriting care and quality improves along with the scarcity of capital. Therefore, historically, risk-adjusted returns in the insurance industry have increased after a capital-depleting event. After Hurricane Andrew in 1992 and after the events of September 11, 2001, property premiums spiked but losses in the ensuing contract years were negligible. Capital has traditionally flowed back into the industry after these events through equity, debt or hybrid capital-raising, or the establishment of new companies to take advantage of the favorable underwriting environment.

Learning from this history, instead of scaling back in the fall of 2005, some insurers and reinsurers looked for additional sources of capital to support additional underwriting in strategic areas. Sidecars provided a novel form of capital that enabled these companies to scale up, increase market share and generate fee income without issuing equity, which can be expensive and dilutive, or taking on financial leverage. At the same time, investors who were interested in the favorable post-KRW property cat environment were keenly aware that the favorable part of the cycle would not last for long, and also became increasingly wary of new companies with untested management. Sidecars offered these investors the potential for equity returns generated by laser-focused exposure to property cat risk, without investing in the equity of insurers and reinsurers. In that environment, over $6 billion of capital was raised in sidecars over an 18-month period.[2] Between the end of 2006 and the end of the first half of 2008, insurance industry capital was rebuilt in the absence of major catastrophes and as a result, premiums declined. The softening market reduced the need for alternative capital as well as investor appeal, and sidecars were not as prevalent during that period.

---

[2] Morgan Stanley estimate.

At the time this chapter is being written (at the end of 2008), the belief that the market is hardening is becoming widespread, and work has begun on the next generation of sidecars to respond to the 2009–2010 environment.

11.2   SIDECAR STRUCTURES

11.2.1   Basic structure

The basic reinsurance sidecar structure (Figure 11.1) involves a special purpose reinsurer (most commonly domiciled in Bermuda) that provides reinsurance capacity to a designated ceding insurer or reinsurer. The 'sidecar' itself is the operating entity and may be established under a holding company, although it is not always necessary to add a holding company to the structure.

The sidecar (or its holding company) raises equity and/or debt capital. Most of the proceeds of the capital raise are deposited in a collateral account to support the sidecar's reinsurance obligations under the reinsurance agreement. A portion of the capital raised may be withheld from the collateral account to fund the sidecar reinsurer's operating expenses including interest expense, if applicable. Premium income from the reinsurance contract can also be deposited in the collateral account to reduce the capital required from investors and increase the structure's leverage.

When the cedant is a US-domiciled insurer or reinsurer, the collateral is typically held in a trust that complies with the credit for reinsurance requirements of the ceding company's state of domicile. As a technical matter, this is not necessary because statutory reserves are typically not required to support catastrophe exposures prior to catastrophe events. Cedants, however, generally prefer that the structure complies with credit for reinsurance rules at the outset so that, upon a cat event and the establishment of ceded reserves, there is no delay or difficulty in obtaining credit for reinsurance.

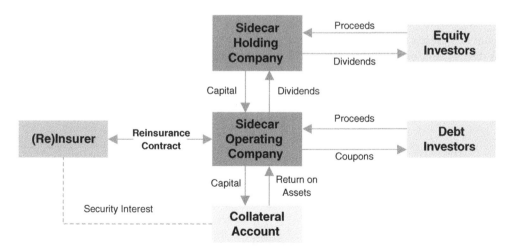

Figure 11.1   Sidecar structure
Source: Morgan Stanley

A credit rating on the sidecar entity is also not required to allow the cedant to receive capital credit from rating agencies. When calculating capital credit, rating agencies take into account the immediate availability of funds and any possible competing interest in those funds. Because most of the assets of the sidecar are held in a trust account that complies with credit for reinsurance rules (and therefore the cedant is the sole beneficiary with a claim on the trust assets that is senior to the sidecar's creditors), rating agencies have been comfortable allowing full reinsurance capital credit to the cedant up to the amount of those assets. Despite the fact that investors do not have an obligation to contribute more capital once the collateral account balance has been drawn down to zero, the dedicated source of capital is enough to secure credit.

Assuming the sidecar is structured as a limited life vehicle, and assuming there are no events that trigger coverage by the sidecar during the exposure period, the assets in the collateral account are distributed back to the investors at the expiration of the exposure period and the sidecar and its holding company may then be dissolved. However, if there is an event that triggers coverage during the exposure period, the assets in the sidecar's trust accounts are used to pay the claims. Because claims and reserves develop over time, there is typically a pre-agreed window after the exposure period during which reserves may be established (these reserves may be known as loss reserves or reserves for expectations of claims that have not yet been reported). At the end of that window, the sidecar either commutes the reinsurance agreement with the cedant, or goes into runoff until all claims are settled. In a commutation, sidecar assets in excess of the reserves are distributed back to investors and loss reserves are paid to the cedant. In a runoff, only assets in excess of reserves (often with some additional hold-back to cover the risk of adverse development) are distributed back to investors, and the sidecar remains in operation until all claims are paid. There are arguments for and against either approach to sidecar wind-up.

While sidecars generally share these characteristics, there are two fundamental types of sidecars – those that directly write reinsurance to the market, and those that provide capacity to the sponsoring company.

11.2.2 Market-facing sidecar

Figure 11.2 depicts a 'market-facing sidecar' which is a special purpose reinsurer that assumes risk directly from one or more cedants. The sidecar does not reinsure the sponsoring reinsurer.

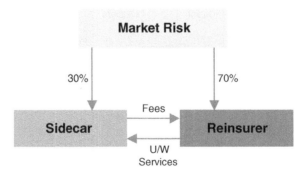

Figure 11.2   Market-facing sidecar
Source: Morgan Stanley

Table 11.1 Increasing capacity using a market-facing sidecar

	Pre-sidecar	Post-sidecar total	Reinsurer share (70%)	Sidecar share (30%)
Contract limit	$100 million	$140 million	$98 million	$42 million

Rather, the sidecar and the sponsoring reinsurer enter into separate reinsurance agreements with underlying ceding companies (either documented separately or together in a single agreement that makes clear that their liability is several and not joint). The sidecar contracts with (and is reliant on) the sponsoring reinsurer for underwriting and servicing of the ceded risks, and the arrangement typically includes a description of qualifying underwriting criteria or line of business. In some versions, in order to align interests between the sidecar and the sponsoring reinsurer and avoid adverse selection, the arrangement obligates the reinsurer, upon assuming any risk meeting the pre-agreed underwriting criteria or line of business requirement, to cede the pre-agreed portion of such risk to the sidecar. In sidecars where a predefined portfolio is ceded at or shortly after inception, such an arrangement is not necessary and the sponsoring reinsurer serves more of a validation and servicing role than a 'sponsorship' role.

Although the cedant faces two separate balance sheets, the structure still allows the reinsurer to increase the amount of capacity it offers. Suppose, for example (see Figure 11.2), the sidecar and the sponsoring reinsurer agree to split qualifying risks 30% to the sidecar and 70% to the sponsor. As a result of using the sidecar's capital capacity alongside its own, the reinsurer is now able to provide total capacity of more than 140% of its pre-sidecar ability (Table 11.1).

The reinsurer provides all of the administration, claim-servicing and underwriting services for the sidecar entity. In return, the reinsurer is paid a fee to cover its costs and is also paid a profit commission based on returns to investors in the sidecar. As a result, the reinsurer is able to generate additional income (assuming profitable underwriting) without using more of its own capital than in previous years.

As noted, in this version of a sidecar structure, the liability of the sponsoring reinsurer and sidecar are several and not joint. The sponsoring reinsurer does not backstop or guarantee the sidecar and has no additional liability in the event the sidecar's capital is exhausted by paying claims.

11.2.3 Non-market-facing sidecar

Figure 11.3 depicts the more common 'non-market-facing sidecar' approach, under which the sidecar assumes risk from a sponsoring insurer or reinsurer in a reinsurance or retrocession agreement. The sponsoring company agrees to cede a predefined portion of its risk to the sidecar, either on a quota share or excess of loss basis. Quota share reinsurance has been more common, but excess of loss is possible, with additional structuring considerations.

As with the market-facing structure, the sidecar typically has no employees or staff; it relies exclusively on the underwriting services provided by the sponsoring company, which is paid a fee to cover expenses, plus a profit commission. Though structured slightly differently, this type of sidecar increases the sponsoring company's capacity by the same amount as the market-facing sidecar. For example, assuming a 30% quota share agreement from the insurer to the sidecar, the sponsoring company can write up to 140% of its previous volume (Table 11.2).

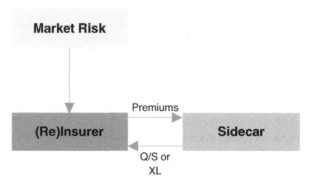

Figure 11.3 Non-market-facing sidecar
Source: Morgan Stanley

11.2.4 Capitalizing sidecars

Typically, insurance companies have the benefit of diversification of risk across business lines and geographies and hold permanent capital equal to only a portion of their total risk exposure. Because sidecars are designed to take targeted exposure to a particular opportunity (e.g., US wind risk during the 2006 season), they generally do not benefit from as much diversification, and are generally collateralized to the full limits written or to a probable maximum loss level.

Figure 11.4 illustrates some capitalization alternatives for sidecars. Total limits written by the sidecar are $1 billion in this simplified example. The modeled risk profile of the sidecar's exposure is such that the 1-in-1000 year risk (0.1% annual probability of exceedance) is $600 million. Given that premiums ($150 million) are used to generate returns on capital, it is likely to be uneconomic to hold capital equal to the total limit ($1 billion) in this case. By holding capital only up to the 1-in-1000 year return period, premium income generates a higher return on capital (25% instead of 15%).

However, in extreme tail scenarios (less likely than 0.1% annually), this could result in a shortfall of capital in the sidecar. Typically this is addressed by having the ceding insurer retain this 'tail risk.' In this example, the sponsoring insurer would assume the risk of the $400 million losses in excess of the $600 million capital held by the sidecar, usually for a small premium.

In most rating agency frameworks, insurers are not required to hold capital to support risks that occur with a modeled annual frequency less than 0.4% (1-in-250 years). Therefore, for the insurer to hold risk above 1-in-1000 years in this case should not cause the insurer any additional capital strain. Typically, the insurer also receives some compensation for retaining this remote risk.

Table 11.2 Increasing capacity using a non-market-facing sidecar

	Pre-sidecar	Post-sidecar total	Remains with (re)insurer (70%)	Ceded to sidecar (30%)
Contract limit	$100 million	$140 million	$98 million	$42 million

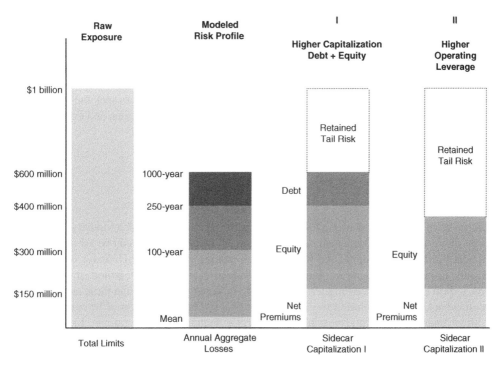

Figure 11.4   Illustrative sidecar capitalization alternatives
Source: Morgan Stanley

11.2.5   How sidecars and catastrophe bonds are different

Because of their common application in the property catastrophe reinsurance markets, sidecars and cat bonds are occasionally confused. While they can both accept property cat risk, the structure and risk content are slightly different. In general, sidecars allow investors to participate in the 'equity-like' risk of specific insurance exposures, with modeled annual attachment probabilities as low as ground-up (first dollar) or 1-in-10 years, for example. A logical extension of the above discussion about capitalization levels is that it can be expensive to hold equity capital behind low-risk layers of exposure (e.g., less frequent than 1-in-250 years). To address this economic challenge, sidecars sometimes look to add leverage by raising debt to support these low-probability risks. It is in these layers that sidecar debt can closely resemble cat bonds. Similar to cat bonds, these risk layers within sidecars do not expect to suffer losses except due to catastrophic events, and carry lower returns than the equity layers as a result. The critical difference between leverage within a sidecar and an indemnity cat bond is that the debt tranches in a sidecar provide leverage to the sidecar's equity investors, while cat bonds provide leverage to the equity investors of the sponsoring insurer (thus complementing the sponsor's traditional reinsurance).

While sidecar issuance tailed off in 2007, catastrophe bond issuance surged. This can be attributed to the different risk profiles and return potential of the two structures relative to the markets they bridge. In a softening reinsurance market, insurers saw little need to access additional capital to support underwriting activity. Given falling premium rates, the underwritten business was unable to generate the 'equity-like' returns on sidecar capital required by investors. At the same time, insurers remained compelled to purchase reinsurance for cat risk. Cat bond spreads softened enough to remain cost effective, though not by as much as the traditional reinsurance market. From an investor point of view, the risk spreads on most capital market products were at all-time lows, leading investors to seek the attractive risk/reward profile of cat bonds. Thus, cat bond activity was able to continue and even grow.

11.3   THE APPEAL OF SIDECARS

11.3.1   From a cedant/sponsor perspective

In the wake of an event (or events) that drain capital from the insurance industry, the first priority of an insurer is to replenish its capital base. As mentioned, this can be accomplished over time by raising premiums and retaining the resulting net income. However, it is often necessary to build surplus more quickly. A traditional capital raise (common or preferred equity, hybrid capital or even long-term debt) could be considered, although these approaches have drawbacks such as dilution to existing shareholders, or the addition of leverage which can affect financial ratios and possibly the insurer's financial strength ratings. In addition, these alternatives are long term (or, in the case of equity, permanent) additions to the insurer's capital base which require commensurate additions to earnings to generate a return on equity consistent with pre-event capitalization levels.

Because sidecar investors contribute capital to a special purpose reinsurer (and not to the sponsoring insurer directly), the capital is not dilutive to the sponsor's shareholders, does not impact the sponsor's leverage ratios and does not affect the sponsor's balance sheet. Also, because sidecar capital is temporary, the sponsor does not have the burden of increasing market share across soft market conditions in order to maintain targeted returns on equity.

Another important benefit of sidecars is fee income for the insurer/sponsor. Investors are dependent on the insurer to source profitable risk and cede it to the sidecar. In return for access to that profitable business and underwriting expertise, investors are willing to share their returns with the insurer in the form of a profit commission. This profit commission comes at virtually no cost to the insurer because the costs associated with underwriting additional business and servicing additional claims are also borne by sidecar investors. Thus, without a direct cost to the insurer, the income from the sidecar generates outsized returns on equity.

Sidecars also confer a relationship benefit to the sponsoring insurer. Using sidecar capacity, the insurer is able to offer greater limits to its clients in a time when capacity from competitors is likely to be constrained. This is an important relationship point for many insurers and reinsurers who have valuable clients they do not wish to turn down.

There can be execution and timing risk to the cedant in sidecar transactions in the event the cedant writes additional business before sidecar capital is fully raised. Additionally, there could be transaction reputation risk in the event sidecar capital is raised but sufficient additional business cannot be written to generate the anticipated returns. These concerns can usually be addressed through thoughtful and careful structuring, however. Perhaps the most significant consideration for sidecar sponsors is the investment of time and corporate resources during the structuring and operational phases of the transaction.

11.3.2   From an investor perspective

Investors have several reasons to value sidecar investments. Whether they put more value on the potential for high risk-adjusted returns or the uncorrelated nature of insurance investments, the rare combination of high returns in an uncorrelated asset is very attractive.

Sidecars offer investors a specific, targeted investment directed at a single insurance exposure over a limited time period. By isolating the pure insurance risk, a sidecar investment eliminates 'noise' associated with an equity investment in an insurance company such as influence from the insurer's other business lines or broad equity market movements. A sidecar is also established to provide reinsurance without creating drag associated with overhead operating expenses. Without employees or infrastructure, the sidecar simply contracts out for limited management, auditing, legal and underwriting services, and does so at minimal cost to cover only the specific services it needs.

Unlike an investment in a startup insurance company, a sidecar gives investors temporary exposure to a particular risk. An investment in a startup insurer is a longer term commitment to insurance risk that some investors may not be willing to assume. Investors who support a new franchise take longer term risk to insurance markets, including underwriting results after the hard market begins to soften. Many investors prefer to define a specific risk period and therefore impose an 'exit date' for their capital. To appeal to some investors' desire to capture a hard market lasting for several years, some sidecars have included features to give investors the 'right of first refusal' on continuing the sidecar's life for another year (or season). In this case, investors retain the right to evaluate market conditions in the future and they may choose to leave their investment intact and allow the sidecar to continue writing business. This option, taken to its limit, would involve turning the sidecar into a 'going concern' after its originally contemplated limited life. Switching to a permanent structure would require significant changes to the sidecar such as installation of a dedicated management team with underwriting capabilities, additional capital and a rating, among other things. Essentially, the sidecar would become a startup reinsurance company and would likely break formal ties to the original sponsoring insurer. While this is possible, it is not often done.

Because most sidecars are structured to accept multiple risks across many geographic regions, a drawback of a sidecar investment (particularly for dedicated ILS investors) is that such an investment could consume risk limits for multiple peak perils (similar to a multi-peril ILS). Another concern, also voiced principally by dedicated ILS investors with multiple access points to insurance risk, is that ceding commissions and profit commissions in sidecars can reduce returns. These investors are able to access similar risk via ILS, ILWs and transformed or collateralized reinsurance and may not have to bear the cost of these commissions. As a result, sidecars have typically attracted capital outside of the dedicated ILS investor universe, such as private equity firms or multi-strategy hedge funds.

11.4   STRUCTURING CONSIDERATIONS

Structuring sidecars requires careful consideration of many issues, including risk content and profile, accounting, tax, regulatory impact, ratings impact, investor appetite and degree of complexity. This complexity can have the negative consequence of deterring cedants or investors from participating. As these considerations are largely situation-specific, there is little benefit to describing all the permutations here. However, there are broad structural elements which may merit brief treatment.

Efficient capital usage is the hallmark of sidecar transactions. Investors make a targeted investment and cedants use the capital for a targeted opportunity. Therefore, many sidecars use 'just-in-time' capital calls to fund the targeted exposure. In the event the cedant has an existing book of business it wishes to cede to a sidecar (in order to release capital supporting that business, for example), investor capital can be used all at once upon closing of the transaction and signing of the reinsurance agreement. However, many sidecars are established on the premise of future underwriting profits due to a hard market. Sidecars that are established to participate in future business do not have risk to capitalize on the closing date. Those sidecars will assume business, and thus require capital, over time (typically a defined underwriting period). These sidecars often feature periodic capital calls from investors to fund capital requirements to support actual business written.

One of the basic structural questions is whether to use a quota share reinsurance agreement or excess of loss. Quota share is inherently easier to define and manage, as it simply passes a pro rata share of the premium and loss on each policy to the sidecar.

Excess of loss reinsurance, however, presents some challenges. In an excess of loss arrangement, the sidecar only accepts remote risk from each policy, with coverage attach ing above a pre-agreed loss amount. The structuring challenge is in pricing, auditing and claims settlements. For assuming a portion of the risk, the sidecar must receive a portion of the premium on the entire policy, but without dedicated underwriting expertise, it has no ability to determine that price itself. Therefore, in some cases, a third party validator and 'watchdog' may be retained to verify or handle these situations. This validator will also likely need to demonstrate some alignment with investors, typically achieved through an investment in the sidecar. On that basis, investors have developed a comfort level with the division of premiums and risk on excess of loss policies.

Leverage is important to many equity investors. Structuring leverage, however, can be challenging, even before considering the price and market conditions for structured debt products. As previously mentioned, one of the crucial elements of structuring a sidecar to accept future business is ramp-up risk – the risk that actual business develops differently than originally anticipated (and modeled). Many debt investors rely on rating agencies to evaluate the modeled risk in their debt investment. Rating agencies, however, are mindful of ramp-up risk, and are hesitant to provide ratings indications before the entire book of business has been written and/or ceded to the sidecar.

11.5   THE OUTLOOK FOR SIDECARS

While 2007 and 2008 have seen limited sidecar activity (as a result of a lack of hard market opportunities), most market participants (insurers and investors alike) anticipate a return of sidecars when capital constraints return to the insurance markets. Both investors and insurers alike anticipate opportunistically using capital to generate high risk-adjusted returns.

As previously mentioned, short-tail lines of business (such as property) tend to lend them-selves best to the limited life of sidecars because investors' investment horizons are typically only a few years long. Commutation of short-tail property claims (i.e., the process of crys-tallizing the post-event loss tail for the sidecar based on an estimation analysis, rather than through actual loss experience) tends to be straightforward in comparison to casualty expo-sures with longer claims tails. There is ongoing discussion about the application of sidecar technology, and therefore sidecar capital, to other lines of business. Commutation will likely be a focal point of any such transactions, and it may take some time for the market to agree on acceptable commutation methodologies. We expect sidecars to be successfully applied to insurance risk other than property catastrophe in the near future as investors and insurers become more comfortable and familiar with the technology.

Without a commutation mechanism, sidecars covering longer tail lines would need to be supported by a more liquid secondary market for their equity and debt capital, allowing investors to sell their holdings at the end of their investment horizon. Such liquidity is unlikely to develop in the near term because of the specialized knowledge needed to evaluate insurance risk and the unique structure of each sidecar.

Another area of development for sidecars is the assumption of unmodeled perils. To date, most non-life capital markets activity has been centered around property catastrophe risk. There have been some securitizations of motor insurance policies in Europe as well as some transactions which have transferred risks such as industrial accident and event cancellation. In order to transfer these risks, which do not benefit from a foundation of scientific research or a history of reliable data on which to build widely accepted loss estimation models, investors will need to rely on due diligence, their own modeling and a strong alignment of interest with the cedant and sponsor.

11.6 CONCLUSION

Sidecars are an efficient way to bring timely capital to capacity constrained insurance markets. They increase capital for insurers and reinsurers who may otherwise be constrained due to recent losses and they have the potential to generate uncorrelated, high risk-adjusted returns for capital market investors. The future of sidecars, while promising, is dependent on their flexibility to address conditions in relevant insurance markets. Longer tail casualty lines may benefit from sidecar technology, but the basic property catastrophe sidecar structure will need to be modified to handle this longer term risk and possible commutation or secondary market liquidity. We continue to evaluate possible applications for sidecar technology given opportunities in insurance markets and look for future growth in the size, scope and term of sidecar transactions.

12

Case Study: A Cat Bond Transaction by SCOR (Atlas)

Emmanuel Durousseau[a]

12.1 INTRODUCTION: SCOR'S RECENT HISTORY

From its foundation in 1970 to its current leading position, SCOR has had a long and rich history including a very distressed situation in 2001–2002.

Further to the arrival of SCOR's current CEO, Denis Kessler, at the end of 2002, it was clear that after the initial reshaping of SCOR ('Back on Track', 2002), and its recovery phase ('Moving Forward', 2004), the time would come to bring SCOR to the next level. SCOR started this transformation in 2006 with the acquisition of REVIOS, a German life reinsurance company. With the acquisition of Converium, which was finalized in early August 2007, just six months after its initial announcement, SCOR set out new objectives in the strategic 'Dynamic Lift' plan, the second version of which was adjusted for the final merger. This second strategic acquisition in two years resulted in a balancing effect with regard to the Group's non-life and life activities and laid the foundations for the new Group.

The resulting new Group is now highly diversified and ranks as the fifth largest reinsurer in the world. The Atlas solutions described below are part of a much larger and deeper ERM strategy, which has been totally (re)developed under the lead of Jean-Luc Besson, SCOR's Group CRO. We invite you to log on to SCOR's website (www.scor.com) for further information about the Group.

12.2 ATLAS III AND IV: BACKGROUND

On the ILS side, SCOR has been an early user of such solutions. Atlas I was launched in 2000 as a multi-class indemnity cat bond. Atlas II was issued in 2002 and the ILS strategy was paused thereafter.

Many internal and external factors drove SCOR to return to this market:

- the recovery phase ('Moving Forward', 2004) and the further acquisition of Converium in 2007 resulted in bringing more risks onto SCOR's growing balance sheet;
- in parallel, the rating agencies hardened the rules used to calculate the cat-driven capital charge;

---

[a]SCOR Group Risk Management, Immeuble SCOR

The Handbook of Insurance-Linked Securities   Edited by P. Barrieu and L. Albertini
© 2009 John Wiley & Sons, Ltd

- it was further anticipated that Solvency II would force some of our clients to buy more cat protection (and some were clearly underprotected) that could later result in higher exposures for SCOR;
- in 2005, the US hurricanes Katrina, Rita and Wilma (KRW) caused many disruptions within the retrocession market that resulted in some illiquidity, exclusions, etc.;
- finally, these events revealed the fragility of some retrocessionnaires and raised concerns about potential issues of counterparty exposure.

At the time of Atlas III (end of 2006), SCOR was mainly a worldwide (excluding US) reinsurance company with two peak exposures: Europe Wind and Japan Earthquake. These two peaks are not numerous enough to bring any statistical leverage or diversification and are either expensive to keep net (i.e. in SCOR's balance sheet without retrocession) or not so cheap to hedge.

As explained above, in the aftermath of KRW, the retrocession markets shrank, became more volatile and rather more fragile. In addition, the returns available in the Florida reinsurance and retrocession markets were so high that they diverted a significant amount of traditional and ILS capacity into this zone. In this context, SCOR took the decision to issue Atlas III, a cat bond that would cover second event Europe Wind or Japan EQ over a three-year period. In addition, to provide some diversification away from the traditional retrocession market, Atlas III allowed SCOR to work with an emerging new retrocession market that was selling one-shot, single collateralized limit capacity. This collateralized capacity would complement Atlas III by providing first event cover.

In parallel, to make the decision to issue a new cat bond, SCOR worked on the characteristics of this new issuance. The main parameters (discussed in Section 12.3) to decide on were:

- type: indemnity, modelled loss, parametric;
- duration, limit, currency;
- localization of the SPV;
- service partners;
- accounting structure and issues: reinsurance, derivative, consolidation, etc.;
- event definition.

As detailed above, a few months after Atlas III was issued, SCOR made an offer to buy Converium. Although friendly in its intention, SCOR's move resulted in some resistance from Converium that ultimately delayed the merger by approximately three months. It was on 8th August 2007, a few weeks away from the Monte Carlo Rendez-Vous (the industry convention), that SCOR became the official owner of Converium. Since, during this additional delay, it was practically impossible to exchange any meaningful information between the two companies, SCOR had only limited ideas regarding Converium's cat exposures.

In actuality, further to its downgrading, Converium lost some business and found itself with excess capital. This excess capital was used to (a) write US cat business on an opportunistic and net basis, i.e. without any retrocessions, and (b) purchase a somewhat reduced retrocession programme for its worldwide (excluding US) exposures. This programme was purchased in USD currency.

Apart from the US exposures which were very limited for SCOR, our immediate concerns went to Europe, where SCOR's own exposures were large and where Converium's hedge was shrinking every day due to the falling US$ (the European exposures were sold in € and hedged out in a US$ denominated retrocession programme).

On top of these concerns, SCOR and Converium used different cat modelling software with significant discrepancies in PMLs and their associated return period.

The Risks Committee and the Board rapidly decided to (a) reduce the US and Caribbean exposures at the next renewal, (b) hedge the European Wind and Japanese Earthquake as soon as it became possible. SCOR decided to continue its diversification strategy and elected to issue another cat bond. Atlas IV, a first-event cover, was issued at the end of November 2007, just before the peak period of European Wind. In order to speed the processes up, it was further decided that (a) we would 'copy and paste' the main structures of Atlas III and (b) we would work with the same service providers. Finally, the original idea to set up a shelf turned out to be incompatible with SCOR's timing, since it would have added another month to the transaction. Figures 12.1 and 12.2 show the Atlas IV transaction timeline and structure respectively.

12.3   ATLAS: MAIN CHARACTERISTICS

- Both Atlases cover our peak exposures: Europe Wind and Japan Earthquake.
- Atlas III offers a €120 million limit while Atlas IV offers €160 million limit. These limits were decided according to the Group's needs (cat capital charge) and offer an overall good fit with our traditional structure. In detail, Atlas IV is actually a layer of 80% of €200m xs €450m and Atlas III is a layer of 60% of €200m xs €450m. The reason for such a structure is detailed below.
- Atlas IV is a first event cover over three years while Atlas III covers second and subsequent events over three years.

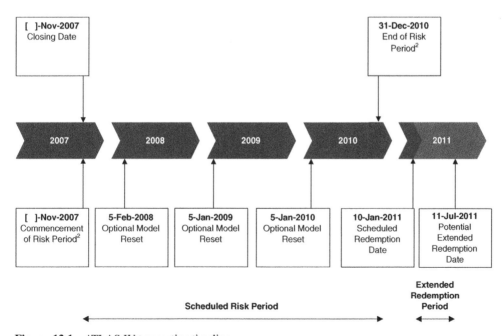

Figure 12.1   ATLAS IV transaction timeline

Source: SCOR

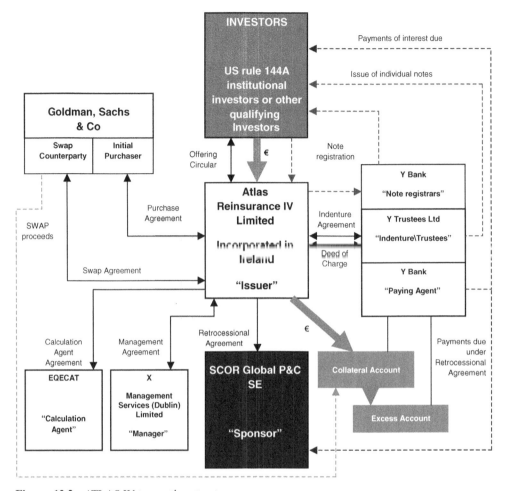

Figure 12.2   ATLAS IV transaction structure
Source: SCOR

- Both are modelled loss portfolios (EQE) and have annual resets, with the option to cancel (call option). As far as the type of cat bond was concerned, three choices were possible: a parametric, a modelled loss or an indemnity cover.
  - A parametric bond was quickly ruled out since it would have meant high(er) basis risk.
  - Indemnity was a real option for SCOR since it would have reduced our basis risk. However, SCOR felt that this structure raised other issues such as potential legal risks. In addition, SCOR would have had to keep a share of its hedged portfolio. This co-insurance along with the risks that were not possible to protect under such a structure, would have resulted in creating another basis risk. Finally, especially for Atlas IV, SCOR did not feel totally comfortable with the required disclosure; the January 2008 renewals were the first renewal of the combined SCOR and Converium portfolios and the disclosure of this renewal which would have been introduced with the January 2008 Atlas Reset, would have resulted in potentially more pressure on SCOR than the Group was ready to assume.
  - SCOR elected to use the modelled loss structure.

- There is a step-up coupon for Atlas III. This was introduced to compensate potential investors with some mark-to-market loss when a first event occurs. When a first event occurs, the probability that Atlas III (second and subsequent events) could suffer a loss increases and the value of the cat bond decreases. In order to overcome this issue and facilitate secondary trading, a step-up coupon was introduced. In reinsurance terms, it is the same as having a second event cover with a lower up-front premium and a second instalment due when a first event occurs. Please see Figure 12.3 for the modelled calculation in Atlas III.
- Since the main currency of exposures to hedge was €, it was decided to issue both Atlas III and IV in €. All the non-€ exposures (mainly Japanese ¥) were translated into € using significantly conservative values. The idea was not to add currency risk to other risks already embedded within such a transaction. In addition, at the time of Atlas III and IV (2007), it was believed that the investors' universe was smaller for Euro-denominated bonds than $ bonds. The additional complexity and cost of currency conversion that would have allowed us to issue in $ and be hedged in € led SCOR to finally issue in €.
- The main place used for cat bond SPV administration is the Cayman Islands. However, as a French-European company, the fiscal constraints did not leave much room as to where the SPV could be located, and Ireland rapidly became the only viable alternative. The main advantages of the Cayman Islands over Ireland are costs, speed of execution and somewhat more flexibility (a shelf, for example, can be structured as reinsurance and derivatives in the Cayman Islands while two separate SPVs would be needed in Ireland).
- Other characteristics such as event definition and extension periods are outlined in the appendix at the end of this chapter.

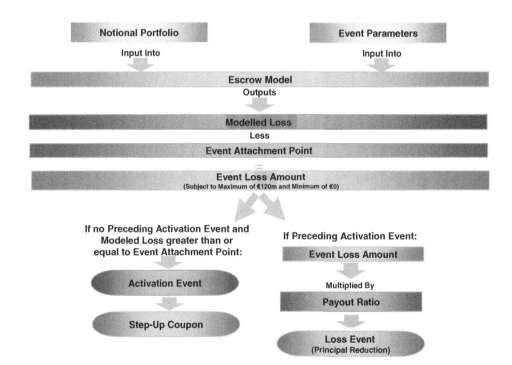

Figure 12.3 ATLAS III modelled loss calculation

Source: SCOR

12.4 BASIS RISK

The aim of the retrocession is to hedge the Group and not to add other risks. It is also important that these transactions provide the highest possible relief in terms of cat capital charge.

Basis risk comes from three main sources: non-modelled contracts; poorly modelled contracts and model inadequacy. Basis risk mitigation at SCOR is achieved via four different and complementary elements:

- reset;
- significant gross up in the modelled portfolio;
- explicit overlap;
- synthetic retrocession cover, described below, in Atlas III and IV.

12.4.1 Reset

Each of the Atlas bonds has an option to perform annual reset. This option was exercised for both Atlas III and Atlas IV in January 2008 in order to ensure that the modelled portfolio perfectly matched SCOR's actual exposures. The idea here is that via the annual reset, the annualized probability of attachment and annualized expected loss are kept constant.

Although issued at the end of November 2007, we included an option to reset Atlas IV at the beginning of 2008. January 2008 was the first renewal of the combined SCOR and Converium book of business and SCOR wanted to make sure that Atlas IV would best reflect the new combined renewed portfolio.

Atlas III reset (based on the combined SCOR and Converium portfolio) went as planned. When originally issued, Atlas III was basically a layer of 100% of €120m xs €250m. After the reset, the layer became 60% of €200m xs €450m. This second event layer is further completed by some traditional structures.

12.4.2 Gross up

The gross up approach is slightly different for Atlas III (second event) and Atlas IV (first event) where, in addition to the portfolio gross up, all the contracts with aggregate deductible have been modelled without aggregate deductible in Atlas III. By doing this, we force these contracts to respond as if they were first loss, although in reality this will not be the case for all of them. This represents an additional gross up of 15% for our French portfolio.

For Europe Wind (see Figure 12.4), a gross up factor of 12% has been applied to take into account non-modelled (per risk and motor damage) and poorly modelled contracts. For the same reasons, a gross up factor of 15% has been applied for Japan Earthquake. Finally, some exposures have been directly grossed up to compensate for some potentially weak damage functions.

12.4.3 Overlap

In addition to the above-mentioned gross up, SCOR included some explicit overlap between its traditional market and ILS solutions. Although modest in size, this overlap cumulates with the synthetic covers described below. One of the main reasons to issue only 80% of €200m

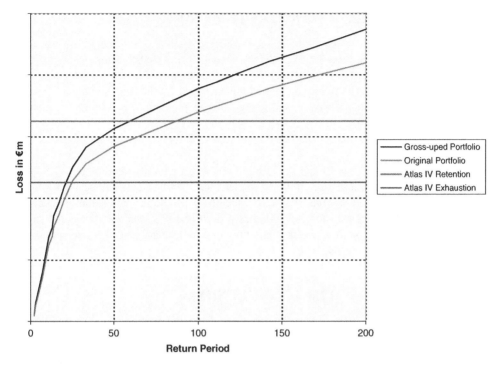

Figure 12.4   Graphical illustration (Europe Wind)
Source: SCOR

xs €450m for Atlas IV was SCOR's willingness to have this explicit overlap where more than the remaining 20% of €200m xs €450m would be purchased from the traditional market. In addition, the reinstatement cover included with this traditional placement considerably reduced the 40% gap left with Atlas III (being 60% of €200m xs €450m – second and subsequent events).

12.4.4   Synthetic covers

For model inadequacy, SCOR has put in place some synthetic retrocession covers that are either directly based on single insurer losses or on a basket of underlying reinsurance covers. The design and selection of such covers are based on nonlinear correlation and an iterative deal replacement optimization process.

The idea here is to be long a cover that is both highly correlated with industry loss and SCOR's own losses. Should the modelled loss (as escrowed in the Atlas transactions) be far from the reality, these synthetic covers, as a basket of actual reinsurance covers, will pick up the model mismatch.

More generally, these synthetic covers were purchased not only to hedge some of the basis risk, as explained above, but also to finance the retrocession reinstatement premium or to lower SCOR's retention for certain types of loss scenarios.

12.5   TOTAL RETURN SWAP

A total return swap (TRS) is a bilateral financial transaction where the counterparties swap the total return of a single asset or basket of assets in exchange for periodic cash flows, typically a floating rate such as LIBOR or EURIBOR +/− a basis point spread and a guarantee against any capital losses. A TRS is similar to a plain vanilla swap except the deal is structured such that the total return (cash flows plus capital appreciation/depreciation) is exchanged, rather than just the cash flows.

A key feature of a TRS is that the parties do not transfer actual ownership of the assets, as occurs in a repo transaction.

Although at the time of Atlas III and IV, TRS did not attract a lot of attention, the TRS is a key element within such a transaction. It is here to guarantee that the assets will be at par when they need to be liquidated to pay the SPV a loss. Ideally, it should provide isolation against market turbulence. The recent history of 2008 has proved that this was not always the case and the market is working on finding a new structure that will satisfy investors and sponsors in terms of flexibility and security.

12.6   CONCLUSION

Atlas transactions provide some diversification away from the traditional markets. Today (2008), approximately one-third of the overall cat capacity purchased by SCOR comes from capital markets or is in a collateralized form.

As a buyer (sponsor), one of the secondary challenges in these transactions is to get the highest possible credit in the capital charge calculations. Basis risks, legal risks and others are difficult to measure or quantify precisely. To achieve our goals in terms of getting this highest credit (in the cat capital charge) from the rating agencies, SCOR has (a) associated with the agencies very early on in the process and (b) put in place the strategies described in Section 12.4.

Atlas are also multi-year covers and provide the double advantages of some budgeting visibility and lower capital charges associated with the risk of not being able to renew the retrocession while still carrying run-off exposures in our balance sheet. Another (conditional) advantage is related to the speed of settlement which should, for modelled loss transactions, generate a temporarily positive cash flow for the Group, enabling SCOR not to sell assets to pay for our clients' losses.

A modelled loss transaction where the reference portfolio reflects the actual underlying portfolio also provides a more objective risk assessment. One of the characteristics of SCOR's portfolio is that within Europe, it is relatively over-exposed in France (our home market). Some quick (and dirty) approaches based on our average European market share cannot properly track down this characteristic and this drives some pricing inadequacy in the retrocession market. As an illustration of the above, Lothar would be a significantly larger loss than the 90A storms for SCOR while being the exact opposite in terms of the Euro amount for the industry as a whole.

One last word regarding modelling: the selection of a single agent (EQECAT for Atlas) translates into some loss of flexibility. Internally, our European exposures are benchmarked against multiple models that are weighted according to the strengths or weaknesses of each. Damage functions can be corrected via inflated or deflated sums insured but it is impossible to change correlations between countries or loss frequencies.

What will be left following the convergence after the 2007–2008 financial crisis remains to be seen. What was advertised as a potentially 'unlimited' market has proven to be temporarily very limited. The non-correlation of cat bonds with financial markets is also under question with the current TRS structures. However, all these issues can be solved with increased transparency, proper isolation from (financial) systemic risks and diversification of TRS providers.

The cohabitation between the traditional market and insurance-linked securities should remain inevitable and is even desirable. When mutualization, diversification or leverage on risks is no longer possible or efficient, this form of 'spot capital' is a good complement to the current insurance/reinsurance structure of the capital. SCOR is currently working on many ILS projects and will continue to contribute to the development of this maturing and exciting market.

APPENDIX A

A.1 Definition of events

Definition of a storm with Europe peak gust wind speeds:

- Higher than 25 metres/second at a minimum of four Europe qualified recording stations within the same hour and a maximum distance of 600 kilometres between any two stations.
- Reported by any of the Europe qualified windstorm reporting agencies.
- Occurring within the boundaries of Europe Windstorm covered territory.
- Occurring during the risk period.
- Storms will be considered to be separate storms if they are given different names by the Institute of Meteorology, University of Berlin, or any other organization performing such a naming role.

Defined as an earthquake:

- Reported by the Japan Earthquake Reporting Agency.
- Occurring during the risk period.
- An earthquake shall not be a Japan Earthquake event if a nuclear explosion reported by a Japanese government agency has occurred:
  ○ within one hour prior to the Japan Earthquake occurrence time; and
  ○ within a distance of ten kilometres from the epicentre of such earthquake to the location of such nuclear explosion.
- If multiple Japan Earthquake events occur within a specific 30-day period and within a radius of 200 kilometres of the Japan Earthquake event starting such 30-day period, the Japan Earthquake event shall be the Japan Earthquake event within such radius with the highest resulting Japan Earthquake modelled loss.

Collectively, the modelled portfolio of property reinsurance business covers:

- Underlying insurance risks in the Europe Windstorm covered territory against the risk of modelled loss arising from Europe Windstorm events; and
- Underlying insurance risks in the Japan Earthquake covered territory against the risk of modelled loss arising from Japan Earthquake events.

A.2   Extension events

Extension event I occurs if the ceding reinsurer elects to require the issuer to extend the maturity of the notes, and an event has occurred in the three-month period prior to the scheduled redemption date. The spread associated with an extension event I is 10bps.

Extension event II occurs if the ceding reinsurer elects to require the issuer to extend the maturity of the notes and the requirements of extension event I have not been met. The spread associated with an extension event II is 250bps.

13

Case Study: Swiss Re's New Natural Catastrophe Protection Program (Vega)

Jay Green[a] and Jean-Louis Monnier[a]

In June 2008, Swiss Re sponsored the first issuance under Vega Capital Ltd. (Vega), an innovative insurance-linked securities program providing multi-peril natural catastrophe protection. The first issuance of Vega, Series 2008-I, introduces a new risk transfer structure for Swiss Re that enhances the efficiency of natural catastrophe protection transferred to the capital markets. Series 2008-I marks an evolution of Swiss Re's insurance-linked securities (ILS) strategy, using new credit enhancement features to reach a broad base of investors for protecting earnings volatility associated with riskier layers of exposure.

As a note program, Vega provides Swiss Re with a flexible platform to access the capital markets on an ongoing basis and to modify the risk transfer structure as Swiss Re's risk management needs evolve. Distribution of notes under the Vega program is subject to US securities laws and regulations and more specifically pursuant to Rule 144A and sold only to investors who are Qualified Institutional Buyers and Qualified Purchasers for US Persons that are residents of, and purchasing and holding in, a Permitted US Jurisdiction or a Permitted Non-US Jurisdiction, as defined in the respective offering materials.

Series 2008-I expands the level and efficiency of coverage available to Swiss Re in the capital markets by using risk pooling and tranching techniques to optimise risk transfer for multiple natural catastrophe risks. Series 2008-I consists of $150 million in four classes of floating-rate notes that are tranched according to seniority of repayment and level of risk exposure. The Series 2008-I notes are rated by Standard & Poor's and Moody's Investors Service.

The 2008-I issuance structure is described in Table 13.1.

13.1 A POSITIVE EVOLUTION OF SWISS RE'S ILS STRATEGY

As a leading and highly diversified global reinsurer, Swiss Re has been a leader in the development and innovation of the ILS market as a means of efficiently managing its exposure to peak natural catastrophe risks. Swiss Re was the first sponsor to utilise a note program to transfer multiple perils to the capital markets in 2002 with the Pioneer program. Since then, Swiss Re's note program strategy for transferring natural catastrophe risk has continuously

---

[a]Swiss Re Financial Products Corporation

Any opinion expressed in this work is the opinion of the author and is not to be taken to represent the opinion of the corporation by which the author is employed.

Table 13.1   2008-I issuance structure

	Class A	Class B	Class C	Class D
Securities sold (millions)	$21.0	$22.5	$63.9	$42.6
Risk period	three years	three years	three years	three years
Rating (S&P/Moody's)	A−/A3	BBB/Baa2	Ba3	Not rated

Source: Swiss Re

evolved, enhancing the amount and efficiency of risk transfer. In 2003, Swiss Re introduced the Arbor Program, and in 2006, Successor, the largest natural catastrophe program to date.

Vega Series 2008-I continues the evolution of Swiss Re's ILS strategy by complementing the coverage provided by Successor and expanding risk transfer to higher risk layers. Whereas Swiss Re's previous ILS programs have focused on solvency protection against severe events, Series 2008-I is designed to provide protection for low, riskier layers that are more exposed to frequency risk.

13.2   SWISS RE ACCESSES MULTI-EVENT NATURAL CATASTROPHE COVERAGE

Series 2008-I provides earnings volatility management to Swiss Re by protecting against the frequency risk of five peak natural catastrophe risks: US Hurricane, Europe Windstorm, California Earthquake, Japan Earthquake and Japan Typhoon. These perils are pooled in a static portfolio based on parametric index, modeled loss and industry loss index-based triggers. The risk profile of each peril trigger is fixed for the entire risk period.

Each peril is subject to an individual sublimit that caps the total amount Swiss Re may recover for each peril within each annual risk period. The sublimits range from $37.5 million to $52.5 million and are fully reinstated at the beginning of each annual risk period. Swiss Re is able to receive multi-event protection for each peril while providing stability to the overall risk pool by limiting the total loss that may occur from an individual event.

All four classes of the Series 2008-I notes are exposed to each peril in the risk pool. Following a triggering event, principal reductions are determined based on the resulting index value and the available sublimit. Principal reductions to the notes resulting from loss payments to Swiss Re are applied in reverse order of seniority. The principal amount of the most junior class of notes will be fully reduced prior to any reduction of the next class of notes in the structure.

This structure provides Swiss Re with multi-event, multi-peril protection while providing investors with diversification across five natural catastrophe risks with the transparency of index-based triggers.

13.3   THE FIRST ILS TO USE A CASH RESERVE ACCOUNT AS CREDIT ENHANCEMENT

Series 2008-I introduces a new approach to credit enhancement in ILS using a cash reserve account to provide subordination to the notes. The reserve account and risk tranching allow for a higher rated structure, increasing participation of more classes of investors and giving Swiss Re access to a broader base of capacity.

Swiss Re makes scheduled payments into the reserve account on a quarterly basis according to a fixed schedule. These proceeds are available to absorb event losses before any principal reduction of any Series 2008-I notes.

The quarterly reserve payments also help in absorbing the timing risk of potential events. If no loss events occur over time, the notes will experience positive credit migration. To the extent loss events occur early in the risk period, future reserve payments may reinstate the outstanding principal of the notes in order of seniority. The reserve account may also provide additional return potential to the most junior noteholders, who will receive any excess proceeds in the account at maturity.

13.4   INNOVATION LEADS TO MORE EFFICIENT PROTECTION

The sponsoring of Vega affirms Swiss Re's leading role in the product innovation in the ILS market. Series 2008-I increases Swiss Re's level of protection for peak natural catastrophe risks while optimising the cost of risk transfer by accessing investors across the credit spectrum.

Part II
Life Securitisation

14

General Features of Life Insurance-Linked Securitisation

Norman Peard[a]

In this chapter the background considerations for and general features of a life insurance-linked securitisation are discussed. The aim is to give an overview since a full technical discussion of the matters raised would result in an entire book for some individual themes and a full technical discussion of the entirety of the subject matter would run to several volumes. Some of these matters are covered in more depth in other chapters of this book. For example, Chapter 20 describes a range of factors pertinent to securitising a single risk associated with much life insurance-related business – mortality (and the closely related risk of longevity). Chapter 15 contains a cedant's perspective on life insurance-linked securitisation, its motivations and the process needed to complete a transaction. Chapter 26 is dedicated to a discussion of regulatory issues.

This chapter is divided into three principal subsections. In the first, a brief description of the different life insurer corporate and business structures is provided. This is relevant to an understanding of the structures within which life insurance-related risks are currently located within the life insurance industry and a brief description of the risks and products is also provided. This in turn is relevant to understanding some of the strictures placed on insurance-linked securitisation which may not be present when securitising business from other sources.

In the second section the various actors are considered. Each of these will be involved at different stages in the process of an insurance-linked securitisation. Their roles interact and sometimes overlap. The sometimes competing, or even conflicting, interests of the various interested parties will impact significantly on the process of the transaction. It is thus somewhat artificial in practice to try to separate the actors from the process, but it is important to do so in any conceptual discussion as an understanding of the interrelationships of the various actors is necessary in order fully to appreciate the process of a transaction.

In the third section matters of what might best be termed 'process' are discussed. These relate to the process of determining what business is to be securitised and how. It will become apparent that there are many potential objectives and that external constraints result in a complex environment within which the securitisation needs to be structured. The interactions between these various constraints and objectives result in the sometimes complex structures used to satisfy the various demands. The process is also discussed from a somewhat different perspective in Chapter 15.

---

[a]Credit Suisse International

14.1   LIFE INSURER CORPORATE AND BUSINESS STRUCTURES, RISKS AND PRODUCTS

In this section the principal corporate structures, life insurance business-related risks and life insurance product categories are outlined and an indication given as to why these are important in relation to life-based insurance-linked securitisations. In summary, though, the corporate structure is important because of associated legal and regulatory restrictions specific to each structure and the business risks determine much of the process of securitisation, whilst the product categories straddle these two aspects.

14.1.1   Mutual life offices

The earliest approach to providing life insurance on a technically sound basis was, in effect, founded on the principle of mutuality. Early examples of life insurance include individuals with a common interest grouping together to provide for each other. For example, individuals working in one of the skilled trades might band together and each pay a regular premium in return for which, if they were to die, a sum of money would be available to pay for a funeral. This commonality of interest lay at the basis of what have developed into the modern mutual life offices. Each of the individuals was, in effect, in modern terminology, simultaneously a member of the mutual and a policyholder. As there was very limited information on which to base the cost of the insurance provided, premiums were often set very conservatively and so resulted in significant profits. Within the framework and philosophy prevailing this did not pose a problem – the profits were either shared by, for example, increasing benefits or reducing premiums for the existing members or were carried forward as a buffer providing additional security for later generations of members. As the members were often small, closely knit groups with common interests, this worked well. As profits resulting from carrying on life insurance business were shared amongst the policyholders in the form of bonuses,[1] the business became known as 'with-profits' business.[2] It also provided the basis for the mutual life insurance offices of today. Today's mutual is, in many respects, very similar to the original mutuals, but there are differences. For this discussion, there are three areas of interest in which today's mutual is a different type of entity.

First, some mutuals have now grown so large, counted amongst the largest life insurance companies, that the members no longer have any clear common interest. So, whilst the principles of mutuality still apply, issues of equity or fairness both between current members and between generations of members have become more complex. This, in turn, has often resulted in closer regulatory scrutiny and the on-going development of the concepts of 'policyholders' reasonable expectations', 'treating customers fairly' and the practical implications of such concepts (to a greater or lesser extent these issues have also arisen in relation to the change in status of some mutual offices to become proprietary offices in a process known as demutualisation, mentioned again below). Due regard to these concepts needs to be had in relation to any life insurance-linked securitisation, but it is of particular relevance where the transaction sponsor is a mutual office or has written significant volumes of with-profits business.

---

[1] Bonuses could be provided in a wide range of approaches, for example an increase in the death benefit which would be paid under the policy. A key feature is the discretionary nature of these bonuses.

[2] Another term used for this type of business is 'participating' business – policyholders participate in the resulting profits.

Secondly, there is nowadays a far greater variety in the range of life insurance products available. This is covered further below, but one key difference is that many policies are written in a manner which no longer includes profit sharing.[3] The policy states what benefits are payable in what circumstances and the office takes on the liability to meet those obligations as they fall due. This, in turn, has two significant implications – first, the profits (or losses) resulting when a mutual office effects these policies continue to be shared amongst the with-profits policyholders and, secondly, a separation between membership of the mutual and being a policyholder comes into clearer relief. As regards the sharing of profits resulting from writing non-profits policies, the with-profits policyholders can be thought of as investing in writing business and sharing in the risks and rewards of so doing. As regards membership, it is often the case that non-profit policyholders are not members of the mutual. The question of membership and membership rights is mentioned for completeness in the context of insurance-linked securitisation – it has significant practical consequences in the context of demutualisation, but for current purposes is of most relevance in drawing comparisons and distinctions between mutual and proprietary offices, as discussed below.

Thirdly, mutual life offices, in common with other life offices, are capital constrained. Generally, mutual offices have very limited access to new capital. Their capital base has been built up over many years from writing profitable business and retaining some of those profits within the company and, unlike proprietary life offices, described below, they cannot raise capital by the issue of shares. No longer is it acceptable to the extent previously observed for mutual offices simply to write business and for the with-profit policyholders to share in the results – now, with technical advances in the field of insurance, mutual offices compete more directly with other forms of provider of life insurance and, indeed, with products of other types provided by other forms of financial service provider and as a result the product offering must be designed to provide an adequate return on capital. As a result, mutuals are, to a greater extent than in the past, being assessed, directly or indirectly, with regard to efficiency in the use of capital. This combination of increased requirements for efficient capital usage on the one hand and constraints on access to capital on the other hand is a feature which makes the use of insurance-linked securitisation of potential interest to the mutual offices.

14.1.2 Proprietary life offices

The second major form of insurance office considered here is the proprietary life office. These are the companies owned by shareholders with limited liability. In these companies the interests of the owners of the company and those of the policyholders are much more clearly differentiated. Ultimately, the owners provide the risk capital and retain the profits and losses resulting from carrying on the business of insurance. These companies are clearly, from a structural perspective, well suited to writing non-profit business. They have often also been established in a manner which permits them to write with-profits business. In order to do so, the assets and liabilities in relation to the with-profits business are tracked separately from the remaining assets and liabilities of the company and this business operates effectively in a manner very similar to the same business written in a mutual office. One major difference is that when bonuses are declared to policyholders, this usually results in the triggering of a transfer to the shareholder assets of some of the profits from writing with-profits business.

---

[3] Such policies are referred to as "non-profit" or "non-participating".

So, both mutual and proprietary offices can (and do) write both with-profits and non-profits business. There are many similarities between the two forms and also significant differences. From a regulatory perspective, and this has implications for insurance-linked securitisation where a proprietary office writes with-profits business, there are potential conflicts of interest between the shareholders and the with-profits policyholders which need to be considered.[4] In principle, these same conflicts exist between members and with-profits policyholders of a mutual, but these two groups often comprise the same or substantially the same individuals and thus the issues are not so acute in the case of a mutual. From a different perspective, proprietary offices have a much more direct route to raising additional capital when required – they can raise it directly from the capital markets, for example through issuing new shares. But raising pure equity capital is not always the most desirable approach for a proprietary office and so insurance-linked securitisation techniques have a role to play in optimising the capital structure of these undertakings. For example, in the United States of America, Regulation XXX or Guideline AXXX deals with the regulatory reserving requirements for certain types of life insurance business – these result in reserve requirements being greatly in excess of what is regarded as economically necessary and securitisation technology provides a route to meeting requirements more efficiently than raising large amounts of equity capital – a case study is given in Chapter 23. In addition, in some jurisdictions, the economic value associated with a block of in-force business (the value of in-force, or VIF[5]), normally treated as an asset with no value from a regulatory perspective, may be monetised using securitisation techniques and recognised for regulatory capital purposes – this is again more efficient than raising equity capital and a case study is given in Chapter 23.

There is another situation when insurance-linked securitisation may have a significant role to play. Reference was made above to demutualisation. There have been occasions on which offices have sought to change their legal structure. Although there have been instances when offices changed their status from that of a proprietary office to a mutual, in the recent past the tendency has been for a change from mutual status to proprietary. The process is referred to as 'demutualisation'. It has been seen to offer a range of benefits, for example providing an opportunity for members of the mutual to 'unlock' their interest in the capital accumulated from profits arising on business written for past generations of policyholders or to provide access to the capital markets in order, for example, to be able to implement plans to meet the ambitions of the mutual office in the developing market environment. The arguments in favour of each of the different forms which an office might adopt are outside the scope of this book, but there are aspects, which can be seen from a consideration of the potential drivers of demutualisation, where insurance-linked securitisation could have a greater role to play than has to date been the case. Two examples are the provision of capital to fund an acquisition of another business, or to unlock the interest of members in the accumulated capital of the company.

---

[4] These and other issues of a regulatory nature are considered in some detail in Chapter 26.

[5] Various descriptors are given to transactions which are based on the monetisation of the VIF – these include 'VIF monetisation', 'VIF securitisation' and 'EV securitisation'. EV refers to 'embedded value', which is usually taken to mean the sum of the VIF and the net asset value of the insurance company, the net asset value not, in fact, playing a significant role in the transaction. The result of the transaction is usually to exchange a portion of the shareholders' interest in the value of the in-force business for cash proceeds, hence the term monetisation. In this chapter, the term 'VIF monetisation' is used for these reasons but colloquially the other terms are used and have been used in other chapters.

14.1.3 Other forms of life office

In the discussion so far, the focus has been on the two principal forms of life insurance office through which the vast majority of business is written. The precise nature of each of these forms of office varies from jurisdiction to jurisdiction around the world. The precise form for determining the amount of profit to be shared between with-profits policyholders and the manner and timing of its distribution varies considerably between jurisdictions and, sometimes, between companies within an individual jurisdiction. Very often historical factors have played an important role in deciding which form is most prevalent. Local differences in the legal and regulatory environment result in varying considerations for the process of an insurance-linked securitisation. However, the broad considerations outlined above remain valid across much of the insurance market globally.

The descriptions above are also helpful in considering the application of insurance-linked securitisation to other company structures. A considerable range of company structures exists. For example, some structures are, in many respects, mutual structures, but in certain circumstances the members may be required to provide additional capital to the company. Another structure is that shareholders have provided capital in the past, but they do not share in the profits and losses of the business except to the extent that it impacts on the ability of the company to pay a fixed annual dividend to the shareholders. These structures demonstrate features, from an access to capital perspective, somewhere between those of a mutual and a proprietary office and this provides a basis from which to consider the value of insurance-linked securitisations for these offices too.

14.1.4 Principal risks associated with life insurance business

Ultimately the role of insurance-linked securitisation is to provide increased efficiency in terms of the allocation of capital. Life insurance offices accept a wide variety of risks when they enter into contracts of insurance with policyholders. To some extent, at least when considered across a large number of policyholders, these risks are predictable. However, the risks are never wholly predictable and therefore in practice result in profits and losses emerging from contracts entered into. Capital needs to be held in order to cushion against the losses when these arise – the individual policyholder will not wish to forego the promised benefits under the contract of insurance because one of the risks has materialised.[6] Capital efficiency requires consideration of the risks, the amount of capital required to be held to provide reasonable security in relation to those risks and the best source for that capital. There are some very big questions here – for example, how is the amount of risk to be measured, what is reasonable security, how is the best source of capital to be decided? The conclusion, however, is that the most efficient approach is not for all the risk to be retained by the insurance office which wrote

---

[6] Perhaps in a very extreme scenario this would be acceptable. Policyholders would perhaps not expect an insurance company to be able to pay out in full in all possible conceivable scenarios, but the nature of life insurance is such that policyholders expect a very high level of certainty and that the certainty be maintained over potentially a very long period of time, perhaps well in excess of 50 years. The scope of this book does not include the economic theory of insurance, but it is clear that to provide the required security, significant amounts of capital are required to be held to meet adverse scenarios. Over time regulatory regimes have been developed which make minimum capital and risk management requirements fundamental to being permitted to write life insurance business. This protects the policyholder and helps ensure the fundamental ability of the insurance industry to continue to play a role in the economy over the long term by providing a mechanism for the secure pooling and redistribution of risks from those seeking protection to those able to provide the capital to bear the associated risks.

the business, but for the risk to be managed and certain elements of the risk to be passed to other economic agents willing and able to bear a portion of the risk. Securitisation plays a dual role here – it permits the parcelling up of portions of the entire risk and enables access to some of the economic agents which would not otherwise be involved in bearing that risk.

As to the risks associated with writing life insurance business, these can be categorised in a number of ways. One frequently used categorisation subdivides the risks into demographic risks, market risks and operational risks.

Demographic risks include mortality, longevity and morbidity risks. Also capable of inclusion within this category (although it may be argued that they do not fit in this category, or fit better in another category, or should be in a new category which relates to interactions with other factors) are risks such as policyholder lapse and option exercise risks. Mortality risks arise in relation to products where an increase in the death rates of policyholders results in a loss to the office. Longevity risks arise where the life office suffers a loss in scenarios where policyholders live longer than anticipated. Morbidity risks arise where the life insurer offers policies which provide benefits to policyholders determined by reference to their state of health.[7] Each of these risks must be considered from a wide range of angles in coming to a proper assessment of the risk.[8] The extent of exposure to the risk is usually assessed in terms which reflect both the likelihood of the risk crystallising and the economic cost of the risk to the insurer in the event that it should crystallise. Each assessment requires the involvement of a range of specialists working together. For example, considering morbidity risk, the economic exposure may depend on the product design, the likelihood of the insured falling into ill health and the likelihood of recovery or death over given timeframes. So a proper assessment of the office's exposure to morbidity risk will require medical, statistical and financial modelling techniques at a minimum. Mortality and longevity risks and their securitisation are discussed in detail in Chapters 20 and 21 and a case study of a mortality (catastrophe) bond is contained in Chapter 22. Policyholder lapse risk relates to the risk of a loss arising when a policyholder, for whatever reason, does not pay a premium when due.[9] Depending on contractual terms and conditions, non-payment of a premium may or may not result in termination of the insurance contract. In addition, technical features mean that the office may suffer an economic profit or a loss in the event of non-payment of a premium (and indeed which applies may vary over the term of a particular type of insurance product). Some life insurance policies include options, which may be of value to policyholders in certain circumstances. Whenever these options are exercised, there is a risk to the office of economic loss and it is not possible to ascertain in

---

[7] Policies exposing an insurer to risks associated with the state of health of the insured are sometimes issued by life insurance offices and sometimes by non-life insurance companies. How the categorisation is arrived at is not a concern for the purposes of this book.

[8] Mortality and longevity risks are described more fully in Chapters 20 and 21. Morbidity risk can be described broadly as the risks to a life insurance office related to the state of health of the insured individuals and may arise because a claim is triggered by reference to this, for example a payment or payments following disability, or diagnosis of cancer. It also includes risks related to the rate of recovery from ill health – some claims are payable on a regular basis until the insured regains a specified level of health.

[9] Many life insurance policies are written on a basis that premiums will be paid regularly over a period of time, perhaps over many years, rather than simply entailing the payment of a single premium. Sometimes the payment of further premiums is optional. Technical distinction may be drawn between situations in which policyholders fail to make one or more premium payments, terminate their policy or transfer the policy to another provider (which is sometimes possible), but for simplicity no distinction is drawn here – the key feature is that the receipt of lower premium volumes than anticipated may cause an economic loss to the insurer and the risk of this happening is referred to here as lapse risk.

advance to what extent the options will be exercised. Accordingly there is uncertainty as to the financial outcome of providing these options and option exercise risk is present.[10] The propensity to lapse or exercise policy options may depend on features such as the economic environment at the time, or the insured's state of health (e.g. a policyholder may have difficulty affording a premium in a difficult economic environment and so be more likely to miss making the payment, but conversely may be more likely to make the premium payment to ensure continued insurance protection if the insured's state of health has deteriorated since the policy was effected and a claim in the near future appears likely). It is features of this nature which indicate why it is difficult to assign these risks to one category or another – the underlying drivers may not fit within a single category.

Market risks most obviously arise in connection with the investment of the life office's assets. The values of equities fluctuate, interest rate changes result in changes in the value of fixed interest portfolios and so on. However, the value of a life insurance office's liabilities also fluctuate depending on market conditions. In part, this is due to the often largely predictable pattern of a significant proportion of liability cash flows. So, a large proportion of the office's liabilities may be considered as behaving as a fixed interest portfolio. This oversimplifies the case, as policy options, profit-sharing mechanisms and some categories of insurance product introduce exposure to other market risks within the liabilities, including equity risk, property market risk and exposure to changes in the volatility of equities or interest rates, just to give some examples. Furthermore, once a full analysis is carried out of the interrelationship between assets and liabilities, the interactions between different categories of market risk and correlations need to be considered, as do the interactions between market risks and policyholder action risks, such as the risk of lapse.

Operational risk may arise in a wide range of guises in a life insurance operation. This is often defined as the risk of loss resulting from inadequate or failed internal processes, people and systems, or from external events. Generally this is taken to include legal risks and exclude risks arising from strategic decisions. For example, if a computer system fails, this could lead to the insurer being unable to process new business. If telephone lines fail during a period of financial market turbulence, this could result in an inability to realign the office's investments, resulting in significant losses. A flaw in product design could result in business being unknowingly sold on loss-making terms. A poorly drafted legal agreement could result in significant unintended claims, or failure to be able to recoup claims from a reinsurer.

One risk which does not fit easily within any of the above categories is liquidity risk. Generally speaking this has not been considered to be a major risk for insurance companies, but this is not necessarily the case. Liquidity risk can be described as the risk that the office does not have, and is unable to realise, cash as required to meet obligations to policyholders and others as they fall due without suffering significant costs. A complicating factor for insurance offices, often referred to as fungibility, is whether liquidity available in one part of the company (or group of companies) can be made available elsewhere in the company (or group). Due to regulatory constraints this is not always the case.

It becomes apparent that a life insurance office is exposed to a wide variety of risks. As a result, from a risk analysis perspective, insurance companies can be amongst the most complex and interesting of businesses. This carries over into consideration of life insurance-linked securitisation.

---

[10] Lapse risk may be considered to fall within option exercise risk, but the latter term is normally reserved for explicit options in the contract to acquire financial or insurance benefits upon exercise of the option.

To conclude this section of the chapter, a description of some of the main categories of life insurance product is provided. From this will be apparent both the wide range of products available from insurance providers and some insight into the nature of the insurance risks likely to be connected with each of the types of insurance product. This is then further considered in the section on the process of a life insurance securitisation.

14.1.5 Principal product types and associated risks

For the purposes of this chapter, the range of products offered by life insurance offices can be considered firstly under three main categories, which are referred to here as linked, with-profits and non-profit. The principal distinguishing feature between with-profits and non-profits business has already been described above: under with-profits business, policyholders share, through a bonus or profit-sharing mechanism, in any profits resulting from the premiums and investment returns thereon being more than sufficient to meet the guaranteed benefits which the office is obligated to provide; whilst, for non-profit business, only the guaranteed benefits are provided. A third category of insurance policy has come to be of major importance, namely the linked insurance policy.

Linked insurance policies are designed so that the policyholder receives benefits which are linked (hence the name) to the performance of a defined basket of assets. Technically there are a number of variants on this theme, but these are not relevant for present purposes. What is relevant is that typically these policies have much in common with investment management contracts provided by other financial institutions and they provide a vehicle for long-term savings under which the policyholder may decide the categories of asset by reference to which the value of the policy and the benefits thereunder are determined. For these policies to qualify as insurance policies, there must also be some element of insurance risk, but the details vary from jurisdiction to jurisdiction. To make this more concrete, such a policy might, for example, provide that, upon payment of a premium, the policyholder would become entitled to a payment on the death of the insured of twice the amount which would result from investing the initial premium in some proportions in equities, property, cash and fixed interest securities.[11] Upon survival of the insured to maturity of the policy, the amount which would result from so investing the original premium would be paid to the policyholder.

There are also life insurance products which exhibit elements of more than one of the above categories. One example is a linked product which provides benefits linked to the smoothed performance of a with-profits fund.

Another way to look at the range of products is to consider the type and extent of demographic risk present within the product. The basic range of policies then includes policies which provide a benefit:

- on the death, incapacity or disability of the insured or suffering by the insured of one of a specified range of illnesses, either within a specified period of time or without this limitation (single payment);
- on the survival of the insured for a specified period of time (single payment);

---

[11] This very simplified example makes no allowance for the various costs associated with providing the policy and so, in practice, the amounts payable to the policyholder would also reflect charges for administration costs, investment management, insurance risk, etc. The precise details vary significantly.

- on either the death of the insured within a specified period of time or survival to the end of this period (single payment);
- regularly for the remainder of the lifetime of the insured, starting immediately (multiple payments);
- regularly for the remainder of the lifetime of the insured, provided the insured first survives some specified period (multiple payments);
- regularly for the remainder of the lifetime of the insured, starting on the incapacity or disability of the insured within a specified period of time (multiple payments).

Variants of these basic products have been developed in each of the linked, with-profits and non-profit formats described above.

14.2   ACTORS AND THEIR ROLES

In what follows, the principal actors likely to be involved are briefly described, together with an overview of the role or roles each plays. Other parties may also be involved and neither the list, nor the descriptions, is intended to be exhaustive. As for the other sections of this chapter, the aim is to give a good flavour of what may be involved rather than attempt to address all potential aspects.

Some actors are present, in one form or another, in any insurance-linked securitisation. In particular, a transaction sponsor and investors (in one form or another) will always be involved. As the insurance industry is highly regulated and insurance-linked securitisation is still innovative, it is highly likely that regulators will have a direct interest and will, in any event, have at least an indirect interest. It is difficult to conceive of transactions being effected without external professional advisers – expertise sufficient to enable the efficient completion of a transaction is still not widespread and so, given the likely size of a transaction in order to be economically viable, given associated costs, it is unlikely that all the expertise required will be available in-house at both the sponsor and investor. Ratings agencies and monoline insurance companies may or may not have a role to play in any individual transaction. Parties such as liquidity and swap providers and calculation agents might or might not be involved, depending on the structural specifics. These parties and their roles are described more fully below.

14.2.1   Sponsor

The sponsor is essential – in order for there to be a life insurance-linked securitisation, there must be a life insurance office,[12] currently exposed to one or more of the risks associated with life insurance business, which it wishes to some extent to pass to other participants in the capital markets. The sponsor, usually together with its advisers, will identify the objectives of the insurance-linked securitisation, retain the necessary external specialist advice, provide the necessary information to enable the structuring of the transaction and, usually, participate in presentations, as required, to other interested parties, in particular to investors, but also to

---

[12] The sponsor might also, for example, be a reinsurance company, which has accepted life insurance risk from a direct writing life insurance office. For the purposes of this chapter this distinction will not be drawn out – the essential point is that there is a source of life insurance business related risk to be transferred from an insurance office (which here includes reinsurance office) to the capital markets.

regulators and rating agencies as relevant. The objective is critical. The primary objective may include one or more of the following:

- raising capital;
- managing capital requirements;
- monetising illiquid assets;
- managing peak risks.

There are also likely to be secondary objectives, which will be returned to in Section 14.3 on process – the objectives are dealt with in greater detail in the next chapter.

Raising capital may be achieved in a number of ways and usually refers to raising either regulatory or ratings agency capital. For example, in order to do so, an asset which is not recognised (or only partially recognised) for regulatory or ratings agency purposes is first identified and cash raised through the insurance-linked securitisation structure, the repayment of which is contingent on the realisation of the value of this asset. These transactions are typified by value in force ('VIF') monetisation transactions. VIF is the value of an in-force portfolio of life insurance policies, which is the economic value of a book of in-force policies, or, expressed differently, the value of the future profits anticipated to emerge in respect of that book of business. A profit is anticipated to emerge since regulatory regimes usually require conservative values to be placed on the insurance liabilities and the assets held to back those liabilities, so that on an economic or market-consistent basis the assets are worth more than the corresponding liabilities and this difference may be expected to emerge over time. Typically this economic value is not recognised for regulatory purposes and is only partially recognised by ratings agencies in carrying out their respective assessments of a life insurance office. Replacing this economic asset by cash may allow this asset to be recognised and, as a result, increase reported capital.

Managing capital requirements may be achieved by transferring, by means of the insurance-linked securitisation structure, some or all of the risks associated with a portfolio of life insurance business to the capital markets. An assessment is first required of the nature and extent of the risks to which the office is exposed. Next an assessment of the amount of capital required to ensure the solvency of the office with a stated level of certainty is required – ideally this assessment needs to be carried out assuming scenarios under which varying proportions of the individual risks are transferred in order to identify the optimal risk transfer. This can be a highly technical exercise, particularly if a full economic analysis of the risks and associated capital requirements, and therefore optimisation of economic capital requirements, is the objective. As regulatory, and indeed ratings, capital assessments may be on a simpler basis than a full economic capital assessment, it is possible that the assessment may be simpler where the objective is to manage regulatory or ratings capital requirements.

Monetising illiquid assets is effectively the use of a life insurance securitisation structure to raise cash in return for transferring an interest in illiquid assets to the capital markets. The VIF monetisation described above is a good example of such a transaction. The economic asset is not readily converted to cash in the sense that the asset cannot simply be sold in the marketplace. However, the value may be realised in cash by means of such a transaction, the cash raised being repaid as the economic value is realised over time, thereby itself gradually becoming liquid.

14.2.2 Investors

Investors are also essential to any life insurance securitisation transaction. The term should probably best be used in a broad sense here. Many life insurance securitisation transactions will result in the issue of debt securities which are acquired by investors. However, in the process of structuring a life insurance securitisation, it may well be that various of the individual risks embedded within the structure are separated out and passed to specialist investors in other forms, such as swaps and other derivative contracts. These other investors may be considered to play a role in facilitating the end result, which is the issue of securities that may be invested in by investors, the term being used in the narrower sense.

The end investor may also take many forms. Some of the typical end investors include specialist funds established to acquire and trade in insurance-linked securities, hedge funds, leveraged finance investors, bond and convertible funds, investment banks, insurance companies, pension funds and high net worth individuals. Each will have its own set of criteria for investment and these need to be considered in arriving at the most appropriate structure for any proposed life insurance-linked securitisation.

14.2.3 Regulators

Regulators[13] will be involved directly or indirectly. Whether or not an insurance-linked securitisation is intended to affect the reported regulatory capital of an insurer, or its regulatory capital requirements, it will impact the office's risk landscape. Regulators will be concerned to ensure that the insurer is fully cognisant of the impacts of the transaction in all scenarios which might reasonably be anticipated to arise in the future. They will wish to ensure that the office's ability to demonstrate solvency in the future will not be adversely affected by unintended effects of the transaction. Where reported capital or capital requirements are affected, it needs to be ensured that the relevant regulatory policy is reflected in the terms of the structure. Since the majority of insurance-linked securitisation transactions involve a significant amount of innovation and, in most jurisdictions, regulators have not yet had the opportunity to review many such transactions, most transactions are currently carried out with close involvement of the regulator. Often questions of policy need to be resolved and the manner of reporting the transaction for regulatory purposes may need to be agreed. Even where the regulatory authority is not actively engaged in the process, a review of the structure, its implications and how it is being reported is likely once the sponsor submits its next set of regulatory returns. This is covered in more detail in Chapter 26.

14.2.4 External professional advisers

External professional advisers, as noted above, are highly likely to be involved. Not only must the sponsor decide on the objective of the transaction, but the treatment of the transaction from regulatory, accounting, tax and, where the sponsor is rated, ratings perspectives will need to be considered. Legal aspects will need to be addressed, often in more than one jurisdiction and across both insurance and securities law. Whilst at this stage in the development of the life insurance-linked securitisation market the main issues have been identified and resolved

---

[13] The term is here being used to include the supervisors of regulated institutions.

and the expertise is to hand from the ranks of the professional advisers, it is still very unusual for the range of expertise to exist in-house. Accordingly it is assumed that external advisers are retained and the principal advisers and their roles are described.

The arranger of the transaction, usually an investment bank, will bring together the full range of actors and coordinate the whole process of the transaction, described in the next section of this chapter. They will bring structuring expertise, knowledge of the investor base, an analysis of the range of different routes to achieving the best execution price and access to other market counterparties which may need to be involved in order to structure the transaction efficiently.

Actuarial advisers provide evaluations of the underlying risks of the transaction, which may be relied upon by other actors. The sponsor will wish to have independent confirmation that the objectives are the right ones and that they are met, and actuarial advisers have a significant role to play here. In addition, investors, regulatory authorities, rating agencies and other market participants are likely to wish to have expert advice on aspects of the transaction. Risk assessment and risk modelling are covered in more detail in Chapter 17

Insurance accounting is a specialist field in its own right. The sponsor's accounts will be subject to audit and insurance-linked securitisation transactions are likely material to the preparation of those accounts. The accounting for these transactions also often involves consideration of aspects of accounting developed in connection with other forms of securitisation which have a longer history. These aspects may not initially be familiar to specialists in insurance accounting. The range of jurisdictions involved in transactions and the international nature of the activities of many sponsors may also mean that more than one accounting regime is relevant, and the accounting treatment may not be identical across accounting methodologies. Accordingly accounting specialists from a range of disciplines may be involved. This becomes even more the case once the accounting treatment of those elements of the transaction in which other market participants are involved is brought into the picture – those other participants will often retain their own advice on this aspect.

Similarly, insurance taxation is a specialist field, varying by jurisdiction and, given that insurance-linked securitisation structures involve not just aspects of insurance taxation but also group, international, securities taxation and the taxation treatment of investors and other market participants, the retention of specialist expertise is often appropriate. Not only will this play a role in structuring the securitisation to optimise the benefit to the sponsor, but it is essential to ensure that there are no obstacles from the perspective of the other market participants. It should not be underestimated how important this aspect is – there are frequently many initial options to be evaluated for the structure of a transaction, but some will be ruled out immediately on the basis of tax considerations and others will need careful evaluation across a range of scenarios before the final structure is decided upon. This aspect is covered in more detail in Chapters 24 and 25.

Legal advisers play a significant role. Each of the actors is likely to have its own internal and, frequently, external legal advisers in relation to a life insurance securitisation. High level considerations will include whether the sponsor can enter into the proposed transaction in the proposed form and whether the documentation achieves the intended effect. Other, perhaps less obvious considerations, include whether the various aspects of the transaction should properly be treated under insurance law or securities law in the relevant jurisdictions. This can affect the ability of investors to participate, for example. Specialist legal advice is required – similarly to the position for other expert advice – in the case of insurance-linked securitisation and, in particular, life insurance-linked securitisation; a range of specialisms within the legal field will be required to be brought to bear. Advisers with expertise in the relevant areas will usually be familiar with a range of possible structures which may potentially be used for the transaction and so will often also play a role in providing important input into the structure of the transaction. Moreover, they will have experience in working together with the relevant regulatory and ratings authorities and may, when not acting for the sponsor, be involved in advising these on aspects of insurance-linked securitisations. In a major transaction, it is quite conceivable that the sponsor, arranger, investors, regulators, ratings agencies, other market participants and the advisers to the various interested parties will all seek internal and external legal advice.

14.2.5   Ratings agencies

Ratings agencies may play a role in a number of contexts within a life insurance securitisation. First, it may be that the sponsor is a rated insurance company, or a member of a group which is rated. In this case the implications of the transaction for the rating will need to be considered. Secondly, it may well be that the securities issued as part of the transaction will be rated. This is important in terms of investor support for the transaction – for example, some investors will (or are permitted to) only invest in securities which have a minimum rating and other investors may take some comfort from a rating even if it is not a requirement for them to invest. For some transactions a rating by a single ratings agency will be sufficient, for others it may be optimal to seek ratings from more than one agency. This subject is dealt with in more detail in Chapter 16.

14.2.6   Monoline insurers

Monoline insurers have played an important role in the success of the early life insurance transactions, but more recently a trend to transactions being executed privately and to transactions being executed without reliance on monoline insurers has been observed. The role of the monoline insurer in these transactions is to wrap the transaction, which in essence means that the transaction will be rated in line with the monoline insurer, rather than at the lower quality rating it would achieve absent a monoline wrap. If the cash flows passed to investors under the terms of the securitisation structure, based on underlying experience of the securitised life insurance business, are insufficient or not timely, then the monoline insurer will make up the difference. In return for this wrap, the monoline reinsurer receives a fee – given that the issued securities then achieve a better rating and the terms on which they may be issued into the capital markets are improved, the net cost to the sponsor may be improved by the presence of the monoline insurer in the structure. In Chapter 23 a case study of a life insurance-linked securitisation involving a monoline wrap is discussed.

14.2.7   Liquidity providers

Liquidity providers may be included where there is a risk that cash flows from the business underlying the securitisation structure will not necessarily arise in time to meet repayment obligations to investors, but are nonetheless expected to arise. The role of the liquidity provider is to provide cash so that timely payments may be made to investors, with that cash being repaid as soon as the cash flows from the business emerge. The period in respect of which the liquidity is provided would normally be short. Essentially, this is a mechanism for smoothing timing differences between actual and projected cash flows where there is a high level of certainty that the cash flows will arise but a risk as to the precise timing. The risk as to the timing is likely, in turn, to arise from volatility related to the underlying risks associated with the securitised business. With a view to making this more concrete, if for example the number of deaths within an insured portfolio over the course of one year is precisely the expected number, but they are not spread evenly throughout the year, without the presence of a liquidity provider this might result in some payments being delayed (or advanced) in early periods and this being corrected in later periods. The presence of the liquidity provider will eliminate this effect from an investor perspective.

14.2.8 Swap providers

Swap providers may play a number of roles within a life insurance securitisation transaction. Some potential roles are given here, but the list is not intended to be more than indicative of the range of possible roles. One potential role is to ensure that, where the structure entails collateralisation, the proceeds of investing the collateral, together with the proceeds of the swap transaction, are a precise set of cash flows with regard to both amount and timing. Another role may be to swap variable interest rate cash flows for fixed rate cash flows, for example where the terms of the securities provide for fixed coupons but the structure results in cash flows from the underlying insurance business which are linked to variable interest rates. This may be important in order to ensure that investors can be paid obligated, fixed cash flows on a timely basis. Yet a further potential role may be to provide a swap where the currency of the securities issued differs from the currency in which some or all of the underlying business is denominated. Recently, developments have also been in the direction of transferring certain demographic risks by means of swap transactions and these, or swap transactions designed to remove market risks, may also be used within a life insurance securitisation transaction structure.

14.2.9 Others

Other parties may also be involved, for example calculation agents, trustees, parties retained to resolve disputes under the terms of the securitisation and others. As mentioned above, the list is not intended to be exhaustive and not all actors will be involved in all, or even the majority of, transactions.

14.3 PROCESS

Not all life insurance securitisations will follow precisely the same process, so the following is intended as a general outline of the main steps likely to be involved. The process is also discussed from a somewhat different perspective in Chapter 21. In any particular transaction, some steps may be omitted, steps may overlap or be combined with one another or may be taken in a different order. The discussion that follows is likely to reflect the main steps present in one form or another in a large proportion of life insurance securitisation transactions. For ease of reading, the steps are numbered, but that runs the risk of ascribing a formality to the steps which may not be apparent in the practical business of putting a transaction into effect.

Step 1: the sponsor decides on the objective of the transaction

As noted above, the objective is likely to fall under the headings capital raising, risk management or monetisation and may involve more than one of these objectives. For example, an insurance company may, following analysis of its book of business, determine that it has greater exposure than it desires to death claims which would result from the outbreak of a major fatal disease epidemic or natural or man-made disaster. The objective would then be to transfer some or all of this risk to others. Secondary objectives may be, for example:

- management of risk exposures so that the risk of unacceptable levels of reported earnings volatility is avoided;
- ensuring that the market consistent embedded value[14] of the life office is not severely adversely affected in stress scenarios;
- implementation of a new business model for accessing capital for new business and the subsequent transfer of the associated risks back into the capital market;
- to be seen as an innovative organisation with the ability to move ahead of the competition;
- to demonstrate that the office has available to it a wider range of tools to access capital and manage its risk exposures than available using only traditional tools.

The objectives are likely to be determined as a result of internal knowledge of the business and analysis carried out internally, but confirmed using input from external advisers, particularly actuaries and investment bankers.

Step 2: structuring advisers are retained and an initial working hypothesis as to the trans-action structure is developed

The structuring advisers are likely to be a team within an investment bank with specialist experience relevant to both securitisation in general and insurance business specifically. Consultants such as actuaries and accountants may or may not be retained at this stage, depending on whether the transaction is still considered to be at an exploratory stage, or whether the sponsor is more committed to carrying it through to completion. Some of the principal issues which will be considered are:

- the risks that are to be transferred under the structure;
- whether only extreme risks are to be transferred or risks which have a significant probability of materialising;
- whether risks are to be fully transferred or, alternatively, to be hedged to a greater or lesser degree with retention of basis risk;
- the duration of the transaction;
- the likely investors;
- whether the sponsor will need to establish any special purpose entities and, if so, the nature of these entities, for example special purpose reinsurance vehicles or other vehicles requiring regulatory approval;
- whether the principal contracts to be entered into by the sponsor in order to transfer risk are required to be reinsurance contracts or can take other forms;
- the extent to which transformation structures will be required to enable insurance risks to be transferred by the sponsor, with those risks being accepted without requiring an insurance licence by the investors and how best this will be achieved;

---

[14] Insurance liabilities are not often traded publicly. The market consistent embedded value of a life insurance office is a measure of the value of the economic interest of the shareholders in the business of that insurance office, determined using techniques which, as far as possible, place values on assets and liabilities which are consistent with values for comparable assets and liabilities traded in the marketplace.

- identification of the other actors that will be required within the structure, such as the monoline insurers and the liquidity and swap providers;
- the extent to which regulatory authorities and ratings agencies are to be involved and the timing for approaching them.

Furthermore, some other practical considerations may need to be considered, for example:

- compliance with data protection legislation;
- ensuring the sponsor is capable of meeting data and other obligations under the terms of the transaction within the constraints of existing system capabilities or without incurring significant system development costs.

Step 3: initial views are formed as to the likely regulatory, ratings, accounting and tax treatment of the transaction

The variety of potential structures is too large to permit a detailed description of what may be involved here. The process of structuring the transaction is likely to be iterative with interactions between Steps 2 and 3 and between Steps 3 and 6 of the process as described here. Structural features will be required that have regard to the perspectives of the investors, regulatory authorities and ratings agencies but also to ensure that accounting and tax considerations are appropriately addressed. An initial analysis of the ability of the proposed structure to meet all required sponsor objectives will be carried out, using internal sponsor expertise and the expertise of the structuring advisers. This analysis will result in an initial view being available to the sponsor covering the efficacy of the proposed transaction to cover the principal objectives as well as an initial analysis of the acceptability of the structure to regulatory authorities, the likely views of any relevant ratings agencies, the accounting treatment and assurance that this will be satisfactory and any tax implications, which should also be satisfactory.

Step 4: the arranger provides an indication as to the likelihood of the securities being successfully placed in the market and some indication of the likely cost of issuance

On the basis of the structure it is possible for the arranger, typically the investment bank which is advising on the structure, to form a view as to the likely investors, the likely level of interest from those investors in the market conditions current at the time and the potential price range at which those investors will be interested. A wide range of information is available to the arranger in reaching its views on these points. For example, given the state of development of the insurance securitisation market, up-to-date information as to the level at which similar securities are trading in the market is now likely to be available, either privately or publicly. Also, the arranger will be in regular dialogue with a wide range of investors and will thus be aware of current appetites. It is also possible that informal soundings be carried out at this stage, with the agreement of the sponsor, in order to confirm the understanding of the arranger as to the likely market response.

Step 5: a decision in principle to proceed is taken by the sponsor

At the end of this step, there should be a clear understanding of what the insurance-linked securitisation transaction is intended to achieve and within which constraints that is to happen, a working hypothesis as to the structure which will achieve this and an initial analysis that confirms, subject to detailed analysis, that the transaction achieves the objectives within the constraints identified and the price at which this is likely to be possible. Assuming this is satisfactory to the sponsor, a decision in principle to proceed with the transaction will be taken by the sponsor and the main work then begins.

Step 6: external professional advisers are retained and the detailed structure is developed in a form anticipated to meet the requirements of all the interested parties

At this stage a full, detailed analysis is carried out. Unless investors are being approached early, and this is only likely if there are special circumstances, for example a requirement for some insurance risk to be accepted by a reinsurance company,[15] then this stage will proceed without the involvement of all those actors who have a direct role within the structure, but who have not been individually identified at this point. At this stage the objective will be to develop a structure, in detail, which will have regard to their likely interests. For each element of the transaction, draft term sheets will be prepared. Research will be carried out in order to decide the best jurisdiction for any vehicles which are required to be established for the structure to operate efficiently. All the elements of the structure will be tested to ensure that they operate correctly in all possible circumstances. Legal advice will be relied upon heavily. The accounting and tax treatment of the structure from the perspective of the sponsor will be confirmed. Where possible, opportunities to optimise the structure will be identified and implemented. Documentation supporting the transaction will be produced.

The documentation referred to immediately above will fall within a number of categories. What precisely will be produced and in what form will depend on the specifics of the transaction, however some items of documentation are produced for most transactions. Usually there will be a risk analysis report, most likely prepared by external actuarial advisers, carried out with the aim of providing information to enable potential investors and, where relevant, ratings agencies to assess the risks and investors the potential returns should they invest. Background information on the sponsor and the reasons for the transaction will be prepared. Draft legal documentation will be drawn up – to the extent possible this will draw on precedent, but a significant amount of new drafting is likely to be required given the still innovative nature of life insurance-linked securitisations. Typically the legal documentation is very extensive. The draft term sheets and legal documentation together with the actuarial analysis will provide the necessary detailed information to permit a full analysis of the tax and accounting aspects of the proposed transaction. On the basis of this, the structure is likely to be further refined. Once this stage has been reached, it is possible to move into the final stages of the transaction, which involve confirming that the regulator has no objections, obtaining any ratings agency assessments and ratings that may be required, ensuring that all other parties directly involved in the structure are identified and the terms on which they will participate and, last but not least, taking the opportunity to the investment community.

Step 7: the regulator and ratings agencies are engaged

It is not unlikely that the regulatory authorities and the ratings agencies will have been approached at some point before this step is reached. Regulatory authorities generally like to be made aware of significant matters affecting the institutions they supervise and so some communication of plans will likely have occurred. However, with the insurance-linked securitisation project reaching a critical stage, it is appropriate that it be presented to the regulator in order that it may raise any questions it may have and, potentially, any objections to the proposed structure which will need to be addressed. The approach to the regulator will be made by

---

[15] The term "investor" is here being used once again in a broad sense.

the sponsor, but in discussions the sponsor is likely to wish to have advisers in attendance – regulatory aspects are covered further in Chapter 26.

As regards approaching the ratings agencies, as mentioned earlier, this may be in order to clarify how the transaction will be viewed from the perspective of the sponsor's rating (if rated), or may be with a view to having a rating assigned to the securities to be issued to investors – more detail is contained in Chapter 16.

Step 8: all other parties required for the functioning of the securitisation structure are identified

The roles of these parties, for example monoline insurers, liquidity and swap providers, have already been described and at this stage those who may fulfil the roles will be approached and the terms for their participation agreed.

Step 9: informal market soundings are taken to confirm the likelihood of successful issuance and indicative pricing levels

The arranger will approach a small number of investors known to be interested in participating in offerings of the specific type represented by the structure. As the structure will have been decided having regard to the needs of these investors, it is unlikely that any significant changes will result. The informal soundings will be used to gauge initial reactions from those who will most likely influence the success of the transaction if proceeded with. They should result in a good indication as to the pricing terms on which the market will absorb the transaction, the likely demand in order to gauge levels of competition amongst investors and the investor appetite, in terms of size, the better to gauge the number of investors likely to take a stake (or needed to take a stake) in the final offering.

Step 10: a formal decision is taken to proceed to close the transaction

Once all other matters have been decided, it now remains for the structure, agreed by all the parties thereto, and having been reviewed by the other interested parties, to be formally agreed by the sponsor and a decision taken by the sponsor to proceed to close the transaction.

Step 11: a roadshow is held to present the opportunity to investors

The investment opportunity is now presented to potential investors. A description of the opportunity, key risks, the transaction rationale and an analysis of returns to the investor in a range of scenarios will likely be presented. Potential investors will have the opportunity to seek clarification and may be able to ask for additional information. Senior representatives of the sponsor will almost certainly take part in the presentations to potential investors. The terms of the offering will be provided and investors will be in a position to decide on their participation.

Step 12: the transaction is closed

All transaction documentation will be signed by the parties to the structure. The bids from investors will be collated and the successful bidders determined in accordance with the offering terms. Securities will be issued and payment received from the investors. A wide range of legal matters need to be attended to immediately prior to and post transaction close, but these are largely routine matters. The transaction has closed and cash flows through the structure in accordance with the governing documentation.

The story doesn't end there though. For the entire duration of the transaction from closing, it needs to be administered and monitored in line with the governing documentation. This, like the structuring of the transaction, may require the involvement of a wide range of parties. Some of those parties may be needed to fulfil active functions throughout the entire duration, whilst others may only become involved in specific scenarios. However, the objectives of the securitisation have been decided, a structure designed, all those directly involved in the securitisation structure have been identified and have taken up their roles within the structure and the investment community has been approached and provided capital, risk transfer and/or liquidity as required.

15

Cedants' Perspectives on Life Securitization

Understanding the key motivating factors of a cedant in an ILS transaction is essential for the development and growth of this market. In this chapter, two major players present and analyse their perspectives, the context, some concrete examples, the challenges and the opportunities of life securitization as an advanced tool for risk mitigation, capital management and as a complement to traditional risk management solutions.

15A   A CEDANT'S PERSPECTIVE ON LIFE SECURITIZATION
Alison McKie[a]

15A.1   Why securitize?

Securitization is one of many tools available to a (re)insurer for risk or capital management purposes. The use of the capital markets to absorb insurance and related financial market risks, through securitization, increases the available capital to support these risks taken by (re)insurers and leads to greater capacity and a more efficient market.

Packaging life insurance risks into insurance-linked securities (ILS) enables sponsors to access additional capital in the fixed-income market, whose players value the ability to diversify risks and assets, and the opportunity to invest in instruments with a range of durations at attractive spreads.

Life ILS typically fall into three broad categories: first, catastrophe cover to manage peak risks, i.e., pandemic protection; second, embedded value (EV) securitizations to help firms manage their capital more efficiently; and third, financing transactions, such as redundant reserve financing, ie, 'XXX' or 'AXXX' securitizations where little or no insurance risk is transferred.

Life catastrophe cover

A good illustration of a life catastrophe cover is the Vita Capital program, which Swiss Re first launched in 2003 to cover its exposure should a lethal pandemic occur across a range of countries where the firm has its highest mortality exposure. The cover provided under the latest program, Vita Capital III, is based on increases in a mortality index during a period of two consecutive calendar years, in an overall risk exposure period of four years. The index is comprised of age- and gender-weighted death rates from publicly available sources covering five geographical regions: United States, United Kingdom, Germany, Japan and Canada. The weights are designed to replicate Swiss Re's current geographic and demographic mortality exposure. The trigger points vary by class of security under the program, with the most junior risk classes issued to date attaching at 110% of the index and the most senior at 125% of the index.

The Vita Capital III structure – also illustrated in Figure 15A.1 – is as follows:

- Swiss Re enters into a derivative contract (the 'counterparty contract') with Vita Capital III, which pays out to Swiss Re in the event the defined index increases above stated thresholds during the risk period.
- Vita Capital III issues floating rate notes (the 'notes') up to the notional amount of the counterparty contract to fully collateralize its contingent payments to Swiss Re.
- A portion of the notes are issued with a financial guarantee whereby a note guarantor promises timely interest and principal repayment to a noteholder.

---

[a]Swiss Re Services Ltd

Any opinion expressed in this work is the opinion of the author and is not to be taken to represent the opinion of the corporation by which the author is employed.

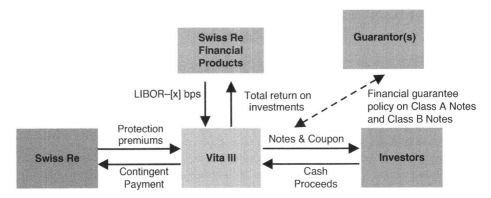

Figure 15A.1   Vita Capital III structure

Source: Swiss Re

- Proceeds of the notes are held in trust and invested in highly rated liquid collateral; the collateral assets and investment income are hedged with a total return swap provider (Swiss Re Financial Products, rated AA−/Aa2).
- If the mortality index value exceeds predefined levels, collateral is sold and a payment is made to Swiss Re; otherwise the collateral is liquidated at the redemption date of the notes and paid back to investors.

This type of securitization, covering the tail risk arising from an extreme mortality event, provides significant risk capital relief in Swiss Re's internal economic capital model.

Structures such as Vita help to build additional capacity into the (re)insurance market and improve efficiency. The value chain as a whole can benefit, in that direct insurers who accumulate mortality risk exposure may derive advantage from ceding a proportion to a reinsurer, who (depending on its scale and business mix) in turn aggregates and diversifies this risk across geographies and risk classes and/or transfers the remaining peak risk to the capital markets.

Embedded value

Embedded value securitizations are closer in nature to whole business securitizations, where numerous risks in the business are transferred to investors, but with issuers retaining a residual interest to ensure an alignment of interest with those buying the securities. Due to the bundled nature of a typical insurance policy, these transactions can cover a wide range of insurance and financial market risks including mortality, persistency, morbidity, interest rates, default and credit spreads.

Alternatively, the financial market risks can be retained by the issuer with only the insurance risks being transferred to investors. These securitizations facilitate efficient capital management and acceleration of the issuer's balance sheet. The structure effectively monetizes a proportion of expected future profits, which are an intangible asset, and enables the insurer to invest the proceeds in new business or other corporate opportunities. The duration of EV deals varies with the underlying insurance risk and product design; generally the weighted

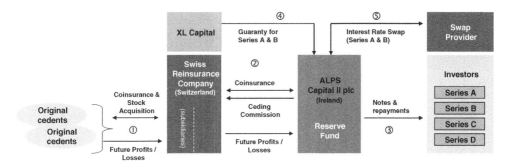

Figure 15A.2   ALPS Capital II structure

Source: Swiss Re

average life of the securities is between five and ten years but may be longer, particularly in more junior classes.

In 2005 Swiss Re sponsored two securitizations of selected blocks of its US Admin Re business – 'Queensgate' and 'ALPS Capital II'. The special purpose vehicles (SPVs) used in the transactions issued notes in various tranches to a range of investors totalling US $615 million and retained US $75 million in liquid assets to protect against short-term liquidity exposures, and to provide protection to Swiss Re against potential adverse performance. The remaining proceeds from the note issuance, US $540 million, were paid as a ceding commission at the inception of the deal to Swiss Re, thereby monetizing the value of the expected future profits. These proceeds, along with the associated capital supporting the business, were then able to be reinvested in new business or for general corporate purposes.

The ALPS Capital II structure – also illustrated in Figure 15A.2 – is as follows:

- Swiss Re acquires US individual life portfolios through Admin Re transactions.
- Swiss Re enters into a 'coinsurance agreement' with ALPS Capital II; at closing, Swiss Re receives a ceding commission of US $325m.
- ALPS issues US $370m of notes to pay the ceding commission and deposits the remaining US $45m into a reserve fund.
- XL Capital guarantees timely payment of interest and ultimate repayment of principal for the Series A and B notes.
- ALPS enters into an interest rate swap to hedge the interest rate risks on the Series A and B notes, which pays floating.

Financing transactions

The most typical financing transactions currently in the market are those used to fund the redundant or excess reserves that US life insurers are obliged to establish under Regulations XXX and AXXX, on either a recourse or a non-recourse basis. These financing-style transactions are not typically aimed at transferring insurance risk to the capital markets, but at providing efficient financing for the redundant reserves. This typically involves the issuance of debt (or surplus notes) from an SPV, with the proceeds invested in a high-quality asset

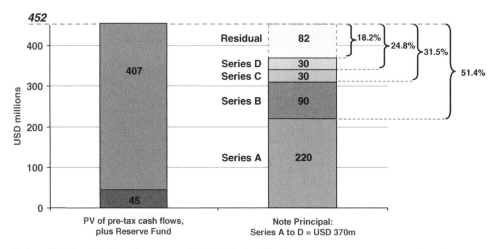

Figure 15A.3   Credit enhancement of ALPS Capital II

Source: Swiss Re

portfolio to back the excess reserves. This type of transaction therefore typically carries more financial market risk than insurance risk, with any insurance risk components being far out of the money. Some of these transactions have recently been adversely impacted due to their exposure to illiquid or lower quality assets. This has reinforced the need for the assets backing the portfolio to be of a high quality with timely reporting by issuers, in order to ensure that investors are able to monitor and mark their investments to market appropriately.

Due to the long-term nature of the liabilities, these transactions tend to have long duration, often in excess of ten-year weighted-average lives for senior securities.

Safeguards offered by issuers

The range of safeguards offered by issuers varies depending on the type of ILS. Given that the structure of the transactions is largely through a retrocession arrangement to an SPV with finite resources, the issuer retains the risk up to the attachment point and again after the exhaustion point. The issuer may also provide protection against financial market risk within the structure.

In an EV deal, the issuer creates credit enhancement by retaining a residual interest in the business. Figure 15A.3 illustrates the credit enhancement of ALPS Capital II where Swiss Re retained an 18.2% residual interest.

Issuers typically retain all the risk relating to the servicing of the business, along with the ongoing client/cedant relationships, and are therefore motivated to ensure that the business is managed on a consistent basis both before and after the securitization. Issuers also maintain their regulatory and legal responsibilities for the operation of the business.

15A.2   Life ILS can be complex

Due to the nature of life insurance risks, understanding the ILS risk profile means having some knowledge of the underlying products and the associated risk drivers. As part of any offering of securities, an independent actuarial consulting firm is engaged by the issuer to prepare a risk

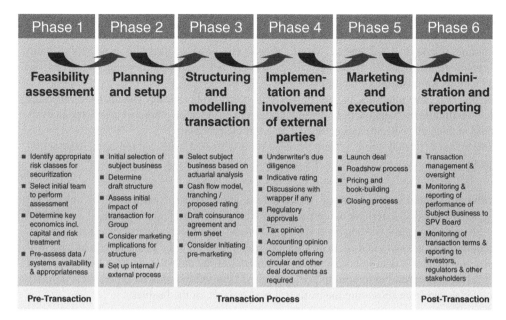

Phase 1	Phase 2	Phase 3	Phase 4	Phase 5	Phase 6
Feasibility assessment	Planning and setup	Structuring and modelling transaction	Implementation and involvement of external parties	Marketing and execution	Administration and reporting
▪ Identify appropriate risk classes for securitization ▪ Select initial team to perform assessment ▪ Determine key economics incl. capital and risk treatment ▪ Pre-assess data / systems availability & appropriateness	▪ Initial selection of subject business ▪ Determine draft structure ▪ Assess initial impact of transaction for Group ▪ Consider marketing implications for structure ▪ Set up internal / external process	▪ Select subject business based on actuarial analysis ▪ Cash flow model, tranching / proposed rating ▪ Draft coinsurance agreement and term sheet ▪ Consider initiating pre-marketing	▪ Underwriter's due diligence ▪ Indicative rating ▪ Discussions with wrapper if any ▪ Regulatory approvals ▪ Tax opinion ▪ Accounting opinion ▪ Complete offering circular and other deal documents as required	▪ Launch deal ▪ Roadshow process ▪ Pricing and book-building ▪ Closing process	▪ Transaction management & oversight ▪ Monitoring & reporting of performance of Subject Business to SPV Board ▪ Monitoring of transaction terms & reporting to investors, regulators & other stakeholders
Pre-Transaction		Transaction Process			Post-Transaction

Figure 15A.4   Key stages of a typical transaction

Source: Swiss Re

analysis report on the subject business. The actuarial firm uses the issuer's data and historic experience of the business to derive its independent view of a base-case set of assumptions, to which it applies stress tests in order to provide investors with a range of possible outcomes during the life of the security.

The granularity of this analysis can vary, depending on what level of risk is being transferred to the market. Depending on the complexity of the risks, investors may employ their own actuarial advisors to review the risks and form their own judgment.

Key stages of a typical transaction

A typical ILS transaction will involve many stages and both internal and external counterparties in order to achieve a successful outcome. The key stages are outlined in Figure 15A.4.

Selecting the subject business   It is important that the sponsor selects the most appropriate subject business for a transaction, i.e. for an embedded value transaction this may be a well-seasoned block with stable experience. The availability of good quality data is very important and the internal cash flow projections should be well modeled. Diversification should be considered, i.e. the degree of geographic/demographic diversification and whether potentially a mix of insurance products should be included; covering a range of different insurance risks, mortality, persistency, morbidity and investment risks.

Given the relatively high cost of ILS issuance, choosing a block of subject business with sufficient scale is very important.

Initial assessments of the structure   An initial assessment of possible economic outcomes from the transaction should be undertaken, including different capital bases (i.e. ratings, economic, regulatory), tax and accounting views. The possible jurisdiction of SPVs should be considered in light of the above analysis, legal and regulatory considerations and the implications for investors of the selection.

Risks that are intended to be transferred need to be clearly identifiable, measurable/quantifiable and capable of being monitored and reported on a timely basis. Risk analysis should include all risks, including those with a remote probability.

Internally a formal project team should be established with agreed-upon transaction objectives.

Involving external counterparties   Once the feasibility assessment has been completed the process of involving external counterparties commences. These include actuarial consultants to perform independent risk analysis of selected blocks of subject business, external legal and, if required, tax advisors and securities underwriters. Typically the actuarial consultants will utilize the sponsor's data to prepare their own model of the cash flows of the business. They will select appropriate assumptions, i.e. mortality, persistency rates based on their industry knowledge and from reviewing the historical performance of the business.

Transaction structuring   The sponsor will work closely with their actuarial consultant on the subject business model to verify the assumptions used, provide necessary data and analysis and reconciliation to internal models. Once the actuarial consultant's model has been created, the underwriters will commence work on the securities cash flow model, including proposed tranching and targeted ratings, targeted spreads and impact on proceeds to be raised, levels of collateralization, indicative capital amounts, taxes and sensitivities. The external legal team will put together an initial term sheet addressing key structural features of the transaction, such as legal entities and/or counterparties involved, notional amounts, cash flow mechanics (i.e. how the investors will receive their expected returns), duration, credit enhancements for investors, representations, warranties and covenants from the sponsor, etc. and first drafts of the key legal documents, including reinsurance agreements.

Structuring should take into account many factors, including the sponsor's commercial drivers, operational risk, regulatory and tax environments, capital and accounting and levels of residual risk, including legal risk being retained. There are many stakeholders to consider involving at this stage, including the sponsor's operational teams who will run the transaction post close, originators, investors, regulators, auditors, tax authorities and rating agencies. The extent of involvement will depend on the size, complexity and novelty factor of the structure being proposed.

Implementation   During the implementation phase the securities underwriter will commence their due diligence process and discussions will begin with rating agencies which may result in changes to the proposed structure, depending on feedback received. The sponsor will typically discuss the transaction in some detail with their home regulator and the regulator of any new jurisdiction being involved to ensure their understanding and support, in advance of formal applications for approval. All transaction documents will be drafted, including, where applicable, the offering circular, with a focus on risk factors, financial disclosure, business description, listing requirements, etc. Any required tax or accounting positions should be agreed with authorities and external auditors as necessary.

At the end of this phase the ratings for the transaction should have been provided, any accounting or tax positions signed off, the offering circular and other transaction documents finalized and approvals obtained from regulators.

It is likely that the underwriters will commence premarketing towards the end of this phase to ensure that the final structure and terms will be acceptable to investors.

Marketing and execution   The external bankers will largely guide the process at this point, with significant involvement from the sponsor, including the formal transaction launch, preparation of and participation in investor roadshows and in the approval of the syndication process, which includes pricing indications and final pricing of the issued instruments as well as monitoring the bookbuilding (size and characteristics of investors' orders) and assessing the impact on the amounts to be issued (transactions can be downsized or – often in ILS – upsized from initial targeted amounts).

Subject to satisfactory terms being met, at the end of this process the formal transaction documents are signed and the closing process, including cash transfers, completes.

Post-close monitoring and reporting   Monitoring and reporting of the subject business needs to be completed on a timely basis and to a materiality standard appropriate for capital market transactions; the necessary processes to support this should be formalized well in advance of the transaction closing in order to ensure good corporate governance. After closing, the transaction should run on auto-pilot to ensure consistency over time, given that some transactions can have a legal final maturity of up to 30 years.

Use of monolines

Historically, most life ILS EV and financing transactions offered to the market have included the guarantee of a monoline insurance company (also defined as a 'wrap') on the high investment-grade tranches, assisting those investors wishing to supplement their own actuarial diligence. Given 2008 market conditions, which affected the credit quality of monoline insurance companies and their appetite for new business, it is not clear whether the monolines will return to play a significant role in future transactions of this nature.

Peak risk transactions have not used a monoline structure in significant volume, given the digital nature of the risk. Vita Capital III did, however, offer a monoline wrap on the more senior tranches to those investors who preferred this approach.

In the future, assuming monolines provide guarantees on future ILS issues, it is likely that issuers will wish to provide flexibility to those specific investors who would like to take advantage of a monoline wrap, rather than simply issuing either with or without.

If the availability of monoline guarantees becomes significantly diminished in the future, organizations will need to engage the necessary specialists to fully consider the risks in more complex structures, such as where a specific portfolio of insurance policies is being securitized (and there are obvious efficiencies in having only a small number of firms doing such work). Equally, investors may prefer to undertake the necessary diligence on their own account in return for the higher yield offered at a lower rating.

Ongoing reporting

An area of key focus for issuers at the moment is the appropriate level of ongoing reporting for investors in ILS, particularly EV and financing transactions, which may carry financial market risk in addition to insurance risk. As this asset class is still evolving, as yet there are no industry-standard disclosure requirements. However, steps are being taken to increase the frequency and detail of regular reporting, particularly on the asset side. In order to enhance the current market development, issuers will need to be highly focused on producing timely, relevant reporting for investors to facilitate better marking to market and trading of securities.

15A.3   Outlook for life ILS

The life insurance industry is a significant contributor to the global economy, with a wide range of traditional and new products available to protect individuals, families and companies against the financial impacts of death, disability, critical illness, medical treatment and care needs – along with products enabling people to efficiently accumulate wealth and to spend it in retirement. With a growing and aging global population, coupled with significant gaps in the amount of protection cover people hold, the life insurance industry has significant growth potential. This will provide a wide and deep pool of insurance and financial market risks for future life ILS issuances.

There are many factors to encourage (re)insurers to focus more on economic capital, including regulatory change and developments in internal risk management and rating agency capital models. Generally, to date, regulatory and rating capital requirements have focused on applying fixed risk-based factors to determine appropriate capital adequacy. This approach is generally determined on a 'ruin theory' basis, which reflects a conservative view of an industry-wide exposure to risk but does not necessarily mirror an individual company's economic capital requirements. Some regulatory environments and ratings tests supplement the risk-based approach with additional stress and scenario testing. Regulators in many markets, along with rating agencies, require companies to establish a solvency margin to satisfy specific adverse events such as a 1-in-200-year mortality shock, or are considering moving towards such an approach.

As (re)insurers increase their focus on economic capital, whether through Solvency II or International Financial Reporting Standards (IFRS) developments in Europe, a greater regulatory focus in the United States, or through changes to rating agency models, the use of tools to manage peak risks is expected to increase, driving more (re)insurers to seek efficient mechanisms to transfer insurance risk from their balance sheets.

While precise details of its planned introduction are not yet available, the widely anticipated move towards principles-based reserving in the United States is expected to reduce the level of excess reserves required, which may limit the volume of redundant reserve financing transactions. However, it is believed that this will not be applied retroactively, and it may not be in effect for at least four years, meaning that a significant volume of excess reserves on business written before the change takes effect will still require reserve financing.

Akin to the banking model, shareholder pressure will continue to encourage (re)insurers to improve capital management and acceleration of the balance sheet. This should increase the volume of EV ILS deals.

These forces will combine to encourage issuers to increase their use of ILS wherever risks can be clearly identified, measured, reported and competitively priced by the capital markets. The regions most likely to see a greater issuance volume in the short term are in the larger (re)insurance markets, i.e. the United States and Europe.

15B A CEDANT'S PERSPECTIVE ON LIFE SECURITIZATION

Chris Madsen[a]

15B.1 Key considerations

Just as there are many different securitization structures, there are many motives for an insurance company (the 'cedant') to undertake a securitization. These motives include risk transfer, capital relief and monetizing an anticipated future profit stream. In the following pages, we take a look at some of the key aspects from the cedant's perspective.

Value creation

In pure economic terms and absent taxes, securitization does not create economic value that did not previously exist. However, regulatory requirements may trap that economic value, making it impossible to use for another purpose. Securitizations can help free this trapped value. In other words, value is not created out of thin air, but value may be recognized if the securitization allows a company to realize 'trapped' economics. Note, one area where value can be created is if the aggregate tax position of all activity relating to the structure is more favorable after securitization. In this case there can be an actual increase in after-tax value even after all the fees.

The fees involved include paying the bankers to place the securities, the lawyers drafting the documentation and the prospectus, the consultants to approve any modeling that is required, the credit enhancer to guarantee some of the tranches, rating agencies and the time of internal staff. The result is that the process of securitization causes some of the economic value to be transferred from the originator and investor to other parties to the transaction. The critical step in the analysis is whether the advantages are worth this cost.

Apart from the more direct value creation, securitization can also be used effectively to increase ROE. As securitizations move risks off the balance sheet, the capital requirements for the remaining business drops, allowing the company to return capital to shareholders, redeploy capital to finance the growth of other business lines or to make acquisitions. Does this create value? Perhaps not directly, but it will allow the company to grow faster (increasing book value) while achieving a higher ROE. The higher ROE will, in theory, afford a higher price-to-book ratio, and since the growth is also growing the book value, the resulting growth in share price should be all the more powerful . . . in theory. In reality, the decision as to whether the securitization creates value comes down to the use of any funds or capital raised. If the funds or capital can be invested more effectively elsewhere, then the securitization creates value. But any entity considering securitization has to be mindful that this is a form of leverage – whether it is considered to be operational or financial.

Impact on liquidity

Securitization can either improve or deteriorate liquidity depending on the structure. The securitization of illiquid asset classes on the balance sheet improves the liquidity of the asset

---

[a]Risk Structuring and Transfer, Group Risk, AEGON NV

The Handbook of Insurance-Linked Securities   Edited by P. Barrieu and L. Albertini

class. This has been the result of the large well-developed mortgage-backed securities market, which nonetheless at the time of writing is experiencing substantial stress. The benefit of securitization is that virtually any asset on the balance sheet can be securitized to raise cash instead of actually selling the asset outright. It may be that the cost of the securitization is prohibitive[1] due to market conditions, but it is an option.

In securitizations that involve blocks of business, the liquidity of the company may actually deteriorate. Upon closing the transaction liquidity is improved when the cash is paid to the originator in exchange for the cash flows transferred to the special purpose entity (SPE). However, if the asset and liability cash flows need to be isolated in an SPE, these assets are no longer available to meet liquidity needs on the balance sheet.[2]

Whether or not the liquidity deteriorates depends on the liquidity profile of what business (assets and liabilities) remains with the company relative to the company liquidity profile before the securitization.

Capital redundancy

Capital redundancy is a current motivator of securitization including XXX reserve issues. The key consideration here is that although one particular block of business may have a capital redundancy, the position of the entire company should be considered before expensive and complicated transactions are executed. An internal economic capital model can help to identify the company's capital position relative to redundant reserves. The goal of capital redundancy securitizations is to improve measures of operating performance (most notably return on regulatory capital).

The basis of these transactions is that the regulatory reserve requirements combined with the regulatory capital requirements tie up more capital than is economically necessary to support the line of business. By securitizing the redundant portion, SPE investors provide debt capital to support the business. This reduces the cost of capital.

The net effect of the debt capital depends on the structure of the securitization. As long as trapped capital in excess of economic capital is released, the securitization adds value. However, if some of the risk remains on the balance sheet and is not fully hedged, there could be increased leverage in the block of business if some capital relief is still allowed. It could also be argued that the blocks of business most often securitized are those that are most stable and therefore most attractive for investors. Once these are removed from the balance sheet, the remaining book is more volatile and operational leverage may have been increased. The key consideration thus becomes the evaluation of regulatory/rating agency capital versus economic capital. A 'XXX' securitization (more on this in the section entitled 'Reserve funding securitizations' later in this chapter) is an example where the regulatory requirement exceeds the economic requirement. By securitizing the business, the redundant excess capital (the excess of regulatory over economic) can be released, allowing both future profits to be realized up front and return on capital to increase. However, this is seldom a one-off consideration; it must be viewed in conjunction with all the other capital considerations in the company.

---

[1] In order to attract a deep investor base, the asset profile that is transferred to the 'special purpose entity' (SPE) must be relatively transparent; otherwise the securities would need to yield a higher price.

[2] This could be mitigated through a 'modified coinsurance' arrangement where the assets actually stay on the balance sheet of the insurer.

Strengthen capital position

A company may need to strengthen its capital position. In such cases, raising cash through securitization is one way to improve capital adequacy by hedging the uncertainty in the future profit stream as well as accelerating the expected outcome. It is important to have debt structure plans in place well in advance of any specific need for capital strengthening, as it takes time (usually 6–12 months) to complete a transaction.

Sources of capital financing have traditionally been restrictive due to the heavy regulation of the insurance industry, but both securitization and any related structured debt issuance help to broaden the opportunities.

Managing concentration

If a company's concentration (or risk exposure) is considered too high in a given geographic area or line of business, it is possible that a securitization may help. As with other considerations, it comes down to weighing benefits and expenses. As long as the cost of capital paid through the securitization is less than the return on the same capital measure achieved through the business, then this type of transaction is practically feasible.[3]

The current typical insurance company structure bears risk in the policies issued and takes risk in the investment of the proceeds from policy issuance. At the other end of the spectrum is the intermediary model – generally used by investment banks. True intermediaries always look to capital market clearing levels to hedge risks that they have taken on. The intermediaries are, in effect, creating a pricing rationality check for the risk initially.

Securitization is a tool to transfer the risks while maintaining the flexibility to retain different forms of risk than were originally sourced on the balance sheet. This can be done by retaining some of the tranches of the SPE that have a different risk profile than the asset in its original form. For this purpose, securitization becomes a strategic management tool.

Divestment of business

A company may choose to exit a market for strategic reasons. For example, the company may feel it lacks the scale to compete effectively. Securitization offers the potential to cash in closed blocks of business, but transparency of such blocks of business is crucial in order to securitize the blocks successfully. Lack of transparency leads to higher spreads paid in the contingent coupons. Further, in order to exit a business entirely (not keeping any residual), the investors need to understand the business and the risk they are assuming very well. The originating company also needs a solid investor story. This can lead to substantial costs that need to be reviewed in a strategic context.

Reaction from rating agencies and regulators

Both regulators and rating agencies need to be consulted in advance to make sure the desired effects are realized. For reasons already mentioned, the regulators don't want to see the remaining policyholders disadvantaged by the transfers to the SPE. Similarly, the rating agencies have concerns for the remaining capital structure of the company.

---

[3] If the cost of capital exceeds the returns on the business, then the company should probably review its pricing.

Impact on financial statements

It is important to fully understand the impact on the income statement and balance sheet, both short-term and long-term. This topic has been touched on already as we discussed the fact that value is accelerated to the originator in return for the SPE investors taking the value over time. Tax considerations play a very important role in the economics but also the financial statement impact.

Deregulation of the financial services industry has put pressure on capital efficiencies. The pressure to use securitization for insurance structures is likely to continue, despite the natural hiccups along the way. The growth of insurance-related securitization is likely to impact financial statements even for companies that have no securitizations themselves. Through market value accounting, a company's assessment of value will be more transparent. Since determining the market value of the business securitized is a natural part of a securitization, market prices of insurance business will become more transparent as the number of securitizations increases. This creates the ability to infer market prices about business that is still on insurance company balance sheets – possibly pressuring companies that are at odds with such value assessments. In the end, securitization allows for a more current market evaluation of the business and it allows companies to hedge risks that previously were unhedgeable.

15B.2   Examples of securitization opportunities

Securitization of future cash flows from a block of business

On the liability securitization side, there is a trade-off between spread paid and the level of transparency and predictability of the risks. Note that liability securitization generally does not transfer the risk in the sale sense – a novation (a complete transfer of obligation) does accomplish this but is a burdensome exercise due to regulatory constraints. Any liabilities that are securitized by an entity do not relieve that entity from its responsibility to pay the policyholder and as such never truly leave the balance sheet. The tail risk that exists when investor funds are exhausted still exists with the company. Securitization of liabilities does transfer some or most of the economic risk, but the extent to which that occurs depends on the final structure.

The securitized block of business is preferred by investors to be profitable and structured to a separation of cash flows (payments and proceeds). This introduces the practical difficulty of identifying the assets to support the block that is both acceptable to investors but does not disadvantage the business that remains on the balance sheet, which would be unacceptable to regulators. One way to accomplish this is through 'modified coinsurance' where the assets remain on the insurer's balance sheet. The asset performance that relates to investors is simply an index-based return in this case. Since the company retains the assets, it can decide to fully hedge its exposure to the index or it may decide to invest assets differently. In the latter case, the company is effectively adding asset risk to achieve a spread return over and above that resulting from the index.

Any business that has high margins is a possible candidate for securitization. Historically, this has only applied to mature blocks of business. But, any block of business that has high up-front expenses that are to be recovered from future profits is a candidate for securitization. Some possible candidate businesses are:

- management and expense fees on unit linked or variable annuity products;
- embedded value of either fee business or traditional life products.

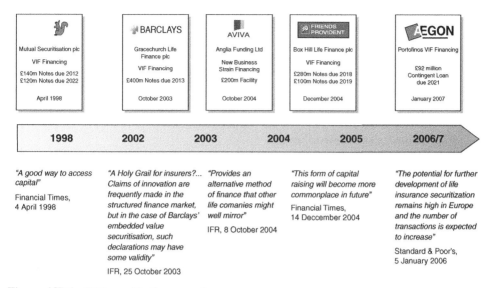

Figure 15B.1 VIF securitization examples

Source: AEGON

As this type of securitization realizes the embedded value of the business or the 'value-in-force' (VIF), these types of securitization are often referred to as VIF securitizations. A few examples are given in Figure 15B.1.

AEGON has executed several VIF transactions. An example is a private UK VIF transaction with Barclays that was completed in January 2007 in the amount of GBP 92 million. In this case, Barclays Capital provided fixed-rate contingent lending to AEGON, where the payment of interest and repayment of principal was contingent on the emergence of regulatory surplus from a closed book of business. Though these transactions are often wrapped and publicly rated to make them more attractive to investors, this was not done in this case. The advantage of doing a private transaction is that these steps were not necessary. There were a number of key considerations to AEGON at both the holding company level and at the local level. These are summarized in Figure 15B.2.

Reserve funding securitizations

The most common reserve funding securitization is the securitization of US Regulation XXX and AXXX reserves. Such securitizations have also been completed by AEGON. For example, in May 2007, AEGON closed an offering of US $550 million of 30-year maturity securities by its wholly owned subsidiary LIICA Holdings LLC. The proceeds from the issuance were used to fund certain statutory Regulation XXX reserves associated with level premium term life insurance policies. So these transactions securitize the expected emergence of mortality-based redundant reserves. Generally, a XXX securitization involves one entity raising funds and transferring the funds to an SPE, which then supports the XXX block of another business, freeing up capital for this business. As a result, the company gets the benefit of lowering the cost of capital associated with this business.

Key criteria for assessing capital management options Comments

AEGON Group level	1. Improve the AEGON Group cash flow and/ or capital position	Capital returned to AEGON NV
	2. Maintain capital leverage within internal tolerance	Does not contribute to capital leverage
	3. Viewed positively by the ratings agencies - Neutral to positive impact on ratings financial leverage - Neutral to positive impact on ratings fixed charge cover	As the financing is non-recourse it does not contribute to measures of financial leverage or fixed charge cover
	4. Improve key measures of AEGON Group financial performance	More cost efficient than equity capital thus will improve financial measures such as ROE and RoEV
Operating unit level	5. Maintain strong capitalisation under rating agencies models	Creates core regulatory capital, converts EV into cash
	6. Maintain strong capitalisation under local reg. cap. requirements	
	7. Improve cash flow position of the operating unit/enable operating unit to pay dividend	Will improve cash flow position of the operating unit and depending on distributable reserves may enable operating unit to pay dividend
	8. Improve return on required capital	May reduce the quantum of required capital for the operating unit and/or the cost of required capital

Figure 15B.2   Key criteria

Source: AEGON

Transactions around redundant reserves have been successful but run the risk of being considered financial leverage if not structured properly.[4]

Current possibilities for reserve funding securitizations include:

- term insurance;
- mortality portion of universal life;
- payout annuities;
- traditional insurance;
- fixed annuities with reserving tied to minimum crediting rates.

Life insurance risk transfer securitizations

True life risk transfer securitizations in the broader sense are more theoretical than practical at this stage of the market development.[5] The most transparent risks would again be the most plausible. There are also some less likely lines of business due to the difficulty of predicting all the drivers of the economics. But it is theoretically possible to securitize the following for the purposes of risk transfer:

- long-term care;
- short-term disability;
- long-term disability.

---

[4] There are also limits to operational leverage enforced by the rating agencies through the ratings review process.

[5] In the non-life market, catastrophe bonds are an example of risk transfer securitizations. The same structure could be applied to extreme mortality events and there have been some examples, but they are hardly commonplace yet.

Under the banner of risk transfer securitizations, a company could issue the debt portion of its capital base on a contingent basis. The debt would be contingent on the performance of an index or the occurrence of an event. If there is a predefined change in the index or a specific event occurs, the obligation to repay the debt investor is partially or totally reduced. This has the effect of improving the quality of the capital base at a time of stress.

Pure asset securitizations

On the asset side, the rapid expansion of securitization allowed almost any asset to be securitized until recently. In addition, recent changes to the rules regarding special purpose entities (SPEs) mean that it is not really possible to securitize an asset class without giving up most of the economics. Almost all asset securitizations now result in the asset being removed from the balance sheet.

However, as with liability securitizations, for units that are skilled at sourcing an asset class, this remains an excellent tool for transferring the risk with a residual gain to the sourcing business. This is very important in terms of risk management since it facilitates liquidity to illiquid asset classes as well as reducing excessive exposures.

Unlike liability-driven securitization, which requires assets and liabilities in a portfolio, asset securitization is done on positively identifiable cash flows. The following are all candidates for asset securitization:

- residential mortgages;
- commercial whole loans;
- private placements;
- investment grade bonds;
- high-yield bonds;
- hedge funds;
- sale and leaseback of real estate (really a hybrid of securitization).

Reinsurance recoverables could also potentially be securitized.

15B.3 Differences between securitization and reinsurance

Insurance companies have traditionally looked at the reinsurance contract as a way of transferring/reducing their risk exposures. Limited availability, increasing reinsurance costs and concerns about exposure to reinsurer credit risk have forced some companies to look into alternative solutions for transferring risk.

Reinsurance has also been the traditional tool to alleviate certain reserve strains. This too has been the subject of concerns as regulators have stepped up efforts to curtail inappropriate finite reinsurance activities.

Securitizing a block of business provides an alternative whereby risk is transferred to the capital markets instead of to reinsurers. The difference really only exists in the form of the counterparty (and thus the credit risk), but in substance they are almost identical and most securitizations in fact involve reinsurance between the SPE and the issuing entity. In either case, the liabilities do not truly leave the balance sheet. Instead, what is created is a receivable from the counterparty. In the case of reinsurance, it is obviously the reinsurer, but in the case of securitization it is the investors via the SPE. It is also possible to achieve the same economic risk transfer via a derivative contract but there could be some regulatory risk, since a regulator may stop the payment from the insurer upon seizure following a deterioration of the insurer below regulatory minimum thresholds.

Reinsurance may offer a few advantages over securitization for risk transfer purposes, but these are counterbalanced by the credit risk issue. Conversely, reinsurance transactions with a reinsurer can normally be entered into quickly whereas a securitization takes time. Finally, costs may be vastly different, and reinsurance treaties can be extremely flexible and incorporate most, if not all, aspects of the transaction. Securitization documentation is much larger in volume and more cumbersome, but it ensures that everything is agreed up front. There is little room for surprises.

In practice, the costs associated with securitization require large transactions to keep the relative costs at a marketable level. The relatively low set-up cost of reinsurance allows for smaller size transactions.

The conclusion is that securitization is a viable alternative that should be evaluated alongside other funding solutions such as traditional debt and reinsurance. Under certain market conditions, securitization is likely the best answer, whereas reinsurance may be preferred under other market conditions. In the end, securitization is another option in a company's capital management toolbox. It has some clear advantages as regulators move to a market-consistent framework, but it is still costly and time-consuming to implement, thus requiring minimum economies of scale.

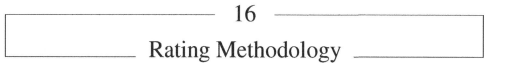

16
Rating Methodology

Harish Gohil[a]

In this chapter, Fitch sets out how it analyses insurance-linked securitization (ILS) transactions from the point of view of rating the notes issued. The impact on Fitch's analysis of the sponsoring insurance company is also touched upon. While the focus of this chapter is clearly on life securitizations, it also briefly covers non-life transactions, partly to put life transactions in context but mainly because Fitch's overall ILS rating methodology aims to be consistent across all types of transactions.

16.1 FITCH'S APPROACH TO THE RATING PROCESS

For informational and pedagogical purposes, Fitch has published a number of criteria papers and sector reports (see references at the end of this chapter). The agency's overarching global ILS criteria paper outlines the broad principles of how ILS transactions are analysed and rated. This is supported by more detailed criteria papers covering specific kinds of transactions, including one on natural catastrophe bonds and one on life insurance reserve financing.

ILS are structured finance transactions that involve insurance risk. Fitch therefore staffs each ILS rating team with representatives from its insurance and structured finance groups. The insurance team members may be either life or non-life analysts depending on the insurance risk transferred. In some cases the team may be supplemented with public finance or sovereign analysts if the sponsor is a government entity.

The rating process of any transaction involves an analysis of the insurance risk, an analysis of the structure and an analysis of the legal risks. The structural and legal review is something that is common to all structured finance transactions, and this is undertaken by the Fitch structured finance group. On the other hand, the analysis of insurance risk is specific to ILS and is performed by the Fitch insurance group.

The rest of this chapter focuses on the insurance analysis aspects of Fitch's rating approach for ILS. However, it should be noted that based on the findings of the structural and legal review, Fitch may then adjust the rating implied by the modelled loss statistics either up or down to reflect structural risks or enhancements to derive the final ratings of the securities issued. In this way, the final rating recommendation reflects the combination of the insurance, structural and legal reviews.

---

[a]Fitch Ratings Ltd

The Handbook of Insurance-Linked Securities   Edited by P. Barrieu and L. Albertini
Chapter 16 © 2009 Fitch Ratings Ltd

16.2   INSURANCE RISK ANALYSIS

The key steps in Fitch's insurance analysis process include the following:

- estimate the probability of loss, through modelling of the risks;
- compare the estimated probability of loss to Fitch's default rate grid to determine the implied rating;
- analyse the risk of the sponsoring insurer.

These and other related aspects are described in the following sections.

16.2.1   Risk modelling

An important aspect of Fitch's rating process is modelling, which is a key part of the process for rating any kind of ILS transaction. Fitch strongly prefers the use of stochastic techniques wherever feasible, rather than the stress tests traditionally employed by rating agencies, which can be arbitrary and difficult to justify or calibrate. An insurance stochastic model involves simulating a variety of risks that are relevant for a given transaction, such as mortality or investment risk, and thereby generating a number of future possible outcomes for the performance of the transaction. Thus, for instance, there may be 10 000 such future simulations generated and one can then consider how many of those simulations would lead to a loss for investors. If there were, say, 50 simulations that led to a loss, the probability of loss would simply be 0.5% (i.e. 50 in 10 000) and this then implies a particular rating level (as described in the next subsection). On the other hand, a stress test approach involves defining, for a given risk, what levels of stress the transaction must be able to withstand, for a particular rating level to be achievable – it is these levels of stress per rating level that can be difficult to justify, other than by reference to expert judgement and intuition, in the absence of a stochastic approach. It is a much more challenging technical task to develop an appropriate stochastic model but Fitch believes it is fundamentally a more sound approach.

However, Fitch can and does use deterministic stresses as a proxy for stochastic modelling, effectively using a stochastic model to help it to come up with the correct calibration for the level of stress to apply. Fitch recognizes, however, that it is not feasible or readily possible to use a stochastic approach for certain risks – policy lapse risk is an important example of such a risk. Policy lapse rates are a difficult factor to model as they depend heavily on policyholders' future behaviour, which in turn can be affected by changes in tax and regulatory environment, and general economic conditions. Indeed, it can be argued that large 'step changes' in lapse experience are more of an issue than random variability around a mean level, meaning that a stress test approach may actually be preferable for this particular risk. One further point regarding lapse risk is that it can be correlated with investment markets. Therefore, where appropriate, Fitch would consider modelling lapses with a dynamic link to investment returns (which themselves may be modelled stochastically).

Fitch has developed its own stochastic insurance capital model, called Prism, that is used, where possible, to support the rating analysis of ILS transactions. Prism has both life and non-life modules that simulate a variety of risks, on an aggregated and correlated basis, to which insurers are exposed, including natural catastrophe risk, mortality risk, investment risk and reinsurance collectibility risk. In addition, the agency also has the capability to build bespoke models where appropriate and necessary. That said, Fitch often uses loss output from models built by qualified third parties, or models that are properly reviewed independently by a third party.

Table 16.1 Ten-year cumulative default table

(%)	1	2	3	4	5	6	7	8	9	10
AAA	0.005	0.017	0.033	0.054	0.078	0.106	0.138	0.172	0.21	0.251
AA+	0.01	0.031	0.058	0.092	0.132	0.176	0.225	0.279	0.336	0.397
AA	0.015	0.046	0.088	0.139	0.2	0.267	0.342	0.424	0.512	0.607
AA−	0.022	0.067	0.128	0.202	0.287	0.383	0.489	0.604	0.728	0.86
A+	0.03	0.09	0.171	0.27	0.384	0.512	0.653	0.806	0.97	1.145
A	0.034	0.104	0.199	0.315	0.45	0.602	0.769	0.951	1.147	1.356
A−	0.047	0.146	0.281	0.448	0.642	0.862	1.105	1.37	1.656	1.962
BBB+	0.189	0.471	0.804	1.173	1.572	1.995	2.44	2.904	3.384	3.88
BBB	0.279	0.698	1.191	1.74	2.331	2.959	3.617	4.302	5.01	5.739
BBB−	0.386	0.956	1.622	2.357	3.146	3.979	4.848	5.749	6.677	7.628
BB+	0.548	1.311	2.178	3.117	4.111	5.148	6.219	7.319	8.442	9.585
BB	0.737	1.795	3.012	4.339	5.747	7.218	8.738	10.296	11.885	13.496
BB−	1.989	4.451	7.086	9.808	12.571	15.348	18.117	20.865	23.581	26.256
B+	3.015	6.325	9.678	13.013	16.3	19.522	22.668	25.73	28.706	31.591
B	5.964	11.25	16.131	20.677	24.932	28.924	32.677	36.211	39.542	42.684
B−	10.867	18.703	25.324	31.111	36.256	40.878	45.062	48.868	52.346	55.535
CCC+	22.274	33.57	41.901	48.519	53.976	58.582	62.533	65.964	68.97	71.624

Source: Fitch Ratings

The important point is that Fitch needs to get comfortable with whatever model is being used and get to a point where the agency has confidence in the model and believes that it is robust and produces a probability loss curve that meets Fitch's rating criteria.

16.2.2 Ratings benchmarks

The primary focus of the insurance analysis is to evaluate the probability that there will be a failure to make a principal or interest payment as scheduled. In other words, in actually assigning ILS ratings to the notes to be issued, Fitch bases the rating on probability of default, i.e. 'first dollar' loss. This approach is used across Fitch for all structured finance transactions. This is in contrast to corporate finance debt issues, where the rating is based on expected loss, i.e. a combination of the probability of default and the loss given default. Each of these approaches reflects established practice in the respective areas.

The default rate grid that is used for ILS purposes to determine the implied rating is the same one used throughout Fitch insurance. In particular, it is used in Fitch's insurance capital model, Prism, for assessing capital adequacy levels. This means there is consistency and symmetry between insurance company ratings and ILS ratings. A ten-year extract of the default grid is shown in Table 16.1 for illustrative purposes. The full 30-year cumulative default table has been published in the criteria papers referred to in the references at the end of this chapter.

One specific point to highlight is that for ILS tranches that are exposed to loss for investors from a single event, the rating would be capped at a level of 'AA', even if the modelled probability of default were low enough to imply a higher rating. This reflects Fitch's understanding that at the highest rating levels investors would not expect to incur a loss simply from the occurrence of a single event. In practice, this is not really a constraint, as transactions that involve the possibility of a loss from a single event (such as natural catastrophe bonds) generally tend to be rated at much lower levels anyway based on the modelled probability of default.

16.2.3   Analysis of sponsor and other counterparties

The analysis of the sponsor is the final part of Fitch's insurance analysis. In most cases, Fitch already rates the insurance entity concerned, so it is not usually a case of Fitch having to do this from scratch as part of an ILS transaction.

The need for, and weighting of, the sponsor analysis could vary greatly depending on the type of transaction. For example, parametric catastrophe bonds might include minimal weighting of the sponsor analysis while indemnity catastrophe bonds, Regulation XXX or VIF life insurance transactions may require significant analysis and have a greater influence on the overall rating.

For VIF transactions in particular, the performance of the portfolio that is being securitized can be very much linked with the performance of the insurance company as a whole. For example, if there were some bad publicity or reputation issue affecting the company, there may well be increased lapses from the securitized book, even though there was no issue with that book as such. This is because, of course, the insurance company continues to manage and service the securitized block of business. In any case, there is no 'true sale' of the portfolio, so it is difficult to see an effective de-linking of the rating of the instrument from the rating of the sponsor.

In terms of life ILS, other key counterparties can include monoline insurers (to guarantee the credit quality of certain tranches of issuance), and the total return swap counterparties.

The development of life ILS deals had always somewhat suffered from investor reluctance to take on lower-rated tranches and was reliant on guarantees from the monoline insurers to achieve high ratings. Since the severe effects of the credit crunch manifested themselves from late 2007 onwards, these monolines are no longer a feature of the market, so it remains to be seen how the VIF market will develop in future.

16.2.4   Surveillance

Life ILS ratings are reviewed at least annually. However, ratings may be reviewed more frequently if warranted, e.g. if a relevant event occurs or if the credit quality of the sponsor or a key counterparty changes. Details on the events which might cause a rating review will vary depending on the type of ILS.

Life ILS ratings can be upgraded or downgraded or placed on 'rating watch'. Rating watches indicate that there is a heightened probability of a rating change in the short term and the likely direction of such a change. These are designated as 'positive', indicating a potential upgrade, 'negative', for a potential downgrade, or 'evolving', if ratings may be raised, lowered or maintained. Likewise, rating outlooks may change – outlooks indicate the direction the rating is likely to move over a one- to two-year period. The events that might trigger a rating watch or changes in rating or rating outlook include, but are not limited to, the following:

• the occurrence of a catastrophe that causes a large loss of life;
• a significant divergence in actual lapse or mortality rates from that assumed;
• a significant divergence in actual interest rate spreads or default rates from that assumed;
• a significant divergence of equity markets from that assumed in the underlying modelling;
• a change in the credit quality of a key counterparty (e.g., sponsor, guarantor or swap counterparty);
• an event of default under the notes' indenture (e.g., a failure to pay premiums or an insolvency proceeding) has occurred.

Fitch maintains ratings on most major insurers, banks and counterparties. Thus, surveillance of those entities occurs in the normal course of maintaining those ratings. However, if the sponsor was not otherwise rated by Fitch, then it is likely that Fitch would have to maintain periodic surveillance of the sponsor.

It is worth adding that, on occasion, Fitch does provide private rating assessments, and it is possible for these to be done on a 'point-in-time' basis, i.e. ratings are assigned and communicated privately at outset to the party that requested the rating (which could be an investor, the arranger or the sponsor, as the case may be), with no subsequent ongoing surveillance and updating of the ratings.

16.3   ZEST: A VIF CASE STUDY

In this section, an example of a VIF transaction is described, to illustrate Fitch's rating approach and methodology. A VIF transaction in essence crystallizes part of an intangible asset, namely the present value of a stream of future profits from an existing block of business. A VIF transaction can therefore be of significant benefit to the sponsoring company. It can enhance financial flexibility, improve liquidity, release tied-up capital and improve return on equity.

However, in assessing the overall benefit to a sponsoring company's ratings, a key consideration for Fitch is the use of proceeds. If a company is monetizing future earnings in order to invest in something comparatively risky, then the overall risk profile of the sponsor may increase and therefore there could, in theory, be an adverse impact on the company's ratings.

A further important point is that the block of business that is securitized in a VIF transaction is likely to be the safest and most stable of the future cash flows. That would leave the riskiest and most volatile book on the company's balance sheet.

In 2008, Zest was the latest development in VIF transactions. In fact, it was the only VIF deal during the year. The sponsor in this case was AEGON, through its main UK subsidiary, Scottish Equitable plc. It was a private transaction, which raised £250m, qualifying as Core Tier 1 capital from a regulatory perspective. There was a single tranche issued, which was rated 'A' by Fitch.

Key features of this innovative transaction included:

• a simple contingent lending structure (as illustrated in Figure 16.1);
• a segmented block of business within an open fund;
• a defined block permitted to 'revolve';
• a model definition of surplus – no expense risk;
• no monoline guarantee.

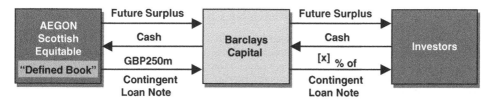

Figure 16.1   Zest structure

Source: Fitch Ratings (transaction documents)

The block of business whose profits are securitized under this transaction is permitted to 'revolve'. More specifically, each year for the first three years, policies that were not initially part of the segmented block of business or new business written during the year would, given certain conditions, be permitted to be moved into the segmented block. This allows Scottish Equitable to maintain the collateral backing the notes rather than amortising the notes. This means that the finance outstanding remains at £250m for four years which, as well as being beneficial for the sponsor, was seen as an advantage for attracting potential investors.

Principal and interest is payable only out of surplus arising on the defined block of business. There is a model definition of surplus for the purposes of the transaction – in particular, expense risk is not part of the Zest transaction, being retained by Scottish Equitable.

The issued notes did not benefit from a financial guarantee insurance policy, but nor was the rating on the notes constrained by the sponsor's rating. As such, the rating was based on:

- volatility of underlying profit sources;
- cash flow stress-test results; and
- transaction cash flow and legal structure.

Fitch's rating process included a review of the embedded value methodology, assumptions and actuarial model developed by Scottish Equitable. Tillinghast, an actuarial consulting firm of Towers Perrin, independently reviewed the models and the assumption set used.

As far as the insurance analysis was concerned, given that expense risk is, in effect, retained by Scottish Equitable, the primary risks considered were:

- investment returns;
- persistency rates;
- 'paid-up policy' (PUP) rates (i.e. percentage of regular premium policies that stop paying premiums but the accrued fund remains invested).

These risks were captured through the derivation of a deterministic stress test. This took the form of a 'day one' crash in asset prices combined with a reduced future investment return on all asset classes and a reduced persistency rate for the term of the projection.

This format was chosen as being practical to apply to the policies while capturing the key risks. The final stress was qualitatively increased to account for the PUP rates risk. The stress was derived from a stochastic calculation performed on a bespoke model built by Fitch and calibrated to the full internal model used by Scottish Equitable.

The final result of this derivation process, for this particular transaction and rating level, was a day one equity and property crash of 45%, future investment returns on each asset class reduced by 100 basis points per annum, and future lapse rates at 205% of the base assumptions.

REFERENCES

The following is a list of selected life ILS-related research that Fitch has published.

Fitch (2005) *Reeling in the Years: VIF Securitisation*, 20 June.

Fitch (2006) *Insurance Securitisation – Coming of Age*, 6 December.

Fitch (2008a) *Insurance-Linked Securities: Ratings Criteria (Global)*, 4 February.

Fitch (2008b) *Catastrophe Bonds (Ratings Criteria)*, 11 March.

Fitch (2008c) *Life Insurance Reserve Finance (Ratings Criteria)*, 8 July.

Fitch (2008d) *Zest: AEGON's Scottish Equitable Value of In-Force Securitisation*, 22 July.

17

Life Securitization: Risk Modelling

Steven Schreiber[a]

In modelling the risks for life insurance securitizations, the actuary develops models to project future insurance cash flows for the business to be covered by the transaction under a wide range of possible future experience. The modelling typically differs between an index transaction, such as a mortality catastrophe bond, and an indemnity transaction, such as a value-in-force (VIF) transaction or an excess reserve transaction.

In a catastrophic mortality transaction, where losses on the bond can be directly related to the actual level of mortality experienced (i.e., there is a specific mortality attachment point at which investors begin to lose principal), the result of the actuarial model is a loss distribution showing the probability of investors losing some or all of their principal.

In a VIF transaction, in contrast to a catastrophic mortality transaction, losses are based on the overall financial condition of the insurance special purpose entity which has reinsured the subject block of business. One cannot form a view about a transaction based solely on the output from the actuarial model, but instead, an investor needs to consider how that output affects the overall transaction. The actuarial model output for an indemnity transaction consists of projections of insurance cash flows and liability items (such as statutory reserves and 'economic' reserves). These outputs are then input into a transaction 'deal model' which models all of the cash flows into and out of the captive insurer, based on the 'waterfall' mechanism defined in the transaction documents. The exact same insurance cash flows in two different transaction structures could result in very different results for investors.

This chapter discusses the modelling approach for both kinds of transactions.

17.1 MODELLING OF A CATASTROPHIC MORTALITY TRANSACTION

There have been six catastrophic mortality bond programmes issued over the past several years. The structure of these transactions follows closely the structure used in the natural catastrophe bond market. These are all index transactions, where investors lose principal if a population mortality index created for the transaction increases above defined attachment levels over defined periods of time. The transaction-specific index reflects the issuing insurance company's country exposure, age exposure and gender exposure, to try to minimize basis risk for the insurer. In addition, there has been at least one mortality catastrophe swap transaction

---

[a]Milliman, Inc.

The Handbook of Insurance-Linked Securities   Edited by P. Barrieu and L. Albertini
© 2009 John Wiley & Sons, Ltd

which has been structured and modelled comparable to the mortality catastrophe bonds. The details of these transactions are discussed elsewhere in this book.

Milliman has been the independent modelling agent for all six catastrophic mortality bond programmes. The modelling approach for these transactions has been developed by Milliman and described in detail in the various offering documents associated with the six transactions. The modelling approach has also been reviewed by several rating agencies, with one agency reproducing the Milliman model so as to allow it to run its own sensitivity tests. There are many possible approaches to project future mortality and the risks presented under these types of transactions. This chapter discusses the approach used by Milliman in its modelling of mortality catastrophe bonds.

The modelling approach Milliman has used is an 'actuarial' approach, which means that Milliman has collected historical mortality data and projected potential future levels of mortality based on such historical data. Historical data have been collected from the various government reporting agencies in the different countries included in the various transactions (e.g., US Centers for Disease Control and Prevention and Census Bureau for US data). Data collected include basic population mortality data as well as population mortality data related to specific causes, such as pandemic deaths and terrorism-related deaths, two areas focused on in the modelling.

The historical mortality data are extrapolated to develop future mortality trends and the potential impact of future pandemic-related and terrorism-related deaths.

The Milliman model separately analyses baseline mortality risk, pandemic risk and terrorism risk. Because of the level at which the attachment points are set for these transactions, the main risk for these transactions is a severe pandemic which could trigger investor losses in the event of hundreds of thousands of additional deaths (though in some cases the attachment point could be reached with an increase in the tens of thousands of additional deaths).

The model can be visualized as three separate mortality models that feed into a combined one to produce a combined mortality index, as shown in Figure 17.1.

The baseline model reflects expected mortality and fluctuations in mortality during normal times. The disease model reflects additional mortality that could occur under certain disease events. The terrorism model reflects additional mortality that could occur under certain voluntary acts of potential human violence.

One million simulations are run for each model and the results are combined to define a loss distribution curve from which the probability of attachment (investor begins to lose principal) and the probability of exhaustion (investor loses all principal) can be estimated.

For the baseline model, historical population mortality rates are analysed for each country in the transaction, reflecting the age and gender mix specified for the transaction. A mortality curve for each country is fit to the historical data and is used to project a baseline expected value mortality curve over the life of the transaction. The difference between the actual historical mortality and the fitted curve defines an 'error component' which is used to project random variation around the mean over the projection period. The mean and standard deviation for the error component are determined separately for each country's model using the mean and standard deviation of the historical difference between the modelled and actual mortality rates.

The approach taken by Milliman in modelling a severe epidemic is to assume a somewhat regularly occurring spike in deaths due to an infectious disease outbreak. Historically the greatest threat has been the influenza virus and this guided the development of the methods and assumptions used in the disease model. The disease-modelling process starts with a random variable that determines if an epidemic has occurred in any given year. If an epidemic has

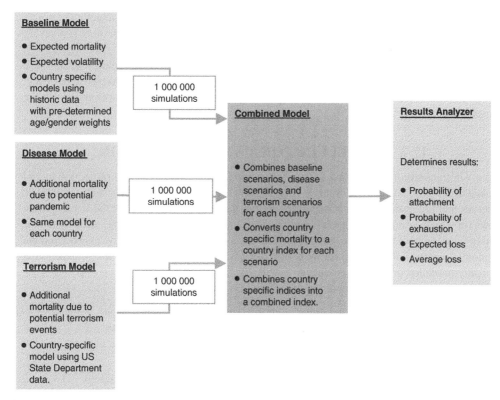

Figure 17.1 Modelling catastrophic mortality
Source: Milliman, Inc.

occurred, another random variable is sampled so as to determine the degree of severity of the epidemic in terms of percentages of excess mortality. Because of the limited amount of historical data available to parametize the disease model, various sensitivity tests need to be considered on both the potential frequency and severity of severe epidemic events.

The terrorism model is designed to assess the potential of a terrorist strike that may result in losses occurring on the bond. The challenge of building such a model is the lack of historical data to assess the probability of such an event. To address this challenge, Milliman designed a multi-level model in the form of a trinomial lattice. The model is split into 20 levels. The increasing levels represent an increasing severity of each potential terrorist event. The model assumes that along with increased severity associated with each level, there is also an increased rarity. Once the terrorists have selected a level of destruction/severity, then there is a probability of success or failure. The approach taken to build the terrorism model is to fit the data that exist at the lower levels to the model structure. The model structure then naturally extrapolates to larger and larger terrorist events that may ultimately cause loss on the bond. The most severe historical data point in the terrorism model is 3000 deaths resulting from the September 11, 2001 terrorist attack in the US.

While the terrorism model extrapolates potentially significantly larger events, they happen at such a low assumed frequency that the terrorism model, overall, adds very little to the expected losses under the mortality catastrophe bond transactions. Given the level of attachment points in the transactions to date, the main driver of potential loss for such transactions is a severe pandemic event.

Both because of the limited amount of historical data available on the main risks in these transactions, and to test the potential for future experience to be different from past experience, it is important to test a wide range of sensitivities on the key underlying assumptions in the transaction.

17.2   MODELLING OF A VIF TRANSACTION

For a VIF transaction or an excess reserve transaction, a traditional actuarial projection model is used to develop projected insurance cash flows and insurance liability items such as statutory reserves and tax reserves. The actuarial modelling may focus either just on the liability cash flows (in which case the deal model would need to incorporate the modelling of the assets) or it may focus on both the liability cash flows and the asset cash flows for the assets backing the economic reserve liabilities. Asset modelling for assets backing surplus in the transaction is typically modelled in the deal model.

The inputs to the actuarial model include:

- in-force records for the policies included in the transaction;
- information about business not yet written to be included in the transaction;
- plan parameters (such as fixed premium rates, policy charges, death benefit patterns, reserving rules);
- projection assumptions (such as assumed mortality rates, lapse rates and expense rates).

The in-force records consist of policy-by-policy information for each policy to be included in the transaction. Such information includes product type, issue age, issue year, underwriting classification, face amount of insurance, any policy account values, reinsurance coverage (if applicable) and other information. The actuarial model may project results for each policy or, as is often done, the actuary may construct a 'model office' representation of the business in force, as well as new business expected. This model office groups together policies with similar characteristics. For example, policies of a particular type issued over the course of one year may be modelled together assuming a mid-year issue date, and policies with a similar age at issue may be grouped together and modelled as one issue age. The model office concept is an historical approach developed when computing power was more limited. As actuaries have gained access to more and more computing power, their models have become more granular (fewer groupings are being performed) and in some cases, results are projected policy by policy on a probabilistic basis.

Whether a model office approach or a policy-by-policy approach is used, the actuary needs to validate that the starting values of the model, such as policy counts, total face amounts and total statutory reserves validate against the company's actual values. This is known as a 'static' validation. This validation should be considered both in aggregate and at subplan levels (e.g., different product types, different issue year groupings).

For future business to be included in the transaction, the actuary needs to reflect the anticipated distribution of business by product type, issue age, underwriting class and other characteristics, as defined by the insurance company. Often, the distribution of business from the most recent year is used, with adjustments to reflect increases or decreases in expected volume.

For each model office 'cell' (where a 'cell' defines the characteristics of the model point, such as policy type, issue age, issue year, underwriting class), both plan parameters and projection assumptions are needed.

Plan parameters include values specific to the cell, such as the premium rate table, the death benefit schedule, the policy charge schedule, cash value formula and policy guaranteed interest rates. The particular types of plan parameters depend on the product design, such as term versus permanent designs. These are data that can be found in the policy form.

Projection assumptions include assumptions such as expected mortality rates, expected termination (or lapse rates), expected premium patterns (for policies with 'flexible' premiums) and expected interest credited rates (rates to be credited to policy values; this may often be defined based on a spread off the underlying rate projected to be earned by the assets backing the block of business).

In setting the projection assumptions, the actuary should consider the company's various assumption sets, such as pricing assumptions, current cash flow testing assumptions and embedded value assumptions, as well as the reasons for any recent changes in such assumption sets. The actuary should also consider the company's actual experience corresponding to the various assumptions. In many cases, credible actual company experience may not be available to support the setting of the assumptions, at least for later durations in the transaction because companies may not have consistent data going back a sufficient number of years due to the introduction of new products or changes in underwriting practices. In such cases, the actuary should consider other potential sources, such as industry data and industry trends, and the applicability of such data and trends to the particular transaction being modelled.

Because of the potential variability of future experience (even if relevant, credible experience exists in support of the assumptions), the actuary should test (and investors should consider) a wide range of variations in the underlying assumptions. Such sensitivity tests may include stochastic analyses (such as stochastic interest rate scenarios or stochastic mortality scenarios) but should also include a range of deterministic scenarios (such as more or less mortality improvement in the future, changes to mortality slope, higher or lower policy lapse rates, etc.).

The outputs from the actuarial model include projected premiums, death benefits, surrender benefits and other values relevant to the block. If the actuarial model projects assets, the projected asset cash flows are also an output of the model.

The outputs from the actuarial model for the baseline projections and for the sensitivity test projections are then included as input into the deal model, which then reflects all of the terms of the proposed transaction (including the tax effects and potential tax allocation arrangements between the captive and its parent company), to determine the availability of cash flows to service the debt contemplated under the transaction. Aside from the sensitivity tests developed as part of the actuarial modelling, which are available for analysis in the deal model, the deal model often has functionality to test other variations, such as changes in asset returns or additional mortality variations (in addition to those developed in the actuarial models).

18

Life Insurance Securitisation:
Legal Issues

Jennifer Donohue[a]

In the last five years there has been significant interest in consolidation activity within the insurance sector. This has resulted in several completed transactions, but also some that stalled at preliminary discussions and others that have never really amounted to anything beyond speculation. Transactions include Resolution's purchase of the life business of Abbey from Santander for £3.6 billion, Aviva's acquisition of AmerUS for £1.6 billion (contrasting with its failed approach for UK rival Prudential) and Swiss Re's acquisition of GE Insurance Solutions. Takeover talk followed Standard Life's demutualisation and there has also been speculation in relation to Scottish Widows.

Interesting innovations have developed to fund acquisitions, for example a mixture of internal resources, external debt and equity (rights issues). A considerable amount of private equity capital has also come into the industry through companies such as Pearl Group and Resolution plc, culminating in £4.5 billion by the Pearl, Royal London offer for Resolution in 2007/2008. Pioneering development of securitisation or monetisation (as is preferred) of the value of in-force policies was seen in the Gracechurch (2003) and Box Hill (2004) transactions. This capital-raising technique has then metamorphosed in to a range of transactions, such as the Avondale securities issue in 2007 involving a revolving book of policies, the privately placed Portofinos loan notes in 2007 and AEGON Scottish Equitable's Zest transaction in 2008.

Despite interest in monetisation as a source of capital, the market appears to have taken a 'wait-and-see' approach; companies have been viewing monetisations from a distance to see how they perform over time. There is also concern over the 'real' outcome of Solvency II requirements. This chapter considers the legal issues and practical effects of monetisation.

18.1 MONETISATION OF FUTURE CASH FLOWS

18.1.1 Some background on monetisation

Monetisation concerns itself with the release of value in force (VIF). VIF is the value of an in-force portfolio of life insurance policies, which is the economic value of a book of in-force policies, or, expressed differently, the value of the future profits anticipated to emerge

---

[a]Simmons & Simmons

The Handbook of Insurance-Linked Securities   Edited by P. Barrieu and L. Albertini
© 2009 John Wiley & Sons, Ltd

in respect of that book of business. A profit is anticipated to emerge since regulatory regimes usually require conservative values to be placed on the insurance liabilities and the assets held to back those liabilities, so that on an economic or market-consistent basis, the assets are worth more than the corresponding liabilities and this difference may be expected to emerge over time.

It is important to note that various descriptors are given to transactions which are based on the monetisation of the VIF – these include 'VIF monetisation', 'VIF securitisation' and 'EV securitisation'. EV refers to 'embedded value', which is usually taken to mean the sum of the VIF and the net asset value of the insurance company; the net asset value not, in fact, playing a significant role in the transaction. The result of the transaction is usually to exchange a portion of the shareholders' interest in the value of the in-force business for cash proceeds, hence the term monetisation. In this chapter, the term 'VIF monetisation' is used for these reasons but colloquially the other terms are used and have been used in other chapters.

18.1.2   The market drivers of monetisation

The Groups Directive, the Solvency II reforms and the decline in equity values have produced both a greater need for capital and greater innovation in ways of raising it. Aside from raising capital for regulatory purposes, increased amounts of capital are necessary for the renewed interest in acquisitions within the insurance sector.

The Groups Directive, amongst other things, introduced arrangements that preclude the double use of the same capital to cover risks in an insurer and its related undertakings. Solvency II and Basel II are the international initiatives that require financial institutions to have a more risk-sensitive framework for the assessment of regulatory capital. Both of these may involve increasing the amount of capital.

Life assurance companies are required to maintain a minimum level of regulatory capital against the risks to which their businesses are subject, to ensure that they are always able to meet their liabilities to policyholders as they fall due. The UK Financial Services Authority (FSA) regulations lay down detailed rules about the amount and quality of capital that such companies must maintain, based in large part on the developing rules for banks following Basel II.

In particular the capital requirements for life assurance companies involve the stratification of capital in terms of Tier 1 (broadly equivalent to equity capital) and Tier 2 (broadly equivalent to long-term debt) in much the same way as the approach used by banks since Basel I. The rules require that at least 50% of the capital is made up of Tier 1 capital. However, equity capital is an expensive form of capital and the increasing demand for this has led life assurance companies to look for cheaper alternatives which nonetheless retain sufficient of the characteristics of equity for them to rank as equity for regulatory purposes.

For similar reasons many banks have, in the past, succeeded in devising debt instruments which have had some equity characteristics, and a number have raised some so-called innovative Tier 1 or hybrid capital. However, there is a significant limitation in the regulations for both banks and life assurance companies in the extent to which such instruments can be treated as equity capital for regulatory purposes. No more than 15% of the Tier 1 capital after deduction can be made up of hybrid capital. So, a couple of years ago we saw the very successful rehabilitation of an idea first tried (rather less successfully) by NPI in the late 1990s, the so-called securitisation of embedded value.

18.1.3   Monetisation in the current climate

Regulatory drivers

Capital requirements will increase under Solvency II, the new framework for enhanced European insurance solvency rules currently under preparation. Monetisation can be used to tackle the issue and smooth the impact of Solvency II on European insurance companies.

Solvency II – what is it and why is it relevant?

Current solvency rules for insurers have suffered from being formulaic and not directing capital adequately to where the risks are. Current regulatory capital is based solely on the volume of business written. The Solvency II objective is that capital requirements are aligned with the underlying risk of an insurance company and to develop a proportionate, risk-based approach to supervision. It is also designed to create a consistent regulatory framework across the EU and to recognise diversification and risk mitigation. It will cover the entire insurance industry (life and non-life, direct writers and reinsurers).

Recent regulatory developments: ISPVs   There are new regulatory developments with the enactment of new rules relating to insurance special purpose vehicles (ISPVs). These ISPVs assume risks from insurance or reinsurance undertakings and fully fund their exposure through debt issuance or another financing mechanism which is subordinate to their reinsurance obligations. Amounts recoverable from an ISPV by an issuer can be taken into account as an admissible asset and treated as reinsurance for the purposes of regulatory capital, but only with a waiver from the FSA. The new regulations are complemented by the Taxation of Insurance Securitisation Company Regulations 2007. They make securitisation easier (in particular regulatory approval) and demonstrate regulatory willingness to consider securitisation.

18.1.4   Some transaction structures

Monetisation transactions involve a number of parties, depending upon the structure. The complement could be as many as the following: originator, rating agencies, arranger, trustee, servicer/subservicer, agents/paying agent, cash manager and account banks. Other secured parties may include the following: swap counterparty, liquidity facility provider, guaranteed indemnity providers or monoline subloan provider. Insurance securitisation often also includes a modelling agent. Some of these dramatis personae are expanded here.

What is value in force (VIF)?

As explained above, the monetisation of 'value in force' on a book of insurance policies (typically life policies) is the monetisation of the present value of the future regulatory surpluses expected to emerge on the book of business.

To date, the public transactions have been: NPI (1998), Gracechurch (2003), Box Hill (2004) and Avondale (2007). The private but reported transactions have been: Portofinos (2007) and Zest (2008).

VIF has no regulatory value but it has an economic value and therefore can be monetised. Cash raised can be taken into account for the purpose of the regulatory capital.

Whilst classic structures such as the Gracechurch and Box Hill transactions involved closed books of business, thereby making the identification of the policies in the monetised pool relatively straightforward, more recent arrivals in the market such as the Avondale Securities issue (2007) or AEGON's Zest transaction (2008) introduced new innovation.

18.2 LEGAL ASPECTS OF LIFE INSURANCE SECURITISATION – SOME KEY FEATURES

18.2.1 Closed book/open book

The early transactions dealt with closed books of business. Here, the benefit was largely in the modelling of the behaviour of the emerging surplus. With no new variables entering the mix from new business, the emerging VIF was more easily predictable.

This contrasts with Avondale, a later transaction, where a 'dynamic' or revolving block of business was monetised; that is, new business written for up to the next five years was accepted into the 'dynamic block'.

18.2.2 Unit-linked policies – not 'with profits' policies

As with closed books of business, the transactions to date have focused on unit-linked, not with profits, policies. This, again, was a means by which the emerging surplus could be predicted with greater accuracy since it was not subject to contagion by stock market fluctuations.

18.2.3 Risk transfer versus no transfer

Under the new Solvency II regime it is expected that capital relied will be given as a specific benefit where genuine risk transfer from the insurer is achieved. The new regime will move away from formulaic calculations for capital to a model-based calculation, meaning that each company may adopt a monetisation in accordance with its individual risk model profile. This will likely act to encourage monetisation.

One of the key documents in risk transfer is the reinsurance treaty ('the treaty'). Careful drafting is needed if a reinsurance treaty is used to achieve risk transfer to the reinsurance vehicle. The treaty has been known to operate to transfer risk and to recapture it. In Box Hill, for example, the reinsurer provided reinsurance of certain liabilities and risks to Friends Provident Life & Pensions (FPLP), which, in turn, was required to pay an annual premium to the reinsurer. In addition to the annual premium to be paid, FPLP was required to recapture liabilities reinsured by the reinsurer, in an amount (the 'recapture amount') corresponding to the amount of the defined book surplus calculated in a given year less the annual premium. This ongoing recapturing of liabilities allowed the reinsurer to release funds held as collateral, and to repay principal under the reinsurer loan and then on the interco loan, which in turn allowed the insurer to repay principal on the notes. Payments to FPLP would occur only when the last liabilities had been recaptured.

18.2.4 Warranties

Another important legal feature in these transactions is the drafting of the warranties. They form a critical part of a triggering mechanism requiring the insurer to make payments to offset an impact of any breach.

The warranties include such matters as:

- origination procedures and servicing of the defined book in a manner expected of a sound and prudent insurance company;
- tax assumptions to remain unchanged;
- responsibility for accuracy of all information;
- requirement to act as a prudent insurer;
- obligation to maintain an inflation hedge fully allocated to the defined book;
- the reinsurer regulatory surplus not being less than the defined book surplus (the conduit covenant);
- the reinsurer meeting regulatory capital requirements (the capital maintenance warranties);
- investment objectives and criteria for the reinsurer assets as per the reinsurer investment management agreement;
- investment of proceeds of the annuity book in accordance with the annuity-backed investment criteria and objectives;
- compliance with laws and regulations, including no mis-selling.

18.2.5   Monoline wrap (payment obligation)

These have been used in a number of the transactions, for example in Gracechurch and Box Hill, AMBAC gave an unconditional and irrevocable financial guarantee. This permitted the rating agencies to improve the rating of the notes.

18.2.6   Recharacterisation risk

There is a major legal issue surrounding the character of the instrument issued by the note vehicle to the market, as explained in Chapter 20. For the smooth and effective use of the instrument, it is important that it, and the trading in it, does not constitute the effecting or carrying out of contracts of insurance.

As the FSA notes in its Regulatory Guidance on the Identification of Contracts of Insurance (PERG 6 FSA Handbook), the courts have not fully defined the common law meaning of 'insurance' and 'insurance business', since they have, on the whole, confined their decisions to the facts before them. They have, however, given useful guidance in the form of descriptions of contracts of insurance. The best established of these descriptions appears in the case of *Prudential v. Commissioners of Inland Revenue* [1904] 2 KB 658. This case, read with a number of later cases, treats as insurance any enforceable contract under which the insurer undertakes:

1. in consideration of one or more payments
2. to pay money or provide a corresponding benefit (including in some cases services to be paid for by the provider) to an insured
3. in response to a defined event, the occurrence of which is uncertain (either as to when it will occur or as to whether it will occur at all) and adverse to the interests of the insured (an insurable interest).

As the FSA points out (PERG 6.5.4.), the courts have adopted the following principles of construction to determine whether a contract is a contract of insurance:

1. More weight attaches to the substance of the contract than to the form of the contract. The form of the contract is relevant, but not decisive of whether a contract is a contract of insurance. *Fuji Finance Inc. v. Aetna Life Insurance Co. Ltd* [1997] Ch. 173.

2. In particular, the substance of the provider's obligation determines the substance of the contract (In *re Sentinel Securities* [1996] 1 WLR 316]). Accordingly, the insurer's or the insured's intention or purpose in entering into a contract is unlikely to be relevant to its classification.
3. The contract must be characterised as a whole and not according to its 'dominant purpose' or the relative weight of its 'insurance content'. *Fuji Finance Inc. v. Aetna Life Insurance Co. Ltd* [Supra].

Among the factors identified by the FSA (PERG 6.6) which the courts have taken into account in deciding whether any particular contract is a contract of insurance are the following:

1. Case law establishes that the provider's obligation under a contract of insurance is an enforceable obligation to respond (usually, by providing some benefit in the form of money or services) to the occurrence of the uncertain event.
2. Contracts under which the provider has absolute discretion as to whether any benefit is provided on the occurrence of the uncertain event are not contracts of insurance. This may be the case even if, in practice, the provider has never exercised its discretion so as to deny a benefit. *Medical Defence Union v. Department of Trade and Industry* [1979] 2 All ER 421.
3. The 'assumption of risk' by the insurer is an important descriptive feature of all contracts of insurance.
4. The recipient's payment for a contract of insurance need not take the form of a discrete or distinct premium. Consideration may be part of some other payment, for example the purchase price of goods. Consideration may also be provided in a nonmonetary form, for example as part of the service that an employee is contractually required to provide under a contract of employment.
5. A contract is more likely to be regarded as a contract of insurance if the amount payable by the recipient under the contract is calculated by reference to either or both of the probability of occurrence or likely severity of the uncertain event.
6. A contract is less likely to be regarded as a contract of insurance if it requires the provider to assume a speculative risk (i.e. a risk carrying the possibility of either profit or loss) rather than a pure risk (i.e. a risk of loss only.)
7. A contract is more likely to be regarded as a contract of insurance if the contract is described as insurance and contains terms that are consistent with its classification as a contract of insurance, for example, obligations of the utmost good faith.
8. A contract that contains terms that are inconsistent with obligations of good faith may, therefore, be less likely to be classified as a contract of insurance; however, since the substance of the provider's rights and obligations under the contract is more significant, a contract does not cease to be a contract of insurance simply because the terms included are not usual insurance terms.

From this list of factors it may be very difficult to predict whether any particular contract will, or will not, be characterised by the courts as a contract of insurance rather than as an insurance-linked security.

Therefore, in all of the structures which result in a market instrument, the structure and the terms of the contracts may have a significant impact on characterisation. The particular categories of financial instruments are very broad, and include a wide variety of structures and documentation. Structuring and the terms of the bond or notes need to withstand a significantly robust test.

18.3   SOME EXAMPLES OF VALUE-IN-FORCE SECURITISATION/MONETISATION

Two UK transactions, Gracechurch (Barclays Life) and Box Hill (Friends Provident), took advantage of a little-known provision in the regulations which enables life assurance companies to treat as equity capital borrowings which are limited recourse to future profits from their existing policies (referred to as the value in force or VIF). Although popularly referred to as securitisations, transactions of this sort do not involve the transferring of title or the giving of security over third party obligations in the way that traditional securitisations do. In effect, there is merely a pledge by the life assurance company that its profits from its existing business as realised each year over the term of the debt will be used to service the debt obligations. Monetisation of the value of in-force business is therefore a more accurate word for these transactions.

18.3.1   A classical VIF structure: Gracechurch

Gracechurch (Figure 18.1) is the 'classical structure', very much still setting the standard. It involved the monetisation of the VIF of the entire book of life policies of Barclays Life, providing equity capital of £400 million. The VIF was reinsured with a Dublin-based captive insurance company, which used it to back a limited recourse loan from a finance vehicle which itself used that to back the notes of £400 million issued to the capital markets. Box Hill, a similar structure, was subsequently adopted where the VIF of a defined book of life policies held by Friends Provident was monetised to provide capital of £380 million. In both cases the notes issued to the markets were wrapped by a monoline to provide a AAA rating.

Both of these transactions related to a closed book of life policies, which made documenting the arrangements relatively easy to achieve. This is particularly true in the case of Gracechurch, where the policies were largely unit linked so that the insurer retained no significant investment

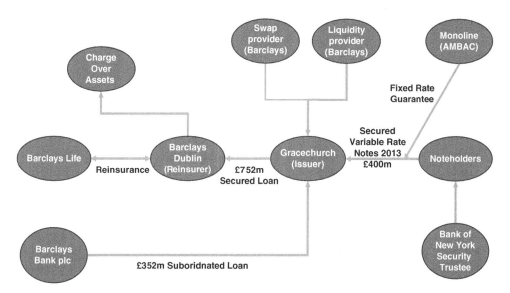

Figure 18.1   Barclays Life – Gracechurch

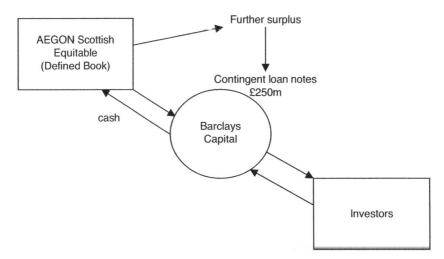

Figure 18.2 The Zest transaction

risk. Further innovative monetisations involving new business – potentially volatile types of business such as annuities – have followed.

18.3.2 A private but reported transaction: Zest

The latest arrivals in the toolbox like Zest (Figure 18.2) involve monetisation of new business strains.

Important features of Zest include:

- £250 m contingent loan;
- interest and principal payable only out defined book surplus;

Additional key features include:

- model definition of surplus;
- insufficient surplus notes written off;
- revolver.

AEGON Scottish Equitable's unit-linked book, including both regular and single policies, was placed into a revolving defined book. For the first three years, instead of using statutory surpluses arising to amortise the loan, Scottish Equitable can retain these profits and bring additional business into the revolving defined book, while ensuring that certain financial and others criteria are satisfied. Once the revolving period has finished, amortisation occurs with regular payments. Following the revolving period, if insufficient surplus emerges over the defined book, the loan notes will be written off and the lender not repaid. Conversely, if a surplus arises more quickly or in greater volume than expected, the notes will be redeemed faster than expected. Base case maturity would have been modelled, as would a worst case scenario.

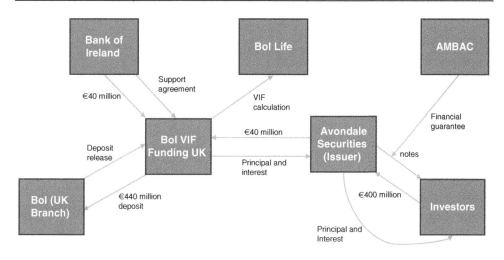

Steps of Transaction

1. Avondale issues €400m of notes wrapped by Ambac (monoline)
2. Avondale lends €400m to BoI VIF Funding vehicle
3. Bank of Ireland lends €40m to BoI VIF Funding (Ltd Partnership) and Support Agreement. €440 then deposited with UK Branch BoI
4. BoI Life calculates VIF and pays principal and interest

Figure 18.3   Avondale 'dynamic book' life securitisation

This allowed AEGON group to support its growth ambitions and to meet three strategic priorities:

1. Reallocate capital toward businesses with higher growth and return prospects.
2. Improve growth and returns from existing businesses.
3. Manage AEGON as an international group.

In addition to Zest, revolving features have also been present with a 'a dynamic book' of business in other transactions, such as Avondale (Figure 18.3), to create the opportunity to provide funding and amortise the transaction costs over a greater period of time. However, this does pose challenges to preserving the integrity of the existing book of business. The investor's perspective will naturally demand not to be diluted by the addition of any new policies which do not satisfy predetermined criteria. These predetermined criteria will often be determined by actuarial requirements.

There have been other private transactions. The trends have been towards initial deferral of 'amortisation' by including dynamic/revolving books in the structure, for example Avondale; simplification by reducing/eliminating the monoline wrap; the development of insurance special purpose vehicle legislation; and a potential demand for riskier tranches than AA/AAA.

18.4   OUTLOOK

With Solvency II approaching for insurers, capital management techniques that are emerging in the banking world following Basel II will inevitably arrive in the world of insurance. Financial institutions are becoming increasingly conscious of the cost of capital and can, in particular

Extreme Mortality	VIF	XXX
Vita 2003	Holdings LLC 2001	INC Money Markets 2003/4/6
Vita II	MONY 2002	Potomac Trust 2004/5
Osiris Capital 2006	Gracechurch Life 2003	Stingray Trust 2005
Tartan Capital 2006	Box Hill 2004	Orkney Holdings 2005
Vita III 2007	Norwich Union 2004	Orkney Capital II 2005
Nathan Re 2008	FLAC 2004	INC Term Securities 2005/6/7
	ALPS Capital II 2005	Ballantyne Re 2006
	Queensgate 2005	Timberlake Financial 2006
	Avondale 2007	Shenandoah 2006
	Portofinos 2007	LIICA Holdings 2007
	Zest 2008	River Lake Ins Co 2007
		SBLI 2008

AXXX	Other Life
Rivermont 2006	AM Skandia 2001
Double Oak Capital 2007	CBC Inc. Rev. 2002
Pine Falls 2008	AMP Life 2002
	Patron's Legacy 2003/4
	Tailwind Holdings 2006
	Northwind Holdings 2007

Figure 18.4   Life deal comparison chart

when using an internal risk-based approach as opposed to the standard credit risk approach, manage their capital by both complying with the regulatory requirements and simultaneously bundling and placing risk in accordance with their needs and resources. For example, A/B structures, where the risk inherent in a loan is split between a senior and a junior piece, a feature well known in the commercial mortgage-backed industry, are becoming increasingly common for other asset classes, allowing the institution to retain an asset portfolio with a reduced risk profile whilst offering earnings potential to outside, unregulated investors.

Given the continuing consolidation drive in the European insurance market, monetisation may also be used as a neat way of raising capital to fund acquisitions. This can be either through the monetisation of existing books of business to raise finance for acquisitions, or partly funding an acquisition or refinancing a bridge loan by monetising some or all of the books of business gained under the acquisition. Going forward, new business generated by the life company may be used to repay other financings.

To end this chapter, we present, in Figure 18.4, a chart showing various transactions, grouped according to type.

19

The Investor Perspective (Life)

Luca Albertini[a]

The objective of this chapter is to offer the perspective of an investor in life insurance-linked securities. A similar analysis was done for the non-life insurance sector in Chapter 9.

To give a little background to readers, I was involved with life insurance-linked securitisation whilst managing Swiss Re's European Insurance-Linked Securities team from 2003 until April 2008. At present I am the Chief Executive of an asset management company which specialises in investing in insurance-linked risk (a 'dedicated ILS fund'). Dedicated ILS funds are active investors in life insurance securitisation alongside other institutional investors.

The first section of this chapter outlines the types of life insurance-linked risk that have been introduced to capital market investors and the development of an investor base for the risk; the second section offers a summary of the key elements investors analyse when investing in life insurance-linked securities; and the last section covers the evolution of the life insurance securitisation market from an investor perspective. Throughout this chapter, references to life insurers are also applicable to life reinsurers, who played an important role in the development of the life insurance securitisation market.

19.1   LIFE INSURANCE-LINKED RISKS AND INVESTOR APPETITE

The life insurance industry (and indeed the non-life insurance industry) has been looking at the capital markets for equity or debt capital for a long time, but the repackaging of life insurance risk into securitised or derivative form has been relatively recent, with only a small number of large transactions. In the early days of this market, the general investor community, which has been comfortable taking insurance risk blended with other risks in the stock market or in debt instruments, has been less comfortable underwriting 'pure' life insurance risk repackaged into securities or derivatives. The originators and the arrangers of the first transactions have therefore had to invest considerable time and resources in explaining the risk components embedded in life insurance securitisation to the investor community.

19.1.1   The role of the monolines

After some pioneering 'unwrapped' transactions, sponsors and banks placing the notes were supported by monoline insurance companies (commonly simply referred to as 'monolines')

---

[a]Leadenhall Capital Partners

The Handbook of Insurance-Linked Securities   Edited by P. Barrieu and L. Albertini

which guaranteed (or 'wrapped') some of the tranches of value in force (or VIF) securitisations, almost all of the US regulatory capital securitisation (defined as 'Regulation XXX') and, at a later stage, select tranches of catastrophic mortality transactions. An investor in a monoline-wrapped note was exposed to a loss only if the transaction generated a loss and the monoline guarantor was bankrupt and unable to honour its guarantee. Monolines were, in effect, doing most of the legwork in analysing each wrapped transaction, and taking all of the risks in the transaction as well as the lion's share of the premium paid by the protection buyer in exchange. Monolines also imposed strict conditions on transactions and influenced some of the structural outcomes. An investor in wrapped securities had access to some information to enable analysis of the insurance risk behind the transaction, but due to the additional security provided by the wrap, investors generally relied on the top-rated credit of the guarantor, and therefore the spread over floating rate available on the notes wrapped by the largest monolines was generally in the low double-digit basis points range, compared with a spread of normally over 100 basis points for unwrapped notes of comparable risks.

Whilst monolines were very useful in supporting the growth of the market and in allowing banks to tap a wider investor base for the placement of large transactions, value investors willing to receive the full premium for the insurance risk have been focusing on unwrapped tranches. In some cases where a securitisation has offered a wrapped tranche alongside an unwrapped one, the unwrapped tranche has seen better investor demand and placed at a more competitive all-in pricing than the wrapped tranche. In those transactions, the monolines played an important role in supporting the risk analysis, as their underwriting was on top of the analysis done by a modelling agency and two rating agencies (in some cases the monolines employed another actuarial firm to double check the modelling done by the modelling firm acting for the transaction).

With the credit and capital issues affecting the monolines in 2008 and with little reasonable chance of recovery in the medium term, little monoline capacity is expected to support the life insurance securitisation sector. This highlights the importance of further investor education, so that more risk-taking investors can be prepared to accommodate the larger deals placed prior to 2008.

19.1.2 Understanding the risk

The education process and investors' understanding of the key risk components of life insurance securitisation have followed similar patterns to non-life insurance risk in certain aspects, and a unique path for others. The process can be divided into two key components:

- risk descriptions;
- risk modelling.

Risk descriptions

Life insurance securitisations can embed a number of risk types, which include:

- **mortality risk:** can be defined as a higher than expected mortality experience and may embed within it pandemic risk and terrorism risk among other factors;
- **longevity risk:** can be defined as a lower than expected mortality experience;
- **persistency or lapse risk:** can be described as the risk of policyholders terminating their life policy sooner or later than expected;

- **market risk:** can be defined as elements of investment risk – which can be equity market risk and/or fixed-income risk – embedded in the emergence of the value in force, or VIF;
- **sponsor counterparty risk:** can be defined as the risk of default of the transaction sponsor, as most life insurance securitisations, with the exception of catastrophic mortality transactions, are expected to suffer material losses (if not a complete loss) in the case of bankruptcy of the sponsoring life insurer;
- **life insurers' counterparty risk:** can be defined as the bankruptcy risk of one or more life insurers and may be incorporated in securitisations of life settlements (i.e. secondary market sale of term life insurance policies) or other secondary market life insurance contracts;
- **marginal risks:** include risks which can arise from the structural features of each transaction, and the counterparty risk emerging from players other than the transaction sponsor, such as the swap counterparties and any guarantor of the notes.

Some of the above-mentioned risks, such as market risk and counterparty risk, are familiar to the general investor community, which has the methodology to be able to assess their fundamental components, and can therefore focus on how such risks could impact each transaction.

Market risk has a different impact on each transaction, according to the structure. Such impact and correlation are, of course, key elements of the investor analysis of the specific structure. In general terms, blocks of life insurance policies backed by fixed-income investments meet more favourable investor response due to their lower volatility than those portfolios backed by equities. Similarly, fixed-interest investments with durations closely matching the duration of the blocks' expected liabilities are also more favourably received by investors The rating of a transaction also reflects the assessment of market risk volatility in each tranche. Last but not least, transactions normally allow a great deal of freedom to the asset management of the ceding life insurer in managing the asset portfolio, to make it very difficult for any investor to be able to hedge or to constantly map its exposure to the market risk in the transaction.

Counterparty risk is not solely limited to bankruptcy risk, and for most life insurance securitisations exposed to counterparty risk, the analysis is more complex. Not only does an investor need to assess whether, for the relevant transaction, the correct measurement is the claims-paying ability or the debt-service ability of the sponsoring insurer, but a careful analysis should also be conducted on how any deterioration of an insurer's credit and rating could impact other risks embedded in the transaction, such as persistency risk. In general terms rating agencies cap the underlying rating (i.e. before any wrap) of the transaction at the rating of the ceding life insurers, thus further underlying the full correlation of life securitisations with the credit of the ceding company, unlike non-life securitisations, catastrophic mortality securitisations and Regulation XXX securitisations, in which the impact of the bankruptcy of the ceding company is the likely default on the premium payment, which would cause an early termination of the notes at par. Also, as to date it is considered to be very difficult (if not impossible) to achieve a true sale in the securitisation of life portfolios, it is assumed that there is a possibility that a liquidator would capture the cash flows payable to the securitisation structure.

Another impact of counterparty risk which goes beyond bankruptcy is any servicing risk associated with a block of securitised life policies in the face of a breach of a contractual obligation by the sponsor as well as due to bankruptcy. Replacing the originator as servicer of a securitised portfolio is expected to be quite cumbersome due to the specific nature of the risks as well as regulatory constraints.

The focus of the educational work on the specific life risk (on top of the impact on each transaction) has therefore been on mortality, longevity and persistency risk.

My experience in roadshows has been that investors have been quicker to grasp the dynamics of mortality risk and have had more difficulty getting comfortable with longevity and persistency risk.

Mortality risk (unlike high frequency and low severity non-life risk) can be analysed with the benefit of a long series of granular data. This feature, together with help from the modelling firms, has made this risk more familiar to structured finance and institutional investors, who are used to long series of granular data in their investments, as well as the lower tail risk embedded in the modelling. In addition, the mortality improvement is such that mortality models for projecting baseline mortality have been, in general terms, reasonably accurate over the long term; any errors made have tended to be on the conservative side, thus not hurting investors. Of course when making such an analysis one must distinguish between national population statistics (such as for catastrophic mortality transactions), which capture the general population (even when weighted by age and gender), and other pools of indemnity securitisations, which are based on the specific portfolio of policyholders of the ceding life company. Large life offices also tend to have a section of the general insured population (which is different from the broader population as not everybody purchases life insurance) and have a long series of granular data, although in some cases this is hard to compile in a consistent way due to a number of factors, such as changes in computer systems and mergers and acquisitions which have changed the shape of the portfolio over time, the impact of which is important to understand for an investor. Some pools, however, may originate in a very specific target market (e.g. wealthy people living in upmarket urban areas, or working class population with manual jobs), where the mortality could be distinctly different from that of the general insured population or the general population. Finally, some portfolios may consist of a relatively low number of high-value life policies (such as, for example, a $200 million portfolio of 100 policies of $2 million each). In such a case, mortality risk is harder to assess with the traditional actuarial instruments applicable to large pools, and supplementary analysis to include medical underwriting analysis of each policyholder becomes much more important. In addition, we must note that modelling mortality risk for extreme events and for shorter durations is less reliable, as the modelling error for a low frequency and high severity risk profile is higher.

Longevity risk analysis offers some similarities to the analysis of mortality risk. Large series of granular data are available, and particular attention must be given to the analysis of the general population, the general insured population and subsets of the population with distinct characteristics. From a pure risk analysis perspective, investors have, however, been slower to support any of the current modelling approaches for longevity risk. Among the various reasons, the key aspects are linked to (i) the fact that the models used by key industry players in the past have consistently underestimated longevity, and (ii) the potential for breakthrough medical improvements (such as more effective cures for heart disease and cancer), which could have a material impact on life improvement. The latter is considered to be more of a concern than the potential for factors like obesity and/or catastrophic mortality events, which could reduce or reverse existing mortality improvements. In summary, whilst mortality risk models generally compare well with observed historical experience (and deviations have generally not been adverse to investors), longevity risk models suffer from the opposite performance history and from questions pertaining to the impact of future medical developments. New models have tried to take all of this into account, such as through the use of stochastic analysis, and structural features have been introduced to cope with some of these issues. Longevity risk has been placed into the capital markets (mainly in swap form, as outlined in Chapter 21), thus showing that progress has been made in meeting investors' questions on risk assessment, but for a wider acceptance of pure longevity risk in capital markets, the current educational efforts by the key market players will need to be continued if not reinforced, and pricing expectations between investors and sponsors must further converge.

Persistency (lapse) risk is influenced by a number of factors, which include not only the policyholders' perceived value of any policy benefits (including any embedded economic guarantees such as minimum earnings yield on investment contracts or locked-in premium rates) but also the competitive position of the protection buyer, pricing competition in the industry, the perceived financial strength of the protection buyer and any incentive by the ceding life insurer to push a policyholder to terminate an existing policy and enter into a new one (the latter not being unusual because new products may be more suitable for a policyholder than an existing one, or, less nobly, the change of policy could earn extra commission for the ceding life insurer and/or for the broker). Some of the elements of persistency risk are less easy for the ceding life insurers to control. On the other hand, there are elements of this risk for which the ceding life insurer is in control (such as the targeting of existing policyholders for new product offerings, and whether those products are distributed using external parties or its own sales force), and investors normally look at structural solutions and representations from the protection buyer to mitigate or completely eliminate the adverse impact of these actions on the notes. Indeed, it would not be desirable for a life insurer to sell the VIF of a block of business to investors, and then push a policyholder to switch to another nonsecuritised policy, so that it benefits from the same policyholder twice and investors suffer a loss. On the other hand, life insurers cannot be straight-jacketed so that they never offer an improved product to their client base. Structural solutions for such a risk have been identified and incorporated into existing structures. Where fewer data are available and it has been more difficult for investors to achieve comfort, is their assessment on persistency of a slow or of a rapid deterioration in the credit strength of the ceding life insurers? What is the impact on persistency of different phases of the competitive landscape in the life insurance industry, and what is the impact of the presence of a retail broker community? It is important for investors to have the information to gain a deep understanding of the particular features of each insurance product and of the historical experience which allows them to take a view on potential policyholder behaviour during key stages of the policy life cycle, especially when exposed to various market environments. Whilst in normal market conditions a lower persistency risk can be observed for a seasoned block of certain types of life insurance business, the lack of policyholder behavioural data during various combinations of market distress (such as the 2008 market environment) does reduce the ability of investors to formulate a view on the persistency risk impact of stress risk scenarios.

Risk modelling

A detailed explanation of the risk modelling has been very important in the development of investors' comfort and acceptance of the various elements of life insurance risk. Many life insurance securitisations include a risk-modelling section in the offering circular in which not only is each risk component defined, but the modelling approach is explained in detail, so that an investor might understand how the modelling firm has reached its conclusions. Modelling for life insurance is normally performed by actuarial firms (please see Chapter 17 for the modelling of life insurance securitisations).

Rating agencies have also been very useful in modelling and explaining securitised life insurance risk to investors. Unlike non-life insurance-linked securities, life securitisations have a predominance of investment-grade tranches for each transaction, with investors requiring one or more ratings to make an investment. For this reason, and due to the fact that some of the transactions have also been fully or partly guaranteed by monolines which normally require a rating from both Moody's and Standard & Poor's as a condition to provide a guarantee, a number of life insurance securitisations have two or three ratings.

The combination of the opinion of actuarial firms, with recognised strong expertise in 'pure' insurance risk, and the second opinion of rating agencies, with strong expertise in market, credit and structured finance risk assessment, has been very important in helping to educate investors and to compare points of view. Also, 'translation' of the risk analysis outcome into a rating offers an investor a common basis to compare this investment with alternative fixed-income securities.

19.1.3   Correlation with other investments

Insurance-linked securities are generally described as having a low correlation with the rest of the portfolio of an institutional investor. As outlined in Chapter 9, it can be observed that the insurance risk in non-life securitisations has showed limited correlation with the rest of the financial markets, whilst the bankruptcy of Lehman Brothers had an impact on those transactions with a total return swap structure provided by the bank. The analysis for life insurance-linked securities from an investor perspective is more complex. Whilst it is true that 'pure' life insurance risk, such as mortality and longevity risk, is seldom available to investors and is a diversifying asset when compared to other fixed-income instruments, life insurance risk and capital markets can show different degrees of correlation.

A full correlation analysis is beyond the scope of this chapter, but to try to provide a general framework for observing correlation, we can look at:

• how a life insurance event might impact the general financial markets;
• how financial markets might influence the life insurance-linked securities.

Impact of a life event on the general financial markets

The life event for the purposes of this analysis would include mortality risk, longevity risk and persistency risk. Market risk and counterparty risk are 'imported' from the financial market in some life securitisation structures.

First of all, if a transaction is covering small portfolios or a very specific sector where the behaviour of a given life risk is not necessarily linked with that of the general life insurance market, then the correlation with the rest of the exposures of a general investor is less obvious. For example, in a settlement portfolio of 200 large US policyholders, the longevity risk could be purely related to these lives and not to the longevity experience in the United States or in a specific state or even a specific age group (e.g. 70–75-year-old policyholders) within a localised region.

When looking at large portfolios representative of the general insured population or of the general population, a material increase in mortality risk could adversely impact the general economy. In particular, a pandemic outbreak (or even the fear of it) in the Western economies could restrict people's movements, and sectors such as transportation, retail, holidays and entertainment could be affected. High levels of actual mortality could also be expected to affect some tranches of securitised unsecured consumer credit (and financial stocks).

A material increase of life expectancy, on the other hand, could affect the market valuations of those corporations with substantial unhedged and unfunded pension liabilities, and would be expected to increase the public deficit of a number of Western governments, with negative consequences for their economies.

Persistency risk is more likely to have effects that are limited to the life insurance industry, thus not contaminating the general financial markets.

A material event arising out of all of the above risks for the general population would obviously affect the stock market valuation of the life insurance industry, at least in the jurisdictions affected.

In summary, whilst it can be argued that material sudden increases in mortality or life expectancy could have some impact on at least some sectors of the general financial markets, it is less easy to imagine the observation of such an impact in the presence of the small volatility of such risks (which could, however, impact some junior tranches of life insurance securitisations), or a gradual shift in actual experience or when looking at the behaviour of small or localised portfolios.

Impact of the financial markets on life insurance-linked securities

Financial market unrest does not seem to have an obvious impact on either mortality or longevity experience.

The persistency analysis is more complex. In a recession, with policyholders experiencing lower disposable income or having a fear for their jobs, there is a higher risk that insurance in general (and life insurance) could be among the regular expenses being reduced. Also, if a cheaper policy can be purchased, the policyholder may be more amenable to reducing their regular expenses and open to new offers. Also, some securitised life insurance portfolios include investment products coupled with insurance cover. If the investment portfolio does not generate the expected returns (or even generates a loss), the risk of termination of the policy increases.

For life insurance securitisations such as VIF structures there is an explicit exposure to the investments backing the life insurance block of business and therefore investors are generally offered (and perform on their own) stress analysis to show the estimated impact of various levels of adverse market developments on the securitisation structure.

Counterparty risk is a component of financial market risks. To better assess its impact on life securitisation structures, the question is what impact can a market downturn have on the credit standing of life insurers? The recent market downturn offers some examples of such impact. The collapse of AIG in autumn 2008 was caused by financial market turmoil rather than an insurance event. Also in 2008 the attention of investors, analysts and regulators focused on the impact of the market turmoil on the insurance sector (and life insurance in particular), with the concern that some asset management losses could have severely weakened the capitalisation of the main insurance companies.

An interesting component of counterparty risk correlation, which is peculiar to the life component of the insurance-linked securities sector, has been that associated with the monolines. As noted above, a number of life securitisation notes have been wrapped by a monoline insurance company. A number of the monolines were downgraded in 2008 (some to non-investment grade level) as a result of losses arising from their non-insurance-linked securities credit wraps. As a consequence of such downgrades, investors in monoline-wrapped notes have greatly suffered in terms of mark-to-market valuation, as investors in secondary market notes in 2008 have tended to disregard the monoline guarantee or even penalise the pricing of the note for having such a guarantee.

In terms of marginal risks, the analysis for life insurance securitisations is similar to that for non-life insurance transactions. In general terms, collateralised structures in which the proceeds of the issuance of the notes are held in trust and invested via a total return swap would need to be revisited in a similar fashion to those collateral structures for non-life insurance-linked securities with frequent mark to market and margining calls on the collateral assets (see Chapter 9 for more details). In many cases, life insurance securitisations embed a number of derivatives (such as interest rate, total return swaps and other derivative structures) and guarantees, which need to be structured to withstand the bankruptcy (or financial distress) of the swap counterparty and of the guarantors.

A final remark is on mark-to-market risk. We have outlined above the negative mark-to-market performance of monoline-wrapped life insurance securitisations due to the issues affecting the monoline insurance industry. During the 2008 credit crisis we have observed some pressure on the mark to market of senior unwrapped life insurance securitisation due to the absence of investor demand for senior securitised paper in general. Such mark to market volatility has been more limited for the non-investment-grade or very low investment-grade tranches due to some sustained demand from investors in insurance-linked securities. The life securitisation sector (like the non-life) has suffered most in the last quarter of the year, when dedicated investors showed more limited capacity to absorb secondary market offers by sellers forced to reduce their exposure to insurance-linked securities due to redemptions in their own funds and to lower availability of leverage. However, to put this in the right context, unwrapped life insurance securitisations for which insurance-linked securities broker dealers release indicative secondary market pricing have been marked with a 10% to 20% discount to par, thus comparing very well with other structured fixed-income investments during the 2008 credit turmoil.

19.1.4 Relative value

Life insurance securitisations offer relative value to investors compared with investments with a similar rating profile. The most visible pricing difference has been observed for un-wrapped tranches of life securitisations. The last placements of life securitisations prior to the 2008 credit crisis were still generally completed at a premium over other securitised paper within the same rating range for most of the senior tranches of notes. For example, notes in the single-A range have been placed at a spread of over 100 basis points over the benchmark rate (LIBOR or EURIBOR) whilst other non-insurance-linked securitised notes (with the exception of some tranches of CDO – not unreasonably in hindsight) were placed well below 100 basis points. Such premium pricing has been achieved for investing in notes which do not directly overlap with other stock market or fixed-income assets in the portfolios of institutional investors, thus representing good relative value.

The expected, much-reduced role of monolines in wrapping insurance-linked securities is likely to require a larger investor skills base for unwrapped paper. In addition, Solvency II in Europe is likely to push sponsors of life insurance securitisations to issue more junior tranches in their securitisations, as the focus would then shift from regulatory capital arbitrage to risk-based capital relief. In this context the full risk premium payable by the notes would be received by the investors (rather than being partly allocated to the monolines), and transactions with a higher risk–return profile would be likely to be placed, thus supporting the absolute returns available to investors in the life insurance securitisation sector.

In summary it can be observed that whilst life insurance securitisation might embed some level of correlation with the general financial markets (which may be minimal or larger according to the structure), it does introduce a new asset class with new risks and therefore could contribute to diversifying a portfolio, reducing the return volatility and increasing the portfolio efficient frontier (i.e. the maximisation of the expected return for a given amount of risk, typically measured by the volatility).

19.1.5 Valuation and liquidity

The traditional insurance-linked securities indicative pricing sheets regularly available to institutional investors do not always provide indicative marks for life insurance securitisations. When available, indicative marks may, in some cases, be limited to catastrophic mortality, and in others to the issues managed by the firm providing the valuations. For the remainder of the issuance, valuations are generally available to each investor from the broker dealer who has placed the securities.

As for non-life insurance-linked securities, there is currently no market making for life securitisations, only indicative secondary pricing. Also, given the relatively limited number of unwrapped life securitisations, and given the structural complexity of some VIF or Regulation XXX structures, secondary market transactions occur between existing investors or with a small number of new investors who are interested in getting into this space and are prepared to start the underwriting process to understand the risk profile and structural characteristics of each issuance.

Monoline-wrapped notes used to be more liquid before the monoline sector suffered a loss of confidence and some severe downgrading in 2008. The current liquidity of monoline-wrapped life insurance securitisations is much lower and, as we noted above, trading levels tend to assume zero value for the monoline wrap.

19.2 KEY TRANSACTION FEATURES FROM THE INVESTOR PERSPECTIVE

The life insurance securitisation sector is rich with structural alternatives for transferring risk to the capital markets. It has been and still is subject to financial innovation, partly as a consequence of a new legal and regulatory environment, particularly in the European markets (see Chapter 26).

In this context, and conscious of the fact that a full and exhaustive analysis would require a book in itself, this section summarises some basic features that have been observed to be the key focus of insurance-linked securities investors, on top of the assessment of the underlying risk being securitised. These include risk assessment of the instrument, the term of the transaction and the pricing and risk–reward profile.

19.2.1 Risk assessment of the instrument

The structure of a catastrophic mortality risk securitisation is very similar to that of non-life insurance-linked securities, and therefore we refer the reader to Chapter 9 for the risk assessment of such structures. In this section we focus on other types of life insurance securitisation.

Legal and tax considerations

Other types of life securitisation tend to be heavily influenced by legal and tax considerations from the jurisdiction of the sponsoring life insurer, which generate different levels of complexity and possible risks for investors. Some structures involve one or more special purpose vehicles and the underlying documentation can be lengthy and complex. Investors in traded life insurance securitisations can only analyse the prospectus, as documentation is normally only available to existing investors. A careful analysis of the prospectus is therefore important to spot any possible legal or tax issue in connection with the transaction, which could cause a loss, an unexpected tax or an early termination of the transaction.

In certain indemnity-based life securitisation structures, investors are repaid via payments from the sponsoring life insurer, which represent emerging surplus from the life insurance block. Unlike other securitisations, it has not yet been possible to have a true sale for such cash flows, and therefore a careful analysis of the structural features for the identification and payment of such cash flows to the securitisation structure is very important. Furthermore, a number of life insurance securitisations have been structured on an actual portfolio of regulated life insurance policies (rather than on a population index for example). As a result, it is necessary for investors to understand the essentials of the life insurance regulatory framework so as to assess any associated regulatory risk.

In addition, the analysis of transactions backed by secondary market life insurance policies should also focus on the title that the securitisation structure has over such policies, as the estates of some deceased policyholders have successfully challenged, and are believed to be able to challenge, the sale of life insurance policies in court, when a number of necessary origination procedures are not carefully followed.

'Indemnity' features and alignment of interest

Most life insurance securitisations (with the exception of extreme mortality transactions) are structured on the actual block of business from the sponsoring life insurer. The 'indemnity' features of transactions therefore require an analysis of the sponsor's underwriting and claims-paying criteria similar to that outlined in Chapter 9 for indemnity non-life insurance-linked securities. The one feature that differentiates some life insurance securitisations from non-life transactions is that in certain cases (such as VIF securitisation) the sponsoring life insurer receives the proceeds of the issuance of the notes and then remits cash flows to the securitisation vehicle typically on a quarterly or a six-monthly basis until the notes have been redeemed. In non-life securitisations (or in some life structures such as catastrophic mortality or Regulation XXX) the proceeds of the issuance of the notes are kept within the securitisation structure and invested in high-quality collateral until maturity.

Structures under which cash flows are remitted to the sponsoring insurer embed an element of credit risk (given the difficulty in achieving a true sale for the securitised cash flows) and servicing risk (similar to that of traditional asset-backed securities), as the repayment of the investor is based on the ability of the originator to correctly identify the surplus generating the obligation to repay the noteholder, and its accuracy in timely remittance of the funds.

Investors in 'indemnity' life insurance securitisations need to look at their alignment of interests with the sponsoring life insurer. This is important not only to ensure the best under-writing and claims-paying processes, but is essential in those structures in which the investors are exposed to the performance of the assets backing the securitised portfolio when such assets are managed by the sponsoring life insurer with discretional or very broad criteria.

Particular care in alignment of interest analysis is needed for structures backed by secondary market life insurance policies. These structures are normally the result of a chain of intermediaries and service providers, sourcing the policies, arranging for the documentation, performing the medical underwriting and, in some cases, assembling the pool of life policies. Investors look carefully at how the interests of such intermediaries and service providers are aligned with their own, as the lack of such alignment in the structure of most asset-backed securities has caused some of the issues affecting the securitisation markets in 2007 and 2008.

Data provided and ongoing reporting

The availability of data, which allows investors a proper understanding of each risk component of the transaction, is of paramount importance. The data should provide a sufficient historical background to allow investors to perform their own modelling stresses to compare and contrast with those of modelling and rating agencies.

The consequences of the 2008 financial turmoil are expected to lead investors to perform extra analysis on each investment and rely less on the opinion of modelling and rating agencies. In addition, with the regulatory trend motivating sponsoring companies who seek capital relief to transfer higher levels of the underlying insurance and market risks in their securitisation programmes, investors in such notes will be requiring extra analysis given their greater exposure to the risks and to volatility.

Ongoing reporting on indemnity transactions should also be as accurate, granular and frequent as possible. Life insurance securitisation notes can be medium to long term. Proper ongoing reporting not only keeps existing investors up to date with the developments of the data pools which were offered to them at issuance, but also allows a prospective investor in a secondary market transaction to be able to underwrite the transaction based on fresh data at any point in time.

Asset management

As some life insurance securitisation structures are impacted by market risk, investors in such transactions need to focus on the relevant investments as well as on the asset management criteria for managed pools of assets.

Whilst it is acknowledged that active management of the pools may benefit all parties in the transaction, investors are keen to be offered a snapshot of the relevant portfolios at the date of launch as well as frequent and timely ongoing reporting of changes to the assets in the securitised portfolio.

Asset management criteria are also important as investors (particularly of the most junior notes) as well as rating agencies are likely to make assumptions and stress scenarios which take into consideration the most aggressive portfolio profile allowed by such criteria. The criteria should therefore be a balancing act allowing sufficient freedom to ensure the best performance in changing markets and at the same time offering sufficient boundaries to avoid unnecessary projected volatility and consequent penalisation in terms of tranching of the capital structure and pricing required by investors.

Volatility of repayment profile

The timing repayment of a number of life insurance securitisation structures is based on the performance of a block of life insurance business, as opposed to structures like catastrophic mortality in which the notes are repaid at the same time subject to the catastrophic mortality event not occurring. This implies that investors have an expected note redemption profile, which may vary over time, either by accelerating or delaying payments in accordance with the performance of the transaction. Such volatility of repayment is very similar to that of a number of asset-backed securities structures in which prepayment of assets accelerates the redemption of the notes and arrears delay such redemption. It is important for an investor to have the tools to analyse this type of volatility as it is directly tied to each risk component in the transaction.

In properly structured transactions, a liquidity facility should be there to ensure timely payments of interest (at least for investment-grade notes) and in some cases to reduce the volatility of principal repayments. Properly structured liquidity features are therefore welcomed by investors.

In addition, given that such life insurance securitisation structures are funded by both fixed and floating rate instruments (and in some cases by both fixed and floating rate notes within the same capital structure), the volatility of the redemption profile has an impact on the investors' hedging strategy as well as on the unhedged cost volatility of the securitisation structure, with a possible consequent erosion of the subordination or the collateral available to investors.

Derivatives

In Chapter 9, we outlined the counterparty risk that non-life securitisation structures can have with swap counterparties, and in particular with reference to total return swaps. Investors in insurance-linked securities prefer structures in which the cross contamination from non-insurance events is minimised. Even if some life insurance securitisation structures embed an element of market and counterparty risk, investors look favourably on frequent mark to market of the liabilities of each swap counterparty, with frequent margin posting for negative mark-to-market positions. The aim is to limit, to the extent possible, the contamination to the structure arising from events such as the sudden bankruptcy of Lehman Brothers in September 2008. Some life insurance structures have total return swaps, others have interest rate swaps and some have inflation-linked swaps and other hedging techniques.

Hedging arrangements will therefore be in the spotlight for insurance-linked investors to help them identify any source of counterparty risk on top of the usual analysis to assess the adequacy of the hedges to cover the volatility of the underlying portfolio and the quantification of any unhedged risk on top of the securitised life insurance risk.

19.2.2 Pricing and risk-return profile

Investors are naturally very focused on pricing and on the risk-return profile of their portfolio. Their task to their own stakeholders is to maximise the return for an agreed risk profile.

In common with all other fixed-income investments in the capital markets, the analysis of comparable investments is a key element in validating pricing for life insurance securitisations. The first source of comparable transactions is, of course, within the life insurance securitisation sector. This is possible both for Regulation XXX transactions and for catastrophic mortality securitisations as there are a sufficient number of transactions in the market to monitor their primary as well as their secondary performance. For Regulation XXX in particular, the secondary performance may be an indicator of the pricing of a similar transaction without the benefit of a monoline guarantee due to the little credit now given to the wrap of most monolines by the investor community.

For VIF transactions the comparison is still possible, but the lack of a sufficient number of transactions in the market and the peculiarity of each underlying block and structure would require supplemental analysis with other structured transactions with similar duration, rating and volatility profile.

Bigger challenges arise when trying to use industry comparables for longevity securitisations and transactions backed by secondary market policies. For the latter, there is significant activity in secondary market trading of policies involving brokers and financial institutions, but not much activity can yet be seen on the securitisation front.

Longevity is starting to be exchanged in capital market form via derivative transactions (see Chapter 21), but derivative transactions normally embed a significant amount of leverage as the counterparty of collateralised swaps posts collateral only for a portion of the total exposure, with margining to take care of the volatility. In addition, whilst elements of longevity risk have been included in some existing securitisation alongside other risks, no pure longevity securitisation has been completed as of the end of 2008.

There are a number of reasons why, despite much research and a number of attempts by market participants, there has been little success in the placement of longevity securitisations. These include:

- **Duration:** structures designed to transfer economic longevity performance (particularly on individuals less than 65 years old) can imply the need for long-dated securities (i.e. greater than 10–15 years) to fully match the exposure of the protection buyer. Long-dated notes are less frequent in the capital markets, particularly for structured paper, and therefore there is a smaller community of investors, who often demand a premium pricing beyond what protection buyers are happy to pay. In addition, the typical investors in long-dated securities are life insurance companies and pension schemes which, themselves, have been less keen to add longevity exposure on their asset management side as it correlates with their own exposure on the liability side of the balance sheet. Equally important, these long-dated structures also embed a very significant mark-to-market risk for investors, as an actual or perceived change in life expectancy could affect the traded notes well in advance of any adverse experience affecting the notes. Some shorter dated structures on actual mortality improvements or on life expectancy have been discussed, but with little success, mainly due to the basis risk perceived by the sponsor in such structures.
- **Modelling:** we have already mentioned that modelling for longevity has been affected by the underestimation of mortality improvements by key models in the past, and by the lack of consensus of modelling of longevity going forward. Model uncertainty and questionable credibility could impact mark-to-market valuations of the notes and they therefore require premium pricing.
- **Pricing:** a pricing gap between the expectations of the protection buyer and investors' interest has been observed when discussing longevity securitisation. This gap was partly due to the possible underpricing of existing longevity liabilities by life insurers and pension providers, but also by the premium from the technical risk which investors require for mark-to-market volatility (due to modelling risk and changes in life expectancy) and duration. In addition, the investor universe in longevity securitisations has been limited to mainly hedge

funds and dedicated ILS investors with minimum return requirements. As mentioned above, a number of deals have been structured as derivatives rather than bonds, as those can partly bridge the pricing gap due to the embedded leverage.

In general terms, dedicated ILS funds show a sustained appetite for life insurance securitisation and in particular for those structures with 'pure' mortality and longevity risk, as such investments have the lowest levels of correlation with the rest of the capital markets among the available life insurance structures, and as they also contribute to diversifying their own investments in non-life insurance securitisation risk. Dedicated ILS funds, however, have their own minimum return requirements and with the conservative leverage facilities available in the medium term expected to be with low gearing, they are likely to be interested mainly in low investment-grade and non-investment-grade securities to maintain a minimum level of absolute return.

19.3   MARKET EVOLUTION: THE INVESTOR PERSPECTIVE

The life insurance securitisation market is comparable in terms of outstanding securities with that of non-life securitisation. The key differences are that:

• the life insurance securitisation market is characterised by a small number of large (or very large) transactions, and from few jurisdictions;
• the majority of the issuance has been investment-grade rated;
• the monolines played an important role in a number of issues.

Regulators and legislators in large markets such as the European Union have been working to create a framework for securitisation of insurance risk, which should lead to increased issuance across a number of markets. Focus on economic risk-based capital and the progressive elimination of regulatory arbitrage in the European Union is also expected to produce a higher volume of non-investment-grade issuance in the life insurance securitisation sector. For insurers in the European Union, the impact of Solvency II should permit better identification and quantification of risks and lead to better risk modelling, data capture and reporting capabilities, therefore allowing sponsors to be better prepared to support the implementation and the ongoing management of a life insurance securitisation transaction.

New markets, new structures and more junior issuance will pose challenges to investors in analysing the issuance, but at the same time will also be the base for a wider, richer market with a range of risk–return profiles able to attract various sectors of the market with different risk appetites.

In the short term the viability of many transactions depends on the ability to place high investment grade notes. As the financial turmoil has caused the market for high investment grade structured paper to shrink significantly and has led to the requirement of premium pricing, transactions have become uneconomical for protection buyers. At the same time, the current absence of the monolines requires a deep market of unwrapped investment-grade investors happy to go through the process of the underwriting of this new asset class and to receive a return which is in line with the risk of the notes.

At the end of 2008 such a market for high investment-grade life insurance-linked securities simply is not there, and therefore significant new issuance of a number of life insurance securitisation structures with investment-grade notes is likely to be deferred to a time of more stable fixed-income market conditions. At such time, institutional investors will be able to look back and see the types of transactions which were at the heart of the turmoil, the structural features they would like to see revised and those assets and structures which have shown a good actual performance within the expectations. At the end of this process, institutional investors alongside dedicated ILS funds should be able to see the benefit of the growth of the life insurance securitisation industry and to allocate a portion of their investment book to a new, well-structured asset class, likely to provide relative value and a degree of diversification benefit.

20

Longevity Securitisation: Specific Challenges and Transactions

Jennifer Donohue,[a] Kirsty Maclean[b] and Norman Peard[c]

20.1 MORTALITY AND LONGEVITY RISK

It is difficult to give a rigorous definition of 'mortality risk' or 'longevity risk'. The terms are usually used in context and the intention is then relatively clear. Instead of attempting to define the terms, a description is given in the following paragraph with the aim of making the meaning of the terms clearer.

From the perspective of an investor, or an organisation such as a life insurance company, or some other economic agent such as a pension fund, it might be said that there is exposure to mortality risk if actual rates of mortality in excess of those expected, or increases in rates of mortality, result in an economic loss. Similarly, exposure to the risk of economic loss resulting from mortality rates being less than those expected, or decreases in rates of mortality (and hence an increase in longevity), is referred to as being exposed to longevity risk.[1]

To make this a little more concrete, economic exposure to mortality rates (and thus exposure to mortality or longevity risk) arises where an obligation to pay (or the right to receive) some amount or amounts arises as a result of the contingency or death or survival of an individual or group of individuals. At this point there is economic exposure to mortality rates – whether it is an exposure to mortality risk or longevity risk depends on the nature of the economic exposure. As an example, in the absence of any contingent rights, an obligation to pay an amount in the event of the death of an individual results in mortality risk exposure, and an obligation to pay in the event of an individual's survival results in longevity exposure. Rights to receive amounts result, in the absence of any contingent obligations, in the opposite exposures – so, for example, the right to receive an amount on the survival of the individual results in a mortality exposure. Many contracts involve rights to receive and pay amounts contingent on survival or death and often also contingent rights and obligations,[2] so there may be exposure to both

---

[a] Simmons & Simmons

[b] Formerly of Simmons & Simmons

[c] Credit Suisse International

[1] The fact that both mortality risk and longevity risk depend on experience in relation to mortality rates often causes confusion. It is the directional change in mortality rates that is key to understanding the terms 'longevity risk' and 'mortality risk' as commonly used. Decreases in mortality rates correspond to increased longevity.

[2] For example, a policyholder may have the right to pay a premium at some future date (if the insured is alive at that date) in return for a payment at later future dates whilst the insured remains alive – whether the insurer is today

mortality and longevity risk, but the risk with the greater exposure is usually referred to alone in such cases.

Whilst this descriptive approach is intended to summarise the usual usage of the terms mortality risk and longevity risk, by comparison with terminology in the financial markets they are relatively lacking in rigour. For example, an investor is exposed to equity risk if either a rise or fall in the level of equity markets would result in an economic loss. In the former case, the investor is said to be 'short' equity exposure and, in the latter, 'long' equity exposure. So it can be seen that 'long' mortality exposure would be equivalent to 'short' longevity exposure under the terminology described above, and one of the terms would be redundant. In addition, longevity risk and mortality risk are usually used to describe the impact of general shifts in the levels of mortality rates – the terms are not usually used with any reference to the term structure of mortality rates as they would be in discussing, for example, interest rate exposures.

Despite the inadequacies, common usage is to use this slightly imprecise terminology for most discussions and it usually suffices, at least in context. That said, as longevity risk is increasingly transferred directly into the capital markets, the terminology used is gradually being influenced by capital market terminology.

20.2   A MARKET FOR LONGEVITY RISK

20.2.1   Potential sources of longevity risk for securitisation

The two most obvious sources of longevity exposure are life insurance offices and pension funds. Life offices which have written annuity business are sources of longevity risk, just like pension funds. However, there are other sources. For example, the second-hand life policy market[3] provides an opportunity. Some life insurance policies carry a contractual term granting the policyholder the right to payment of an encashment or surrender value should the policyholder cease paying premia. This payment may not always reflect the full economic value of the policy at the time of encashment or surrender. Policies may be assigned to a third party, that third party taking over the premium payment obligations and the rights to receive the payments payable contingent on the death or survival of the life insured. The third party may pay the policyholder an amount in excess of the encashment value in return for assignment of the policy and this is in the economic interests of both. The market for such transactions is referred to as the second-hand market. An investor may acquire a significant number of such policies. The investor will be exposed to longevity or mortality risk, depending on the nature of the policies acquired in this manner and this market is now large enough that the exposures may be considered for securitisation. In particular, a number of brokers and financial institutions are currently active in the US Life Settlements market, in which a number of high value insurance policies written on older lives are sold in the secondary market. Securitisation of such policies would embed longevity risk in relatively medium-term notes (but would typically not fully transfer longevity risk, which would generally require longer-dated securities and would also embed a number of other risks, including, for example, credit risk to the issuer of the insurance policy, legal risk in relation to the perfection of the assignment of the life policy and risks associated with potential challenge from the estate of the deceased policyholder).

---

exposed to mortality risk or longevity risk depends on the adequacy of the future premium to meet those contingent obligations.

[3] This is often referred to as the 'life settlement market'.

Governments also tend to be exposed to longevity risk. State retirement provision results in an obligation on central government to make life-long payments to a large proportion of the population in many developed nations.

Many, if not most, corporations are exposed to changes in rates of mortality, not just as a result of pensions provision for their employees, but because of the impacts of mortality on the potential size of their customer base. It is worth noting that this latter impact may be very difficult to disentangle from other factors affecting the corporation, many of which will be of much greater immediate significance.

20.2.2   Demand for longevity risk

Demand from investors for longevity risk has, to date, been limited. Some specialist funds have been established to invest in insurance-linked securities, but these have tended to invest in relatively short-duration securities. This has meant that there has been limited scope to transfer mortality/longevity risk other than catastrophe mortality risk.

Banks and fixed-income investors seeking diversification have invested in value-in-force (VIF) securitisations,[4] which, as discussed below, have included both mortality and longevity risk for a long duration, but alongside a range of other insurance risks. Some VIF securitisation structures were, in addition, wrapped by monoline insurers and so, whilst long-duration mortality and longevity risk has, on occasion, been transferred from insurance companies to the capital markets, these securities did not result in investors accepting pure mortality or longevity risk exposure.

Longer term investment, as regards both pure mortality and longevity risk, has been relatively slow to develop. Longevity exposure arising from life settlement business, described above, has been transferred to the books of a number of financial institutions, mostly for warehousing for subsequent distributions or to the high net worth retail investor market, principally in the US but also in Europe. Typically this has been achieved by issuing securities entitling the investor to payouts depending on death rates for lives insured for underlying death benefit policies – the earlier the underlying lives assured die, the earlier the policy benefits are received within the structure and the benefit passed to the investor. So, the investor is exposed to longevity risk. It is worth noting that the underlying policies expose the insurer to mortality risk and so whilst investors have accepted longevity exposure, these transactions have not served to transfer longevity risk from insurers or pension funds into the capital markets.

A limited but growing investor base that will accept the long-duration mortality and longevity risk which insurers or pension funds wish to transfer now exists in the form of specialist hedge funds. The funds will invest in both index- and indemnity-based structures. Increasingly a trend is developing for these specialist funds to retain specialist skills, such as relevant actuarial experience, in-house in order to assess and price the risks associated with opportunities presented to them.

Despite such positive developments and a growing investor base, there is not yet a liquid market for longevity risk, which is still characterised by an excess of demand for longevity risk protection over the available protection supply. This should point to the potential for market growth in response to new and advanced structural solutions as and when market conditions allow.

---

[4] See Chapter 14.

20.3   KEY STRUCTURAL ASPECTS OF LONGEVITY RISK SECURITISATION

There are a number of aspects to take into account when looking at longevity risk securitisation. In this section we summarise some such aspects.

20.3.1   Isolating longevity risk

The market has been developing towards 'pure' longevity risk transfer solutions.[5] When reference is made to 'pure', it indicates that the primary objective is transfer of longevity risk. This distinguishes these solutions from, for example, transactions using VIF monetisation structures which transfer a range of insurance-related risks – such transactions may include longevity risk transfer, but not as the primary feature determining the outcome to investors.

It is worth noting, though, that it is impossible to isolate longevity risk from all other risks. For example, longevity risk exposure cannot be separated from interest rate risk exposure.[6] If future mortality rates[7] for a group of lives were known with certainty today, then for a very large group of lives the cash flow profile of the payment obligations could be predicted with a great deal of certainty. The cash flows could then be precisely matched by investing in suitable fixed-interest instruments, for example.

If this portfolio of hedging assets is purchased, it might at first glance be thought that interest rate exposure has been separated from longevity risk exposure when determining the value of the liability to meet the payment obligations. This is not, in fact, the case. To see this, since the future mortality rates cannot, in reality, be known with certainty, suppose now that the level of mortality rates changes. This will result in a change in the amount of the obligations to be paid in any particular future time period. This means that the amount of fixed interest investment purchased to precisely match the payment obligation for this future date will turn out to be excessive, or insufficient.

More significantly, changes in the overall level of mortality rates away from those assumed will typically also increase or reduce the average duration of the obligations.[8] As a result, the purchased portfolio will turn out to have insufficient or excess duration.

So there is exposure to both longevity risk and interest rate risk. If the longevity risk is transferred, then the related exposure to interest rate risk is transferred too.

For many purposes the fact that longevity risk cannot be entirely separated from other risks is not a material issue, but it cannot always be ignored and should be assessed.

---

[5] For example, swap transactions may reference mortality in order to determine the floating leg payments. Whilst the payments are determined purely by longevity experience, this does not, in fact, mean that longevity risk has been isolated from other risks.

[6] This statement holds even on the assumption that there is no cause and effect type relationship between longevity and interest rates. However, it is likely that there is also such a relationship. For example, an increase in life expectancy in economies with material state pension scheme deficits could have an impact on the general economic policy for the country with direct and indirect implications for interest rates. So, at a macroeconomic level, there is likely also an interaction between life expectancy and interest rates.

[7] Probabilities of death at each age, at each future date, for the group of lives concerned.

[8] If the obligation is to make a single payment to each individual within a group who survives a specified period, then a reduction in mortality rates increases the total amount to be paid at the end of the period. If this is extended to a book of annuity business, under which payments are made regularly to each survivor at each future date, then the impact of a reduction in mortality rates will be proportionately more significant for dates in the far distant future and this results in an increase in the average duration of the liabilities.

20.3.2   Analysis of longevity risks

Where is the exposure?

Commercial pressure is increasing on governments, pension funds, life insurance companies and individuals to deal with the problem of longevity risk. The sophistication of annuity and pension products is being tested by these developments at the retail end and significantly at the wholesale end of the insurer. Historically, there have been few obvious ways for pension funds and insurance companies to hedge the risks they face. A pension fund could ask a life assurance company to 'buy out' the liabilities, but the conversion of the defined benefits to annuities is expensive and insurance capacity has, in the past, been limited, particularly where deferred annuities are involved. Here there is a transfer of the legal liability to pay pensions to an insurer. The set-up may take various forms, however the key underlying model is that companies transfer the portfolio of pension contracts to an external investor that will assume the contractual obligations. In the last few years, the UK has seen the establishment of a number of new investment companies specialising in these buy-outs. These should be distinguished from 'buy-ins', where trustees purchase one or more insurance policies and use proceeds to meet liabilities. Reinsurers' appetite for this type of risk is not high, unless for an existing client and part of an overall package of risks, while capped at a fairly low level, although more significant volumes of business have been transacted recently.

Alternatively, longevity risk may be hedged or reduced through balancing products. For example, the holder of longevity risk enters into a contract with a term assurance portfolio, thereby combining a conventional level of annuity with a whole-life assurance to the value of cost of the annuity. The resulting combination (or homogenising) of the off-setting underlying risks (mortality and longevity risk) would then reduce an insurer's exposure to future increases in longevity, consequently permitting a reduction of capital reserves held in respect of this risk.

Financial markets have also produced 'solutions' by providing a variety of vehicles to hedge longevity risk effectively, thereby assisting insurers in achieving their objective of managing their regulatory capital efficiently. The early 2000s saw the first survivor or longevity bond products. These took the form of annuity bonds whose annual coupon payments were tied to the survivorship index of some reference population. As members of the population gradually died, the coupon payments would gradually fall, and it has been suggested by some commentators that this would be a useful hedge for the annuity book of a life company. Before long, other longevity derivatives were being considered including longevity swaps, options and futures.

Who is buying longevity risk?

Other than providing insurance companies and pension funds with a means of hedging longevity risk, longevity bonds and derivatives offer speculative investors the opportunity to acquire a part of this exposure. Investors in the capital markets, seeking a portfolio disassociated from conventional risk factors, in order to achieve diversification, are the usual candidates. This appealing characteristic of longevity bonds is, however, not fully developed. There are still only a limited number of investors in longevity risk. These investors need to be attracted by offering competitive and sophisticated returns. There is also a significant education need as to the meaning and legal analysis of these risks. Transactions, although limited, have shown investors are currently taking a wide range of views as to future longevity experience and some are interested in investing without requiring a significant premium, i.e.

in effect they are prepared to accept longevity risk at rates in line with those required by direct writers of annuity business, but a very large transaction would need an additional premium to attract a wider range of investors. Another challenge in relation to establishing a market for longevity bonds is that the underlying characteristics differ significantly from some of the more asset-backed issuances. These other bonds often reference indicators which are more frequently updated than longevity experience, which is more attractive to investors.

One other recent development has been the interest of hedge funds (using longevity/mortality as a strategy in taking on this investment). Similarly, we have seen proprietary trading and asset management groups at investment banks operating in this market.

Who is arranging?

The major players in managing sellers and buyers have traditionally been reinsurers and banks. Reinsurers are not offering risk transfer solutions in isolation, but want some role in the structure. Banks, however, will often be prepared to warehouse some risk but have essentially taken the role of arranging transactions.

20.3.3   Longevity risk – legal explanation

The most difficult legal issue surrounding these transactions involves the line between security and insurance contract. The importance of avoiding a bond or derivative being recharacterised as an insurance contract cannot be overstated. The following explanation relates to the UK market, which is one of the most active markets in longevity risk transfer.

As the UK Financial Services Authority (the FSA) notes in its Regulatory Guidance on the Identification of Contracts of Insurance (PERG 6 FSA Handbook), the courts have not fully defined the common law meaning of 'insurance' and 'insurance business', since they have, on the whole, confined their decisions to the facts before them. They have, however, given useful guidance in the form of descriptions of contracts of insurance.

The best established of these descriptions appears in the case of *Prudential v. Commissioners of Inland Revenue* [1904] 2 KB 658. This case, read with a number of later cases, treats as insurance any enforceable contract under which the insurer undertakes:

1. in consideration of one or more payments
2. to pay money or provide a corresponding benefit (including in some cases services to be paid for by the provider) to an insured
3. in response to a defined event the occurrence of which is uncertain (either as to when it will occur or as to whether it will occur at all) and adverse to the interests of the insured (*an insurable interest*).

As the FSA points out (PERG 6.5.4.), the courts have adopted the following principles of construction to determine whether a contract is a contract of insurance.

1. More weight attaches to the substance of the contract than to the form of the contract. The form of the contract is relevant, but not decisive of whether a contract is a contract of insurance. *Fuji Finance Inc. v. Aetna Life Insurance Co. Ltd* [1997] Ch. 173.
2. In particular, the substance of the provider's obligation determines the substance of the contract (in *re Sentinel Securities* [1996] 1 WLR 316). Accordingly, the insurer's or the

insured's intention or purpose in entering into a contract is unlikely to be relevant to its classification.

3. The contract must be characterised as a whole and not according to its 'dominant purpose' or the relative weight of its 'insurance content'. *Fuji Finance Inc. v. Aetna Life Insurance Co. Ltd [Supra]*.

Among the factors identified by the FSA (PERG 6.6) which the courts have taken into account in deciding whether any particular contract is a contract of insurance are the following:

1. Case law establishes that the provider's obligation under a contract of insurance is an enforceable obligation to respond (usually, by providing some benefit in the form of money or services) to the occurrence of the uncertain event.

2. Contracts under which the provider has absolute discretion as to whether any benefit is provided on the occurrence of the uncertain event are not contracts of insurance. This may be the case even if, in practice, the provider has never exercised its discretion so as to deny a benefit. *Medical Defence Union v. Department of Trade and Industry*.

3. The 'assumption of risk' by the insurer is an important descriptive feature of all contracts of insurance.

4. The recipient's payment for a contract of insurance need not take the form of a discrete or distinct premium. Consideration may be part of some other payment, for example the purchase price of goods. Consideration may also be provided in a non-monetary form, for example as part of the service that an employee is contractually required to provide under a contract of employment.

5. A contract is more likely to be regarded as a contract of insurance if the amount payable by the recipient under the contract is calculated by reference to either or both of the probability of occurrence or likely severity of the uncertain event.

6. A contract is less likely to be regarded as a contract of insurance if it requires the provider to assume a speculative risk (i.e. a risk carrying the possibility of either profit or loss) rather than a pure risk (i.e. a risk of loss only.)

7. A contract is more likely to be regarded as a contract of insurance if the contract is described as insurance and contains terms that are consistent with its classification as a contract of insurance, for example, obligations of the utmost good faith.

8. A contract that contains terms that are inconsistent with obligations of good faith may, therefore, be less likely to be classified as a contract of insurance; however, since the substance of the provider's rights and obligations under the contract is more significant, a contract does not cease to be a contract of insurance simply because the terms included are not usual insurance terms.

From this list of factors it may be very difficult to predict whether any particular contract will, or will not, be characterised by the courts as a contract of insurance rather than as a insurance-linked security. Therefore in all of the structures which result in a market instrument, the structure and the terms of the contracts may have a significant impact on characterisation. The particular categories of financial instruments are very broad, and include a wide variety of structures and documentation. Structuring and the terms of the bond or notes need to withstand a significantly robust test.

20.3.4   Examples and legal aspects of transaction structures

The basic mortality risk transfer structure, by way of illustration, is usually set up as follows. A special purpose vehicle (SPV) is formed and an insurer makes payments equal to expected mortality costs under a block of policies to the SPV and, in exchange, receives payments based on the actual mortality experience under the block. The SPV is funded, as usual, by issuing notes to investors, who receive LIBOR plus a risk premium to compensate for bearing the mortality risk. The bond may, for example, be structured to follow the actual experience on a specified block of life insurance policies or the experience of an index based on national statistics. Essentially, the structure covers only the mortality risk and not the other risks which affect the overall profitability of the block.

Longevity securitisations

In terms of capital market innovations that can be used to hedge mortality and longevity risk, trades have been relatively few. The early Barclays Life Assurance Company transaction (Gracechurch, 2003) successfully securitised £400m of a defined book of unit-linked life and pensions business. It included a notable percentage of mortality/longevity risk in the defined business. Friends Provident (Box Hill, 2004) followed with longevity and mortality risk transfer to the capital markets. Whilst these transactions included mortality and longevity risks (longevity relating to annuity business) amongst the principal risks to which investors were exposed, they did not transfer purely mortality or longevity risks, as they also transferred other insurance and market-related risks.

A further development to transfer purely mortality risk, pioneered by a private financial institution, was the Swiss Re mortality bond in December 2003 (Figure 20.1). Swiss Re offered a $400 million bond programme ($250 million initial issuance with an option to offer $150 million in additional notes) with a three-year maturity whose principal payment was tied to an index tracking mortality rates in five countries: France, Italy, Switzerland, UK and US.

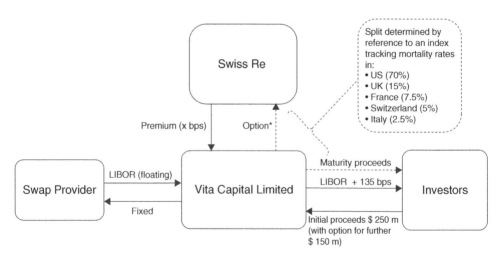

* The option payoff is the (initial proceeds) x ((Index % - 130%)/(150 %−130%)), but not exceeding the initial proceeds

Figure 20.1   Structure of Swiss Re Vita I

The bond was priced at LIBOR + 1.35% in return for accepting the risk of a reduced principal payment in the event of a catastrophic mortality deterioration such as that associated with the Spanish flu pandemic of 1918. The principal was repayable in full if the mortality index did not exceed 1.3 times the 2002 base level during any of the three years of the bond's life. It would, however, be reduced by 5% for every 1% increase in the mortality index above the threshold, and would not be repaid if the index surpassed 150% of the base level.

The instrument offered has a number of characteristics similar to a catastrophe bond, where principal repayments are reduced if the trigger event (usually adverse mortality experience) occurs. This noteworthy transaction, based directly on mortality risk, is simpler to model and understand than transactions involving all of the cash flows on a whole block of life insurance policies. The transaction did not require a third-party guarantee to obtain a high credit rating, (as had been the case with Gracechurch and Box Hill), owing partly to its simplicity and transparency. The bond allowed Swiss Re to lay off some of its extreme mortality risk and release capital that would otherwise have needed to be held to cover its life and health insurance liabilities in the event of a major mortality event. The bond was well received by investors.

In November 2004, a longevity bond to be issued by the European Investment Bank (EIB) was announced by BNP Paribas, in conjunction with Partner Re (Figure 20.2). The bond, with a value of £540 million and a maturity of 25 years, was intended for UK life insurance companies and pension funds with exposure to longevity risk. Payments under the bond were linked to a cohort survivor index based on the realised mortality rates of males aged 65 in England and Wales. The base coupon of £50 million was scaled by the percentage of the reference group who were still alive (or, more specifically, were alive two years prior, due to the time lag in gathering the data).

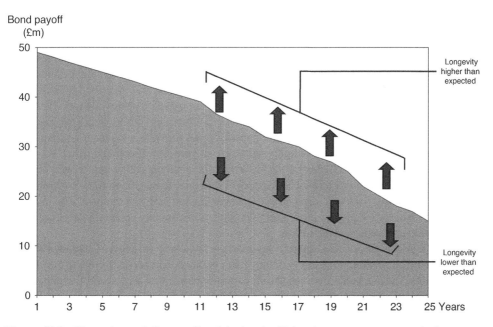

Figure 20.2 Illustrative cash flow profile of the bond utilising the government actuary's department projections

Under the structure, BNP was to bear the investment risk and the longevity risk would be covered by Partner Re. The bond was set to be AAA rated, equivalent to the EIB rating at the time, thus offering potential investors lower risk to counterparty. The issue was withdrawn in late 2005 predominantly because the pension industry found the price of coverage on longevity risk too high.

Studies have shown that many factors contributed towards the failure of the bond structure. First, it has been suggested that longevity risk is a long-term risk with low volatility and is an economic risk different from interest rate or inflation risk. Second, asset–liability matching rules and other regulatory requirements are not effective in encouraging pension funds to hedge this aggregate risk. The UK pension funds subscribing to this longevity bond could not therefore take any regulatory benefits. It has been reported that there were problems with the design of the issue; the fact that it ran for 25 years meant there was a 'tail risk', in that there was no feature built in to hedge the costs of pensions to members who survived more than 25 years after retirement.

Longevity swaps

The emergence of a market for longevity swaps has been slow to date, however bearing in mind the wealth of knowledge and product development emanating from a cast of major financial institutions as set out below, it is apparent that the trend toward trading in the life market is beginning to take hold. Development has so far favoured index-based transactions.

In December 2005 Credit Suisse announced their Longevity Index (based on US lives), which aims to provide a benchmark longevity index against which longevity derivatives of various forms can be calibrated. The Credit Suisse Longevity Index ('the Index'), the first of its kind, was designed specifically to enable the structuring and settlement of longevity risk transfer instruments such as longevity swaps and longevity structured notes. The Index markets itself as 'a standardised measure of the expected average lifetime for general populations based on publicly available statistics'.

2007 saw J.P. Morgan, along with advisors Watson Wyatt and Pensions Institute at Cass Business School, put together LifeMetrics, a toolkit for measuring and managing longevity and mortality risk for pension plans, sponsors, insurers, reinsurers and investors. LifeMetrics enables these risks to be measured in a standardised manner, based on observed mortality rates as published by the UK government's Office for National Statistics (ONS), aggregated across different risk sources and transferred to other parties. It also provides a means to evaluate the effectiveness of longevity/mortality hedging strategies and the size of residual risk.

Following on from this, the Goldman Sachs Group, Inc. announced the launch of a family of indices, called QxX, said to allow participants to measure, manage and trade exposure to longevity and mortality risks in a standardised, transparent and real-time manner. The indices roll on an annual basis and are therefore said to produce a continually updated reference pool, market evolution and underwriting trends.

In 2008, Deutsche Börse also entered this market, launching a range of indices (Xpect Indices) tracking population trends in Germany, with planned equivalents for other European countries. Deutsche sources its own data from local municipalities and is said to update the indices monthly.

By way of illustration, the closing of the first publicly acknowledged longevity swap in a transaction conducted by Lucida and J.P. Morgan took place in February 2008. The deal with J.P. Morgan to hedge Lucida's longevity risk occurred through a derivative contract linked to the investment bank's LifeMetrics Longevity Index. The swap, called a q-forward contract (q is the symbol in standard actuarial notation for a mortality rate, 'forward' refers to a forward contract) is thought to be in the region of £100 million and has a ten-year maturity.

Following on from this, September 2008 saw the UK division of insurer Canada Life enter into a transaction to hedge £500 million worth of longevity exposure with J.P. Morgan. This long-dated swap, with a maturity of 40 years, offers investors increased payment if the Equitable annuitants live longer than expected. The swap also allows investors the option to resell the investment back to J.P. Morgan throughout the duration of the swap and the present value of expected cash flows under the swap is updated monthly.

In light of new mortality guidelines proposed by the UK pension regulators in early 2008, pension funds too may find the prospect of using such derivatives attractive.

Other longevity risk transactions in the UK in 2008 included the £1.7 billion deal between insurer Friends Provident and Swiss Re, using a reinsurance mechanism.

20.4   SOME FEATURES OF LONGEVITY RISK

20.4.1   Model risk

There are various ways in which longevity risk may be assessed. Two principal features of the assessment will be considered here: (i) the error in assessing the level of mortality underlying the experience to date in respect of a book of business, and (ii) the possible future experience.

In order to determine the level of mortality underlying the experience to date in respect of a book of business, it is necessary to compare the number of deaths to the number of lives exposed to risk of death. Whilst conceptually this is very simple, in essence being a comparison of numbers of deaths with numbers of policies in force, in practice it is not so simple. There may be practical difficulties, for example data quality may be less than ideal (either legacy databases are missing desirable data or potentially, particularly in the case of reinsured business, only summary data are available to the reinsurer in relation to the underlying business). Even when data are complete and accurate, the analysis is a statistical exercise and so the data can only provide an estimate of the underlying mortality process applicable to the insured portfolio.[9] In addition, several approaches to a full analysis can be taken.

It has been found that mortality rates vary not only by reference to factors such as age, sex and whether or not the individual smokes, but also other factors such as, for example, the size of the policy.[10] Analyses reflecting these factors are generally considered in arriving at an estimate of past experience in relation to the portfolio in question. Even for large blocks, it is usually the case that there is significant variation in mortality experience from year to year and the observed experience volatility over shorter periods may be quite significant. All of these factors (and others) play a role in estimating the level of mortality underlying the experience of the particular portfolio of business.

Figure 20.3 illustrates the extent of the variance in mortality rates for males by reference to one of these factors in the case of pension benefits. The rates have been expressed as

---

[9] An exaggerated example will clarify this. If the portfolio consisted of just one life, then the experience would result in a sample estimate probability of death of either 0 or 1. So there is an estimation error in assessing the underlying experience. This estimation error decreases as the size of the insured portfolio increases.

[10] By and large (but not always), insured lives with policies providing for larger death benefit amounts or larger regular annuity payments experience lower mortality rates.

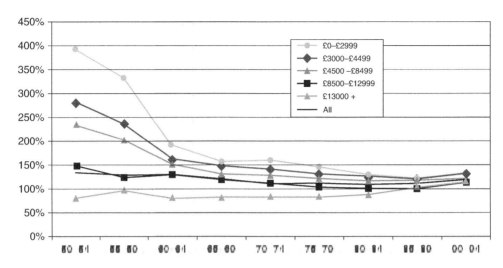

Figure 20.3 Mortality rates – illustrative relationship to size of pension

Source: Continuous Mortality Investigation

percentages of a standard mortality table. Rates of mortality experienced at ages 50–54 are approximately four times as high for pensioners with an annual pension of under £3000 as they are for pensioners with an annual pension in excess of £13,000, for example. Note that the relationship (the four times multiplier) itself varies with age. The experience analysis is based on UK data.

The possible future experience then needs to be addressed. For large portfolios, this will be the most significant contributor to the mortality or longevity risk associated with the block of business. Observations are that, for much of the 20th century, rates of mortality have been decreasing in most major economies, across all ages and for males and females. The trend has not been uniformly decreasing and has varied in magnitude and timing depending on age, sex, occupation, income and other factors. The improvement has been greater at some ages than at others and in some time periods than others. The causes are only partially understood. This last point is key – there is, ultimately, no full understanding as to the drivers of mortality, either in the population as a whole or in an insured portfolio. Some of the improvements relate to medical advances, some to improved living conditions, some to changes in lifestyle, but it is not possible to link past improvement definitively to causative factors. So it is impossible to give a certain prediction as to what the future may hold for mortality rates. Developments in medical science continue apace. Insights from the field of gerontology are, on the one hand, helpful in terms of scientifically explaining the aging process, whilst on the other hand unhelpful in introducing further uncertainty as experimental evidence in relation to animal species suggests significant increases in life expectancy may be achievable – but not the extent to which this can be achieved for *Homo sapiens*. Furthermore, the levels of obesity in Western civilisations are reaching epidemic proportions and must be expected to result in some offset to future mortality improvements.

Figure 20.4 indicates the variation in mortality rates across a range of industries. As in the previous figure, the rates are expressed in terms of percentages of a standardised table. The experience is shown based on two separate analyses, one by reference to numbers of

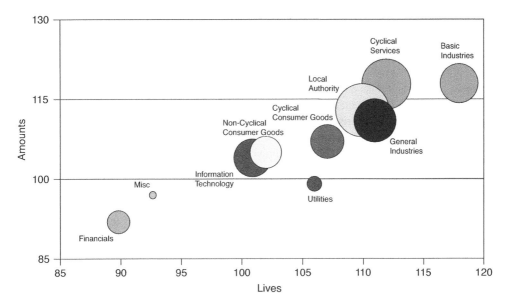

Figure 20.4   Mortality rates – illustrative relationship to industry

Source: Continuous Mortality Investigation

individuals, the other by reference to the size or amount of pension.[11] The circles indicate the relative sizes of the underlying mortality databases. The graph clearly demonstrates the significant variation across different portfolios and is indicative of some of the potential shortcomings in terms of basis risk attaching to risk transfer on an index basis. The experience analysis is based on UK data.

One of the significant features of longevity risk is the long duration of typical exposures. An insurance company or pension fund providing an annuity for life may still be paying benefits in 40 years' time to some of those individuals currently aged 60 or 65. In order fully to hedge the exposure, risk transfer is required over a similar period. For some forms of contract, exposures may be much longer – for example, an individual currently aged 30 may have earned entitlement to an annuity commencing at age 65 to be paid for the remainder of life. The expected duration[12] of these payments may be of the order of 50 years, but the potential duration could be in excess of 70.

Before leaving this section, it is worth mentioning that even where an insurance company is exposed to both longevity and mortality risk as a result of writing a range of different policies, it is not the case that these risks are natural hedges. As alluded to above, rates of mortality do not move in the same direction at the same time at all ages. There is a partial natural hedge effect over time, but it is not perfect. Accordingly, life insurance securitisation may be used to hedge exposures to mortality and longevity arising from an insurer's total business, even when both risks are present.

---

[11] See the third paragraph of Section 20.4.1.

[12] This is used in the mathematical sense of a probability-weighted average.

20.4.2 Ratings

In the last few years demand has grown for mortality- and longevity-linked securities to be issued in rated form. Ratings agencies have retained relevant expertise and, as described below, modelling has become more sophisticated. This combination has enabled securities to be rated. Mortality catastrophe bonds have been the first to be rated, in line with the pattern described above in the section on demand for mortality and longevity risk. Transactions that embed longevity risk alongside other risks (such as the two aforementioned transactions Gracechurch and Box Hill) have been rated. Although, at the time of writing, no pure longevity security has been rated, it ought now to be possible to achieve a rating.

20.4.3 Pricing

It was mentioned above that mortality experience varies significantly by reference to a large number of factors and fluctuates over time. Even for groups of lives as large as national populations, rates of mortality at a specific age may show significant variation from year to year. They may rise from one year to the next, despite the overall trend for many years having been for rates to fall.

Quantitative modelling is applied with the aim of fitting past data and making projections as to potential future experience under a range of assumptions. For example, the year-to-year fluctuations might be smoothed using various established curve-fitting techniques, or, where mortality is considered as a function of age and cohort, i.e. year of birth,[13] for example, surface-fitting techniques. Whilst the technical aspects are outside the scope of this chapter, it is worth noting that there is a large range of assumptions, including assumptions as to the correct model to use to fit past data and assumptions as to the appropriateness of the model for projecting the future. It is possible for a model to produce a close fit to past data but, when used to project future mortality rates, to produce highly implausible results, so both mathematical expertise and experience in the field of mortality are required. There have been significant developments in recent years in modelling mortality and it is possible to produce a range of plausible outcomes for future experience. Under certain assumptions, a number of models also enable probabilities to be associated with various outcomes – of course, if the assumptions are invalid, those probabilities are wrong. Given that a range of different models can be applied to produce plausible results for individual data sets, but no model produces plausible results for all data sets and model outputs can be highly sensitive to assumptions and the calibration data set, there is, as yet, no consensus as to which model to adopt. However, advances in modelling, together with approaches which have been used successfully for many years in the traditional life insurance markets, enable informed judgement to be applied, potential outcomes, risk capital requirements and costs of capital to be assessed and risk pricing to be achieved.

As previously discussed, a number of factors influence the ability to establish a clearing price for mortality and longevity risk in the capital markets. There is a supply/demand imbalance for longevity risk. The technical features of the risk mean that specialist knowledge and advice are likely to be needed prior to any investment decision regarding mortality or longevity risk. Risk modelling and pricing are demanding, particularly for long-duration transactions which

---

[13] The rate of mortality for 65-year-old males born in 1844, for example, was much higher than for males currently aged 65, born in 1944.

would enable the transfer of risk over long future periods. However, ratings are becoming possible.

The uncertainty as to future improvement trends, in particular, has proved to be a hurdle to longer-dated transactions transferring mortality and longevity risk, although this has been changing very recently. Transaction sponsors and potential investors have maintained significantly different views as to the appropriate basis for pricing long-duration risk. Particularly in the longevity risk transfer arena, this has led to the price that sponsors are willing to pay to offload risk being substantially less than the price at which capital market investors have been willing to accept that risk. Recently several factors have operated to close this gap. Regulators have been looking to insurers to give more consideration to the adequacy of reserves for longevity risk-exposed business. A market has been developing in the aggregate liabilities of pension schemes, and specialist investors have become active as corporates (for whom pension scheme-related risks are non-core) seek to reduce their exposures. As a result, pressure to offload longevity exposure has been increasing, whilst specialist insurance-linked securities investors have, to some extent, tightened their pricing bases. Consequently, pure longevity risk-based trades are now being transacted, although, to date, in derivative form rather than structured as insurance-linked securities.

21

Longevity Risk Transfer: Indices and Capital Market Solutions

Longevity risk is the risk that people outlive their expected lifetimes. It poses a significant risk to defined benefit (DB) pension plans and their sponsors, as well as insurance companies that provide retirement annuities. For these institutions, the longer people live, the greater the period of time over which retirement income must be paid and, therefore, the larger the financial liability.

This chapter focuses on the longevity risk associated with the provision of retirement income. It addresses solutions for transferring longevity risk via the capital markets from hedgers (pension plans and insurers) to end investors, and reviews two kinds of longevity risk transfer transactions that have been implemented over the course of 2008 and are in the public domain. Both of these transactions involved hedging the longevity risk associated with pension liabilities using financial derivatives. The first is a standardized index-based longevity hedge that was executed by Lucida, a UK pension buyout insurer, and the second is a customized longevity hedge that was executed by Canada Life in the UK.

These transactions would not have happened without the development of longevity indices and longevity toolkits, both of which facilitated analysis and valuation by providing the necessary tools and standardization to enable all parties to reach a common understanding of price and risk. These transactions also show that a new market is emerging in longevity risk transfer and, whilst this book focuses on insurance-linked securities (ILS) and no known pure longevity risk transfer has been made in securitized form to date, the analysis of the indices and solutions implemented to date is relevant for ILS market players. Also, it is important to realize that further education and standardization is still required to allow the market to develop meaningful liquidity.

We begin in the next section with a discussion of longevity risk, how it differs from other risks and how the longevity associated with pension plans and annuity portfolios is

---

[a] Managing Director, Pension ALM Advisory, JPMorgan

[1] Guy Coughlan is Managing Director and Global Head of Pension ALM Advisory at J.P. Morgan. Additional information is available upon request. This chapter was prepared by the Pension Advisory Group and not by any research department of J.P. Morgan Chase & Co. and its subsidiaries ("J.P. Morgan"). Information herein is obtained from sources believed to be reliable but J.P. Morgan does not warrant its completeness or accuracy. Opinions and estimates constitute J.P. Morgan's judgment and are subject to change without notice. Past performance is not indicative of future results. This material is provided for informational purposes only and is not intended as a recommendation or an offer or solicitation for the purchase or sale of any security or financial instrument.

The Handbook of Insurance-Linked Securities   Edited by P. Barrieu and L. Albertini
© 2009 John Wiley & Sons, Ltd

different from that associated with life settlements. Then Section 21.2 reviews the market for longevity risk transfer and the needs of different market participants. Section 21.3 examines the importance of longevity indices, toolkits and standards. Section 21.4 discusses the different types of instruments for transferring longevity risk in capital markets format. The following section compares customized and standardized hedges of longevity risk. Then Sections 21.6 and 21.7 discuss case studies of customized and standardized hedges respectively.

21.1   THE NATURE OF LONGEVITY RISK

Longevity risk is a demographic risk different from the kinds of risk that are normally encountered in the financial markets. It is a cumulative long-term risk that is largely uncorrelated with existing asset classes.

As it applies to DB pension plan and insurer annuity exposures, longevity risk reflects the uncertainties in future mortality rates for different ages. In particular, the upward trend in the longevity of males and females observed in the developed world over several decades has been driven by a persistent downward trend in mortality rates. People are living longer because mortality rates are falling (i.e., improving).

The cost of providing a pension or annuity depends on the expected long-term trend of future mortality rates. If the realized trend involves higher mortality improvements (i.e., lower mortality rates) than expected, then the cost of that pension or annuity can be significantly higher than expected. So longevity risk is not so much a 'volatility' risk (as most investment risks are) but a 'trend' risk. Moreover, it is a slowly building, cumulative trend risk. Mortality rates in future years depend on the cumulative mortality improvements between now and then, which only become significant over long timescales.

The precise nature of longevity risk depends not only on the type of exposure (e.g., pension plan, annuity liability, or life settlement investment), but also on the population or 'pool' of individual lives to which the exposure relates. Any pool of lives is characterized by two things:

- number of lives in the pool;
- profile of the individuals in the pool.

Small pools with small numbers of lives suffer from sampling risk, which means (i) it is difficult to measure the true underlying mortality rate for the pool with any accuracy, and (ii) the realized mortality experience in any period can be significantly different from expectation (even if the expected mortality rate were known to a high degree of accuracy). By contrast, in a large pool of lives (e.g., national population for a large country), there is little sampling risk for most ages, but future mortality rates (and hence longevity) are still uncertain because the underlying process for the evolution of future mortality is uncertain.

Life settlements typically involve small pools of lives (generally hundreds of lives), whereas pension plans and annuity portfolios can involve larger pools (thousands, tens of thousands, hundreds of thousands or more). So sampling risk is a large component of the risk attached to life settlements, compared with pension and annuity exposures. But that isn't the only difference between them: members of life settlement pools have been selected on the basis of medical underwriting, which is not the case for pension plans and typically not the case for most annuity portfolios.[2] This 'selection' biases the nature of individuals within the pool and changes the pool's longevity characteristics.

While longevity risk is common to life settlements, pension plans and annuity portfolios, life settlements, by virtue of their small pool size and the selection inherent in the underwriting process, face a different kind of longevity risk. Pension plans and annuity portfolios have more exposure to the systematic, undiversifiable longevity risk that underlies the whole of a national population, necessitating a very different kind of analysis.

For more information on longevity risk, see Richards and Jones (2004).

21.2 THE MARKET FOR LONGEVITY RISK TRANSFER

The development of a market for longevity risk transfer via the capital markets has faced a number of challenges. These include the unfamiliarity of longevity risk for most market participants, the exaggerated perception of complexity, the lack of common language across different market participants and the novelty of transferring longevity in capital markets format. Nevertheless, these challenges are being addressed by education, increased visibility, regulatory changes, the provision of open source toolkits[3] and the publicity associated with successful indices and with successful hedging transactions.

As a result, the market is expected to develop significantly in the coming years as more and more hedgers seek to reduce risk and improve capital efficiency, and more and more investors seek low-correlation returns from new asset classes, such as longevity.

This market involves three primary kinds of participants:

- **Hedgers:** insurers (annuity providers) and pension plans that naturally have longevity risk and are seeking to reduce or eliminate it.
- **Investors:** financial institutions that are potentially end holders of the longevity risk. They include insurance-linked securities (ILS) funds, hedge funds, endowments and even insurers and reinsurers.
- **Financial intermediaries:** banks and other financial institutions that facilitate risk transfer and, in many cases, stand in the middle between hedgers and investors.

The process of risk transfer takes place as illustrated in Figure 21.1.

21.2.1 Hedgers

For hedgers, transferring longevity risk using capital market instruments provides a complementary alternative to using insurance instruments and specifically delivers:

- **Additional capacity for bearing longevity risk:** the universe of end holders of the risk is expanded beyond insurers and reinsurers to include financial investors.
- **Greater diversity of counterparties:** hedgers are not restricted to transacting just with insurers and reinsurers, but can also transact with investment banks, exchanges and other intermediaries.

---

[2] There can be elements of selection in pension plans and annuity portfolios if, for example, they involve voluntary participation, or if they are aligned to particular industries or socio-economic classes. But the selection effect in life settlement portfolios is typically much greater.

[3] Examples of such toolkits are discussed in Section 21.3 of this chapter.

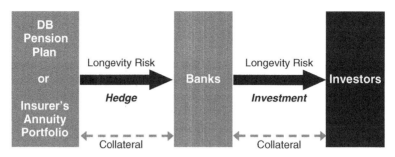

Figure 21.1   Longevity risk transfer in the capital markets
Source: J.P. Morgan

- **Liquidity:** insurance contracts are not liquid, whereas capital market contracts, appropriately designed, have the potential to be highly liquid
- **Fungibility.** longevity hedges or investments transacted with one bank may be unwound with another.
- **Potential for reduced counterparty exposure:** longevity hedges transacted as derivatives are always fully collateralized on an economic basis to reduce counterparty credit exposure. This is generally not the case with insurance instruments.

For a hedger contemplating transferring its longevity risk via the capital markets, there are two important choices that must be made:

- **Metric:** cash flow hedge of liabilities vs. value hedge of liabilities;
- **Type:** customized hedge vs. standardized index hedge.[4]

Over the course of 2008, two different hedging transactions have been made public that span these choices. In January, Lucida, a UK pension buyout insurer, executed a standardized index hedge designed to hedge liability value (see Lucida, 2008; Symmons, 2008). Then in July, Canada Life in the UK executed a customized hedge of its liability cash flows (*Trading Risk*, 2008; *Life and Pensions*, 2008).

Consider the first choice above between hedging cash flow and hedging value. Cash flow hedges involve hedging each liability cash flow, so that the uncertainty in each pension payment is reduced or eliminated. Most insurance-based solutions are cash flow hedges, e.g., a lifetime annuity provides a cash flow hedge for a DB pension liability. Clearly, to hedge all the liability cash flows in this way requires a very long-maturity cash flow hedge that runs until the last liability payment is made.

By contrast, value hedges involve hedging the liability value at a specified point in time called the hedge 'horizon' (say, ten years in the future), so that the uncertainty associated with the liability valuation at that time is reduced or eliminated. A value hedge effectively hedges all the liability cash flows beyond the hedge horizon in value terms at the hedge horizon. One advantage of a value hedge is that it can, in principle, be implemented for any hedge horizon, yet still provide a highly effective degree of risk reduction. This leads to effective hedges that can be of much shorter maturity than the long maturities required for cash flow hedges.

Now consider the second choice hedgers must make, namely that between a customized hedge and a standardized hedge. In any hedging situation, there is a tension between pursuing

---

[4] These alternatives are referred to as 'indemnity' and 'parametric' respectively in the catastrophe risk industry.

a hedge customized to the precise risk characteristics of the exposure and a more standardized, index-based hedge that hedges the majority of the risk more cheaply and more conveniently. We call these two approaches to hedging the 'indemnification' approach and the 'risk management' approach respectively. They are described in greater detail in section 21.5.

Hedgers of longevity risk will, other things being equal, always have a preference for a customized hedge solution, not just because it provides an exact hedge, but also because it mimics the way hedging has been done until now and is, therefore, a familiar approach. Longevity risk in pension plans has traditionally been hedged with annuities, which are insurance products that provide a customized, long-maturity cash flow hedge.

But standardized index hedges offering additional benefits (such as lower cost, etc.) are now being recognized as viable alternative solutions, which may be preferred in certain situations.

21.2.2 Investors

For investors, longevity offers the prospect of earning a risk premium in a new asset class that is (largely) uncorrelated with traditional asset classes. In fact, increasing numbers of investors of various kinds are in various stages of evaluating this asset class and many are indicating that they intend to take on some longevity exposure in their portfolios. Despite current market conditions, many investors have capital ready to be deployed at the right price. For example, in July 2008 J.P. Morgan successfully placed a large customized longevity risk position (originating from the Canada Life hedge mentioned above) with several investors via a long-dated survivor swap. This transaction is discussed in greater detail later in this chapter, but it is important to note its significance. Despite being the first of its kind and despite having many features that were not ideal from an investor perspective, such as very long maturity, customized longevity risk, lack of liquidity, uncapped downside risk and a requirement for complex analytical diligence, this transaction was nonetheless successfully placed with a number of investors at a very challenging time for the capital markets. This is very encouraging indeed for the development of this market.

Despite the success in the Canada Life transaction, investors as a whole (other things being equal) prefer to invest via standardized index-based hedges, in which longevity exposure is transferred in a form that is well-understood, in which the transaction can be of shorter maturity (e.g., ten years) and in which there is the potential to be far more liquid than a customized hedge. The investor base for longevity risk in this format should always be greater than that for long-maturity, customized longevity risk.

There are several challenges for investors wishing to enter the longevity market. The most important of these is the unfamiliarity of longevity risk, which is qualitatively different from financial risks. This has not been helped by the lack of familiarity with actuarial concepts and jargon, which has historically impeded education and created an unwarranted perception of excessive complexity. As a result, education has become an important element for market development and was an important factor behind the development of open source longevity toolkits (See Section 21.3).

21.2.3 Intermediaries

The role of banks in this market will largely be one of intermediation, standing in the middle between hedgers and investors. They are not likely to hold significant longevity positions over the long term, although it will be necessary for them to warehouse temporarily quantities of longevity risk in order to facilitate the market in the early stages and match buyers and sellers of this risk. Intermediation in this way is highly desirable for three reasons:

- **Liquidity provision:** by providing liquidity to both sides of the market it is not necessary for hedgers to wait until the right investor comes along before hedging, and vice versa. Furthermore, the hedge remains in place if an investor redeems its longevity investment.
- **Credit intermediation:** by fulfilling the role of counterparty to both hedgers and investors, management of credit counterparty risk is simplified and undesirable situations are avoided (such as a pension plan having as counterparty a thinly capitalized hedge fund).
- **Repackaging:** many investors want to take longevity risk in different forms from that in which hedgers want to shed it. By standing in the middle, banks can slice and dice exposures into different parcels to meet the specific needs of different investors and hedgers.

Banks are not the only possible intermediaries for longevity risk transfer transactions, but they are likely to be the dominant intermediary in the early stages of market development. Other intermediaries may include insurers, reinsurers, interdealer brokers and exchanges.

21.3 IMPORTANCE OF INDICES, TOOLS AND STANDARDS

The development of the market for longevity risk transfer has been supported over the past few years by the development of tools designed to improve the degree of transparency, education and standardization. These tools include:

- **Longevity toolkits:** these include the projection library and mortality projection software provided by the UK's Continuous Mortality Investigation (CMI) and the LifeMetrics Toolkit which provides analytics, frameworks, data and software for longevity and mortality risk management.
- **Longevity databases:** these include ClubVita which was launched by UK pension consultant Hymans Robertson to pool data on the mortality experience of UK pension plans. Other examples include the data provided by the CMI on UK assured lives and pension mortality, as well as Deutsche Börse's Xpect Data, which provides data on German and Dutch mortality.
- **Longevity indices:** these include the LifeMetrics Longevity Index, the Credit Suisse Longevity Index, the Xpect Index and the QxX index (see below), which provide a visible and consistent snapshot of current mortality rates and life expectancy, together with historical levels.
- **Standardized instruments for transferring longevity risk:** these standardized risk transfer instruments have been successfully developed and traded. This standardization is vital in developing a liquid market and ensuring low-cost hedges for pension plans.

21.3.1 Longevity indices

Indices play an important role in the development of any new market and longevity is no exception. Longevity (and mortality) indices help this market in several ways:

- by increasing the visibility of longevity and the level of familiarity among potential market participants with this very unfamiliar type of risk;
- by providing a transparent benchmark for mortality and longevity;

- by providing historical data to aid in pricing and risk assessment;
- by encouraging standardization, which is essential for building liquidity in a new market;
- by providing a credible, unbiased and unambiguous reference parameter (index) that can be used in the settlement of longevity and mortality derivatives and securities.

The first longevity index was launched by Credit Suisse in the US in December 2005. (For more details, see Credit Suisse, 2005; Gore, 2006). It is a broad-based index based on mortality data for the US national population, with actuarial firm Milliman acting as the index calculation agent. The index is broken down by age and gender and includes (subjective) projections for future mortality, as well as current and historical levels. Data and documentation on the index are available from the website (http://www.credit-suisse.com/ib/en/fixed_income/longevity_index.html) and from Bloomberg (LIFF).

Then, in March 2007, JPMorgan launched the first international longevity index called the LifeMetrics Index, as a key component of the LifeMetrics Longevity Toolkit (see J.P. Morgan, 2007). The LifeMetrics Index covers four countries: the US, the UK (actually England and Wales), the Netherlands and Germany. Like the Credit Suisse index, it is based on national population mortality statistics. But unlike the Credit Suisse Index and the other indices discussed below, the LifeMetrics Index is nonproprietary, fully transparent, open source and freely available. It is fully documented (see Coughlan et al., 2007a, 2007c and 2008) and includes a framework for risk management, research publications, analytics and software for mortality forecasting and stochastic simulation. The calculation agent for the index is Watson Wyatt and the index is overseen by an independent advisory committee comprising consultants, academics and industry practitioners. All data, documentation and software relating to LifeMetrics are available publicly from the website (www.lifemetrics.com), with data also being available from Bloomberg (LFMT).

In December 2007, Goldman Sachs launched a proprietary index of a very different kind called QxX (see Goldman Sachs, 2007). This index is based on the mortality experience of a specifically selected pool of what was originally 46 290 de-identified US individuals aged over 65 who have life insurance policies. This index is designed for facilitating transactions associated with 'life settlements', which involve portfolios of life insurance policies on the individuals in the pool. Some documentation is available publicly from the website (www.qxx-index.com). However, detailed index data are not available without a client subscription.

In March 2008, Deutsche Börse launched a longevity and mortality data service that it calls Xpect Data (Deutsche Börse, 2008a), which initially delivered monthly data on life expectancy for Germany, but was later extended to include the Netherlands. Xpect is a proprietary and non-public data set which is available on a subscription basis. In December 2008 the company announced the launch of Xpect Indices based on this dataset (Deutsche Börse, 2008b), with the indices being available for both Germany and the Netherlands. Xpect Indices are calculated for closed portfolios (Xpect Cohort Indices) and for open portfolios (Xpect Age Indices).

All Xpect Indices are based on the Xpect Data which are provided as generational life tables and updated on a monthly basis from a combination of official and proprietary sources. While Xpect offers a very rich data set that complements the various indices from other providers, there are currently few data available directly from the website and few details about the data sources and calculation methodologies. The website can be found at http://deutsche-boerse.com/.

21.3.2 Trading and liquidity

Indices play an important role in encouraging trading and developing liquidity in any market by virtue of the standardization and transparency they bring. In serving as a reference for settling longevity-linked instruments, longevity indices can provide a transparent window on valuation and the nature of the risk being transferred. In a new market such as this they also serve as a signal of market credibility and assist in the education process. But regardless of which index is being used for a particular transaction, other mortality/longevity data sources can also play a valuable role in analyzing the risk versus the expected return/expected cost of that transaction.

When it comes to creating liquidity, it is important that, in the early stages of market development, trading is concentrated in a small number of standardized contracts. As a result it is important that risk transfer instruments are standardized and that reference indices or subindices are highly aggregated (e.g., males aged 70–79, females aged 80–89, etc.). While more granular data can be useful for analysis, instruments based on indices that are more granular that this will severely inhibit the emergence of liquidity.

Liquidity is also greatly encouraged by (i) the education of market participants and (ii) the standardization of documentation, measurement, analytical concepts, language (definitions), instruments and the approach to valuation. Longevity toolkits, such as those mentioned above, can help to catalyze both the education and standardization processes.

21.4 CAPITAL MARKET INSTRUMENTS FOR LONGEVITY RISK TRANSFER

21.4.1 Longevity bond

The first type of capital market instrument proposed to transfer longevity risk was a longevity bond. Blake and Burrows (2001) proposed a bond that made payments on the basis of the survival rate for an underlying reference population. The expected evolution of a survival rate used in such a bond is illustrated in Figure 21.2.

In the case in which retirement income is the same for all lives, the survival curve in Figure 21.2 also reflects the expected benefit cash flows that are paid over time.

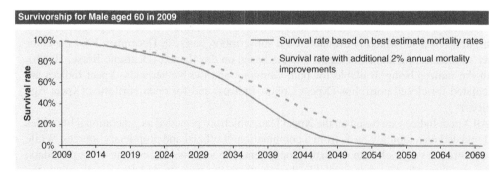

Figure 21.2 Evolution of the survival rate for a closed population of 60-year-old males
Source: J.P. Morgan

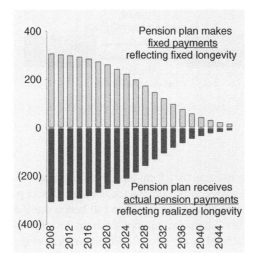

Figure 21.3 Survivor swap cash flows
Source: J.P. Morgan

Since then there have been many papers written on longevity bonds, addressing various aspects of the structure and pricing of these instruments – see, for example, Cairns *et al.* (2005), Lin and Cox (2005), Blake *et al.*(2006a), Blake *et al.* (2006b) and Denuit *et al.* (2007). Then, in 2005, the European Investment Bank (EIB), working with BNP Paribas, attempted to issue such a longevity bond based on the survival rate of the cohort of UK males initially aged 65 (Azzopardi, 2005). Unfortunately, the bond issue was ultimately unsuccessful for several reasons related to the structure and the prevailing level of education of market participants.

21.4.2   Survivor swap

A survivor swap is a derivative version of the longevity bond, which involves exchanging a series of payments based on the actual realized survival for a series of pre-agreed fixed payments (see Figure 21.3).

This instrument is also widely discussed in the academic literature – see, for example, Dowd (2003), Lin and Cox (2005), Blake *et al.* (2006a), Dowd *et al.* (2006) and Sweeting (2007). Furthermore, Mott (2007) discussed using longevity swaps to hedge the systematic (or 'beta') longevity component of life settlement pools. Derivative structures, such as survivor swaps and q-forwards, have emerged as more favorable than bonds for longevity risk transfer because the requirement to invest a large amount of capital up front in purchasing the bond is eliminated. As a result, both pension funds and annuity portfolio managers do not have to change their asset allocations, thereby reducing their expected returns, to hedge this risk. For more details on the survivor swap as an instrument for longevity risk transfer, see the case study in Section 21.6.

21.4.3   q-forward

The simplest type of longevity/mortality risk transfer instrument is a mortality forward rate contract, which is referred to as a 'q-forward' (Coughlan *et al.*, 2007b). It is so named because the letter 'q' is the symbol used by actuaries to denote mortality rates.

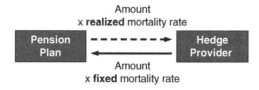

Figure 21.4   For a q-forward, cash flows based on fixed vs. floating mortality rates are exchanged at maturity

Source: J.P. Morgan

q-forwards are important because they form basic building blocks from which other, more complex, life-related derivatives can be constructed. In particular, a portfolio of q-forwards, appropriately designed, can be used to replicate and to hedge the longevity exposure of an annuity or a pension liability. Similarly, an appropriately designed portfolio of q-forwards can be used to hedge the mortality exposure of a life assurance book. In addition, portfolios of q-forwards can hedge many of the life-contingent risks associated with life settlement investments and reverse (or equity release) mortgages.

A q-forward is an agreement between two parties to exchange at a future date (the maturity of the contract) an amount proportional to the realized mortality rate of a given population (or subpopulation), in return for an amount proportional to a fixed mortality rate that has been mutually agreed at inception. In other words, a q-forward is a zero-coupon swap that exchanges fixed mortality for realized mortality at maturity. This is illustrated in Figure 21.4. The reference rate for settling the contract is the realized mortality rate in a future period as determined by the appropriate index.

In a fair market, the fixed mortality rate at which the transaction takes place defines the 'forward mortality rate' for the population (or subpopulation) in question. If the q-forward is fairly priced, no payment changes hands at the inception of the trade. At maturity, however, a net payment will be made by one counterparty or the other.

Table 21.1 gives an example term sheet for a q-forward transaction, where the reference population corresponds to 65-year-old males in England and Wales. The q-forward payout is determined by the value of the LifeMetrics Index for this subpopulation at the maturity of the contract.

This transaction is a ten-year q-forward contract initiated on 31 December 2008 and maturing on 31 December 2018. It reflects part of a longevity hedge provided to a UK pension plan. At maturity the hedge provider (the fixed-rate payer) pays to the pension plan an amount proportional to a fixed mortality rate of 1.2000%.[5] In return the pension plan pays to the hedge provider an amount determined by the reference rate at maturity, which corresponds to the most recent value of the LifeMetrics Index reflecting the realized mortality rate for 65-year-old males in England and Wales. Because of the lag in the availability of official data, settlement on 31 December 2018 will be based on the LifeMetrics Index level for the reference year 2017.[6]

The settlement that takes place at maturity is based on the net amount payable and is proportional to the difference between the fixed mortality rate (the transacted forward rate) and

---

[5] Note that this rate is for illustrative purposes only and does not reflect prevailing mortality forward rates.

[6] In practice settlement usually takes place on the average of the reference rates over more than one reference year; for example, in this case averaging over the rates in 2016, 2017 and 2018 to give an average for the 2017 mortality rate.

Table 21.1   An illustrative term sheet for a single-age q-forward instrument showing the key terms

Notional Amount	GBP 1,000,000
Trade Date	31 December 2008
Effective Date	31 December 2008
Maturity Date	31 December 2018
Reference Year	2017
Fixed Rate	[1.200%]
Fixed Amount Payer	ABC Investment Bank
Fixed Amount	Notional Amount × Fixed Rate × 100
Reference Rate	LifeMetrices graduated initial mortality rate for 65-year-old males in the Reference Year for the England and Wales national population.
Floating Amount Payer	XYZ Defined Benefit Pension Plan
Floating Amount	Notional Amount × Reference Rate × 100
Settlement	Net Settlement = Fixed Amount − Floating Amount

Source: J.P. Morgan

the realized reference rate. Figure 21.5 shows the settlement for different potential outcomes for the realized reference rate. If the reference rate in the reference year is below the fixed rate (i.e., lower mortality) then the settlement is positive, and the pension plan receives the settlement payment to offset the increase in its liability value. If, on the other hand, the reference rate is above the fixed rate (i.e., higher mortality) then the settlement is negative and the pension plan pays the settlement payment to the hedge provider, which will be offset by the fall in the value of its liabilities. In this way the net liability value is locked-in regardless of what happens to mortality rates. The plan is protected from unexpected changes in mortality rates.

21.4.4   Survivor forward

Another possible building block which is slightly more complex than the q-forward is what we call a 'survivor forward,' or 'S-forward.' It is exactly like a q-forward, except that it is linked to a survival rate rather than a mortality rate. As such it involves the exchange of (i) a notional amount multiplied by a pre-agreed fixed survival rate in return for (ii) the same

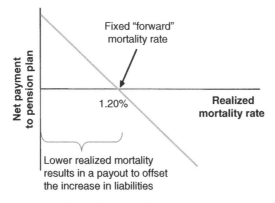

Figure 21.5   Net payout from a q-forward at maturity

Source: J.P. Morgan

Figure 21.6 Survivor-forward or S-forward. Cash flows based on fixed vs. floating survival rates are exchanged at maturity only

Source: J.P. Morgan

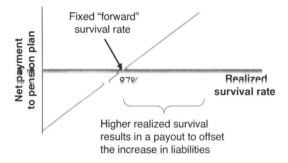

Figure 21.7 Net payout from an S-forward at maturity

Source: J.P. Morgan

notional amount multiplied by the realized survival rate for a specified cohort over a given period of time. This is illustrated in Figures 21.6 and 21.7, where it should be noted that the fixed and floating arrows point in opposite directions to those for a q-forward, because paying realized survival is equivalent to receiving realized mortality.[7] Note that a survivor swap can essentially be thought of as a string of S-forwards with different maturity dates, so the S-forward is clearly a building block for survivor swaps.

The S-forward is a more complex instrument than the q-forward, as it is essentially a function of several mortality rates at different ages and different times. Nevertheless, S-forwards can be very useful as building blocks for developing longevity hedges of the value of retirement liabilities in a similar way to q-forwards.

21.4.5 Instruments and liquidity

The longevity risk transfer instruments that will develop the greatest liquidity will be those that best meet the needs of all market participants: hedgers, investors and intermediaries (market-makers). While hedgers may favor a bespoke hedge based on the concept of survival rates, investors and intermediaries favor more standardized instruments which are easier to analyze and more conducive to the development of liquidity. This latter requirement

---

[7] To understand this, consider that over a single year the survival rate for a cohort is equal to one minus its mortality rate. So exchanging survival rates is equivalent to exchanging mortality rates with the flows in opposite directions.

suggests that for longevity/mortality risk transfer to develop into a liquid market requires (Loeys *et al.*, 2007):

- Having a standardized index which is objective and transparent, and can be used as an unbiased reference by all participants for the transfer of longevity and mortality risk.
- In the early stages of the market's development, restricting transactions to a limited number of standardized contracts into which liquidity can be concentrated.

Reconciling these requirements with the conflicting requirement of hedgers for customization suggests a solution for transferring longevity risk based on standardized building blocks. In this approach, customized hedges are built out of standardized index-based building blocks, as illustrated later in this chapter.

But even if a liquid market develops along these lines involving standardized index-based risk transfer instruments, there is still likely to be demand for other kinds of transactions, including customized hedges based on survival rates. Although these transactions will not be liquid and command an illiquidity premium, they may better meet the needs of some hedgers in certain situations.

21.5 CUSTOMIZED VS STANDARDIZED LONGEVITY HEDGES

Earlier we introduced the distinction between customized hedges and standardized index-based hedges of longevity risk. In this section we describe these two types of hedges in more detail and review their advantages and disadvantages.

21.5.1 Customized longevity hedge

A customized longevity hedge is a risk transfer instrument that is tailored to reflect the actual longevity experience of the specific pool of individuals associated with the exposure. For example, for a pension plan it reflects the actual, realized longevity experience of the plan members and other beneficiaries (e.g., spouses and dependants), whereas for an insurer's annuity portfolio it reflects the longevity experience of the annuitants and other beneficiaries if relevant. Such a hedge typically aims to completely eliminate the risk and represents what is called the 'indemnification paradigm' for hedging longevity. Customized hedges are typically structured as cash flow hedges in such a way that the net cash flow (liability cash flow + hedge cash flow) is fixed with respect to changes in longevity/mortality. Ideally the maturity of the customized hedge would be such that it continued until the runoff of the last liability payment, but in practice there may be a fixed but distant maturity date. Economically, a customized hedge is essentially equivalent to an insurance contract and delivers the same benefits, but in capital markets format.

21.5.2 Standardized index-based longevity hedge

By contrast, a standardized index-based hedge is based on the longevity experience of a broad index (e.g., an index of national population mortality), but calibrated to match the sensitivity of the actual liability (corresponding to the specific pool of individuals) to changes in mortality rates. Such a hedge does not involve indemnification, but rather risk reduction. It represents the 'risk management paradigm' for risk transfer. This means the degree of risk reduction, while significant, will be less than 100% and there will be some residual risk remaining after hedging.

A standardized hedge would generally be structured as a hedge of value, rather than a hedge of cash flow, so that any increase in the value of liabilities due to changes in mortality rates would be offset by a compensating payment provided by the hedge. In other words, the net value of the liabilities at a future date (liability value + hedge value) is locked in. The maturity of a standardized index hedge might typically be five, ten or twenty years – much shorter than that of the customized hedge. But don't be misled by the relative shortness of this maturity. Because it is a hedge of value, it provides protection against the impact of increasing longevity on all cash flows beyond the maturity of the hedge.

21.5.3 Advantages and disadvantages

The case for a customized hedge is clear: it has the distinct advantage of providing complete removal of longevity risk and is a set-and-forget hedge. While this is very desirable for any hedger, it does have some disadvantages. A customized hedge is likely to be more costly, more credit intensive and more cumbersome to adjust or unwind than a standardized hedge. It also requires detailed data on the benefit structure, demographics and mortality experience of the pension plan (or annuity portfolio) to be disclosed to both the hedge provider and potentially end investors. This data disclosure is required both prior to the pricing of the transaction and on an ongoing basis. A standardized hedge, on the other hand, is likely to be more economical, less complex, potentially much more liquid and does not require disclosure of data. The key disadvantage is that it does not completely eliminate longevity risk, but it can reduce it significantly. In particular, a standardized hedge will always leave a residual exposure to population basis risk. This refers to the mismatch between the longevity experience of the specific pool of individuals associated with the exposure and the longevity experience of the index used in the hedge. However, this basis risk can generally be minimized through careful construction of the hedge, leading to high levels of hedge effectiveness and a small manageable residual risk. For any standardized hedge, the level of risk reduction achieved and the amount of residual risk remaining should be measured in a hedge effectiveness assessment (see Section 21.7).

21.6   CASE STUDY: CUSTOMIZED LONGEVITY HEDGE

In July 2008 J.P. Morgan executed for Canada Life in the UK a £500 million customized longevity swap hedge for a portfolio of UK annuitants (see the reports in *Trading Risk,* 2008 and *Life and Pensions,* 2008). The following discussion is based on public information concerning the transaction.

The transaction involves a 40-year maturity survivor swap to hedge on a pro rata basis part of the portfolio of annuities Canada Life bought from Equitable Life in 2006. In this survivor swap J.P. Morgan pays Canada Life the actual payments due to annuitants based on their realized longevity experience and in return Canada Life pays a series of fixed payments based on the expected longevity plus a margin or risk premium. Hence, the swap provides the insurer with a long-maturity, customized cash flow hedge of its longevity risk.

The longevity risk transferred in this transaction from Canada Life to J.P. Morgan was then sold on to a group of investors with mirrored back-to-back survivor swaps (see Figure 21.8).

This leaves J.P. Morgan with no net longevity risk, but with credit counterparty exposure to Canada Life and each of the investors. All the swaps are fully collateralized, with all parties required to post collateral based on the prevailing value of the swap at any point in its life.

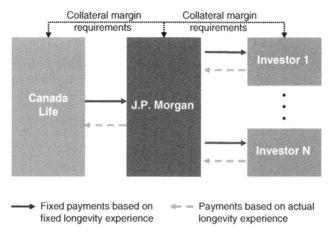

Figure 21.8 Transaction diagram for the Canada Life customized survivor swap
Source: J.P. Morgan

The survivor swap provides investors with exposure to longevity risk in return for the risk premium mentioned above. The expected return on the investment is calculated from the risk premium they receive relative to the amount of collateral they expect to post over the life of the transaction.

Despite the fact that the swap is not based on the LifeMetrics Index but the actual longevity experience of the annuitants, elements of the LifeMetrics Toolkit were important in other aspects of the transaction. For example, the graduation methodology for the observed annuitant mortality rates and the projection of future mortality rates for valuation and collateral calls included LifeMetrics analytics and software.

21.7 IMPLEMENTING A STANDARDIZED INDEX-BASED LONGEVITY HEDGE

As already mentioned, Lucida executed a standardized index-based longevity hedge in January 2008. This hedge involved q-forwards linked to the LifeMetrics Longevity Index for England and Wales.

We now describe the construction and implementation of a standardized index-based hedge of longevity risk. This description is generic, but based on the author's experience with a number of different pension and annuity portfolios.

The framework we use for index-based hedging involves the seven steps listed in Table 21.2. The framework involves a building-block approach to construct a hedge which is tailored to reflect the specific nature of the liability in terms of:

- benefit structure, including, where relevant, benefits for spouses and dependants, as well as death benefits;
- demographics of pension plan members/beneficiaries (gender, age, etc.);
- mortality tables (both mortality base tables and mortality improvements).

The individual building blocks are standardized index-based hedges for males and females of specific ages (such as q-forwards). By combining these standardized building blocks in

Table 21.2   Framework for hedging longevity risk using standardized index-based hedges

Step	Description
1. Setting Hedging Objectives	Define "hedging horizon" over which the liability value is to be hedged and the amount of longevity risk to be targeted by the hedge (e.g., aim to hedge as much as possible or, say 50 percent of the risk, or hedge only the longevity risk of deferred members).
2. Data Collection	Acquire data on the benefit structure, demographic profile, mortality experience and mortality tables (base tables and projection tables).
3. Liability Valuation	Project the "best estimate" liability cash flows and value those cash flows today and at the hedging horizon.
4. Sensitivity Analysis	Measure the sensitivity of the liabilities to changes in mortality rates for different ages, different genders and different subgroups of the beneficiary population. We call this sensitivity "q-duration" (see Coughlan *et al.*, 2007a, p. 83), which is explained more fully below.
5. Hedge Calibration and Optimization	Use q-duration to design a hedge that matches the sensitivity of the liability value to unexpected changes in mortality rates.
6. Hedge Effectiveness Analysis	Implement hedge effectiveness tests to evaluate the effectiveness of the hedge under both stress scenarios and stochastic simulations. This quantifies the degree of risk reduction and the level of residual risk. For a discussion of hedge effectiveness tests in general, see Coughlan, Kolb and Emery (2004).
7. Implementation	Finalize documentation, details of mark-to-model valuation, collateral posting, etc.

Source: J.P. Morgan

a manner tailored to each particular pension plan (or annuity portfolio) liability, a highly effective hedge of longevity risk can be constructed. Such a hedge provides protection against the *unexpected improvements* in mortality rates and their impact on all future cash flows and valuation (See Figure 21.9).

21.7.1   Liability sensitivity and hedge calibration

The key step in the framework involves measuring the sensitivity of the liabilities to changes in mortality rates, or more precisely, changes in mortality rates relative to best estimate mortality rates. This sensitivity is measured by a concept called 'q-duration' which quantifies the change in the value of the liability corresponding to a change in *the trend of future mortality improvements* of, for example, 0.1% per year. Note that q-duration is not based on a uniform shift in mortality rates, but on what is essentially a compounded shift in mortality rates corresponding to a change in the trend of future mortality improvements. This is because our objective is to hedge the value of the liability, which is determined by the trend of mortality improvements from the hedging horizon onwards. The key steps in the calculation of q-duration are described in Table 21.3.

The sensitivity analysis involves evaluating the impact on liability cash flows and value of unexpected improvements in the mortality rates for each age and each gender for different categories of individuals. This leads to a liability sensitivity matrix expressed in terms of q-duration, from which an effective longevity hedge can be constructed by matching the sensitivities of different hedge building blocks to the sensitivities of the liabilities. What this

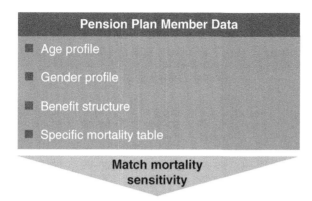

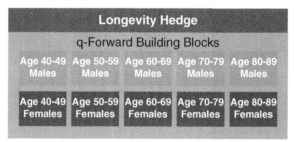

Figure 21.9 Standardized index-based hedges involve calibrating a portfolio of building block hedges to match the sensitivity of the liabilities

Source: J.P. Morgan

means in practice is identifying the correct notional amount of each hedge building block that provides the same sensitivity to changing mortality rates (but in the opposite direction). This is illustrated schematically in Figure 21.10. Note that, at maturity, all q-forwards have the same fixed q-duration of 100 for each unit of notional, which simplifies the calibration of hedges.

We have found that only a small set of standardized q-forward contracts referencing the LifeMetrics Index is needed as building blocks to provide a highly effective hedge of the liabilities of DB pension plans and annuity portfolios. In particular, just ten contracts with

Table 21.3 Steps involved in calculating q-duration

Steps in evaluating q-duration
1. Calculate the value of the liability using best estimate mortality projections at the hedging horizon (H).
2. Reduce the level of the relevant mortality rate over time by applying a shock of 0.1% per year improvement.
3. Calculate the change in the liability value, ΔL, at the hedging horizon.
4. Calculate the change in the relevant mortality rate, Δq_x, at the hedging horizon.
5. Calculate q-duration as $D_x^q(H) = \Delta L / \Delta q_x$.

Source: J.P. Morgan

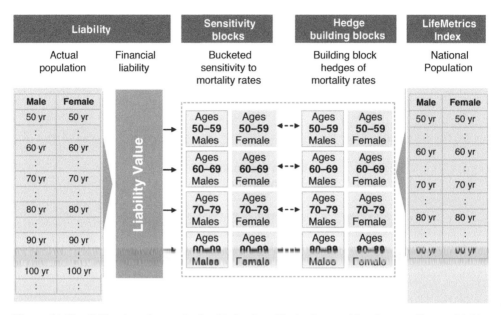

Figure 21.10   Calibration of a standardized index-based hedge by matching the mortality sensitivities of the hedge to those of the liability value

Source: J.P. Morgan

the following characteristics are all that are needed for the vast majority of cases:

- q-forwards of fixed maturity (e.g., ten years);
- split by gender (male and female);
- five age groups (40–49, 50–59, 60–69, 70–79, 80–89).

With these ten contracts the matrix of liability sensitivities can be adequately matched to ensure that the hedge is effective in reducing longevity risk. Note that even for an all-male pension plan, the hedge comprises significant amounts of female q-forward contracts, owing to spouses' pensions, which are paid when the plan member dies, being part of the benefit structure.

21.7.2   Hedge effectiveness analysis

Because standardized index-based hedges do not remove all of the longevity risk associated with a particular pension plan or annuity portfolio, it is important to evaluate the degree of hedge effectiveness and the degree of risk reduction that is achieved. This requires measurement of the residual risk that remains after hedging in monetary terms. For a general discussion of hedge effectiveness testing, see Coughlan *et al.* (2004).

In any hedging situation, hedge effectiveness tests must be designed to reflect the original hedging objectives. In this case it means making sure the hedge effectiveness test reflects the appropriate hedging horizon (e.g., ten years), the appropriate performance metric (e.g., liability value at the hedging horizon) and the appropriate designated risk (i.e., longevity risk corresponding to unexpected improvements in the downward trend of mortality rates). Simply

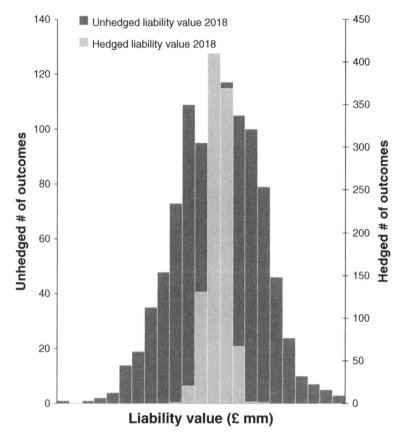

Figure 21.11   Stochastic hedge effectiveness test showing the distribution of liability value at the horizon both before and after hedging

Source: J.P. Morgan

calculating correlations between annual changes in mortality rates for the hedging instrument and the member population of a pension plan is *not* suitable as a hedge effectiveness test.[8]

One important residual risk that cannot be hedged with standardized hedges is population basis risk. This is the risk that the mortality improvement experience of the underlying pension plan or annuity portfolio differs from that of the index used in the hedge. Basis risk is caused by the mismatch in the demographics between the two. As this kind of hedge is designed to hedge against unexpected mortality improvements, it is the basis risk associated with mortality improvements that is key, not the basis risk associated with the underlying level of mortality rates (base table).

With appropriately chosen hedging building blocks, the basis risk with respect to age and gender can be virtually eliminated, leaving a basis risk relating to differences in the socio-economic profiles of the two populations. If the average relationship between the mortality improvements for both populations is known, this residual basis risk can be minimized through

---

[8] Longevity is a long-term cumulative risk that emerges over time and, as a result, short-term (year-on-year) correlations are both irrelevant and contain so much noise as to be misleading.

the calibration of the hedge by determining the optimal amounts of each hedge building block that are required, taking account of the mortality improvement mismatch.[9]

The degree of hedge effectiveness achieved in stochastic effectiveness tests of index-based longevity hedges implemented in this way has typically been in the range 80–90% when basis risk is taken into account. Note that this is comparable to the degree of effectiveness achieved by interest rate and inflation hedges over long horizons. Figure 21.11 shows the result of a stochastic mortality test, showing the distribution of future liability values in 2018 both with and without the standardized hedge. In this case the hedge effectiveness result is 86% risk reduction including basis risk.[10] So a high degree of hedge effectiveness was achieved from the building block index hedges.

21.8   CONCLUSIONS

Longevity risk transfer via the capital markets is now a reality for defined benefit pension plans and annuity providers. Transactions have been executed both customized and standardized index based products. The key players in this new market are hedgers (pension plans, insurers and reinsurers), intermediaries (investment banks) and end investors (ILS funds, endowments, hedge funds, etc.). We have argued that the development of liquidity in this market requires the acceptance of longevity indices as the basis for hedging and the development of standardized instruments to transfer this risk. The market still requires further education and standardization, but these are now being addressed by the provision of open source toolkits for longevity risk management.

REFERENCES

Azzopardi, M. (2005). The Longevity Bond, *First International Conference on Longevity Risk and Capital Markets Solutions*, Cass Business School, 18 February.

Blake, D. and Burrows, W. (2001) Survivor Bonds: Helping to Hedge Mortality Risk, *Journal of Risk and Insurance*, **68**, 336–348.

Blake, D., Cairns, A. and Dowd, K. (2006a) Living with Mortality: Longevity Bond and Other Mortality-linked Securities, *British Actuarial Journal*, **12**, 153–197.

Blake D., Cairns, A., Dowd, K. and MacMinn, R. (2006b) Longevity Bonds: Financial Engineering, Valuation, and Hedging, *Journal of Risk and Insurance*, **73**, 647–672.

Cairns, A., Blake, D., Dawson, P. and Dowd, K. (2005) Pricing Risk on Longevity Bonds, *Life and Pensions*, October, 41–44.

Coughlan, G.D., Emery, S. and Kolb, J. (2004) HEAT (Hedge effectiveness analysis toolkit): A consistent framework for assessing hedge effectiveness, *Journal of Derivatives Accounting*, **1**(2), 221–272.

Coughlan, G.D., Epstein, D., Ong, A., Sinha, A., Balevich, I., Hevia-Portocarrera, J., Gingrich, E., Khalaf-Allah, M. and Joseph, P. (2007a) LifeMetrics: A Toolkit for Measuring and Managing Longevity and Mortality Risks, Technical Document, London: J.P. Morgan, 2 July [http://www.lifemetrics.com].

Coughlan, G.D., Epstein, D., Sinha A. and Honig, P. (2007b) q-Forwards: Derivatives for Transferring Longevity and Mortality Risk, London: J.P. Morgan, 13 March [http://www.lifemetrics.com].

---

[9] See Coughlan *et al.* (2007a, pp. 80–82) for an empirical analysis of basis risk between two populations. This involved using a backtesting methodology to show that an appropriately calibrated LifeMetrics hedge (reflecting the national population of England and Wales) provides effective long-term longevity risk reduction for the pensions of a group of 65-year-old males (based on the demographics of individuals within the population who have life insurance). These reflect two very different demographics and two different mortality data sets, yet nonetheless the hedge is shown to be effective when evaluated with actual historical data.

[10] To put this into context, assuming there was no basis risk, the hedge effectiveness was 97%.

Coughlan, G.D., Epstein, D., Hevia-Portocarrera, J., Khalaf-Allah, M., Watts, C.S. and Joseph, P. (2007c) LifeMetrics: Netherlands Longevity Index, Technical Document Supplement, London: J. P. Morgan, 22 October [http://www.lifemetrics.com].

Coughlan, G.D., Epstein, D., Watts, C.S., Khalaf-Allah, M., Joseph, P. and Ye, Y. (2008) LifeMetrics: Germany Longevity Index, Technical Document Supplement, London: J. P. Morgan, 7 April [http://www.lifemetrics.com].

Credit Suisse First Boston (2005) Credit Suisse First Boston Introduces Credit Suisse Longevity Index, *CCN Matthews*, 12 December.

Denuit, M., Devolder, P. and Goderniaux, A.-C. (2007) Securitisation of Longevity Risk: Pricing Survivor Bonds with Wang Transform in the Lee-Carter Framework, *Journal of Risk and Insurance*, **74**(1), 87–113.

Deutsche Börse (2008a) *Deutsche Börse Launches Business with Longevity Data*, [http://deutsche-boerse.com/].

Deutsche Börse (2008b) *Deutsche Börse Launches Longevity Indices*, 1 December, [http://deutsche-boerse.com/].

Dowd, K. (2003) Survivor Bonds: A Comment on Blake and Burrows, *Journal of Risk and Insurance*, **70** (2), 339–348.

Dowd, K., Blake, D., Cairns, A. and Dawson, P. (2006) Survivor Swaps, *Journal of Risk and Insurance*, **73**, 1–17.

Goldman Sachs. (2007) *Goldman Sachs Launches Tradable Index for Longevity and Mortality Risks*, [http://www.qxx-index.com/]

Gore, G. (2006) Credit Suisse Launches Longevity Index, *Risk*, **19** (1), January.

JP Morgan Chase & Co. (2007) *JP Morgan Launches Longevity Index: Investment Bank Creates Life-Metrics Platform*, 13 March, [http://www.lifemetrics.com].

Life and Pensions (2008). Canada Life hedges Equitable longevity with JP Morgan swap, *Life and Pensions*, October, p. 6.

Lin, Y. and Cox, S.H. (2005) Securitisation of Mortality Risks in Life Annuities, *Journal of Risk and Insurance*, **72**, 227–252.

Loeys, J., Panigirtzoglou, N. and Ribeiro, R.M. (2007) *Longevity: A Market in the Making*, London: J.P. Morgan, 13 March.

Lucida plc. (2008) *Lucida and JP Morgan First to Trade Longevity Derivative*, 15 February, [http://www.lucidaplc.com/en/news].

Mott, A.R. (2007) New Swaps to Hedge Alpha and Beta Longevity Risks of Life Settlement Pools, *Journal of Structured Finance*, Summer, 54–61.

Richards, S.J. and Jones, G. (2004) Financial Aspects of Longevity Risk, *Staple Inn Actuarial Society* meeting, London, England.

Sweeting, P. (2007) Pricing Basis Risk in Survivor Swaps, *Life and Pensions*, September, 44–48.

Symmons, J. (2008) *Lucida Guards against Longevity*, 19 February, [http://www.efinancialnews.com].

Trading Risk (2008) JP Morgan longevity swap unlocks UK annuity market, *Trading Risk*, **5**, September/October, 3, [http://www.trading-risk.com].

22

Case Study: A Cat Mortality Bond by AXA (OSIRIS)

Sylvain Coriat[a]

'AXA announces today the implementation through a special purpose vehicle, 'OSIRIS Capital plc', of a Euro 1 billion shelf program to transfer mortality risk to the capital markets. This shelf program is a flexible and efficient structure to diversify sources of cover for the Group's mortality risk exposure by benefiting from the broad capacity of capital markets. In this framework, AXA also announces the successful placement of notes indexed to mortality levels in France (60% of the combined index), Japan (25%) and the US (15%), for a total amount of circa Euro 345 million.'

AXA press release,[1] 13th November, 2006

22.1   CATASTROPHIC PANDEMIC RISK

This project started in 2005 with an internal risk management review of life risk. This shed light on the explicit exclusion of pandemics in most of our catastrophic reinsurance treaties. Operational entities, supported by the Group's risk management team, then expressed the wish to find an alternative to reinsurance to hedge that risk. The significant expertise in securitization within the Group was, for the first time, put at the service of its life business, for a very satisfactory and efficient outcome.

The reluctance of reinsurers to get involved is justified by the true nature of pandemic risk. The reinsurers cannot mutualize this risk. In fact, the ease and speed of transportation make it certain that any potential fast-spreading disease will hit each and every developed country. The only partial hedge actually in the hands of reinsurers comprises business lines that benefit from an excess mortality – pension funds and fixed annuity business. These lines are, however, usually not reinsured.

The first thing that was needed was a set of consistent hypotheses to apply to different portfolios in different countries. The reference paper published by the French Institute for Public Health Awareness – InVS (Doyle *et al.*, 2006) was used as a very satisfactory starting point. It allowed us to account for the very different structures of portfolios among countries, be it in terms of gender, sum at risk, age distribution, etc. It also helped us realize the structural lack of information we have in Group life business as far as the individuals insured are concerned.

---

[a]Global Head of Life Operations, AXA Cessions
[1] http://www.axa.com/lib/en/uploads/pr/group/2006/AXA_PR_20061113.pdf

---

The Handbook of Insurance-Linked Securities   Edited by P. Barrieu and L. Albertini
© 2009 John Wiley & Sons, Ltd

This approach helped us quantify the peril for the Group, which was close to EUR 1.5 billion – a figure similar in magnitude to a severe European storm. Most of all, beyond the claim assessment, it allowed us to reflect on five other major unknowns:

1. **Assets:** in the case of a major pandemic, what would the reaction of investors and financial markets look like? Several hypotheses were made, but we held for a fact that liquidity, asset pricing and the global ability of the financial market to put a price on the simplest instrument, such as a stock of a Fortune 500 company, would be at risk. Some sectors, such as pharmaceuticals, might benefit from the outbreak, but this is not certain.
2. **Embedded value and deferred acquisition costs:** the sudden death of many insured people would force life insurers to write off part of the business and reduce expected premiums. It would also jeopardize our ability to amortize deferred acquisition costs of existing policies. An additional accounting loss would be created; this should be anticipated.
3. **Operational risks:** in the case of a pandemic outbreak, and as a consequence of reduced staff mobility, how could we limit the operational impact on our activities and work abilities, including our ability to face a potentially quadrupled number of claims?
4. **Behaviour of other business lines:** how can we anticipate the potential impact of a pandemic on those business lines with no direct connection with mortality – motor insurance, savings, travel insurance? Would freedom of movement be limited to avoid the spreading of a disease? Would martial law be imposed on some regions? In both cases, the impact on the number of car accidents is expected to be significant.
5. **Model risk:** contrary to property and casualty insurance models on storms or earthquakes, the models used to assess the probability of a pandemic are quite simplistic. We know very little about pandemics, and the best way to assess the probability of outcome is to rely on the number of pandemics known to have occurred in recent centuries. There have been 31 pandemics in 420 years, giving the basis for an estimate of the yearly probability of outcome. As for the severity curve to anticipate the impact of a pandemic once declared, it is interpolated on six known observation points. The model is, therefore, objective, but simplistic.

The juxtaposition of these uncertainties convinced AXA of the opportunity to hedge the risk and complete the first securitization transaction of this type launched by a direct insurer.

22.2   CONSIDERED RISK TRANSFER TOOLS

In the case of major mortality shocks, life insurers selling protection products are at risk. The reason is that life insurance is priced on the assumption that death hits people randomly. Some of us are more likely to live longer (namely young and healthy, non-smoking women), but apart from that life insurance does not price extreme shocks such as war, atomic terrorism or pandemic. For war or war-like operations, another protection is set up, by excluding the event from the scope of cover, with the blessing of the regulator. But it seems difficult to exclude death triggered commonly by a deadly disease. Death certificates usually do not specify the reason for the death.

Another layer of complexity lies in the timing of a potential virus attack. If the deadly mutation is linked to a traditional flu attack, then the most likely period of occurrence would be between October and February, and a yearly approach could lose this two-year dynamic.

The natural tool to hedge this type of mortality shock is 'excess of loss' or 'stop loss' reinsurance. This contract would allow a company to be protected against any event beyond a given economic impact. The reinsurance market has some key advantages when dealing with insurance companies:

- **Flexibility of adaptable contractual clauses:** as it is a traditional contract between professional parties, the reinsurance contract is highly flexible and can be fine-tuned to meet exactly the needs of the ceding company. It is also less standardized than a 144A transaction (a US securities law type of private placement).
- **Better understanding and pricing capacities:** reinsurers are expert pricers as far as insurance risks are concerned and can elaborate using their knowledge of each market and product.
- **Time to execution:** it usually takes less than a month to structure a reinsurance contract.
- **Cost:** reinsurance usually does not require external advisors, such as investment banks, actuarial services and legal firms, which has a significant impact on final price.
- **Perfect fit:** the hedge is the perfect fit for the insurance risk (no basis risk, no duration gap).
- **Regulatory treatment:** insurance regulation is tailored to the reinsurance contract, which triggers solvency relief, reserve benefits and other positive side effects.

Four issues made this natural approach unsustainable for pandemic risk cover:

- **Event definition:** reinsurers do not accept event definition encompassing pandemic or disease-like events.
- **Burden of proof:** specifically pandemic-related cover could raise the question of the burden of proof. Who should be forced to prove that the death is pandemic related? What sort of proof might be acceptable?
- **Cost:** non pandemic-related covers, such as stop loss, are usually extremely expensive. The cost of capital of such a cover usually exceeds the risk premium and this type of protection is therefore not cost effective.
- **Counterparty risk:** traditional reinsurance is usually massively exposed to mortality (this exposure is partially offset by some longevity books but mortality remains higher in their net exposure). Any pandemic-type event would shake their own reserves and cast doubt on their ability to pay the corresponding reinsurance claims.

Conversely, securitization has several advantages as a risk management tool, most specifically as far as nondiversifiable risks, such as pandemic, are concerned:

- Capital markets have significantly greater capacity than reinsurance markets. As far as pandemic is concerned, the lack of reinsurance capacity is patent.
- Better pricing in some cases where the reinsurance market has a limited number of providers, which is the case for life reinsurance.
- Removes counterparty credit risk through collateralization of assets.
- Increases diversification of protection sources and offers multi-year protection, which is not common practice in catastrophic reinsurance.

22.3   DETAILED STRUCTURE

The securitization structure is extremely conventional and similar to that presented in other chapters of this book (Figure 22.1).

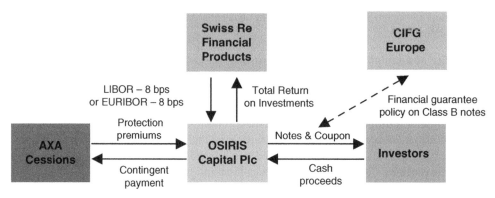

Figure 22.1   OSIRIS plc structural outline

Source: AXA

AXA Cessions is the sponsor of the securitization. It enters into an ISDA swap with OSIRIS plc, an Irish-based special purpose vehicle. The swap is based on a combined mortality index, calculated by an independent agent upon request of the sponsor, and that replicates the exposure of AXA in several countries. The historical index values are shown in Figure 22.2.

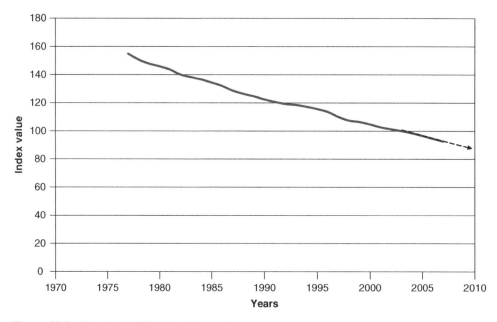

Figure 22.2   Historical OSIRIS plc index values

Source: AXA Cessions

22.4   RISK ANALYSIS

Extensive portfolio review was performed upstream to identify key exposures by product line, gender, age bands and countries. This analysis was done using the numerous models available, and notably the INVS[2] indicated above.

In order to mitigate the need to have an index that is manageable and easy to monitor on the one hand, and close to the actual exposure of AXA as a Group, the decision was made to use regional proxies, notably three 'proxy hedge' countries (France, Japan and the US); publicly available mortality data (French INSEE, US Center for Disease Control, Ministry of Health of Japan) tailored to AXA's selected portfolio composition was used.

22.4.1   Modelling approach

A traditional frequency/severity model was applied to a baseline mortality projection over four years. Frequency was assessed using all known pandemics (31 identified in the last 420 years). Severity was estimated using a fit on the six known data points for which the intensity of the pandemic is reliable. The severity curve was then fitted by using exponential and tangent functions:

- The 1918 data point (excess mortality of 32%) is placed at the 3.2 percentile level, which is equivalent to a 1-in-420 year event given the 7.4% annual frequency of a pandemic.
- Other data points (corresponding to historical epidemic events which occurred in 1957, 1968, 1977 and 2003) are attached at higher percentile levels corresponding to events of lower severity.

The upper end of the curve is unrestricted (hence the tangent): this disease model *does not* simulate a theoretical maximum excess mortality.

A numerical simulation of 350 000 draws was then run to ensure an adequate convergence of all risk indicators, and to allow the assessment of attachment probability and exhaustion probability of all tranches, as well as expected loss.

22.4.2   Index construction

The exposure to mortality shocks is expressed as a deviation to a reference mortality level (for OSIRIS, the 2004/2005 average mortality level is the base 100). Mortality shocks are measured on a rolling two-year basis to overlap year-end (data available with 18 months' lag).

This type of operation involves a good understanding of basis risk and its implications. In our case, basis risk relies on the difference between the actual pandemic and the one that was modelled to assess exposure. This bias is expected to highlight the 'benefit of being insured' and be in favour of the insurer.

Another important feature was the drawback of the natural mortality improvement that can be seen in Figure 22.2. This natural phenomenon was making the attachment risk more remote year after year, since the gap between expected future baseline mortality and the attachment point is widening year after year. This type of 'mortality bond' is therefore naturally expected to receive a rating upgrade after three to four years of existence, and especially in the last year,

---

[2] http://www.invs.sante.fr/publications/2005/pandemie_grippale_170205/estimation_impact_pandemie_grippale.pdf (in French).

where the index is partially known to be low (remember the index is a moving average of the last two years. Any given year with an index value of 96 requires the index of the following year to reach 116 to cross the average value of 106 required to attach the lower tranche).

22.5 INVESTORS' REACTION

'This first offering was nearly 4 times oversubscribed. To date, AXA is the first primary insurer to put in place such an innovative risk management tool and to transfer a sub-investment grade mortality risk layer to capital markets.'

AXA press release[3], 13th November, 2006

The reaction of the investors (profiled in Figure 22.3) was extremely positive. It should be noted, however, that European investors placed orders for investment-grade series, while US investors expressed interest in the non investment-grade bonds (Figure 22.4).

22.6 SPREAD BEHAVIOUR

It is interesting to analyse, with hindsight, the behaviour of mortality bonds in a difficult financial environment. Figure 22.5 shows the movement in the observed secondary market implied spread of OSIRIS B notes (initial rating A−) with and without the wrap of CIFG (the latter being initially rated AAA).

These bonds show a natural decreasing risk with time, and the normal spread behaviour is to decrease each time a year has passed without triggering the warranty.

The bonds were, therefore, behaving nomally in 2007, until the end of July. At that point, the difficulties of Lehman Brothers shook the market and confidence in the wrap benefit started to fade away. The spread kept on soaring, with some trades identified in 2008 (although not material enough to be reflected in Figure 22.5) at a spread where the wrapped tranche was actually more affordable than the unwrapped same risk. This phenomenon was explained by the need of some large investors to get rid of any monoline exposure.

22.7 NEXT STEPS

While extreme mortality is now less of an issue, most of the OECD states having implemented effective emergency plans against a pandemic threat, the interest of market players (issuer, banks, rating agencies) has shifted towards longevity insurance.

Longevity risk is gaining greater consideration from US and UK pension and life insurance companies (press attention on reform of pension schemes, mergers and acquisitions activity took into account the pension risk arising for niche players interested mainly in pension books). This is supported by the existence of an untapped market of more than USD 30 trillion of pension liability that could potentially be hedged on the market against longevity drift and insufficient asset yield.

Many players have tried to standardize the market to make it more accessible to nonprofessional investors, allowing for independent valuation of longevity trends through standardized life indices (Credit Suisse, JP Morgan). These indices cover, in order of priority, the US, UK and the Netherlands and have the benefit of creating liquidity, providing two-way prices and allowing for basic derivative solutions (forwards, swaps, etc.).

---

[3] http://www.axa.com/lib/en/uploads/pr/group/2006/AXA_PR_20061113.pdf.

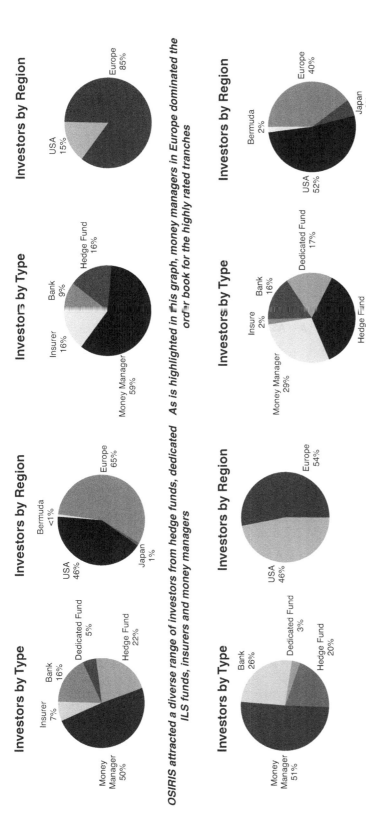

Figure 22.3 OSIRIS plc investor profile

Source: AXA Cessions

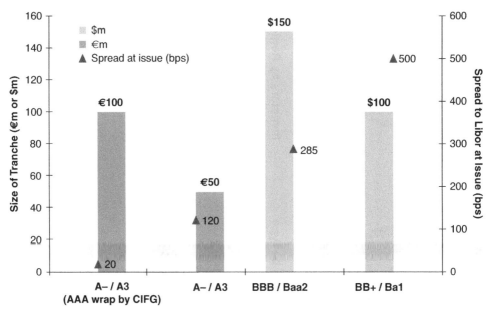

Figure 22.4 OSIRIS plc pricing

Source: AXA Cessions

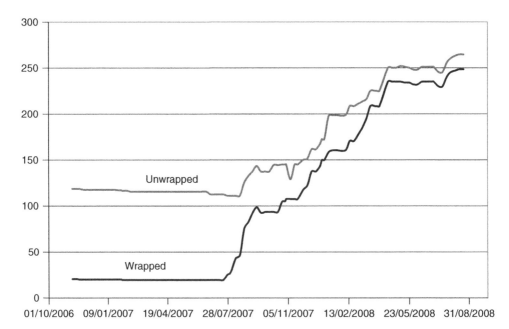

Figure 22.5 Indicative secondary market implied spread of the OSIRIS B tranches

Source: AXA Cessions

Despite these attempts and the commitment of major players, transactions are still limited. Many private equity transactions have taken place, but there have been very few known public capital market transactions. Four main reasons explain this situation:

- Very efficient pricing from reinsurers. Reinsurers have in-depth knowledge of the longevity risk and are massively exposed to mortality. The accumulation of longevity risk, and potentially the management of huge annuity reserves, is therefore a natural match for them.
- One-way exposure of investors. There is no 'natural' buyer of longevity risk. All known economic activity benefits from people living longer (except funeral homes). It is not a structuring issue, but it makes it difficult to find catalysts to generate sustainable long-term demand.
- However, interest is gaining momentum as longevity is seen as a diversifying asset if priced with the 'right' risk premium (hedge funds, dedicated ILS investors, P&C and life insurers). The first transactions in life settlements among institutional investors show that longevity can be purchased if priced reasonably.
- Pension funds and life insurers will need to diversify their counterparties in longevity transactions, to manage efficiently their credit risk and their regulatory capital. As many of the life reinsurers have already accumulated billions of exposure, the need for capital market solutions is clearly becoming more important than ever.

REFERENCE

Doyle, A., Bonmarin, I., Lévy-Bruhl, D., Le Strat, Y. and Desenclos, J-C. (2006) Pandemic influenza: modelling the impact with and without intervention in France, *Journal of Epidemiology and Community Health*, **60**, 399–404.

Case Study: Some Embedded Value and XXX Securitisations

Michael Eakins[a] and Nicola Dondi[a]

Life securitisation transactions have been mainly implemented in Western Europe and in the US due to the fact that the level of complexity of such transactions requires a sophisticated and well-developed level of reporting and can achieve the objectives of the sponsors only in certain jurisdictions where the regulatory framework is advanced enough to allow for such transactions.

The technology has developed at a tremendous pace over the last decade or so, particularly with the growing participation of monoline insurers. However, with the current financial market turmoil, monolines in particular have been badly affected and this will bring about even more structural changes, which will be reflected in the new generation of securitisations.

Insurance companies have executed life securitisation transactions for a number of purposes:

- **Capital rationale**
  - **Optimise capital base:** release encumbered capital at either Insurance Operating Company ('OpCo') level or Group Holding Company ('HoldCo') level and therefore increase the OpCo and/or HoldCo capital base.
  - **Increase regulatory available capital:** provide regulatory additional capital at either OpCo or HoldCo level and thereby improve the solvency position.
  - **Increase economic available capital:** provide economic capital benefit at either OpCo or HoldCo level by structuring the transaction in a manner that provides significant downsize protection.
- **Valuation/market perception rationale**
  - **Return on capital employed:** the monetisation of an in-force portfolio of life insurance policies provides additional capital resources that can be used to reduce shareholders' capital deployed within the insurance business.
  - **Funding new business:** the proceeds raised through a securitisation can be effectively redeployed to fund the writing of new business and therefore increase new business profit.
- **Other rationale**
  - **Group liquidity:** securitisations can be structured in order to provide cash at a Group level and hence increase the liquidity of the Group, which is a strong incentive, particularly

---

[a]Goldman Sachs International

The Handbook of Insurance-Linked Securities   Edited by P. Barrieu and L. Albertini
Chapter 23 © Goldman Sachs International – 2009. By Micheal Eakins and Nicola Dondi, employees of Goldman Sachs International

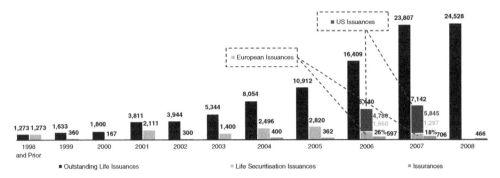

Figure 23.1   Total life linked transactions ($million)

Source: Goldman Sachs

during times when alternative sources of liquidity, e.g. senior and subordinated debt and equity, are either scarce and/or expensive.

o **Acquisition financing:** securitisation can be used as a strategic tool in order to provide acquisition financing as part of the acquisition consideration for any M&A transactions.

Sponsors often look to combine several/all of the above objectives in order to maximise the benefit derived by executing such transactions. This has resulted in very different and bespoke types of structures being executed in different jurisdictions for different sponsors. There is, therefore, no unified and simple technology that can be applied 'off-the-shelf' across jurisdictions, as is the case, for example, with vanilla senior and subordinated debt instruments. Each transaction is unique in nature, depending on the sponsor's objectives and on the specific jurisdiction in which it is implemented.

In terms of transaction volumes brought to market, we have observed a significant drop in issuance volumes due to a number of factors, mainly the disappearance of monoline reinsurers and the broader contagion coming from the wider capital markets turmoil.

Figure 23.1 provides an overview of the volumes of life insurance securitisation transactions executed since the inception of the market. Figure 23.2 breaks these transactions down into types for the period 2001–2007.

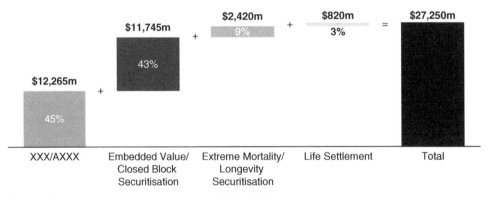

Figure 23.2   Overview of transaction types (2001–2007)

Source: Goldman Sachs

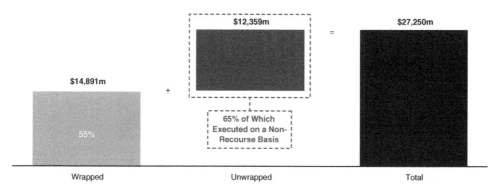

Figure 23.3   Wrapped vs. unwrapped transactions (2001–2007)
Source: Goldman Sachs

It is worth noting that, without the benefit of monoline guarantees and without recourse to the life insurer, the volume of syndicated life insurance securitisations has fallen to extremely low levels over the past 12 months and that a number of full-recourse and monoline-wrapped transactions were completed in the last quarter of 2007. Specifically, those segments of the life market that relied heavily on monoline insurers and auction rate note markets for their successful functioning from 2001–2007 (Figure 23.3) are now effectively closed. The recourse segment of the market continues to function, often in size (over $3 billion in the last quarter of 2007), but pricing is significantly higher, as is the case with issuance spreads for all types of financing instruments.

In this chapter, we will focus on two specific segments of the life insurance securitisation market, specifically embedded value (EV) securitisation and XXX securitisation, by providing specific case studies relating to each.

23.1   EMBEDDED VALUE SECURITISATION – AVONDALE S.A.

As part of an EV securitisation, an insurance company looks at monetising the value-in-force (VIF) of a segment of its overall book of insurance business. VIF is defined as the present value of future expected profits from a block of insurance policies. We have included in Figure 23.4 a schematic representation of a typical embedded value securitisation structure.

The primary objective of the Avondale S.A. transaction was to increase Bank of Ireland's (BoI) Equity Core Tier 1 capital through the synthetic securitisation of the VIF at BoI's subsidiary New Ireland Assurance, trading as Bank of Ireland Life (BoI Life).

VIF arising on contracts classified as insurance in accordance with IFRS 4 (Insurance VIF) is not included within BoI's Core Tier 1 (it is included within Tier 2 capital). VIF classified as investment contracts for IFRS 4 purposes (Savings VIF) is not recognised on the balance sheet of Bank of Ireland Group.

These objectives have been achieved through:

• The issuance through an SPV of synthetic VIF-linked securities that reference the surplus arising on unit-linked contracts within a portfolio defined as the 'dynamic defined block' written at BoI Life.

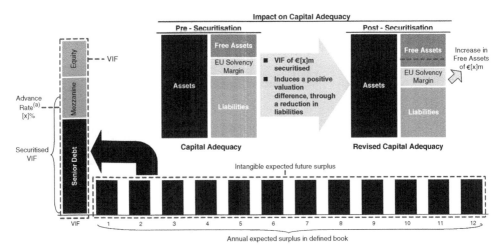

Figure 23.4 Embedded value securitisation – indicative mechanics

Source: Goldman Sachs

- 95% of the securities have been guaranteed by Ambac Assurance Corporation (Ambac), whilst a subordinated tranche of notes equal to 5% of the notes in the transaction have been sold unwrapped to a single investor.

We have included in Figure 23.5 a schematic representation of the Bank of Ireland transaction, which is further described in Tables 23.1 and 23.2.

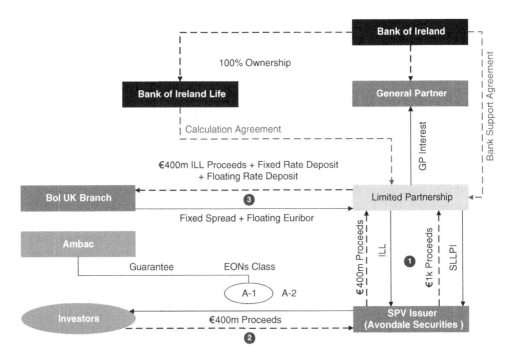

Figure 23.5 Transaction overview

Source: Goldman Sachs

Table 23.1 Description of the transaction

- The Limited Partnership borrows €400m of an insurance-linked loan (ILL) and issues €1000 of savings-linked limited partnership interests (SLLPI) to an SPV issuer (Avondale Securities).
  - Payments on the ILL reference the surplus arising on the emergence of insurance VIF.
  - Payments on the SLLPI reference the surplus arising on the emergence of savings VIF. Payments on the SLLPI will only be made to the extent that insurance VIF is impaired to a level below the notional of the ILL. These SLLPI payments will be at BoI's discretion, however if payments are not made BoI will be subject to a dividend stopper.
  - Floating EURIBOR payable on both instruments will not be contingent on sufficient surplus emerging (only the fixed spread component is contingent).
- Investors purchase €400m of notes in two tranches issued by Avondale Securities:
  - €380m Class A-1 notes (guaranteed by Ambac)
  - €20m A-2 notes
  Avondale Securities' principal assets will be the ILL and the SLLPI, and any cash flows received on these assets will be applied to payments on the notes (subject to senior expenses and other senior payments).
- The Limited Partnership uses the proceeds raised by the issue of the ILL and SLLPI to subscribe for a demand deposit issued by BoI UK branch.
  The demand deposit will be subject to a downgrade trigger, whereby the General Partner will be required to move the funds into eligible collateral should BoI be downgraded below an S&P rating of A− or Moody's rating of A2.
  BoI Group will provide €40m to be deposited with the Limited Partnership, which will also be subject to the downgrade trigger. The fixed yield and principal relating to the €40m will be used to pay the fixed spread on the ILL and SLLPI.

Source: Goldman Sachs

Table 23.2 Note characteristics

Issuer	• Avondale Securities S.A.
Securities	• €380 million Class A-1 floating rate emergence offset notes (EONs) due 2032 (EON to be defined) • €20 million Class A-2 floating rate EONs due 2032
Ratings	• Class A-1: AAA (Standard & Poor's) / Aaa (Moody's) – guaranteed by Ambac • Class A-2: A− (Standard & Poor's) / Baa1 (Moody's)
Weighted avg. life	• Class A-1: 7.8 years – driven off the five-year dynamic feature of the defined block • Class A-2: 11.6 years – driven off the five-year dynamic feature of the defined block
Interest	• Class A-1: 3-month EURIBOR + 75bps • Class A-2: 3-month EURIBOR + 309bps
Expected amortisation	• The principal projected to be repaid will be the projected surplus from the dynamic defined block (DDB) calculated after the initial five year non-amortising period or upon an earlier acceleration event, after deductions for spread and expenses. This is scheduled to be paid each year to redeem first the Class A-1 EONs in full, then the Class A-2 EONs
Acceleration events	• Sale of BoI Life by BoI • Partial sale of DDB (>50%) • Loss of BoI Life authorisation/licence • Breach of dividend stopper • Dissolution event
GS role	• Structuring advisor and joint bookrunner

Source: Goldman Sachs

The Avondale S.A. transaction involved a number of unique innovative market features that are capable of being transferred to other structures in the future. These features include:

- **Index-based EV securitisation:** as part of the Avondale S.A. transaction, the cash does not need to leave the insurance company to pay interest or principal. Instead, the emergence of VIF is tracked on an index basis by BoI Life acting as a calculation agent for the transaction. The notes are then served by Bank of Ireland using Group proceeds.
- **Application of new business for five years from inception to replace emerged VIF:** this specific feature has been named the 'dynamic defined block of business' (DDB) and ensures that for five years from the date of inception, new business written by BoI Life is added to the DDB referenced in the transaction, subject to a number of requirements being met, in order to ensure that the capital benefit achieved by Bank of Ireland through the transaction will be available for at least five years. We have included in Figure 23.6 a representation of the mechanics relating to the DDB.

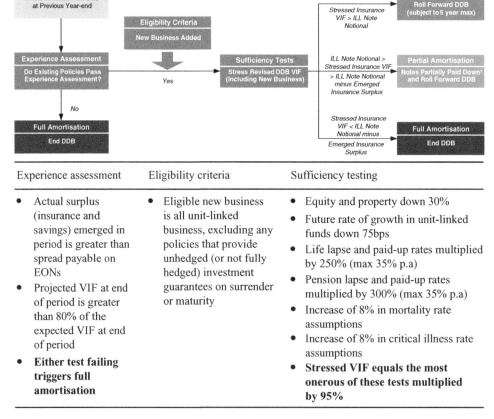

Experience assessment	Eligibility criteria	Sufficiency testing
• Actual surplus (insurance and savings) emerged in period is greater than spread payable on EONs • Projected VIF at end of period is greater than 80% of the expected VIF at end of period • **Either test failing triggers full amortisation**	• Eligible new business is all unit-linked business, excluding any policies that provide unhedged (or not fully hedged) investment guarantees on surrender or maturity	• Equity and property down 30% • Future rate of growth in unit-linked funds down 75bps • Life lapse and paid-up rates multiplied by 250% (max 35% p.a) • Pension lapse and paid-up rates multiplied by 300% (max 35% p.a) • Increase of 8% in mortality rate assumptions • Increase of 8% in critical illness rate assumptions • **Stressed VIF equals the most onerous of these tests multiplied by 95%**

Figure 23.6 Overview of DDB mechanics. Notes are paid down with the amount required so that stressed VIF covers the note notional

Source: Goldman Sachs

23.2   XXX SECURITISATION

XXX securitisation is related to the implementation by the US state insurance regulators of a specific regulation, called Regulation XXX, which requires insurance companies writing term life insurance policies in the US to hold statutory reserves significantly in excess of economic reserves. Figure 23.7 provides an indicative overview of typical economic reserves and XXX reserves.

The XXX reserve requirements create a capital need for insurers that can be more efficiently funded through the capital markets than through equity or other funding alternatives. A number of alternatives are available to insurers looking to execute XXX transactions, including:

- **Offshore reinsurance collateralised with a letter of credit:** the business is reinsured to an offshore reinsurer who collateralises the excess reserves with a letter of credit (LoC) and passes costs through to the parent.
- **Fund with full recourse debt:** the Holding Company (HoldCo) or affiliate issues debt and contributes the proceeds to replace the surplus, which is credited to XXX reserves with recourse to the HoldCo.
- **Fund through non-recourse securitisation:** the business is reinsured to a special purpose captive reinsurer (special purpose financial captive or 'SPFC') and a debt issuance funds a trust to collateralise reserves.
- **Funded trust:** the business is reinsured to an SPFC and a debt issuance from the SPFC funds a trust to collateralise reserves.
- **Onshore letter of credit:** the business is reinsured to an onshore reinsurer who collateralises its obligation with an LoC, subject to regulatory approval.

In Table 23.3 we have included a summary of the key implications of each of the above structures.

As a specific example, we have included below a transaction description for Orkney Re II plc, a Regulation XXX Reserve Relief Transaction sponsored by Scottish Re Group Ltd. (Scottish Re) in 2005.

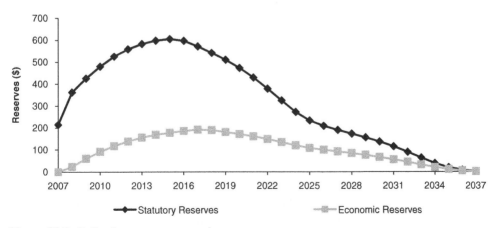

Figure 23.7   Indicative reserves progression

Source: Goldman Sachs

Table 23.3 Reserve relief alternatives

	Reinsure offshore and collateralise with letter of credit	Fund with full recourse debt	Fund through non-recourse securitisation	Funded trust	Onshore letter of credit
Examples	• Most insurers	• Prudential Financial, AEGON, Lincoln	• Scottish Re, Genworth, Banner Life	• Prudential Financial	• Select insurers
Balance Sheet Impact	• GAAP: none • Statutory: reserves ceded	• GAAP: debt consolidated • Statutory: none – capital contribution offsets surplus erosion	• GAAP: debt consolidated • Statutory: surplus contributed is zeroed at life company level and returns over time. Excess reserves (funded by debt) do not impact statements	• GAAP: debt consolidated • Statutory: surplus contributed zeroed. Excess reserves do not impact statements	• GAAP: none • Statutory: reserves ceded
Tax Impact	• Tax losses not consolidated if captive is not owned	• Tax deductions preserved	• Tax deductions preserved	• Tax deductions preserved	• Tax deductions possible
Rating Agency Impact	• Critical of large short-term LoC balances outstanding. Longer term LoCs should receive more favourable treatment • LoC taken out under company name	• Off-credit if demonstrate proceeds are funding redundant reserves; all proceeds could be financial leverage if risk of draw is not de minimis • Proceeds counted towards normal operating leverage limits for S&P and IIP bucket for Moody's	• Off-credit if costs self-contained in vehicle and non-recourse • Proceeds counted towards normal operating leverage limits for S&P only and not counted towards the IIP bucket for Moody's	• Parent guarantees or keepwell agreement results in operating leverage treatment • If the risk of draw is not de minimis, may result in financial leverage treatment	• Critical of short-term LoCs, but longer term LoC may receive favourable treatment • LoC taken out under company name
Other Issues	• LoC renewal risk • Subject to credit risk of bank • Recourse to LoC guarantor	• Complexity of initial execution • May consume investor capacity under company name	• Complexity of initial execution	• Recourse to parent • Moderate structural complexity • Marking-to-market issues	• LoC renewal risk • Regulatory review • Recourse to LoC guarantor

Source: Goldman Sachs

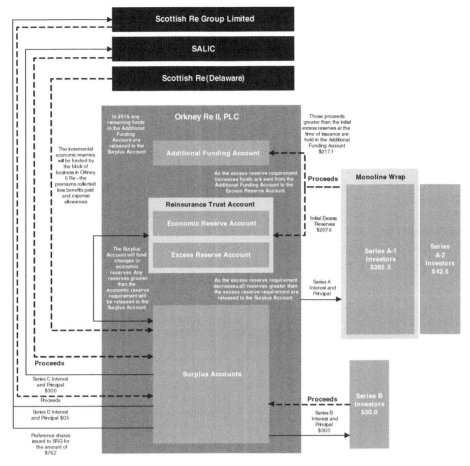

Figure 23.8 Transaction diagram

Source: Goldman Sachs

Table 23.4 Transaction summary

- Scottish Re (US) set up a special purpose financial reinsurer in Ireland, Orkney Re II
- Scottish Re (US) entered into an Indemnity Coinsurance Agreement with Orkney Re II and ceded it all its premiums, reserves and claims on a going forward basis
- Scottish Re funded Orkney Re II with $76.2 million in preference shares and $1.0 million in initial charitable contribution, which was partially used to fund deal expenses and $22.3 million in initial economic reserves
  - Scottish Re was also the initial purchaser of $30.0 million in Series C notes and $500 000 in Series D notes
- Orkney Re II issued securities and used a portion of the proceeds to fund initial excess reserve requirements
- The remaining proceeds from the issuance of notes are held in reserve within Orkney Re II for the sole purpose of funding future excess reserve requirements of Orkney Re II
- Orkney Re II posted a reinsurance trust for the sole benefit of Scottish Re (US)
- The regulatory approval process included Form D filings with Delaware, and formal SPV approval with Ireland
- Residual interest in Orkney Re II is retained by Scottish and the structure is consolidated for GAAP purposes
- Repayment of the notes is based on a 'cash-sweep' system and will depend on the financial performance of Orkney Re II
- Scottish will administer and service the vehicle, and J.P.Morgan Investment Management will invest its assets, each under a fixed cost contract

Source: Goldman Sachs

Table 23.5   Note characteristics

	Series A-1	Series A-2	Series B
Issuer:	Orkney Re II, plc	Orkney Re II, plc	Orkney Re II, plc
Offered notes:	Floating rate insured notes	Floating rate notes	Floating rate notes
Principal amount ($ million):	$382.5	$42.5	$30.0
Initial price:	100.0% of principal	100.0% of principal	100.0% of principal
Coupon:	3mL + 42.5 bps	3mL + 73 bps	3mL + 300 bps
Public ratings (S&P/Moody's):	AAA/Aa1	A−/Aa2	BBB+/Baa2
Maturity:	21 December, 2035	21 December, 2035	21 December, 2035
Weighted average life:	12.6 years	12.6 years	18.0 years
Note guarantee:	Assured guaranty (UK)	Uninsured	Uninsured
Issuer redemption:	• The notes are non-callable for the first year unless there is (i) recapture of termination of an underlying reinsurance agreement in the defined block of business or (ii) change in regulation. Any such redemption will be at a 3% premium • After the first year, redeemable at a 3% premium in the second year declining to 0% by the twelfth year	• The notes are non-callable for the first year unless there is (i) recapture of termination of an underlying reinsurance agreement in the defined block of business or (ii) change in regulation. Any such redemption will be at a 3% premium • After the first year, redeemable at a 3% premium in the second year declining to 0% by the twelfth year	• The notes are non-callable for the first year unless there is (i) recapture of termination of an underlying reinsurance agreement in the defined block of business or (ii) change in regulation. Any such redemption will be at a 3% premium • Following a redemption in full of the Series A notes, redeemable at a 3% premium in the second year declining to 0% by the twelfth year
Transfer rights:	To qualified institutional buyers pursuant to Rule 144A who are 'qualified purchasers' as defined in Section 2(a)(51) of the Investment Company Act		
Lead manager and sole bookrunner:	Goldman, Sachs & Co.		
Co-managers:	Scottish Re Capital Markets, Lehman Brothers, HSBC, RBS Greenwich Capital		

Source: Goldman Sachs

The transaction provided Scottish Re with relief for the excess reserves associated with the term life policies forming the defined block of business at a stable and competitive cost for 30 years with no rollover risk. The transaction involved the issuance of debt with recourse only to Orkney Re II and no recourse to other Scottish Re entity and is hence excluded from financial leverage by S&P and Moody's and from operating leverage by Moody's.

We have included in Figure 23.8 and Tables 23.4 and 23.5 an overview of the transaction structure.

Part III

Tax and Regulatory Considerations

24

The UK Taxation Treatment of Insurance-Linked Securities

Adam Blakemore[a] and Oliver Iliffe[b]

This chapter explores the UK taxation treatment of certain insurance-linked securities (such as securities issued by insurance special purpose vehicles as well as catastrophe bonds), with attention being drawn to how particular insurance risks may be securitised using both UK tax resident and non-UK tax resident vehicles. The securitisation of insurance risks can be potentially attractive to cedant insurers, offering access to cheaper capital market funding, allowing insurance companies to release embedded capital and reduce solvency ratio requirements in their insurance businesses and possibly allowing a lower level of credit risk than conventional insurance.

However, despite the potential advantages of securitising insurance risks, significant legal, tax and regulatory barriers have existed historically to using insurance-based structured finance. Even simple intra-EU jurisdictional structures have struggled to unite in an efficient and flexible manner the prevailing local regulatory and prudential requirements while allowing reinsurance coverage to be funded by the capital markets. In this environment, the introduction of the European Reinsurance Directive (EC/68/2005) ('the Directive') has aimed to remedy the historical lack of common regulation of reinsurance in Europe by the adoption of a harmonised prudential regulatory framework for reinsurance activities in all EU Member States.

This chapter considers how the possibility for the establishment of insurance special purpose vehicles (ISPVs) under the Directive has led directly to UK taxation changes which contemplate and facilitate insurance-linked securitisation by UK tax resident reinsurance undertakings. Very broadly, an ISPV is an undertaking which assumes risks from insurance or reinsurance undertakings and which fully funds its exposure to such risks through the issue of debt securities or some other funding mechanism, and includes a reinsurance securitisation vehicle.[1] It is considered that, despite the difficult capital markets environment which exists at the time of writing, there is considerable opportunity for the use of such vehicles in the near future as part of the ongoing evolution of the insurance-linked securities market.

In addition to considering the possibilities that exist for securitising insurance risk through the use of ISPVs, this chapter also considers the UK taxation treatment of insurance-linked

---

[a]Tax Partner, Cadwalader, Wickersham & Taft LLP
[b]Tax Associate, Cadwalader, Wickersham & Taft LLP
[1] Article 2.1(p) and Article 46 of the Directive.

The Handbook of Insurance-Linked Securities   Edited by P. Barrieu and L. Albertini
© 2009 John Wiley & Sons, Ltd

securities which are issued from non-ISPVs and which fall outside the scope of the Directive, with particular attention to structures akin to catastrophe bond transactions.

24.1 THE DIRECTIVE AND THE TAXATION OF UK ISPVS

The Directive introduces a unified minimum standard for harmonised prudential supervision of reinsurance across the EU in advance of implementation of the Solvency II directive. The aim of the Directive is to establish a framework to remove certain regulatory problems preventing the European insurance industry from accessing EU-based reinsurance structures.

24.1.1 The implementation of the Directive in the UK

In summary, the key innovations of the Directive are the requirement for reinsurers[2] to be supervised in their home state by a relevant authority (hence permitting 'passported' operation throughout the EU) as well as the introduction of a solvency regime and general principles on asset investment and abolition of collateral requirements. A key element of the Directive which is especially pertinent for taxation purposes is the permission for Member States to establish a new system of regulation for ISPVs. The Directive permits separate Member States to enact the provisions under local law and regulatory practice, allowing each Member State some flexibility in designing the detail of the regime governing ISPVs in that jurisdiction. In the UK, the proposals of the Financial Services Authority (FSA) for introducing ISPVs were outlined in June 2006 in Consultation Paper CP 06/12 'Implementing the Reinsurance Directive' ('CP 06/12') and it is the adoption of these proposals that has led to the UK taxation changes considered below.

The Directive has been transposed into UK law and regulatory practice by a number of measures. The Reinsurance Directive was initially implemented by the pre-existing provisions of the Financial Services and Markets Act 2000 and has been supplemented by both the Financial Services and Markets Act 2000 (Reinsurance Directive) Regulations 2007 (SI 2007/3255)[3] and the FSA's amendments to the FSA Prudential Sourcebook for Insurers (INSPRU) to accommodate the Directive.

24.1.2 Implementation of the ISPV framework in the UK

An ISPV is an EU Member State reinsurance undertaking, the exposures to risk of which are funded by debt issuance or another financing mechanism through the capital markets. As such, ISPVs are the potential successor to a number of reinsurance special purpose vehicles which have been used by European cedant insurers for many years to raise capital market finance while managing underwriting risk. The use of these vehicles has not, however, been straightforward

---

[2] The Directive affects pure reinsurers, namely those writing reinsurance business including captive reinsurers which only accept reinsurance business from a single firm, and special purpose vehicles. It does not apply to direct insurers carrying on reinsurance business which are already within the scope of existing EU insurance directives, although the provisions on solvency margins in the Directive will apply to the reinsurance business of an insurer if the volume of reinsurance activities represents a significant part of that business.

[3] The Financial Services and Markets Act 2000 (Reinsurance Directive) Regulations 2007 came into force on 10 December 2007 and addressed a number of important amendments to the existing legislation and regulatory framework, introducing consequential amendments to existing regulations to complete the implementation of the Directive, in particular as regards transfers of reinsurance business and the 'passporting' of rights for pure reinsurance business.

owing to certain difficulties for cedant insurers in obtaining solvency credit from the FSA through reinsurance using special purpose vehicles. One aim of introducing ISPVs is to clarify the treatment of ISPVs in the solvency calculations of European cedant insurers and reinsurers and regulatory balance sheets, while offering a viable regime with authorisation and prudential requirements that are proportionate to the reinsurance risk adopted.

With these aims in mind, an ISPV is required to be fully funded with paid-up debt or other financing, with the ISPV's reinsurance liability being subject to a maximum aggregate limit covered by its assets. Contingent funding is not permitted. This requirement operates as a very simple solvency rule and broadly prevents the ISPV being required to hold a minimum amount of capital or 'free assets' or retain any other solvency margin. The consequence of the solvency rule is that payments to holders of capital market securities issued by the ISPV and payments of other liabilities will be subordinated to an ISPV's reinsurance liabilities, a requirement which has consequences from a UK tax perspective (as described further below). The simple capital and solvency rules for an ISPV assist in making such a vehicle potentially attractive to cedant insurers.[4]

A number of other ISPV features included in the Directive are intended to prevent commercial barriers to their use. Provided certain conditions are met, cedant insurers should benefit from full solvency credit on the reinsurance provided by the ISPV.[5] In addition, ISPVs will be subject to minimal regulation.[6]

Although the Directive and the amendments to INSPRU are directed to the use of an ISPV as a securitisation vehicle, the FSA has confirmed that the use of an ISPV is not limited to such transactions. A company providing reinsurance solely to other group companies can be an ISPV if it funds its exposure to risk as required under the Directive and INSPRU. In addition to securitisation ISPVs, group reinsurance ISPVs can therefore be established. However, these group reinsurance vehicles are outside the scope of this chapter.[7]

A diagrammatic representation of the structure of an ISPV is shown in Figure 24.1.

In this structure:

- Capital market investors subscribe for note tranches issued by a UK incorporated ISPV. The notes carry a fixed or floating LIBOR-based return, but payment of interest and principal is subordinated to the ISPV's reinsurance liabilities (INSPRU 1.6.11 R, as revised).

---

[4] From the cedant's perspective, protection is achieved by the ISPV's liabilities being fully funded, together with the return of the funding or any other payment during the life of the IPSV being subordinated to the ISPV's insurance liabilities. In this regard, a contrast might be drawn with certain non-European special purpose reinsurance vehicles involving more complex ownership structures which are intended to distance the cedant from the vehicle owing to the reinsurer's solvency capital requirements.

[5] ISPVs should permit credit to be obtained on a cedant's regulatory balance sheet, provided that the cedant ensures risk transfer principles are met and an appropriate waiver is obtained from the FSA following the cedant providing the FSA with information about the ISPV on the cedant's individual capital assessment. Solvency credit should therefore be available if the cedant demonstrates to the FSA that an amount of insurance risk has been effectively transferred to the ISPV or has been subject to adequate risk transfer by means of, for example, a credit default swap, total rate of return swap or other form of risk transfer.

[6] The FSA emphasis in CP 06/12 was on the reduction of information required by the ISPV and greater emphasis on self certification and quicker authorisation. The ceding firm is responsible for ensuring the legal efficiency of the ISPV arrangement and for ensuring that all associated risks (including insurance, liquidity and credit) are accurately assessed and included in the ISPV's individual capital assessment. In addition, an ISPV will not be required to prepare an FSA regulatory return.

[7] See further HMRC Life Assurance Manual (HMRC LAM) paragraph 2.115 et seq.

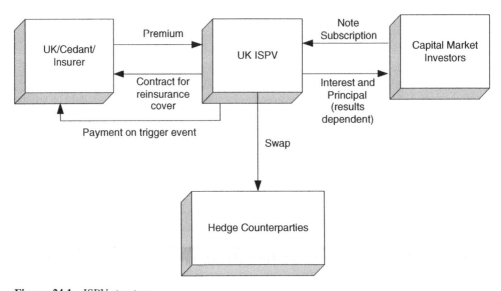

Figure 24.1 ISPV structure

Source: Cadwalader, Wickersham and Taft LLP

- The UK-based cedant enters into a reinsurance contract to transfer certain insurance risks to the ISPV, paying a premium to the ISPV as consideration for the transfer. The reinsurance provided by the ISPV is crystallised on the occurrence of a determined event (a 'trigger event').
- In the event that a trigger event takes place, the ISPV makes payments to meet its reinsurance liabilities. Any payment made will reduce debt service on the ISPV's notes, resulting in the loss of some or all of the interest and principal entitlement of the noteholders. If no trigger event occurs, the capital market investors will receive a return dictated by the degree of risk taken under the notes.

24.1.3 UK tax treatment of ISPVs

The FSA had expressly recognised in CP06/12 the importance of aligning the regulatory changes under the Directive with initiating corresponding changes to the UK tax regime.[8] While the FSA's own consultation was launched during a period when draft legislation on securitisation companies was being generally considered by HM Revenue & Customs (HMRC), early consideration was also given as to whether ISPVs should fall within one of the specific regimes for UK securitisation companies.[9]

Following the transposition of the Directive into UK law and practice, several UK tax issues were perceived as potentially preventing the use of ISPVs. A number of these issues were germane to UK securitisation companies generally. One particular difficulty related to the potential impact of International Financial Reporting Standards (IFRS) fair value accounting

---

[8] See CP 06/12 at paragraph 3.3, page 17.
[9] Details of the UK regime for securitisation companies are discussed further below.

(whether under international accounting standards or UK generally accepted accounting practice (GAAP) which is converged with IFRS) on the taxable profits of UK resident securitisation vehicles. As the taxable profit for UK corporation tax purposes arising from a debt or derivative depends, to a significant extent, on the profit shown in a company's *solus* accounts, changes to accounting standards directly impact UK corporation tax liability. The effect of IAS 39 (which, very broadly, prescribes the principles for recognising and measuring financial instruments) in accordance with the gradual alignment of UK GAAP with IFRS, and in particular the incorporation into the converged FRS 26 of IAS 39, is that changes in fair value should be taken as the accounting profit for certain debt and derivatives including swaps. As IFRS fair value accounting is required for any UK company issuing listed securities on an EEA exchange (which would include any UK-based ISPVs issuing capital market securities in EEA markets), the additional volatility to the taxable profit of a UK securitisation company created by fair value accounting of certain debt and derivatives would be unwelcome. The fair value profits recognised in respect of debt or derivatives to which the ISPV is a party could be taxable, but without a cash profit being realised from which such tax could be paid. The position raised the spectre of securitisation vehicles, which would lack substantial cash reserves, being subject to tax liabilities without the cash to pay them. This uncertainty was clearly a concern as regards the credit rating of the capital market bonds issued by the securitisation vehicle. While regulations were introduced by HMRC in late 2004 under which tax liabilities arising from fair value fluctuations under IFRS could be disregarded,[10] it was generally considered that these were not capable of providing the certainty of tax treatment in all circumstances which would be required by the rating agencies on a securitisation.

To address these concerns, HMRC introduced an interim regime in the Finance Act (FA) 2005 (the Interim Regime) which allowed securitisation companies to use UK GAAP as it stood at 31 December 2004 instead of the new IFRS (or IFRS converged) accounting standards. The Interim Regime was not intended by HMRC as a permanent solution.[11] A permanent regime (the Permanent Regime) was subsequently designed to replace the Interim Regime, being introduced under the Taxation of Securitisation Companies Regulations 2006 (SI 2006/3296) (the TSC Regulations). The Permanent Regime provides, very broadly, that UK securitisation companies will be taxed on their 'retained profit' computed by reference to a formula prescribed by statute rather than their accounting profit, thereby achieving the reduction of the impact of fair value accounting on the taxable profits of UK securitisation vehicles.

The TSC Regulations have effect for periods of account beginning on or after 1 January 2007. A company formed on or after 1 January 2007 which meets the conditions for being a securitisation company is automatically and mandatorily taxed under the Permanent Regime. However, the Permanent Regime does not accommodate all UK companies engaging in securitisation transactions. A securitisation company is defined in the Regulations as a company

---

[10] The Loan Relationships and Derivative Contracts (Disregard and Bringing into Account of Profits and Losses) Regulations, as amended (Statutory Instrument SI 2004/3256, as amended).

[11] Although it is understood that discussions were held between HMRC and the securitisation industry regarding the temporary FA 2005 regime being retained on a permanent basis, this was ultimately rejected owing to the complexity of retaining old UK GAAP accounting for securitisation companies at a time when IFRS was becoming more universally adopted. A combination of amendment to FA 2005 and further statutory instruments have resulted in it being possible for the Interim Regime to apply for accounting periods ending before 1 January 2017 (see The Securitisation Companies (Application of Section 83(1) of the FA 2005: Accounting Standards) Regulations 2007 (SI 2007/3338)).

that has a retained profit and is a 'note-issuing company', an 'asset-holding company', an 'intermediate borrowing company', a 'warehouse company' or a 'commercial paper funded company'. These definitions provide a reasonably comprehensive basis for encompassing the main types of companies that might be involved in a securitisation of financial assets (basically being defined in accordance with the meaning of 'financial assets' for accounting purposes). However, such definitions are not suitable for other securitisations, including the securitisations of insurance risks where ISPVs may hold assets other than 'financial assets'.[12]

Accordingly, it was difficult for UK ISPVs to be formed under the general corporation tax rules governing UK tax resident companies or the specific rules for UK securitisation companies. Without any targeted tax legislation focused on ISPVs, such ISPV companies would be taxed under the general principles of UK corporation tax, with potential difficulties arising, in particular, regarding the deductibility of financing costs where debt service is subordinated and limited in recourse to the securitisation company's assets[13] and from the volatility introduced into the taxation computations of the ISPV arising from, among other instruments, any hedging arrangements. What was required was an adjustment to the Permanent Regime which removed the requirement for UK companies formed as ISPVs to utilise IFRS fair valuation of financial instruments for calculating their corporation tax profits but which also ensured that the ISPV was itself not precluded from constituting a 'securitisation company' within the Permanent Regime.

With this aim in mind, two statutory instruments came into force on 28 December 2007, having effect for periods beginning on or after on 1 January 2007 and being current on 4 December 2007.[14] The first statutory instrument, The Taxation of Securitisation Companies (Amendment No. 2) Regulations 2007 (SI 2007/3401) (the TSC Amendment Regulations), amended the TSC Regulations to extend the existing Permanent Regime to certain insurance securitisations. The TSC Amendment Regulations amend the scope of a 'securitisation company' under the TSC Regulations. Under the TSC Amendment Regulations, a 'securitisation company' was amended to include a 'note-issuing company'[15] within the TSC Regulations which is not itself acting as a reinsurance undertaking but which lends the proceeds of the issue of securities into the capital markets to an 'insurance securitisation company'. Effectively, this means that such a note-issuing company and intermediate borrowing company would be taxed only on their retained profit from the transaction.[16]

---

[12] The categories of 'securitisation companies' place various requirements (for a 'note-issuing company') on the company as regards its activities. These requirements would have precluded an ISPV, which would carry on different reinsurance activities, from falling within the scope of these provisions. For example, as originally drafted in the TSC Regulations, and before the amendments discussed later in this chapter, an ISPV would not be a 'note-issuing company' within paragraph 5 of the Regulations as it would not have undertaken activities of acquiring, holding or managing financial assets forming the whole or part of the security for a capital market arrangement or of acting as a guarantor of loan relationships and other financial instruments.

[13] Such subordination of debt service to an ISPV's reinsurance liabilities is expressly required under the Directive and under the relevant FSA practice: see INSPRU paragraph 1.6.11R.

[14] It is noted that 4 December 2007 was the date that both statutory instruments SI 2007/3401 and SI 2007/3402 were made, both statutory instruments being laid before Parliament the following day.

[15] The definitions of 'note-issuing company' and 'intermediate borrowing company' in the TSC Regulations are closely articulated. A 'note-issuing company' is required to, among other things, issue securities to investors in the form of a capital market investment that is part of a capital market arrangement. An 'intermediate borrowing company' would typically include an SPV whose only business is to act as a lender to a company holding the financial assets which are subject to the securitisation or, following the TSC Amendment Regulations, a lender to an ISPV.

[16] See paragraph 2(3)(b) of SI 2007/3402, now included as paragraph 5(5)(b) of the TSC Regulations.

The second statutory instrument, entitled The Taxation of Insurance Securitisation Companies Regulations 2007 (SI 2007/3402) (the ISC Regulations) provides a substantive framework for securitisations utilising ISPVs and includes the key definition of 'insurance securitisation company'.

The ISC Regulations define an 'insurance securitisation company' as being an ISPV[17] which is either (i) a borrower under relationships owed wholly or mainly to a note-issuing company or an intermediate borrowing company under the Regulations; or (ii) being a note-issuing ISPV in its own right. Accordingly, an 'insurance securitisation company' under the ISC Regulations could either be a reinsurance undertaking which is itself funded by securitisation companies or a company issuing securities into the market. This latter class of 'insurance securitisation company' would be required to meet qualification tests[18] similar to those which would be required from a non-insurance securitisation company within the TSC Regulations which issues notes to capital market investors, but without the restriction on the types of business in respect of which a general securitisation company can undertake. This relaxation is less advantageous than may appear at first sight to be the case; as a practical matter the INSPRU guidelines will limit the activities of the ISPV to reinsurance business. Very broadly, the qualification tests require an insurance securitisation company to act as debtor to a capital market investment which is part of a capital market arrangement[19] under which securities[20] are issued wholly or mainly to independent persons.[21] The capital market investments made under these arrangements would need to have a total value of at least GBP 10 million. These conditions are imported for insurance securitisation companies in the same way as they apply to UK securitisation companies holding financial assets.

Where an ISPV falls within the scope of an 'insurance securitisation company' for the purposes of the ISC Regulations, the ISPV is required to compute its corporation tax profits in accordance with UK generally accepted accounting practice as it applied for an accounting period ending on 31 December 2006, with the important exclusion of Financial Reporting Standard 26 issued in December 2004 by the Accounting Standards Board in the UK.[22] Rather

---

[17] For these purposes, ISPV is defined under section 431(2) ICTA using language which broadly replicates the language of Article 2.1(p) of the Directive, requiring that the ISPV is an undertaking which assumes risks from insurance or reinsurance undertakings and which fully funds its exposure to such risks through the issue of debt securities or some other funding mechanism. An ISPV is excluded from being an 'insurance company' for UK tax purposes, with the effect of disapplying the corporation tax life assurance rules applicable to insurance companies in Chapter 1, Part 12 of ICTA 1988.

[18] The qualification tests are set out in paragraphs 4(2) to 4(4) of the ISC Regulations.

[19] The terms 'capital market investment' and 'capital market arrangement' carry the meaning set out in section 72B(1) of the Insolvency Act 1986.

[20] 'Securities' are not defined in SI 2007/3402 or the Regulations. It is considered that the term is capable of very wide construction and that, for practical purposes, should include securities listed and admitted to trading on a stock exchange which is designated by HMRC as a 'recognised stock exchange' in accordance with section 1005 of the Income Tax Act 2007.

[21] The term 'independent persons' is defined in the ISC Regulations to mean 'persons who are not connected with a company' (paragraph 2(1) of the ISC Regulations). This ostensibly simple definition is, however, complicated materially through a further definition of what the expression 'connected' means. Very broadly, a person could be connected with another when it could exercise 'control' over the other, especially through shares, votes, rights to distributions or rights to assets on a winding up. This broadly worded provision can cause some difficulties in a securitisation context. Although loan creditors cannot exert 'control' for the purposes of the 'independent persons' test in the ISC Regulations, considerable care must still be taken in any circumstances where the cedant is to subscribe for a proportion of notes to be issued by the ISPV.

[22] Regulation 6 of the TSC Regulations.

than compute the corporation tax profits by reference to a statutory formula and an amount of retained profit (as in the TSC Regulations), the ISC Regulations result in taxation based around profits as measured under 'old UK GAAP' as it stood before convergence with IFRS took place. In this regard, therefore, the taxation of an 'insurance securitisation company' is closely related to the taxation of more general securitisation companies under the Interim Regime.[23] The effect of this treatment is that the ISPV is taxed on whatever profit is shown in its *solus* accounts, subject to any modification if it does use FRS 26. There remain some difficulties with this approach. ISPVs would need to manage the administrative burden of producing 'old UK GAAP' compliant accounts (absent FRS 26) for the purposes of computing UK taxable profits as they would have been computed as at 31 December 2006. This burden is likely to be more pronounced as time progresses, memories fade, new auditors are appointed and pre-IFRS information becomes more scarce. Such a solution, as contemplated in the Interim Regime for general securitisation companies, was not intended (or desired) to be a long-term solution and it is possible that a permanent regime for UK ISPVs will eventually replace the regime set out in the ISC Regulations at some point in the future.

Certain provisions are also included in the ISC Regulations which, if applicable, could prevent an ISPV from coming within the favourable tax regime under the ISC Regulations. Broadly, these are equivalent to exclusions from the existing TSC Regulations that prevent a securitisation company obtaining the benefits of being within the TSC Regulations where it has, or at any time has had, an 'unallowable purpose', this being one where the purpose for which the company is party to the capital market arrangement or a related transaction or a transaction in pursuance of that arrangement is not among the business or other commercial purposes of the company. A main purpose of avoiding tax through the securitisation would be such an unallowable purpose. However, in practice the circumstances where a company which is party to a securitisation could have such a main purpose of tax avoidance should be very rare indeed.

Importantly, ISPVs which are 'insurance securitisation companies' also benefit from the removal of the UK's interest recharacterisation rules in section 209(2)(b) to (f) of the Income and Corporation Taxes Act 1988 (ICTA 1988). This is particularly important in the context of the removal of section 209(2)(e)(iii) ICTA 1988, this being the provision recharacterising limited recourse interest paid to a recipient outside the scope of UK corporation tax as a non-deductible distribution for a UK tax resident company. The removal of this provision is an important feature of the TSC Regulations, allowing the use of limited recourse notes by securitisation companies which only pay interest to the extent that funds are available for debt service. Qualifying ISPVs which are 'insurance securitisation companies' together with note-issuing and intermediate borrowing companies should therefore be able to issue and be party to limited recourse loans without prejudicing the tax deductibility of interest arising under such loans. This should allow limited recourse notes to form part of the debt structuring of a UK ISPV, this being a requirement of importance given that the definition of 'insurance special purpose vehicle' in section 431(2) ICTA (by reference to which 'insurance securitisation company' in paragraph 4(1) of the ISC Regulations is defined) is based around the financing by debt or some other financing mechanism 'where the repayment rights of the providers of

---

[23] It is noted that an 'insurance securitisation company' is not expressly excluded from section 83 FA 2005 (although the first HMRC draft of what is now SI 2007/3402 did originally include such an exclusion). It is considered that any ISPV would not fall within section 83 FA 2005 as it would be unlikely to fall within the requirements of a 'securitisation company' in section 83(2) FA 2005, hence the need to expressly exclude an 'insurance securitisation company' from section 83 FA 2005.

such debt or other financing mechanism are subordinated to the reinsurance obligations of the undertaking'. Certain other UK corporation tax rules are also 'switched off' for ISPVs within the ISC Regulations, including the group relief and chargeable gains intra-group transfer rules and the loan relationships and derivative contracts group transfer rules.[24]

Some differences between the Permanent Regime and the ISC Regulations relate to the difficulty of simply treating ISPVs as 'securitisation companies' within the TSC Regulations for general securitisation companies. 'Securitisation companies' within the TSC Regulations are required to meet the 'payments condition' in Regulation 11. This Regulation is designed to ensure a 'securitisation company' does not simply hoard cash from its securitised assets and act as a money box, receiving and retaining cash tax free and paying it out at a later date. Accordingly, a 'securitisation company' under the TSC Regulations is required to pay out all cash received within 18 months of the end of the accounting period of receipt, unless such cash is required to be provided against losses or to maintain or enhance the securitisation company's credit worthiness. As noted above, the 'payments condition' does not apply to an ISPV. Bearing in mind the INSPRU requirements regarding an ISPV's assets and liabilities, the 'payments condition' in the TSC Regulations is not replicated in the ISC Regulations in order to prevent a UK ISPV being effectively forced to offer reinsurance over a greatly reduced time period.

In summary, the ISC Regulations complement the changes introduced by the FSA following the transposition of the Directive into UK law. The key achievement of the ISC Regulations is to ensure that any accounting uncertainties which could be created as a result of IFRS recognition of movements in the fair value of financial instruments are not crystallised into tax volatility. As noted above, residual concerns remain that the ISC Regulations are a temporary solution, which may gradually become unsuitable in the future as a method of taxing UK ISPVs in the event that compiling the ISPVs' accounts on the basis of UK GAAP as it stood at 31 December 2006 (absent FRS 26) becomes progressively more difficult with the passage of time. These residual concerns militate in favour of a more permanent solution being devised along the lines of the Permanent Regime for general securitisation companies, although such a solution may well be complicated by the nature of the reinsurance business which the ISPV would be carrying on. It is also important to remember that, notwithstanding the integration of ISPVs into the regime for UK securitisation companies, there remains the potential for anomalies to exist regarding the treatment of ISPVs under other legal and regulatory requirements.[25] It is considered that ending such anomalies may be just as challenging as solving any tax complexities which still relate to the use of ISPVs.

24.2 NON-UK INSURANCE SPECIAL PURPOSE VEHICLES

While the foregoing discussion has concentrated on the United Kingdom regime for ISPVs, it should be noted that, at the date of writing, the favoured structure for insurance-linked

---

[24] See HMRC LAM paragraph 2.127. The removal of the provisions of section 209(2)(b) to (f) ICTA 1988 for UK securitisation companies under paragraph 16 of the Regulations has also been supplemented by the new section 79(7B) FA 1986 (introduced by section 101(3) FA 2008) providing a complementary relaxation for limited recourse debt issued in respect of a capital market instrument for stamp duty and stamp duty reserve tax purposes. It is considered that the stamp taxation relaxation in section 79(7B) FA 1986 should apply to both a 'securitisation company' under the TSC Regulations and an 'insurance securitisation company' under the ISC Regulations.

[25] Such anomalies might arise, for example, in the event that an ISPV is considered to be undertaking insurance business from the perspective of the INSPRU rules, thereby necessitating consideration from transaction counterparties as to whether they have the necessary permissions to undertake business with the ISPV.

securities is the issuance of catastrophe bonds by non-UK offshore vehicles. As described in other chapters of this book, these issuers will be typically established and tax resident in tax haven jurisdictions such as the Cayman Islands or Bermuda and will complement traditional reinsurance or retrocession by transferring low-probability, high-impact risk to capital market investors.[26] However, some issuers of catastrophe bonds have also been established in Ireland.

Despite the offshore status of these catastrophe bond issuers, a number of UK tax issues may still arise depending on the connection between the catastrophe bond issuer and the UK. These issues are considered below and, broadly, comprise the tax residence status of the issuer, the tax residence status of the issuer's agents, the location of the issuer's assets and the manner in which the issuer manages those assets to the extent that any of them are situated in the UK.

24.2.1 Tax residence status of the issuer

The first key point in relation to a catastrophe bond issuance has been the need to maintain the residence of the issuer outside the UK to avoid potentially adverse tax consequences which could result from the issuer being resident in the UK.[27] The corporation tax scheme brings the worldwide income, profits and gains of all companies within the scope of corporation tax under section 6(1) ICTA 1988 and then excludes, under section 11(1) ICTA 1988, companies which are not resident in the UK from the scope of that charge unless they are trading in the UK through a 'permanent establishment'.[28] A primary concern for every offshore catastrophe bond issuance is therefore that the issuer should be tax resident outside the UK.

In UK tax law, 'residence' is a case law-based test which depends on where the 'central management and control' of a company exists.[29] This will not necessarily be the place where the issuer is established[30] and is to be distinguished from the place where the main operations of a business are found (see paragraph 11 of HMRC Statement of Practice SP 1/90), but ultimately will be a question of fact based on all the circumstances. The general rule of thumb is that the place of central management of control is the place where the directors meet as a board and make the management decisions of the company in accordance with the constitution of the company. However, the place where the board meets is unlikely to be conclusive unless it is the directors who make the important and substantive decisions concerning strategy and policy of the issuer and they do so only at board meetings.[31]

As a consequence of the legal uncertainty created by this vein of case law, there are certain nonexhaustive guidelines that directors of catastrophe bond issuers usually follow in practice. The directors will maintain their tax residence outside the UK. They will hold board meetings outside the UK and not take part in those meetings from the UK by telephone. They will make

---

[26] The reasons for establishment of the issuer in a tax haven are mainly driven by the US tax treatment of the catastrophe bond transaction (please refer to Chapter 25).

[27] Careful structuring is otherwise needed to ensure that a UK tax resident issuer gains the necessary protections and dispensations afforded by the ISC Regulations, as considered in Section 24.1.3.

[28] See Section 24.2.2.

[29] The leading English case on this is *De Beers Consolidated Mines v Howe* [1906] AC 455. Note, however, that a company incorporated in the UK is generally deemed to be resident in the UK for tax purposes. See section 66 of FA 1988.

[30] Under UK tax law it is possible, for instance, for a company to be registered in the Cayman Islands and tax resident in Bermuda.

[31] See, for instance, the case of *Unit Construction Co Ltd v Bullock* [1960] AC 351 where the House of Lords found that the board of a company established overseas had been usurped by its parent which was tax resident in the UK.

all the important strategic and policy decisions of the company at those board meetings and will not delegate powers to make those decisions to directors or third parties who are resident in the UK. They will hold board meetings regularly and document the proceedings so that they can demonstrate, if necessary, that control of the issuer rests with them and that they have sufficiently deliberated and understood the decisions that have been made.

If there is a real risk of a catastrophe bond issuer ceasing to be resident outside the UK (and therefore becoming tax resident in the UK), one practical approach is to structure the transaction in such a way that the issuer could in such a situation meet the requirements of being a note-issuing ISPV in its own right within Regulation 4(1)(a) of the ISC Regulations. Such an approach would require attention to be paid not only to the actual accounting treatment of the issuer in the jurisdiction of its incorporation, but also how the issuer's accounts would be used to calculate its UK corporation tax liability in the event that the issuer was treated as being UK tax resident.[32] Complexities might well arise where, in the future, the issuer's accounts prepared under an offshore GAAP are to be construed on the basis of UK GAAP as it stood at 31 December 2006, ignoring FRS 26, such accounts forming the basis of a UK corporation tax computation.[33]

As mentioned above, where a catastrophe bond issuer is not tax resident in the UK its profits, income and gains will only be chargeable to corporation tax to the extent that the issuer carries on a trade in the UK through a 'permanent establishment' in the UK.[34] Where this is the case, the issuer will generally be chargeable to corporation tax only on trading income arising from or through the permanent establishment, income from property or rights of the permanent establishment and chargeable gains arising from trading assets and other assets held by or acquired for the permanent establishment.[35]

24.2.2   Tax residence status of the issuer's agents

Section 148 FA 2003 defines a permanent establishment as being 'a fixed place of business through which the business of the company is wholly or partly carried on, or an agent acting on behalf of the company [that] habitually exercises their authority to do business on behalf of the company'. Catastrophe bond issuers will not generally have a 'fixed place of business' in the UK but problems could arise if such an issuer were to employ agents in the UK. In practical terms these UK agents could include the account bank (at which the issuer holds its accounts) and the total return swap provider. It is highly unlikely that any factors will point to the account bank as being a permanent establishment of the issuer, as it should simply not have authority to conduct business on behalf of the issuer. The position of the total return swap provider might be more complex.

The role of the total return swap provider involves the investment of the proceeds of the catastrophe bond issuance and the provision of a return. Proceeding on the assumption that there is no other relationship between the total return swap provider and the issuer, the issuer will want to ensure that a total return swap provider in the UK is an 'agent of independent status acting in the ordinary course of his business' under section 148(3) FA

---

[32] Very broadly, the issuer would be required to compute its UK corporation tax profit in accordance with current UK GAAP, even if the issuer has previously prepared accounts, and kept its books, under the GAAP of the relevant non-UK jurisdiction.

[33] Regulation 6 of the ISC Regulations.

[34] Section 11(1) ICTA 1988.

[35] Section 11(2) and 11(2A) ICTA 1988.

2003; in such a situation, an agent would not amount to a UK permanent establishment of the nonresident issuer. However, depending on the role undertaken by the total return swap provider, particularly to the extent that any management of investments is undertaken by such swap provider on the issuer's behalf, further detailed UK tax requirements in Schedule 26 FA 2003 might need to be considered in order for the swap provider to be identified as an 'agent of independent status'.[36] The provisions in Schedule 26 FA 2003 are supplemented by HMRC Statement of Practice SP 1/01 (as revised) and amplify the more general requirements of section 148(3) FA 2003 regarding independent agents. While the detail of the provisions is outside the scope of this chapter, broadly speaking they provide for a series of tests which would need to be met by a UK total return swap provider providing investment management services to the issuer in order for that total return swap provider to be treated as being an 'agent of independent status' and therefore exempt from being a UK permanent establishment of the issuer. In the event that these provisions are relevant, close examination will be required of the relationships of the issuer with both the total return swap provider and also any person connected with it.

Where a catastrophe bond issuer conducts its business in the UK exclusively through a UK total return swap provider which is not a 'permanent establishment' (for example where it meets the requirements of section 148 FA 2003 as an agent of independent status and has no other UK permanent establishment), the tax on profits arising from that business should be limited to income tax, computed under section 815 ITA 2007.[37]

24.2.3 Location and management of the issuer's assets

Accordingly, the catastrophe bond issuer may need to take steps to ensure that its investments adhere to strict eligibility criteria to limit the incidence of UK income tax withholding at source on the issuer's assets. Typically this may involve selecting quoted Eurobonds, gilt-edged stock, bills and interest-bearing securities with less than 12 months' maturity.[38]

Alternatively, the issuer might simply avoid investing in assets which pay interest with a UK 'source'. This is because there is only a liability to withhold income tax from interest payments if those payments 'arise' in the UK. HMRC have stated that they consider the two most important factors in determining the source of interest as being the residence of the debtor and the location of its assets.[39]

---

[36] This issue will only arise where the issuer is trading through the total return swap provider, as discussed further below.

[37] Note that relief under a double taxation convention between the UK and the jurisdiction of residence of the issuer may be available, although this will not be relevant where the catastrophe bond issuer is resident in a tax haven (with which the UK has no double taxation treaty).

[38] Quoted Eurobonds are bonds which are issued by a company, listed on a recognised stock exchange (and admitted to trading on its regulated market) and carrying a right to interest (see section 987 ITA 2007). Gilts are exempt from withholding tax under section 877 ITA 2007 and bills have a maturity of less than one year, meaning that, together with interest-bearing securities of a similarly short maturity, they will not pay 'yearly interest' which falls within the duty to withhold on account of income tax under section 874 ITA 2007.

[39] See HMRC Savings and Investment Manual paragraph SAIM 9090. The residence of the debtor is not the tax residence but rather its jurisdictional residence (i.e. its jurisdiction of registration). Other factors which HMRC will consider include, (a) the place of performance of the contract and the method of payment; (b) the competent jurisdiction for legal action and the proper law of contract; and (c) the residence of any guarantor and the location of the security for the debt. These factors are said to derive from the decision in *Westminster Bank Executor and Trustee Company (Channel Islands) Ltd v National Bank of Greece SA* (1970) 46 TC 472.

Any payments made by the total return swap provider under the total return swap should not generally be subject to any UK income tax withholding.[40] Finally, interest accruing on the accounts of the issuer in the UK should not be subject to a withholding requirement provided that the account bank is a 'bank' within the meaning of section 991 of the Income Tax Act 2007 (ITA 2007).

On the basis that the typical catastrophe bond issuer will be a company which is resident outside the UK for tax purposes and will not have a permanent establishment in the UK, such an issuer should not be subject to corporation tax in the UK. As briefly noted above, the extent of a catastrophe bond issuer's income tax liability in such circumstances is limited by section 815 ITA 2007 to the aggregate of two amounts. The first amount can be equated, very broadly, to income tax deducted at source (such as income tax deducted from interest and annual payments and tax credits on dividends). The second amount is the income tax chargeable on the issuer's income other than interest, annual payments and income arising through UK investment managers and brokers within the meaning of Schedule 26 FA 2003.

Identifying this second amount can sometimes be problematic. There are residual concerns that a catastrophe bond issuer could be directly assessed for income tax by HMRC in the event that it was alleged by HMRC to be trading 'within' the UK (as opposed to merely trading 'with' the UK).[41] These concerns become particularly relevant where the issuer is tax resident in a tax haven jurisdiction which does not have a double taxation convention with the UK, as is often the case with catastrophe bond issuers. In such circumstances, the absence of an applicable double tax treaty prevents the elimination of such an income tax charge under the business profits article. It should be noted that, provided the relevant UK agents of the issuer do not amount to permanent establishments of the issuer (see above), HMRC should not be able to assess such agents for the UK income tax of the issuer. Any UK income tax liability would need to be assessed directly against the issuer itself, despite the practical and jurisdictional difficulties created by the non-UK tax residence of the issuer, which are outside the scope of this chapter.

It should be noted that even where the investments of a catastrophe bond issuer form part of a static portfolio and are not 'traded' in a commercial sense, income arising from those investments will be regarded as 'trading income' by HMRC because the purpose of the investments is to meet the potential claim of the cedant.[42]

An income tax liability would only arise for the catastrophe bond issuer in circumstances where the issuer was carrying on a trade 'within' the UK, as opposed to merely trading 'with' the UK. The decision of the Court of Appeal in *Greenwood v F. L. Smidth & Co* is authority for the need to examine whether, in substance, the trading operations giving rise to a profit

---

[40] A UK total return swap provider is likely to make payments under a swap within a specific exemption from withholding of income tax (section 980 ITA 2007). Payments by a non-UK swap provider are unlikely to be subject to withholding of income tax for a number of reasons, such as where such payments do not 'arise' in the UK.

[41] Section 18(1)(a)(iii) ICTA 1998, provides that income tax is chargeable on profits or gains arising or accruing 'to any person, . . . although not resident in the United Kingdom from any property whatever in the United Kingdom or from any trade, profession or vocation exercised within the United Kingdom' under Schedule D. See also section 6(2) of the Income Tax (Trading and Other Income) Act 2005.

[42] See HMRC Business Income Manual, paragraph BIM 40805. HMRC practice is based on the decision of the House of Lords in *Nuclear Electric plc v Bradley* [1996] STC 405 at 411, where Lord Jauncey of Tullichettle stated '*Whether income from investments held by a business is trading income must ultimately depend upon the nature of the business and the purpose for which the fund is held. At [the trading income] end of the scale are insurance companies and banks, part of whose business is the making and holding of investments to meet current liabilities.*'

take place in the United Kingdom.[43] An attempt could be made to ensure, in a catastrophe bond transaction, that all contracts, including the purchase and sale of the investments of the catastrophe bond issuer and the supervening investment contracts such as the total return swap, are concluded outside the UK. This might be achieved by a UK agent adopting the role of adviser and passing on offers and details of potential trades to the issuer or one of its non-UK tax resident agents for consideration and acceptance.[44] It may also be the case that, even where income is generated from activities of the issuer (for example, under a total return swap), such income would not be sufficient to result in a profit as computed in accordance with UK GAAP.

Nevertheless, it is considered that where no protection from a double taxation treaty is available, in some particular circumstances it can be challenging to categorically eliminate all risks of an income tax liability on the catastrophe bond issuer. Much can be done to eliminate such risks through consideration of the accounting treatment of the issuer in respect of its actions under the transaction documents and through careful drafting of any contracts under which the issuer may be construed as taking actions 'within the UK'.

24.3   INDIRECT TAXES AND WITHHOLDING OF INCOME TAX

Since a counterparty contract between the protection buyer and the issuer should be categorised as a contract of reinsurance under paragraph 1 of Schedule 7A of FA 1994 in transactions structured on an indemnity basis, it should be exempt from insurance premium tax.[45] If the counterparty contract is structured as a credit derivative contract under ISDA documentation, as may be the case in a transaction on a non-indemnity basis, it should also be exempt from insurance premium tax because a credit derivative should not constitute a contract of insurance for legislative purposes or as a matter of common law.

Elements of an ISPV securitisation or an offshore catastrophe bond issuance may also have value added tax (VAT) aspects. There are three relevant areas:

1. The provision of reinsurance by an ISPV to a counterparty should be a supply of services which is exempt from VAT under Item 1 of Group 2 of Schedule 9 of the Valued Added Tax Act 1994 (VATA 1994).
2. The relationship between an intermediate ISPV and a note-issuing company should simply be one of debtor and creditor, with the note-issuing company on-lending the proceeds of issuance to the ISPV. Accordingly, the granting of credit by the note-issuing company should be exempt from VAT under Item 2 of Group 5 of Schedule 9 of VATA 1994. A recent

---

[43] *Greenwood v F. L. Smidth & Co* (1922) 8 T.C. 193 at 204, later followed by *Firestone Tyre and Rubber Co v Llewellin* (1957) 37 T.C. 111 at p142.

[44] Although the directors of the issuer must be capable of evaluating the investment advice critically, as following such advice slavishly may result in the issuer becoming UK tax resident if the board of directors could be said to have surrendered central management and control to the investment adviser.

[45] The term 'contract of reinsurance' is not defined in FA 1994, but the HMRC Lloyd's Manual, HMRC Insurance Policyholder Taxation Manual and the HMRC General Insurance Manual; each define reinsurance as 'the insurance of the risks assumed by or potential losses of another insurer (the direct insurer) whereby the latter covers a proportion of the risks assumed or the eventuality of atypically large losses'. Notice IPT 1 on Insurance Premium Tax of March 2002 also provides guidance on what HMRC regard as not constituting reinsurance, namely: (i) transfer of obligations and rights to future receivables attaching to the original insurance business, (ii) partnership and agency relationships between insurers and (iii) direct contracts of insurance used in tandem with self-insurance (see paragraph 5.3). Considerable care will therefore be required in drafting the counterparty contracts, which also will need to take into account qualification for capital relief and the scope of a UK insurer or reinsurer's regulatory permissions.

High Court decision confirmed that it is possible to have a supply of 'securitisation services' by a securitisation company to an originator.[46] It is considered that there is strong support for the argument that the service provided by an ISPV to a cedant can be distinguished from the supply of 'securitisation services' in the context of that decision, although the question is untested before the courts. Even if such a supply were to be identified, it is considered that such a supply should be capable of constituting a supply of services which is exempt from VAT under Item 1 of Group 2, Schedule 9 VATA 1994.

3. The issue of bonds by an ISPV fulfilling the role of a note-issuing company should not amount to a supply by the ISPV for VAT purposes.[47]

Payments by a cedant of reinsurance premiums to a UK ISPV or by a cedant or counterparty to a catastrophe bond issuer should not be subject to any withholding for or on account of income tax.[48]

FURTHER READING

Cummings, J.D. (2008) Cat Bonds and Other Risk-Linked Securities: State of the Market and Recent Developments, *Risk Management and Insurance Review*, **11** (1), 28.

Gill, R., Goodlud, S., Portas, J. and Riley, J. (2007) The Reinsurance Directive – Some Key Features and Practical Implications, *Insurance and Reinsurance Law Briefing*, **124** (Feb), 1–5.

Harrison, J. (2007) Securitisation of Insurance Risks, *Financial Instruments Tax and Accounting Review*, September, 4–8.

Landon, P. (2007) *VAT and the City, Banking Finance and Insurance*, sixth edition, CCH.

MacLeod, J.S. and Levitt, A. (1999) *Taxation of Insurance Business*, fourth edition, Butterworths.

Noussia, K. (2008) The Impact of the Reinsurance Directive 2005/68: So far so good?, *Journal of Business Law*, **5**, 415–431.

Wattman, M., Parker, C. and Navias, M. (2007) Catastrophe Bonds, *Journal of International Banking and Financial Law*, **9**, 532.

Whiteman, P.G. (with Goy, D., Sandison, F. and Sherry, M.) (2003) *Whiteman on Income Tax*, third edition, 2001 and fourteenth cumulative supplement to the third edition, 2003, Sweet & Maxwell.

---

[46] *MBNA Europe Bank Limited v Commissioners of HM Revenue & Customs* [2006] EWHC 2326 (Ch).

[47] In light of the decision in *Kretztechnik AG v Finanzamt Linz* (C-465/03) and HMRC's position in Business Brief 21/2005.

[48] A number of factors can be cited for the absence of any withholding of income tax on reinsurance premia, including that the premia arise outside the UK and that the premia are not qualifying annual payments within Chapter 6, Part 15 of ITA 2007.

25

The US Federal Income Taxation Treatment of Insurance-Linked Securities[1]

David S. Miller[a] and Shlomo Boehm[a]

This chapter discusses the US federal income tax treatment of a foreign corporation that enters into one or more 'insurance-linked instruments' relating to a natural catastrophe risk with an unrelated counterparty, and the US federal income tax consequences to the US and foreign (i.e., non-US) investors that purchase notes issued by the foreign corporation.[2] In this chapter, we generally refer to the notes issued by the foreign corporation as 'catastrophe bonds'; the foreign corporation that issues the catastrophe bonds as the 'issuer' or the 'protection seller,' and the issuer's counterparty as the 'protection buyer.'[3]

Generally, the insurance-linked instruments entered into by the issuer are either documented as 'reinsurance agreements,' 'retrocession agreements,' or as swaps on standard ISDA (International Swaps and Derivatives Association) forms. In general, a reinsurance agreement is an agreement pursuant to which a party agrees to indemnify an insurance company for all of or a portion of loss that the insurance company sustains under insurance policies it has written. A retrocession agreement is a similar agreement entered into with a reinsurance company that, in turn, has reinsured an insurance company.

These insurance-linked instruments generally provide the issuer with an annual (or more frequent) periodic payment equal to a fixed or floating rate (e.g., 5% annually, or a LIBOR-based rate) times a notional amount that is equal to the principal amount of the catastrophe

---

[a]Cadwalader, Wickersham & Taft LLP

[1]This chapter focuses on the US federal tax treatment of insurance-linked instruments; the tax treatment of various cedants or counterparties can be complex and falls outside the scope of this chapter, except where specifically referred to.

[2] In this chapter, 'US investor' refers to an investor that, for US federal income tax purposes, is an individual and is a citizen or a resident of the United States or is treated as a corporation and is created or organized in or under the laws of the United States or any State thereof (including the District of Columbia), 'non-US investor' generally refers to an investor that, for US federal income tax purposes, is a nonresident alien individual or a corporation that is not created or organized in or under the laws of the United States or any State thereof (including the District of Columbia), and 'Foreign Corporation' refers to a corporation that, for US federal income tax purposes is not created or organized under the laws of the United States or any state thereof (including the District of Columbia).

[3] This chapter does not address all of the US federal income tax considerations that may be relevant to an investor, or special considerations and treatment that may be relevant to particular investors. Any person that seeks to enter into an insurance-linked instrument or invest in a catastrophe bond issuer should seek advice from a tax advisor based on the particular circumstances.

The Handbook of Insurance-Linked Securities   Edited by P. Barrieu and L. Albertini
Chapter 25 © 2009 Shlomo Boehm and David Miller

bonds issued by the issuer.[4] In return, under the insurance-linked instrument, the issuer agrees to make a payment to the protection buyer upon the occurrence of a specified geologic or meteorological event (e.g., a hurricane, windstorm, or earthquake).[5] The amount payable is typically calculated based on a predetermined formula. If the event occurs and the issuer makes a payment, the principal amount payable on the catastrophe bonds is reduced by an equal amount.

The issuer generally invests the proceeds from issuing the catastrophe bonds in highly rated securities that serve to collateralize its potential obligation under the insurance-linked instrument. These securities are often referred to as 'directed investments' or 'permitted investments.' In addition, the issuer will often enter into a 'total return swap' under which the issuer pays to the total return swap counterparty all amounts it receives on the directed investments plus, at maturity, any appreciation with respect to the directed investments. In return, the total return swap counterparty pays to the issuer a periodic payment equal to a fixed or floating rate times a notional amount that is equal to the principal amount of the notes plus, at maturity, any depreciation with respect to the directed investments. The economic effect to the issuer of purchasing the directed investments and entering into the total return swap is the same as if the issuer bought a note issued by the swap counterparty that bore interest at the fixed or floating rate, and which was secured by the directed investments (which, in turn, would be treated as owned by the swap counterparty).

The total coupon paid on the catastrophe bonds is equal to the periodic payments received by the issuer under the insurance-linked instrument and the total return swap, less the issuer's administrative costs (which are generally not significant).

Section 25.1 of this chapter discusses steps that issuers take to ensure that they are not treated as engaged in a trade or business in the United States for federal income tax purposes. If an issuer is treated as engaged in a trade or business in the United States, it is potentially subject to US corporate income tax. Section 25.2 of this chapter discusses US withholding tax and excise tax issues associated with the payments made by the protection buyer to the issuer under the insurance-linked instrument. Finally, Section 25.3 of this chapter discusses the federal income tax considerations and consequences for an investor that purchases a catastrophe bond.

25.1 AVOIDING US CORPORATE INCOME TAX FOR THE ISSUER

25.1.1 Overview

A foreign corporation that is treated as being 'engaged in a trade or business' in the United States for federal income tax purposes is required to file US tax returns and is subject to a US corporate income tax (currently at a maximum marginal rate of 35%) on its income that is 'effectively connected' to the US trade or business,[6] possibly state taxes, and possibly a 30%

---

[4] The 'notional amount' is a fixed dollar amount (e.g., $100 million) and is the maximum amount that the issuer may have to pay the protection buyer under the insurance-linked instrument. The notional amount is generally equal to the principal amount of the notes.

[5] For example, very generally, an insurance-linked instrument might provide that if a hurricane occurs in Florida and the amount of industry-wide losses in Florida exceeds $1 billion, then the issuer must pay the protection buyer the notional amount of the insurance-linked instrument.

[6] Section 882 (a foreign corporation that is 'engaged in trade or business within the United States' is subject to federal income tax on its income effectively connected with the conduct of that trade or business). Unless otherwise indicated,

branch profits tax on its after-tax income.[7] A catastrophe bond issuer will typically avoid US federal income tax by scrupulously ensuring that it and any person who could be viewed as its agent does not engage in any substantive activity within the United States.[8] In rare instances, the activities of catastrophe bond issuers may qualify for protection from the corporate income tax under a 'safe harbor' contained in section 864(b)(2) (generally referred to as the 'section 864(b)(2) safe harbor'). Section 864(b)(2) generally provides that a foreign corporation that limits its activities to merely trading in stocks or securities or entering into derivatives is not treated as being engaged in a US trade or business. If a catastrophe bond issuer qualifies for the section 864(b)(2) safe harbor, its activities and the activities of its agents could be conducted in the United States. However, the section 864(b)(2) safe harbor is not available for an issuer that enters into a contract that is treated as insurance for federal income tax purposes. The balance of this section describes when a foreign corporation is treated as being engaged in a trade or business in the United States, and the section 864(b)(2) safe harbor.

25.1.2   Trade or business in the United States

The nature and extent of a foreign corporation's activities within the United States determine whether it is engaged in a US trade or business.[9] In general, a foreign corporation must be engaged in regular and continuous business activities in the United States to be treated as being engaged in a US trade or business,[10] and preparatory and ministerial activities are disregarded.[11]

---

references in this chapter to section numbers, are to sections of the Internal Revenue Code of 1986, as amended, and to the Treasury regulations promulgated or proposed thereunder. In general, if an issuer is treated as engaged in a trade or business in the United States, its US source income (and, for insurance companies, also certain foreign source income) is treated as effectively connected to its US trade or business if that income satisfies either the 'asset-use' test or 'business activity' test. In general, the asset-use test is satisfied if the income, gain or loss is derived from assets used in, or held for use in, the conduct of the US trade or business. The business activity test is satisfied if the management of the investments in the United States constitutes the principal activity of the issuer. Because the sole activity of the issuer is the maintenance of the directed investments and entering into the total return swap and insurance-linked instrument, if these activities are conducted from within the United States, it is likely that all of the issuer's income would satisfy the asset-use and business activity tests, and would be treated as effectively connected to its trade or business in the United States.

[7] Section 884 (imposing a 30% tax on all or a portion of the earnings and profits of a foreign corporation that are effectively connected to a trade or business in the United States).

[8] The activities of an agent are generally attributed to its principal for purposes of determining whether the principal is engaged in a trade or business in the United States. *See, for example, Adda v. Commissioner*, 10 T.C. 27d (1948), *aff'd* 171 F.2d 457 (4th Cir. 1949) (taxpayer was engaged in a US trade or business because of the activities of its agent.)

[9] *See* Revenue Ruling 88-3, 1988-1 C.B. 268 (the determination whether a taxpayer is engaged in a trade or business within the United States is highly factual).

[10] *See, for example, De Vegvar v. Commissioner*, 28 T.C. 1055 (1957) (taxpayer's trading activities too sporadic to be considered to give rise to conduct of US trade or business); *compare de Amodio v. Commissioner*, 34 T.C. 894 (1960), *aff'd without deciding this issue*, 299 F.2d 623 (3rd Cir. 1962) (foreign owner of US real estate was engaged in US trade or business by virtue of activities of local real estate agents performing considerable, continuous and regular activity on its behalf); *Jorge Pasquel*, Tax Court Memorandum 54002 (December 23, 1953) (foreign investor's participation in a single transaction in the United States was insufficient to qualify as a trade or business within the United States); *Linen Thread Co.*, 14 T.C. 725 (1950) (two isolated transactions were insufficient to qualify as a trade or business within the United States).

[11] *See Aktiebolaget Separator v. Hoey*, 40 AFTR 1346 (S.D.N.Y. 1949) (space rented by foreign corporation merely for receipt of dividend income from domestic corporations was not conduct of US trade or business); *Scottish American*

However, a single event or a limited number of events have been held to give rise to a trade or business. For example, a boxer's participation in three fights over two years within the United States was held to be sufficient activity in the United States to be engaged in a trade or business in the United States.[12] And the Internal Revenue Service (IRS) has held that the entry of a race horse in a single race or a boxer participating in a single match is sufficient to subject the horse owner or the boxer to US income tax.[13] Therefore, it is possible that the IRS could successfully argue that a catastrophe bond issuer that conducts substantive activities in the United States is engaged in a US trade or business. Because airplane tickets are relatively inexpensive and a US corporate tax potentially devastating, catastrophe bond issuers typically assume that the limited nature of their activities could be sufficient to cause them to be engaged in a trade or business, and therefore take strict measures to ensure that neither they nor any person that could be treated as their agent conducts any activity on behalf of the issuer while physically located within the United States.

23.1.3 Procedures followed by catastrophe bond issuers to avoid substantive business activities in the United States

A catastrophe bond issuer will typically require that all people who work on its behalf be physically outside the United States whenever they engage in substantive discussions or negotiations on behalf of it. In addition, all people who execute any document on behalf of the issuer are required to be physically outside the United States when they sign. And,

---

Investment Co. v. Commissioner, 12 T.C. 49 (1949) (quantitative and qualitative analysis of the activities performed by or on behalf of the taxpayer is required to determine presence of US trade or business, and while volume of activity is to be considered, the nature of the activities are determinative); *Spermacet Whaling & Shipping Co.v. Commissioner*, 30 T.C. 618 (1958), *aff'd*, 281 F.2d 646 (6th Cir. 1960) (activities that were ministerial and clerical in nature, involving very little exercise of discretion and business judgment did not cause the taxpayer to be treated as engaged in a trade or business in the United States); *Linen Thread Co.*, 14 T.C. 725, 737 (1950) (activities performed by the corporation's New York office were merely clerical). Preparatory activities generally do not give rise to a trade or business. *See Abegg v. Commissioner*, 50 T.C. 145 (1968), *aff'd*, 429 F.2d 1209 (2d Cir. 1970), *cert. denied*, 400 US 1008 (1971) (efforts on behalf of foreign corporation in investigating eleven going concerns, with a view towards a purchase of a stock interest in one or more, did not constitute conduct of US trade or business). The standards applied to determine whether there exists a US trade or business are similar to those applied to determine the deductibility of expenses of domestic corporations at the outset of business activity. *See Abegg v. Commissioner*, 50 T.C. 145 (1968), *aff'd*, 429 F.2d 1209 (2d Cir. 1970), *cert. denied*, 400 US 1008 (1971) (citing cases dealing with deduction of ordinary and necessary business expenses in support of proposition that mere preparatory activities on behalf of taxpayer does not constitute engaging in a US trade or business). Thus, expenses incurred in preparation to pursue an intended business activity, including legal fees, licensing fees, engineering fees, and expenses in soliciting potential clients and raising capital, are not treated as conducted of a trade or business and are not generally deductible. *See Radio Station WBIR v. Commissioner*, 31 T.C. 803 (1959) (expenses incurred by taxpayer seeking to operate radio station were not deductible to extent incurred prior to the grant of broadcasting permit and actual broadcasting); *Polachek v. Commissioner*, 22 T.C. 858 (1954) (expenses incurred by taxpayer to attract capital and associates in planning investment advisory services business not deductible prior to actual conduct of such business). No authority of which we are aware suggests that the mere raising of capital in the United States should be treated as causing a foreign corporation to be treated as being engaged in a US trade or business.

[12] *See, for example, Johansson v. United States*, 336 F.2d 809 (5th Cir. 1964) (participation in three prize fights over a period of two years held to be a US trade or business).

[13] Revenue Ruling 58-63, 1958-1 C.B. 624, *amplified in* Revenue Ruling 60-249, 1960-2 C.B. 264 (entry of a race horse in a single race in the United States found to be a US trade or business); Revenue Ruling 70-543, 1970-2 C.B. 172 (foreign boxer participating in a single boxing match and foreign race horse owner entering its horse in a single race treated as a US trade or business).

finally, all corporate functions are required to be performed by people physically outside the United States.

Typically, the first step in a catastrophe bond offering is a kick-off meeting outside of the United States. Generally, representatives of all parties will attend in person abroad although, as mentioned below, representatives of the protection buyer and total return swap counterparty could remain in the United States and participate by telephone. During this meeting, the material terms of the offering, the insurance-linked instrument and the total return swap are discussed, and attempts are made to resolve substantive points.

Subsequently, counsel for the issuer who is physically present in the United States may reflect the substantive agreements in legal documents, because the act of a scrivener is regarded as ministerial. Counsel for the issuer is also permitted to advise the issuer from within the United States because talking to yourself (which is how talking to your agent is treated for US tax purposes) is not considered substantive activity. The issuer's counsel may also have nonsubstantive conversations with counsel for the other parties (e.g., to arrange scheduling or document distributions, or communicate similar ministerial items) while within the United States. However, if a substantive item arises after the initial offshore meeting, a subsequent meeting is generally arranged outside of the United States to discuss and resolve the new item.

Issuers allow underwriters to conduct roadshows in the United States to market the notes because raising capital is not regarded as a business activity. Similarly, issuers often permit calculation agents physically present in the United States to apply factual data (e.g., wind speed and geographical location of a hurricane) in order to determine whether a specified event occurred and the amount of the required payment under the insurance-linked instrument, because this work is also regarded as ministerial.

Although the underwriter may properly be viewed as representing only itself when it negotiates the terms of the notes, because these efforts benefit the issuer and are not adverse to it, the underwriter is typically required to travel outside of the United States to engage in negotiations and other substantive activity. On the other hand, the protection buyer and total return swap counterparty are adverse to the issuer. These parties seek to minimize the payments they make to the issuer and to maximize the likelihood that it will receive a payment. Therefore, protection buyers and total return swap counterparties are not treated as agents of the issuer and may therefore remain in the United States when they negotiate with the issuer, or the underwriter on the issuer's behalf.

Although some issuers treat the directed investments as belonging to the total return swap counterparty for tax purposes,[14] because this treatment is uncertain, many issuers require that the total return swap counterparty either manage the directed investments only from outside the United States, or that management of the directed investments be automated (e.g., there is a predetermined pool of directed investments and a formula to choose between the various directed investments).

Finally, all corporate functions and communications by the issuer are required to be performed outside the United States.[15]

---

[14] This topic is discussed in Section 25.3.

[15] For example, catastrophe bond issuers typically ensure that the corporate functions contained in Treasury regulations section 1.864-2(c)(2)(iii) are conducted outside the United States. Although these regulations are no longer effective, they provided the rules for determining whether an entity's principal office was treated as within the United States. They prohibit the following functions from occurring within the United States: (a) communicating with the issuer's equityholders (including the furnishing of financial reports); (b) communicating with the general public; (c) soliciting sales of the issuer's equity; (d) accepting the subscriptions of new equityholders; (e) maintaining the issuer's principal

25.1.4   Section 864(b)(2) safe harbor

Section 864(b)(2)(A)(ii) provides a safe harbor under which a foreign entity is not treated as being engaged in a trade or business in the United States, even if a representative or agent of the foreign entity conducts activity for the foreign entity while physically located within the United States, so long as the business of the foreign entity is limited to trading in 'stocks' or 'securities' or, under certain proposed regulations, entering into derivatives for its own account.[16] However, the section 864(b)(2) safe harbor is not available for an issuer that enters into a contract that is treated as insurance for federal income tax purposes. So, if an issuer enters into a reinsurance or retrocession agreement, the section 864(b)(2) safe harbor is not available (because these instruments are typically treated as insurance for federal income tax purposes). However, if an issuer enters into a swap that is treated as a derivative (or 'notional principal contract') for federal income tax purposes, the safe harbor may be available. As discussed in Section 25.2, the distinction between a derivative and insurance is often unclear.

25.2   WITHHOLDING TAX AND EXCISE TAX

25.2.1   Overview

Foreign persons that are not engaged in a trade or business in the United States (such as catastrophe bond issuers) are subject to a 30% withholding tax on certain US source 'fixed or determinable annual or periodical' (FDAP) income.[17] However, the withholding tax generally does not apply to (i) insurance premiums that are subject to a US excise tax,[18] (ii) foreign-source income,[19] or (iii) US-source income that is not FDAP.[20]

If an insurance-linked instrument is treated as insurance or reinsurance for federal income tax purposes, the periodic payments paid by the protection buyer to the issuer are subject to a 1% or 4% excise tax (described below), but not to withholding tax.[21]

---

corporate records and books of account; (f) auditing the issuer's books of account; (g) disbursing payments of dividends, principal, interest, legal fees, accounting fees, and officers' and directors' salaries; (h) publishing or furnishing the offering and redemption price of the equity issued by the issuer; (i) conducting meetings of the issuer's equityholders and board of directors; and (j) making redemptions of the issuer's equity.

[16] Proposed Treasury regulations section 1.864(b)-1. See also the preamble to the proposed regulations in Federal Register Volume 63, Number 113, page 32164 (June 12, 1998) ('For periods prior to the effective date, taxpayers engaged in derivative transactions may take any reasonable position with regard to the section 864(b)(2)(A)(ii) and (B)(ii) safe harbors. Positions consistent with these proposed regulations will be considered reasonable.').

[17] *See* section 1441 (providing that the section 881 gross basis tax is to be enforced through withholding at the income's source); section 1442 (applying the withholding rules of section 1441 to foreign corporations). In general, FDAP is defined to include all gross income other than gain derived from the sale of property (including option premium). *See* Treasury regulations section 1.1441-2(b) (defining FDAP); Treasury regulations section 1.1441-2(b)(2)(i) (gains derived from the sale of property (including option premium) are not FDAP).

[18] Treasury regulations section 1.1441-2(a)(7) ('Amounts subject to withholding do not include ... [i]nsurance premiums paid with respect to a contract that is subject to the section 4371 excise tax.').

[19] Section 881(a) (imposing US tax on foreign corporations that are not engaged in a trade or business in the United States only on US source income); Treasury regulations section 1.1441-2(a) (withholding generally applies only to US source income).

[20] Section 881(a) (imposing US tax on foreign corporations that are not engaged in a trade or business in the United States only on FDAP or other similar income); Treasury regulations section 1.1441-2(a) (withholding applies only to FDAP income).

[21] Treasury regulations section 1.1441-2(a)(7) ('Amounts subject to withholding do not include ... [i]nsurance premiums paid with respect to a contract that is subject to the section 4371 excise tax.').

If an insurance-linked instrument is treated as an option or a 'notional principal contract' for federal income tax purposes, the periodic payments made by a US protection buyer to a catastrophe bond issuer are treated as foreign source income and, in the case of a put option, non-FDAP income, which are not subject to federal withholding tax (or excise tax).[22] However, if an insurance-linked instrument does not qualify as a notional principal contract or insurance, the analysis becomes more difficult and, if the protection buyer is a US entity (or a non-US entity engaged in a trade or business in the United States), the payments made by the protection buyer could be subject to a 30% withholding tax.

Insurance

In general, premiums paid to a non-US person that is not engaged in a trade or business in the United States with respect to reinsurance policies written to protect a US person (or a non-US person engaged in a trade or business in the United States) against property and casualty hazards, risks, losses, or liabilities within the United States are subject to a 1% excise tax (or 4% in the case of insurance that is not reinsurance).[23]

There is no statutory or regulatory definition of insurance for federal income tax purposes. However, in *Helvering v. Le Gierse*,[24] the Supreme Court identified four relevant factors to determine whether a contract is insurance: (i) the form and regulatory treatment of the contract,[25] (ii) the existence of 'insurance risk',[26] (iii) the transfer or shift of that risk,[27] and (iv) the pooling and distribution of the insurance risk by the party assuming it.[28] Reinsurance and retrocession agreements are generally in the form of insurance and are treated as insurance for regulatory purposes. In addition, reinsurance and retrocession agreements directly reference insurance risks borne by the ceding insurance company, so that there appears to be the existence of insurance risk, the transfer or shift of that risk (from the underlying insureds to

---

[22] *See* Treasury regulations section 1.863-7(b) (the source of notional principal contract income is determined by reference to the residence of the recipient as determined under section 988); section 881(a) (imposing withholding tax only on a foreign corporation's US-source income); Treasury regulations section 1.1441-2(b)(2)(i) (option premium is not FDAP); Treasury regulations section 1.1441-2(a) (withholding applies only to FDAP income); section 865(a)(2) (income from the sale of personal property by a nonresident is foreign-source income); section 865(g) (defining nonresident to include a corporation organized under the laws of a country other than the United States); Treasury regulations section 1.1441-2(a) (withholding generally applies only to US source income).

[23] Section 4371 (imposing a 1% or 4% tax on premium paid on certain policies of casualty insurance and reinsurance issued to an insured or reinsured, as defined in section 4372(d); section 4372(d) (defining 'insured' to include 'a domestic corporation or partnership, or an individual resident of the United States, against, or with respect to, hazards, risks, losses, or liabilities wholly or partly within the United States').

[24] 312 US 531 (1941).

[25] *Id.* at 540 ('Congress used the word "insurance" in its commonly accepted sense.').

[26] *Id.* at 539 ('We think the fair import of subsection (g) is that the amounts must be received as a result of a transaction which involved an actual "insurance risk" at the time the transaction was executed.').

[27] *Id.* at 539-40 ('That these elements of risk-shifting and risk-distributing are essential to a life insurance contract is agreed by courts and commentators... Accordingly, it is logical to assume that when Congress used the words "receivable as insurance" in section 302(g), it contemplated amounts received pursuant to a transaction possessing these features.').

[28] *Id.* at 539-40 (same). *See, for example, Sears, Roebuck & Co. v. Commissioner*, 96 T.C. 61, 100-02 (1991, *aff'd*, 972 F.2d 858 (7th Cir. 1992) (listing insurance risk, risk shifting, risk distribution, and the presence of forms commonly accepted as insurance in the trade, as the hallmarks of insurance); *AMERCO, Inc. v. Commissioner*, 96 T.C. 18, 38 (1991), *aff'd*, 979 F.2d 162 (9th Cir. 1992) (reciting the elements of insurance derived from *Le Gierse*).

the insurance company to the issuer), and the pooling and distribution of that insurance risk.[29] So, reinsurance and retrocession agreements appear to satisfy all four *Le Gierse* insurance criteria, and the periodic payments paid by the protection buyer to the issuer would constitute premiums that are subject to the 1% excise tax, but not to a 30% withholding tax.

Derivative instruments

As discussed above, an insurance-linked instrument that is written as a reinsurance or retrocession agreement is typically treated as insurance for federal income tax purposes. However, insurance-linked instruments written on standard ISDA forms generally fail to satisfy a number of the insurance criteria established by the *Le Gierse* case.

More specifically, these instruments are not in the form of insurance or regulated as insurance, do not appear to involve insurance risk (because they are not linked to actual losses of the protection buyer) and do not involve the transfer of insurance risk.[30] The balance of this section assumes that insurance-linked instruments written on standard ISDA forms are not treated as insurance for federal income tax purposes.[31]

25.2.2 Descriptions of insurance-linked instruments written on standard ISDA forms

In general, there are three common insurance-linked instruments that are written in swap form: index contracts, modeled loss contracts, and parametric loss contracts. (For further information, please refer to Chapter 4.)

Very generally, under an index contract, upon the occurrence of a specified event (e.g., a hurricane in Florida), the issuer is required to pay the protection buyer an amount equal to the

[29] In Revenue Ruling 2005-40, 2005-2 C.B. 4 (17 June, 2005), the IRS held that a purported insurance arrangement in which the insurer was exposed only to the risks of a single insured (possibly analogous to the issuer reinsuring a single protection buyer) did not constitute insurance for US federal income tax purposes, because the activities lacked adequate 'risk distribution.' However, the revenue ruling did not address risk distribution in the context of reinsurance or retrocession insurance. Many issuers believe that the revenue ruling is not intended for reinsurance or retrocession insurance that reflects adequate risk distribution of the underlying risks. In support of this position, some issuers point to *Alinco Life Ins. Co. v. United States*, 373 F.2d 336 (Ct. Cl. 1967), in which the court held that a taxpayer was an insurance company even though the taxpayer reinsured the interests of only a single party. However, if reinsurance and retrocession agreements are not insurance for federal income tax purposes, they are also unlikely to qualify as notional principal contracts (for the reasons discussed below). If so, the avenues to eliminate a 30% withholding tax are limited to the put option and Bank of America analyses discussed below.
[30] *See Allied Fidelity Corp. v. Commissioner*, 66 T.C. 1068, 1074 (1976) ('an insurance contract is an agreement to protect the insured . . . against a direct or indirect economic loss arising from a defined contingency'), *aff'd*, 572 F.2d 1190 (7th Cir. 1978); *Home Title Insurance Co. v. United States*, 50 F.2d 107, 109 (2d Cir. 1931) (in order for a contract to be a contract of insurance, 'the insured must have some interest at risk'). We note that these instruments are generally designed to correlate to a protection buyer's actual losses, and the actual losses suffered by underlying insureds of the protection buyer. Moreover, the case law does not require an actual correspondence between the loss and payment under the insurance contract, and an insured may collect from an insurer more than the actual loss. *See Home Title Insurance Co. v. United States*, 50 F.2d at 109 (providing that a contract can qualify as insurance for federal income tax purposes even if it allows the insured to collect more than its actual loss).
[31] Section 4372 provides that the form of an instrument is not relevant to its characterization for purposes of imposing the excise tax. Therefore, if an instrument fails to qualify as insurance strictly because of its form, an excise tax may still be imposed. In this case, as discussed earlier in this section, US withholding tax does not apply to the periodic payments under the instrument.

lesser of the principal amount of the notes and an amount based on a percentage of all insured industry property losses within a specified area that occur upon the occurrence of the event, as determined by an independent company that tracks losses caused by natural events using objective criteria to assess the loss amounts, and is widely available and used by a substantial number of clients (such as Property Claim Services – 'PCS' – for the US insurance industry). More specifically, an index contract might provide that if a hurricane has occurred in Florida, the issuer is required to pay an amount (capped at the principal amount of the notes) that is equal to a specified percentage of the amount of industry-wide losses in Florida in excess of $1 billion, as determined by PCS, multiplied by specific personal, commercial, automobile or other line factors.[32]

Very generally, under a modeled loss contract, the protection buyer provides an independent catastrophe risk assessment company (such as EQECAT, Inc.) with a 'notional portfolio' (e.g., insured residential property in Florida). The risk assessment company then establishes a model that simulates the potential relevant event, for example, a hurricane in Florida, in thousands of specific locations within the larger specified geographical area, and simulates the key meteorological characteristics, such as the wind speed, radii of maximum winds, rate of hurricane movement and the storm track for each simulated storm, which together determine the damage that would generally result from the hurricane, and estimates the expected loss that would be suffered on the notional portfolio if the event were to occur. Upon the occurrence of the event specified in the contract (e.g., a hurricane in Florida), the issuer is required to pay an amount equal to the lesser of the principal amount of the notes and the losses that the model projected for such event based upon physical characteristics of the hurricane (e.g., latitude, longitude and wind speed) input into the computer model by an independent calculation agent.

Under a parametric loss contract, upon the occurrence of the specified event, the amount that the issuer is required to pay the protection buyer is the lesser of the principal amount of the notes and an amount based on the physical characteristics of the specified event using certain predetermined criteria. For example, very generally, a $125 million parametric loss contract relating to Florida hurricanes may provide that if a hurricane with wind speeds in excess of 150 miles per hour occurs in a given latitude and longitude, the issuer will pay $100 million to the protection buyer, and if the wind speeds exceed 160 miles per hour, the issuer will pay $125 million.

25.2.3 Federal income tax definition of notional principal contracts

A notional principal contract is generally defined for federal income tax purposes as (i) a financial instrument (ii) that provides for the payment of amounts by one party to another at specified intervals (iii) calculated by reference to a 'specified index' upon a 'notional principal amount' (iv) in exchange for (a) specified consideration or (b) a promise to pay 'similar amounts.'[33]

The Treasury regulations define a 'specified index' to include a 'fixed rate' or an index that is based on 'any current, objectively determinable financial or economic information that is not within the control of any of the parties to the contract and is not unique to one of the

---

[32] For example, if the personal loss factor for Florida is 0.7, the personal losses suffered in a Florida hurricane, as determined by PCS, would be multiplied by 0.7.

[33] Treasury regulations section 1.446-3(c)(1) (defining notional principal contract).

parties' circumstances (such as one party's dividends, profits or the value of its stock).'[34] The regulations refer to this type of information as 'objective economic information.' A 'notional principal amount' is defined in the regulations as a 'specified amount of money or property that, when multiplied by a specified index, measures a party's rights and obligations under the contract, but is not borrowed or loaned between the parties as part of the contract.'[35]

Insurance-linked instruments that are documented on ISDA forms and do not constitute insurance are clearly 'financial instruments.'[36] They also provide for the payment of amounts by one party (the protection buyer) to another (the issuer) at specified intervals (at least annually and, generally, quarterly), and these payments are calculated by reference to a floating or fixed rate (i.e., a 'specified index') times a notional principal amount. So, the first three criteria of a notional principal contract are satisfied, and if the potential obligation of the issuer to make a payment to the protection buyer if the specified catastrophic event occurs qualifies as 'specified consideration' or a 'promise to pay a similar amount,' the fourth condition is satisfied as well.

If the term 'specified consideration' includes any conditional obligation to make a payment under a contract, an insurance-linked instrument satisfies this condition. However, it is possible that the term 'specified consideration' in the definition of a notional principal contract could be limited to specified consideration that is based upon objective economic information.[37] If so,

---

[34] Treasury regulations sections 1.446-3(c)(2) and 1.446-3(c)(4)(ii). Often an insurance-linked instrument is designed to hedge the protection buyer's risk under the insurance or reinsurance contracts that it writes. However, because the insurance-linked instrument does not reflect the profits or losses of any protection buyer, the determination that the issuer is required to pay the designated amount will be objectively determined without any reference to the buyer, the insurance or reinsurance it has written, or its actual losses, and the insurance-linked instrument references geological or meteorological events (i.e., events that are not within the control of any person), the insurance-linked instruments do not appear to be 'unique' to any person. This position is bolstered by the fact that there is generally expected to be significant 'basis risk' or difference between any protection buyer's losses and the amount of the issuer's payment.

[35] Treasury regulations section 1.446-3(c)(3). Because no payments are guaranteed under an insurance-linked instrument, the notional principal amount of the insurance-linked instrument should not represent an amount borrowed or loaned. *See, for example, Gilbert v. Commissioner*, 248 F.2d 399, 402 (2d Cir. 1957) ('The classic debt is an unqualified obligation to pay a sum certain at a reasonably close fixed maturity date along with a fixed percentage of interest payable regardless of the debtor's income or lack thereof.'). Regulations section 1.446-3(c)(3) also excludes from the definition of notional principal contract a futures contract, a forward contract, a section 1256 contract and an option. Insurance-linked instruments generally do not fit within any of these categories, with the possible exception of an option, discussed below.

[36] *Cf.*, section 954(c)(2)(C) ('forward contracts, option contracts or similar financial instruments (including notional principal contracts and all instruments referenced to commodities)'); section 988(c)(1)(B)(iii) ('forward contract, futures contract, option or similar financial instrument'); Treasury regulations section 1.263(a)-4(c)(1)(iii) (using the term 'financial instrument' to include notional principal contracts, foreign currency contracts, futures contracts, forward contracts, options and any other financial derivative).

[37] The natural reading of the phrase 'specified consideration' in the definition of a notional principal contract is broader than merely a fixed amount of money or property. However, if 'specified consideration' were to include *any* consideration, then, arguably, as long as one leg of a contract provided for fixed or floating payments at specified intervals based upon a notional principal amount, payments on the other leg of the contract would always be treated as 'specified consideration' and the contract would generally qualify as a notional principal contract. Under this reading, a notional principal contract could provide that one party pays a fixed rate times a notional amount and the other party pays amounts equal to its dividends, profits or the value of its stock (i.e., as 'specified consideration'). However, the definition of a specified index specifically excludes payments based on a party's dividends, profits or the value of its stock, which implies that the drafters intended to exclude from the definition of 'notional principal

the payments on some insurance-linked instruments will satisfy this definition of a 'specified consideration' but others will not.

For example, the payments by an issuer to a protection buyer under an index contract appear to qualify as 'specified consideration' based on 'objective financial information' because they are based on current objectively determinable economic or financial information – the dollar amount of losses suffered by insureds in each specified jurisdiction multiplied by the applicable factors – and this financial information is not within the control of any of the parties to the contract or unique to one of the party's circumstances. So, index contracts appear to satisfy all four criteria for notional principal contracts.

However, payments by an issuer under a parametric contract or a modeled loss contract based solely upon the occurrence of a natural event may not qualify as being based on 'economic' or 'financial' information.[38] Nevertheless, there are significant arguments why modeled loss contracts and parametric loss contracts should qualify as notional principal contracts. First, as discussed above, the fourth notional principal contract criterion is satisfied if the issuer pays 'specified consideration' or 'similar' payments. Even if payments on a modeled loss contract and parametric loss contract do not directly reference economic or financial information and are not 'specified consideration,' they are 'similar' to payments that do,[39] and are intended and designed to reflect actual economic and financial losses suffered by insureds within the particular geographic area.[40]

Second, it appears that the 'specified index' in the notional principal contract definition is defined by reference to 'financial or economic information' in order to distinguish notional principal contracts from mere wagers.[41] Since the insurance-linked instruments have a direct economic impact on the protection buyer, are entered into for non-tax reasons (i.e., to hedge the protection buyer's business and economic risk) and do not reference a sporting event, game of chance or similar subject of a wager, it appears consistent with the purpose and intent of the regulations to treat the payments made by an issuer under them as based on objective financial information and therefore as satisfying the fourth condition of a notional principal contract.

---

contracts' contracts whose payments reference the dividends, profits or the value of a party's stock. If so, 'specified consideration' must have been intended to have a narrow scope. In addition, the definition of a notional principal contract is widely viewed as excluding wagers. However, if one leg of a contract provided for fixed rate payments based upon a notional principal amount, the other leg of the contract could technically reference the winner of a sporting event.

[38] From a tax policy standpoint, there is no evident reason to disqualify weather-based derivatives from notional principal contract treatment simply because payments are not based upon 'financial' or 'economic' information.

[39] For example, a notional principal contract may provide that one party is required to make periodic payments equal to a LIBOR-based or fixed rate times a notional principal amount and the other party is required to make specified payments (not to exceed the aggregate principal amount of the contract) if the S&P 500 closes at or below a specified level. This contract would satisfy the definition of a 'notional principal contract.' The payments by the issuer are similar to the S&P 500 payments in this example. If the level of the S&P 500 is set low enough, the economic profile of the contract would resemble that of the modeled loss contracts and the parametric loss contracts in the sense that one party makes periodic payments and in a very unusual circumstance may receive a payment back.

[40] The payments by the issuer do not refer to actual losses, because determining actual losses could take months, if not years, after a particular event, whereas modeled or parametric losses are determinable immediately after the conclusion of the event.

[41] See, for example, Humphreys (1998) (definition of notional principal contract excludes wagers from notional principal contract treatment). Thus, an index based upon the number of wins of a specific baseball team clearly would fail to satisfy the definition of objective financial information.

Third, because a modeled loss contract and a parametric loss contract perform similarly to other contracts – such as the index contracts and equity swaps – that satisfy the definition of notional principal contracts,[42] it would be anomalous to treat them differently.[43]

25.2.4 Put options

Options are generally described as a contract to buy or sell property.[44] It is unclear whether insurance-linked instruments satisfy this definition. On the one hand, insurance-linked instruments that are documented on standard ISDA forms do not provide (directly or indirectly) for the right to buy or sell any property. On the other hand, these insurance-linked instruments economically resemble a cash-settled put option with respect to a reference index that is purchased by the protection buyer from the issuer and provides for periodic payments.[45] If the insurance-linked instruments that are documented on standard ISDA forms are treated as put options for federal income tax purposes, the periodic payments by the protection buyer would likely be treated as non-FDAP income and/or foreign source income, and in either case as exempt from US withholding tax.[46]

25.2.5 The *Bank of America* case (income not clearly described within any other generally recognized category)

In general, if insurance-linked instruments are not treated as insurance, notional principal contracts or put options, then the periodic payment made under them would not be described within any other generally recognized category of income. If so, under the *Bank of America* case,[47] the source of the payments made by the protection buyer would be determined under the rules for analogous financial instruments.[48]

---

[42] As described above, because the index contracts are based on objective economic information, they satisfy the literal language of the definition of a notional principal contract.

[43] If the contracts were treated differently, taxpayers could create tax-advantaged offsetting positions. For example, a taxpayer could enter into a modeled loss contract or parametric loss contract under which it receives periodic payments, and an index contract based on identical risks under which it is required to make periodic payments. If the index contract is treated as a notional principal contract and the modeled loss contract or parametric loss contract is not, the taxpayer could claim deductions for the periodic payments it makes under the index contract (under Treasury regulations section 1.446-3(d)), but could presumably defer inclusions under the modeled loss contract or parametric loss contract under the 'open transaction doctrine' (also referred to as the 'wait-and-see' regime). *See Burnet v. Logan*, 283 US 404 (1931) (tax consequences of a transaction are deferred until the resolution of all contingencies associated with determining the actual amounts paid or received).

[44] *See* Revenue Ruling 78-182, 1978-1 C.B. 265 (describing an option as a contract under which the holder has the right, but not the obligation, for a specified period of time to buy or sell a specified amount of property at a fixed or determinable price).

[45] Although modeled loss and parametric contracts do not reference any actual property, and the relevant index, with respect to an index contract, is not itself property and does not represent direct interests in property, as does a stock index, all of these contracts are generally intended to correspond to a measure of damage to actual property.

[46] *See* Treasury regulations section 1.1441-2(b)(2)(i) (option premium is not FDAP); Treasury regulations section 1.1441-2(a) (withholding applies only to FDAP income); section 865(a)(2) (income from the sale of personal property by a nonresident is foreign-source income); section 865(g) (defining nonresident to include a corporation organized under the laws of a country other than the United States); Treasury regulations section 1.1441-2(a) (withholding generally applies only to US source income).

[47] *Bank of America v. United States*, 680 F.2d 142 (Ct. Cl .1982).

[48] In the *Bank of America* case, Bank of America received fees from various foreign banks for (i) committing to pay the face amount of letters of credit issued by foreign banks to US persons in certain circumstances where the foreign bank does not itself pay such face amount, (ii) actually extending its credit for the benefit of the foreign banks' letters

As discussed above, the insurance-linked instruments are most similar to notional principal contracts, insurance and options. If the best analogy for insurance-linked instruments is to notional principal contracts or put options then, under *Bank of America*, payments on the insurance-linked instruments would not be subject to US withholding tax because, as discussed above in this section, payments on notional principal contracts and options are not subject to withholding tax.

If the best analogy for insurance-linked instruments is to insurance, the analysis is slightly more complicated. Although underwriting income (including premium payments) derived from issuing or reinsuring insurance in connection with United States risk is generally US-source income,[49] Congress specifically excluded insurance premiums from withholding tax.[50] Nevertheless, because the current regulations specifically exclude insurance premiums from withholding tax only if they are subject to the excise tax,[51] it is possible that a court could analogize payments on insurance-linked instruments to insurance premiums, conclude that they are US-source income that is not subject to the excise tax and therefore subject them to US withholding tax. However, because Congress did not intend for insurance premiums to be subject to withholding tax, it appears inconsistent with the statute and Congressional intent to apply *Bank of America* in a manner that would cause payments that are analogous to insurance premiums to be subject to withholding tax.

25.3 US FEDERAL INCOME TAX TREATMENT OF AN INVESTOR IN A CATASTROPHE BOND ISSUER: OVERVIEW

25.3.1 US investors

Catastrophe bonds are almost always treated as equity interests in the issuer for federal income tax purposes because the bonds are generally subordinated to all other liabilities of the issuer

---

of credit and (iii) checking the terms of letters of credit to determine if the beneficiary thereof should receive payment. The court held that the fees received under (i) and (ii) were not interest, but should be 'sourced by analogy to interest' because Bank of America's role was similar to that of a lender, and the fees were, in essence, fees to compensate Bank of America 'for the use of [Bank of America's] credit.' The court held that the fees received under (iii) were to compensate Bank of America for checking 'to see whether the documents the beneficiary presents conform to the terms of the letter of credit,' and were thus best analogized to charges for personal services that are sourced where the services are performed (which, for Bank of America, was in the United States). *See also* Revenue Ruling 2004-75, 2004-2 C.B. 109 (same); and *Howkins v. Commissioner*, 49 T.C. 689 (1968) (determining the source of alimony payments through analogy to classes of income with specified statutory rules).

[49] Section 861(a)(7) (underwriting income derived from issuing or reinsuring insurance in connection with United States risk or in connection with an arrangement whereby another corporation received a substantially equal amount of premium in connection with issuing or reinsuring insurance in connection with United States risk is US source).

[50] *See* Revenue Ruling 80-222, 1980-2 C.B. 211 ('The legislative history of the stamp tax [which preceded the excise tax] . . . demonstrates that Congress did not believe that any income tax, including a withholding tax, was applicable to insurance premiums paid to foreign insurance companies not engaged in a trade or business in the United States.'), *modified and superseded by* Revenue Ruling 89-91, 1989-2 C.B. 129 and *obsoleted by* T.D. 8734, 1997-2 C.B. 109; General Counsel Memorandum 38052 (20 August, 1979) ('insurance premiums are not an appropriate item for taxation under [sections 871(a) and 881(a)]'); Message From the President of the United States (Exhibit VIII), Doc. No. 140, 87th Cong., 1st Sess. 289-290 (1961) ('a 30% withholding tax would destroy a normal and essential channel of the insurance business, which is important to the American economy where only a foreign company is equipped to handle the risk.'). Although the definition of FDAP includes 'premiums,' General Counsel Memorandum 38052 explains that the term was intended to refer to a payment for services.

[51] Treasury regulations section 1.1441-2(a)(7) ('Amounts subject to withholding do not include . . . [i]nsurance premiums paid with respect to a contract that is subject to the section 4371 excise tax.').

and there is no other 'true equity.'[52] In Section 25.3.4 below, we discuss when catastrophe bonds may be treated as indebtedness for federal income tax purposes and the consequences of that treatment. However, for now we assume that the catastrophe bonds are treated as equity interests in the issuer for federal income tax purposes. Although the discussion that follows is lengthy (because investors in catastrophe bonds are subject to complicated 'anti-deferral' taxing regimes, and because the tax treatment of the total return swap entered into by the issuer is unclear), the final conclusion for most US investors in catastrophe bonds is intuitive: they are taxable each year on an amount of ordinary income equal to the coupon they receive on their catastrophe bonds.

The CFC and PFIC anti-deferral regimes

The United States has two different 'anti-deferral' regimes that apply to US investors owning equity interests in a foreign corporation (such as US investors that own catastrophe bonds). The first anti-deferral regime comprises the 'controlled foreign corporation' (or CFC) rules, which generally apply only to US investors who own 10% or more of the voting stock of a CFC (these shareholders are referred to as 'United States shareholders'). In turn, a CFC is defined as a foreign corporation whose United States shareholders, in the aggregate, own more than 50% (or, for a foreign insurance company, 25%) of its value.[53] The CFC rules generally deem the United States shareholder to receive dividends equal to the passive 'subpart F income' (such as interest, dividends, notional principal contract income and insurance income) of the foreign corporation, even if that income is not actually distributed.[54] All of the income of a catastrophe bond issuer is generally subpart F income. Thus, if a catastrophe bond issuer qualifies as a CFC, US investors that own 10% or more of the principal amount of the catastrophe bonds generally report their allocable share of the catastrophe bond issuer's income. Deemed dividends from a CFC are treated as ordinary income.

The second anti-deferral regime applies to 'passive foreign investment companies' (or PFICs). Very generally, this regime applies if the passive income (such as interest, dividends, notional principal contract income and insurance income) of the foreign corporation exceeds 75% of the foreign corporation's total income, or 50% of the assets of the foreign corporation

---

[52] For local law reasons, the issuer is typically required to issue a nominal dollar amount of equity 'shares.' These shares are not entitled to any economic interest in the issuer (other than for the return of their principal amount) and have no meaningful voting or other rights. In fact, issuers generally donate the shares to a charitable organization organized in the jurisdiction of the issuer. Because the shares reflect no economic or other interest in the issuer, they are not viewed as equity for federal income tax purposes and are generally disregarded.

[53] Section 957 (defining 'controlled foreign corporation' and 'United States shareholder'). *See* sections 952(a) and 954(c) (defining subpart F income).

[54] *See* section 951 (providing for the general tax regime of a United States shareholder in a CFC). Subpart F also contains special 'related party insurance income' (or RPII) rules that deem all US holders (including those that own less than 10% of the voting stock) to report their share of RPII if the insurance-linked instrument is treated as insurance for federal income tax purposes, the CFC receives more than 20% of its insurance premiums from related persons and at least 20% of either the voting power or value of the notes are owned by persons that are directly or indirectly insured or reinsured by the issuer or that are related to such insureds or reinsureds. RPII is income (investment income and premium income) from the direct or indirect insurance or reinsurance of any United States person who holds equity of the issuer directly (or indirectly through foreign entities) or a person related to such United States person. It is somewhat unusual for the RPII rules to actually be satisfied. Moreover, as discussed in the text, there is little substantive difference between the federal income tax treatment of United States shareholders in a CFC and holders in a PFIC that have made a QEF election, in the context of a typical catastrophe bond.

produce passive income.[55] All of the assets of a catastrophe bond issuer are treated as passive assets for this purpose, and therefore catastrophe bond issuers are treated as PFICs. The PFIC regime applies to all US investors (and not only to 10% voting shareholders). If both the CFC and PFIC rules apply to a particular investor, the CFC rules trump.[56]

US investors in a PFIC typically make an election (known as a 'qualified electing fund' or 'QEF' election) to include all of the income of the PFIC in income annually (even if it is not distributed).[57] The QEF election is available only if the PFIC agrees to provide the relevant information to the US investors; virtually all catastrophe bond issuers agree to provide investors with the relevant information. If a QEF election is made, the US investors include in income as long-term capital gain any long-term capital gain of the issuer, and all other income of the issuer as ordinary income.[58]

Treatment of US investors

US investors in catastrophe bonds are generally subject to either the CFC or PFIC regimes but, fortunately for United States shareholders in CFCs and PFICs, for investors that make QEF elections, the rules are very similar and straightforward. In each case, US investors report their allocable share of the income of the catastrophe bond issuer in income currently. If a catastrophe bond issuer earns long-term capital gains, QEF PFIC holders may report their allocable share of long-term capital gains as such on their return,[59] while United States shareholders in a catastrophe bond issuer that is a CFC report their entire allocable share of the issuer's income as ordinary income.[60] When a catastrophe bond is redeemed at maturity, or the investor sells its bond prior to maturity, the investor is generally taxable on an amount of gain or loss equal to the difference between the amount received by the investor and the amount the investor paid for its notes.

Since United States shareholders in a CFC or other US investors in a PFIC that make a QEF election are taxable on their allocable share of the foreign corporation's income, it is necessary to discuss the federal income tax treatment of the insurance-linked instruments, total return swap and directed investments.

---

[55] Section 1297(a) (defining 'passive foreign investment companies'). Certain income derived in the 'active' conduct of an insurance company is not treated as passive for this purpose, but catastrophe bond issuers are rarely sufficiently active to qualify for this exception.

[56] Section 1297(d).

[57] *See* section 1293 (describing the tax regime of a QEF). Generally, a US investor makes a QEF election on an Internal Revenue Service Form 8621 and attaches a copy of such form to its US federal income tax return for the first taxable year for which it held the notes. US investors that fail to make a QEF election are subject to a penalty regime when they sell their shares in the PFIC or receive an 'excess distribution.' Under the penalty regime, all income is treated as ordinary income and is subject to additional tax in the nature of interest (at a very high rate). Most investors in a catastrophe bond issuer that is a PFIC make the QEF election in order to avoid the alternative penalty regime.

[58] *See* section 1293.

[59] *See* section 1293. Catastrophe bond issuers generally do not expect a meaningful amount (if any) of long-term capital gains.

[60] A US investor is not eligible for the dividends received deduction in respect of its income from the notes or to the preferential 15% rate allowed to individuals for dividends from US and certain foreign corporations. See section 243(a) (dividend receive deductions apply only to dividends of domestic corporations); section 245(a) (providing dividends received deductions for dividends of certain foreign corporations, but not for PFICs).

25.3.2 Timing and character of income and gain of the issuer with respect to the permitted investments, the total return swap and the insurance-linked instrument

Treatment of the total return swap and the directed investments

The federal income tax treatment of the total return swap and directed investments is not entirely clear. Economically, the total return swap represents a loan made by the issuer to the swap counterparty that pays interest at a rate equal to the fixed or floating rate on the total return swap, the proceeds of which are used by the swap counterparty to purchase the directed investments, which are, in turn, posted to the issuer as collateral for the loan. Moreover, in many cases, the swap counterparty manages the pool of directed investments and controls the voting rights of the directed investments. Many issuers treat the total return swap and directed investment exactly in this matter for federal income tax purposes. Often the issuer and the total return swap counterparty include an explicit statement in the swap documents agreeing to this treatment.[61]

If the total return swap qualifies as a loan to the swap counterparty for federal income tax purposes, the tax treatment is simple and intuitive – the 'interest' (i.e., the fixed or floating payments) is reported as it accrues. In this case, the accrual of income by the issuer under the directed investments and the total return swap will generally equal the portion of the total coupon amount that is derived from the directed investments and total return swaps.

However, if the total return swap is treated in accordance with its form as a swap, and the issuer is treated as owning the directed investments, the issuer's (and the catastrophe bond investors') treatment becomes much more complicated. First, the total return swap may likely be subject to certain proposed 'contingent swap' regulations, which may require the issuer to accrue income in excess of the periodic payment received from the swap counterparty.[62] If so, US investors will have to report this excess amount in income, even though it does not correspond to their economic income and is in excess of the portion of the coupon paid on the notes that is derived from the directed investments and total return swap.[63] Moreover, it is possible that this excess income inclusion may not be corrected until maturity or an earlier sale of the catastrophe bonds and, at this time, may be reflected as a capital loss. Capital losses unfortunately are not generally available to offset ordinary income.

Treatment of the insurance-linked instrument

The treatment of an insurance-linked instrument is also unclear. As discussed above in Section 25.3, the most likely characterizations for an insurance-linked instrument are either as a notional principal contract or as insurance. Under either characterization, the periodic payments made under the insurance-linked instrument would be recognized as ordinary income to the issuer at the time the payment is accrued. Because there is no accrual in excess of payments

---

[61] Consistent treatment by the parties helps to ensure that the IRS is not 'whipsawed' by parties claiming inconsistent treatment. *See Commissioner v. Danielson*, 378 F.2d 771 (3d Cir. 1967) (taxpayer cannot successfully challenge the form of its agreement absent a showing of mistake, undue influence, fraud, duress, etc.).

[62] *See* proposed Treasury regulations 1.446-3 (providing for the taxation of contingent swaps).

[63] However, to the extent that the issuer does not reasonably expect to receive any payment under the total return swap other than the fixed or floating payment, it is generally unlikely that the proposed contingent swap regulations will result in excess income.

actually received by the issuer (which are, in turn, paid out as coupon), no phantom income arises.[64]

25.3.3   Foreign investors

In general, payments on the catastrophe bonds are not subject to US withholding tax.[65] In addition, foreign investors are not subject to any US federal income tax as a result of owning their catastrophe bonds, so long as their income and gain on the catastrophe bonds are not effectively connected with a trade or business conducted by the investor in the United States.[66]

25.3.4   Notes that are treated as indebtedness for federal income tax purposes

If the catastrophe bonds are treated as indebtedness for federal income tax purposes,[67] the investor will not be subject to the CFC or PFIC rules. Instead, a US investor would include the coupon payments as ordinary income as it accrues or upon receipt, depending upon whether the investor is a cash method or accrual method taxpayer.[68] Upon the sale or redemption of the catastrophe bond, the US investor will generally recognize capital gain or loss equal to the difference between the amount received by the investor (other than amounts in respect of accrued and untaxed interest, which will be taxable as ordinary interest income) and the investor's purchase price.

REFERENCE

Humphreys, T. (1998) *Gambling on Uncertainty – The Federal Income Tax Treatment of Weather Swaps, Cat Options, and Some Other New Derivatives*, Tax Forum No. 528, 2 November.

---

[64] As mentioned above, it is possible that certain insurance-linked instruments may be treated as put options for federal income tax purposes. If so, the periodic payments would not be recognized by the issuer as income until the maturity of the insurance-linked instrument. If so, this characterization would not result in phantom income for investors, and may reduce the amount that investors would recognize in income for taxable years prior to the maturity of the insurance-linked instrument.

[65] Because the issuer is not a US person, the payments are not US source and not subject to US withholding tax. *See* sections 871 and 881 (imposing withholding tax only on US source income); section 862(a)(2) (dividends paid by a foreign corporation that is not engaged in a trade or business in the United States is treated as foreign source).

[66] *See* sections 871(b) and 882(a) (foreign investors subject to net income tax only on their income effectively connected to their trade or business in the United States). In addition, if a foreign individual is present in the United States for more than 182 days in the taxable year of the sale and has a tax home in the United States, the foreign individual may be subject to tax on any capital gain. *See* section 871(a)(2).

[67] Very generally, notes are more likely to qualify as debt for tax purposes if, for example, the notes have an investment-grade credit rating, are debt form (such as notes, rather than shares), are senior to a tranche that provides meaningful equity capitalization and the equity tranche is endowed with some meaningful equity-like rights that are not shared with the senior tranche. (It is beyond the scope of this chapter to cite and analyze the sources for these 'debt-for-tax' criteria.) The last criterion may be satisfied, for example, by providing the equity tranche with the right to purchase the debt tranche at par while a meaningful term to maturity remains.

[68] This paragraph discusses tax treatment that is relevant to a note that is purchased for its principal amount and that pays a coupon at least annually. Other rules apply to notes that are issued at a discount or premium.

26

Regulatory Issues and
Solvency Capital Requirements

Mark Nicolaides,[a] Simeon Rudin,[b] Rick Watson[c] and Katharina Hartwig[d]

This chapter outlines regulatory issues and solvency capital requirements in connection with the origination and investment in insurance-linked securities (ILS), and is structured as follows:

- Section 26.1 summarizes the general regulatory questions that are relevant for the sponsors of an ILS transaction.
- Section 26.2 summarizes current solvency requirements within the European Union (EU) and describes how ILS transactions are taken into account in determining an EU insurance or reinsurance undertaking's regulatory capital (including regarding the treatment of contingent loans and special purpose vehicles).
- Section 26.3 summarizes the solvency capital requirements under the draft Solvency II directive and the 'level 3' regulatory convergence proposals that have been made for the solvency treatment of alternative risk mitigation tools.

26.1 REGULATORY ISSUES RELEVANT FOR ILS SPONSORS

26.1.1 Solvency capital

If the sponsor of an ILS transaction is an insurer or reinsurer, it is subject to solvency capital requirements. Besides the impact of the transaction on internal risk capital, the sponsor will ideally also want to receive solvency credit (Figure 26.1) for the risk transfer, thereby reducing its solvency capital requirements. Because of the generally higher solvency ratio maintained by reinsurers, the solvency capital treatment will be of more relevance in transactions where the sponsor is a primary insurer.

Currently, some regulatory regimes allow an insurance or reinsurance undertaking to reduce its solvency capital requirement as a result of an ILS transaction based on an economic view on the risk transfer. Most regulatory regimes, however, in particular the current Solvency I

[a]Latham and Watkins
[b]Freshfields Bruckhaus Deringer LLP
[c]European Securitisation Forum
[d]Allianz

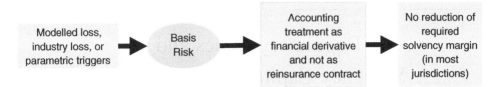

Figure 26.1   Basis risk, accounting treatment and solvency credit

directive[1] adopted by the EU member states (Member States), only allow reductions of an undertaking's solvency capital requirement as a result of risk transfer instruments that can be qualified as reinsurance. Qualification as reinsurance depends on the treatment according to the applicable accounting rules and is generally only achieved in indemnity-based transactions. The situation in the US is very similar, although the 'double trigger' mechanism frequently used in industry loss warranties (ILW) transactions can achieve reinsurance treatment.

According to the Reinsurance Directive,[2] amounts recoverable from special purpose vehicles established within a Member State may, under certain conditions, be deducted as reinsurance in the calculation of the required solvency margin. However, for various reasons, the special purpose vehicle will not always be located in the EU.

Thus, the current solvency regime for insurance and reinsurance undertakings is materially different than the regulatory capital regime applicable to financial undertakings (including banks) insofar as the legislation within the EU implementing the Basel I and Basel II regulatory capital accords allows credit institutions to release regulatory capital through the transfer of credit risk to the capital markets.

A more economics-based view of alternative risk mitigation tools is envisaged in the development of potential future 'level 2' technical implementation measures for the draft Solvency II directive, as described in Section 26.3 (see especially Section 26.3.3).[3] However, further details will have to be specified and one of the most important challenges in that respect will be the assessment of basis risk and the allocation of solvency capital to it. The development of generally known and recognized methods for the assessment of basis risk will therefore be a key element for the further opening of regulatory regimes to ILS structures.

26.1.2   Recognition of sponsors' claims against SPV as eligible assets

Insurance and reinsurance undertakings must cover their technical provisions (as described below) with matching assets that are subject to certain investment restrictions (eligible assets). These restrictions are designed to maintain the safety, yield and marketability of the investments as well as an adequate level of mixture and diversification, while ensuring the insurance undertaking's liquidity at all times. Member States can allow these technical provisions to be covered by claims against reinsurers, subject to certain limits. The qualification as eligible assets of claims against special purpose vehicles resulting from an ILS transaction, however,

---

[1] EU Directives 2002/13/EC, 2002/83/EC and 2005/68/EC (Solvency I).

[2] EU Directive 2005/68/EC.

[3] See also CEIOPS, Call for Advice on QIS4, Annex: QIS4 Technical Specifications (Markt/2505/08), March 2008 and CEIOPS' Report on QIS4 for Solvency II, November 2008 (CEIOPS-SEC-82/08).

depends on the jurisdiction of the special purpose reinsurance vehicle and the funding of the structure. For example, § 66 para. 6a of the German Insurance Supervisory Act specifies that claims against an insurance special purpose vehicle (ISPV) domiciled outside the EU/EEA will only qualify automatically as eligible assets if the ISPV is regulated in its home state and meets solvency requirements that are comparable to those stipulated for special purpose vehicles (SPVs) located in Germany.

26.2   SOLVENCY I

26.2.1   Overview

When looking at the solvency capital requirements in an insurance-linked securitization, it is necessary to consider the solvency position of the insurance originator (the 'insurer' or 'reinsurer'), any SPV and any investor in ILS which is an insurance undertaking. The following focuses on the originator and deals with the position of certain SPVs.

Insurance solvency calculations depend on local regulatory regimes. In the US each state has its own solvency capital requirements. In certain offshore centres (such as the Cayman Islands and Bermuda) the regulation of solvency capital depends on the nature of the insurance business being carried on, with some solvency capital requirements being very light while others are more onerous. In the EU, each Member State is required to have implemented the solvency capital regimes established under the principal EU Directives. It is not possible in a book of this nature to describe each different regime, nor to describe in detail the complexities of any individual regime. However, it is possible to show the approach that needs to be taken to solvency capital in connection with ILS by reference to a single regime and this section describes the position under the EU Directives with particular reference to their implementation in the United Kingdom.

The EU Directives on insurance solvency requirements deal separately with direct life insurance, direct non-life insurance and reinsurance carried out by pure reinsurers. The direct life insurance rules also apply to the reinsurance activities of direct insurers. Some companies (commonly referred to as 'composite insurers') may carry on both life and non-life insurance. In general they can only do this where they were authorized to do so before the insurance directives were adopted in the 1970s, except for a few classes of general insurance business (referred to below) which may be carried out by all life insurers. Pure reinsurers, whenever they were first authorized, may carry out both life and non-life reinsurance business.

As solvency margin calculations go beyond the introductory scope of this chapter, we do not deal with them further.

The principal directive concerning life insurers is the European Parliament and Council Directive concerning life assurance (2002/83/EC) (the 'Life Assurance Directive').

The principal EU Directives concerning the solvency position of non-life insurers are:

- the First Non-Life Co-ordination Directive (73/239/EEC), as amended by
- the Third Non-Life Co-ordination Directive (92/49/EEC) and
- the Solvency I Non-Life Directive (2002/13/EC).

These are referred to as the 'Non-Life Directives'.

The principal EU Directive concerning pure reinsurers' solvency is the European Parliament and Council Directive on reinsurance (2005/68/EC) (the 'Reinsurance Directive').

UK regulations on solvency requirements for life and non-life insurers and reinsurers as well as group solvency requirements are contained in the following FSA rulebooks:

- the General Prudential Sourcebook (GENPRU);
- the Prudential Sourcebook for Insurers (INSPRU); and
- the Interim Prudential Sourcebook for Insurers (IPRU(INS)).

These are derived in part from EU Directives but in part contain provisions which supplement ('gold plate') the EU Directive requirements. The effect is that a level playing field for insurers and reinsurers does not yet exist, as some jurisdictions have implemented these EU Directives in different ways and interpret some provisions differently.

The first thing to note about the EU Directives is that none of them specifically refers to securitization as a form of risk transfer (this can be contrasted with the equivalent solvency capital rules in the banking sector which deal extensively with securitization). In part this is because there is a conceptual difference between bank securitization and insurance securitization; securitization by banks is a transfer of risks inherent in assets (loans or other forms of financing advanced); securitization by insurers is a transfer of risks inherent in liabilities undertaken (i.e. the insurance policies). In part it is due to the insurance solvency framework significantly lagging behind innovations in the markets; it is to be noted that the UK's FSA has sought to remedy this deficiency by providing certain rules in relation to securitization.[4]

The closest that the EU Directives come to contemplating securitization as a form of risk transfer which is to be taken into account as part of an insurer's or reinsurer's solvency position is the ISPV regime permitted under the Reinsurance Directive (see the section entitled 'The ISPV regime in the UK' later in this chapter). Accordingly, the structures that have been developed in the life and non-life sectors have been developed to fit within a legislative framework which is ill-suited to them. Nonetheless, structures have been developed in both the life and non-life sectors through financial innovation.

It will be seen from the following that the calculation of solvency margin is mechanistic and does not necessarily reflect the economic position of an insurance enterprise; it was with this in mind that the Solvency II project was undertaken – this is (currently) expected to be implemented in 2012. Until such time, the following summarizes the relevant provisions in the EU Directives as implemented (and enhanced) in the UK.

26.2.2   Requirement to maintain a solvency margin

Insurers are generally required to maintain a solvency margin. In simple terms, the actual solvency margin is the excess of assets (to the extent permitted in the calculation) over liabilities (as determined by reference to the relevant business). Insurers are generally required to make sure that the actual solvency margin exceeds the required solvency margin. The solvency margin is generally related to the type of business conducted by the insurer (life or non-life and by reference to various subcategories of insurance business).

To benefit the capital position of a sponsoring insurer, an ILS needs to increase the actual solvency margin (in effect, add to the assets of the insurer without giving rise to a corresponding liability) or reduce the required solvency margin (in effect, reduce the liabilities required to be covered by assets, thereby showing a better capital ratio).

---

[4] See INSPRU 1.2.77A-89, for example.

The way that the life, non-life and reinsurance solvency capital positions are calculated varies; however, the basic premise behind them is conceptually similar. Insurance companies are required to maintain an adequate solvency margin. The minimum margin required to be maintained is the required solvency margin. The actual solvency margin, which must at least equal or exceed the required solvency margin, under the relevant EU Directives consists of the 'assets of the insurance undertaking free of foreseeable liabilities, less any intangible items including a number of specified capital instruments such as common shares, certain preference shares and subordinated debt with the requisite characteristics'.[5]

Conceptually, therefore, the capital ratios of an insurer will be improved by any transaction that reduces liabilities without reducing assets or increases assets without increasing liabilities.

Before looking at how ILS feed through into the calculation of the actual solvency margin, it is necessary to look briefly at how the required solvency margin is determined.

Required solvency margin for non-life insurers

The calculation of the minimum solvency margin for non-life companies under the relevant EU Directives is derived from Articles 16a and 17 of the First Non-Life Co-ordination Directive. These require capital to be held equal to the higher of the minimum guarantee fund and the required solvency margin.

The required solvency margin is determined on the basis of the higher of the annual premium amount and the average burden of claims for the preceding three years (or seven financial years in the case of an insurer which essentially underwrites only one or more of the risks of credit, storm, hail or frost).

The annual premium amount is based on the higher of the gross written premiums and gross earned premiums – gross meaning that premiums are ascertained before taking into account any reinsurance. Premiums for certain classes of business (aircraft liability, liability for ships and general liability insurance (other than motor vehicle liability insurance)) are increased by 50% in making the calculation. The premiums due in respect of direct business and premiums accepted for reinsurance in the last financial year are aggregated and from this the total premiums cancelled in the last year are deducted (along with certain other items). The annual premium amount before reinsurance is calculated as the sum of 18% of the amount up to €50 million and 16% of the excess over €50 million.

The claims amount is determined – before taking into account the benefit of any reinsurance – as the sum of the claims paid in the direct business plus claims paid in respect of reinsurance or retrocessions accepted in the preceding three (or seven as applicable) financial years, together with the amount of provisions for outstanding claims established at the end of the last financial year for both direct and reinsurance business. From this amount, recoveries effected in the last three (or seven, as applicable) financial years are deducted. From this, the amount of provision for claims outstanding at the commencement of the second (or sixth, as applicable) financial year preceding the last financial year is deducted. A third (or seventh, as applicable) of the amount so determined is calculated and the claims amount before reinsurance is calculated as the sum of 26% of the amount up to €35 million and 23% of the excess over €35 million.

As noted above, neither of these amounts yet takes into account reinsurance. Each amount is reduced by the 'reinsurance ratio', though in neither case can it be reduced by more than 50%

---

[5] See Article 16 73/239/EEC in the case of non-life insurers and Article 27 2002/83/EC in the case of life assurers.

(the Non-Life Directives refer to the reinsurance ratio itself not being less than 50%). The reinsurance ratio is, in the case of the premium amount calculation and the claims amount calculation, the ratio in the last three financial years of the amount of claims borne after deduction of amounts recoverable under reinsurance over the gross amount of claims.

These requirements are reflected in the UK in the FSA's GENPRU and INSPRU. GENPRU 2.1.13 provides that a general insurer 'must maintain at all times capital resources equal to or in excess of its capital resources requirement'. The capital resources requirement for a general insurer is equal to its minimum capital requirement (MCR).[6] The MCR in respect of general insurance business is the higher of the base capital resources requirement for general insurance business applicable to that firm and the general insurance capital requirement.[7]

The base capital resources requirement corresponds to the minimum guarantee fund in the Non-Life Directives. For a non-mutual liability insurer, for instance, it is €3.2 million. The general insurance capital requirement is defined as the highest of the premiums amount, the claims amount and the brought forward amount.

The premiums amount is:

- 18% of the gross adjusted premiums amount[8] less 2% of the amount, if any, by which the gross adjusted premiums amount exceeds €53.1 million; multiplied by
- the reinsurance ratio.[9]

The claims amount is defined in INSPRU 1.1.47 as:

- 26% of the gross adjusted claims amount; less 3% of the amount, if any, by which the gross adjusted claims amount exceeds €37.2 million; multiplied by
- the same reinsurance ratio as in the premiums amount.

The brought forward amount is aimed at insurers in run-off and will not be dealt with further.

The reinsurance ratio is the ratio (expressed as a percentage of claims incurred (net of reinsurance) in the last three financial years to gross claims in that period; if it is less than 50% it is deemed 50%; if it is in excess of 100% it is deemed to be 100%.[10]

Required solvency margin for life assurers

For life insurance the required solvency margin is a more complex calculation depending in part on the types of business. In somewhat simple terms, however:

(a) for life policies where the insurer bears the investment risk (such as endowment policies which are not unit-linked and do not have guarantees or annuities), the amount is 4% of the mathematical provisions relating to direct business and reinsurance gross of reinsurance ceded multiplied by the reinsurance ratio. The reinsurance ratio is the ratio for the last financial year of the mathematical provisions net of reinsurance to the mathematical provisions gross of reinsurance and cannot be less than 85%;

---

[6] GENPRU 2.1.17.

[7] GENPRU 2.1.24R.

[8] A complex calculation defined in INSPRU 1.1.56.

[9] A complex ratio of premiums net of reinsurance to gross premiums set out in INSPRU 1.1.54R.

[10] INSPRU 1.1.54R.

(b) for policies on which the capital at risk is not a negative figure (e.g. term assurance) the amount is 0.3% (or 0.1% if the policy is for a maximum term of three years and 0.15% if for three to five years) of the capital underwritten multiplied by the reinsurance ratio; in this case, the reinsurance ratio is the ratio for the last financial year which the total capital at risk after taking account of reinsurance bears to total capital at risk before reinsurance;

(c) to the extent a life assurer carries on classes of general insurance business supplementary to its life business (e.g. insurance against personal injury including incapacity or insurance against death arising from an accident or disability insurance, but which is not in (d) below) the calculation is as for general insurers (see above);

(d) for permanent health insurance which cannot be cancelled, the amount comprises an amount calculated in (a) above plus an amount calculated in (c) above; and

(e) for unit-linked policies, (i) to the extent of any investment risk borne by the insurer, the amount is as in (a); (ii) if not in (i) and if management expenses are fixed for a period exceeding five years, the amount is 1% of the technical provisions or, if expenses are not fixed for a period exceeding five years, 25% of the last year's net administrative expenses of that business; or (iii) to the extent of any term assurance included in the contract, the amount is as in (b) above.

The calculation provided for in the UK is similar for a firm which is not a 'realistic basis firm' (in simple terms, one which has de minimis levels of with-profits business). The FSA has, however, for a 'realistic basis firm' (i.e. one with more than a de minimis level of with-profits business) introduced a regime which requires the minimum solvency margin to be calculated based on the higher of the MCR and the 'enhanced capital requirement' (ECR).

The MCR for a realistic basis firm is the higher of the base capital resources requirement for long-term insurance business applicable to that firm (which is a fixed amount) and the long-term insurance capital requirement. The long-term insurance capital requirement substantially reflects the calculations above.

For a realistic basis insurer carrying on long-term insurance business, the ECR (or 'regulatory peak') in respect of that business is the sum of the long-term insurance capital requirement and the with-profits insurance capital component.

The with-profits insurance capital component is a complex calculation. It is designed to ensure that the insurer holds adequate financial resources for the conduct of its with-profits insurance business.

The need for the with-profits insurance capital component arises because capital in excess of the mathematical reserves provided for under the relevant EU Directives may be needed. The purpose of this excess is to ensure that final bonuses can be awarded to policyholders, paying due regard to the interests of the policyholders and the requirement to treat them fairly. The mathematical reserves for a realistic basis life assurer are not currently required, in the EU Directives, to include provision for expected (but not contractually agreed) future annual bonuses or final bonuses.

The other side of the 'realistic' approach to valuing assets and liabilities is that in some respects it involves applying a more realistic and thus less ruthlessly prudent value to some other liabilities and assets. In some cases this results in the value of the liabilities going down (compared to the approach for the MCR) and the value of assets going up. This counterbalances the requirement to provide more generously for bonuses and to write up other liabilities and write down other assets. The calculation is complicated and beyond the scope of this chapter (not least because few have tried to securitize with-profit policies).

Required solvency margin for reinsurers

The Reinsurance Directive provides for non-life reinsurers' required solvency margin to be calculated in a way which is substantially similar to that of non-life direct insurers. Life reinsurers, conversely, rather than use a method similar to direct life insurers, use the higher of premium amounts and claim amounts as non-life reinsurers do, though Member States may, for certain classes of business, apply the provisions of the Life Assurance Directive.[11]

26.2.3 Structuring ILS under EU Directives to enhance solvency margins

From the above it can be seen that the only form of risk transfer expressly contemplated by the EU Directives is that of reinsurance. Accordingly, ILS seeking to obtain regulatory capital relief in the EU have tended to be structured using reinsurance contracts.

The risk transfer arrangement may not constitute a reinsurance contract. This may be the case, for example, where the transaction involves a parametric payout to the insurer. The effect here is not to remove from the required solvency margin calculation the risk transferred (after taking into account any basis risk between the expected loss to the insurer if the event occurs and the expected receipt under the parametric contract – which would be the true economic position). Commonly, therefore, ILS using risk transfer contracts with a parametric payout are unlikely to obtain significant regulatory capital benefits (they may have economic capital and rating benefits, however). To obtain regulatory capital benefits it has been necessary to use an indemnity payout (reinsurance) contract. Some benefit may be obtained if the contract is an asset of the insurer for which some value may be given in calculating the solvency margin. This will be the case, for example, if it meets the admissible asset criteria. This is likely, however, to be of relatively minor regulatory benefit.

There is an implicit form of risk transfer recognized in EU Directives. This arises from the basic requirement that an insurer's solvency margin is its 'assets . . . free from foreseeable liabilities'. If it is possible to establish an arrangement where an asset is received on terms that any liability in respect of it is not foreseeable, that will have the effect of creating solvency margin. It is this concept on which the embedded value transactions – in particular (but not exclusively) in the UK – have been based. The premise is as follows: where the obligation to pay interest on and repay principal of a loan is limited to surplus (profit) emerging on a defined book of long-term insurance contracts, that obligation will be ignored as the payments are not (in actuarial terms) foreseeable; however, the cash advanced is an admissible asset and, accordingly, an asset without a corresponding liability (until the relevant surplus emerges) is created, giving, in effect, capital.

This is recognized in the calculation of capital by the FSA. GENPRU requires Tier 1 capital resources of an insurer to be calculated in accordance with the capital resources table for insurers at GENPRU 2 Annex 1R for insurers. Stage F of that calculation includes 'positive valuation differences' referred to in GENPRU 2.2.105R. GENPRU 2.2.105 states that: 'Valuation differences are all differences between the valuation of assets and liabilities as valued in GENPRU and the valuation that the insurer uses for its external financial reporting purposes, except valuation differences which are dealt with elsewhere in the capital resources table. The sum of these valuation differences must either be added to (if positive) or deducted from (if negative) an insurer's capital resources in accordance with the capital resources table'.

---

[11] See Article 38 of the Reinsurance Directive.

GENPRU 2.2.106 states: '. . . contingent loans or other arrangements which are not valued as a liability under INSPRU 1.2.79R (2) (Reinsurance) result in a positive valuation difference'. For general accounting purposes, a contingent loan would be regarded as a liability in external financial reporting. However, valuation differences dealt with elsewhere permit it to be valued in accordance with those provisions. The provisions of INSPRU 1.2.77A-89 set out a regime for reinsurance 'and analogous non-reinsurance financing agreements, including contingent loans, securitizations and any other arrangements in respect of contracts of insurance that are analogous to contracts of reinsurance in terms of the risks transferred and finance provided'. A number of embedded value securitizations (starting with the Mutual Securitization transaction in 1998, the Gracechurch Life Finance transaction in 2003 and the Box Hill Life Finance transaction in 2004) have been structured to take advantage of this concept.

ILS transactions in the EU that have sought solvency margin benefits have therefore been structured either as reinsurance arrangements or using contingent loan structures (the latter being common on the life (embedded value, rather than longevity) securitizations).

ILS reinsurance structures

The need to have a reinsurance contract as the form of risk transfer arrangement in order to obtain solvency margin benefits has historically resulted in special purpose reinsurance entities being set up in offshore financial centres (such as Bermuda, the Cayman Islands and the Channel Islands) where the regulatory regime allowed favourable treatment of certain types of reinsurer – in particular those that carried out a single activity – or, in one or two life insurance securitizations, in jurisdictions that did not regulate reinsurance (as opposed to direct insurance) activities (such as Ireland).

The Reinsurance Directive was required to have been implemented by Member States by 10 December 2007. A number of Member States have yet fully to implement it. The directive requires reinsurance carried on in the EU to be regulated and, subject as follows, means that EU-based entities are unlikely to be attractive as part of any ILS using reinsurance as the risk transfer contract.

The Reinsurance Directive, however, permits a special purpose reinsurance company regime to be established by Member States. So far, regimes taking advantage of this have been established in the UK, France, Germany and Ireland. The effect of reinsurance from a special purpose reinsurer established under the Reinsurance Directive is that the reinsured may – depending on how the regime has been implemented – obtain capital benefits in respect of the reinsurance provided while there is no corresponding capital cost for the special purpose reinsurance company.

It should, of course, be noted that the effect of the various reinsurance ratios used in the calculations of required solvency margin is to limit the benefit that reinsurance can provide to the extent that the ratio is subject to limits.

The ISPV regime in the UK   In the UK the special purpose reinsurance company regime has been established; the vehicles are referred to as 'insurance special purpose vehicles' or 'ISPVs'. The regime is substantially based on the provisions of the Reinsurance Directive.

An ISPV is an SPV which assumes risks from insurance undertakings or reinsurance undertakings and which fully funds its exposure to such risks through the proceeds of a debt issuance or some other financing mechanism where the repayment rights of the providers of such debt or other financing mechanism are subordinated to the reinsurance obligations of that vehicle. As it is fully funded to meet its reinsurance liabilities, it is not subject to insurance risk to the same extent as other reinsurers (having, in effect, pre-funded its risk). The Reinsurance Directive permits ISPVs to be subject to different rules to those applying to other reinsurers.

The 'fully funded' requirement means, according to the FSA's rules, that the ISPV must actually have received the proceeds of issue of the relevant debt securities it issues – a mere contingent right (for example under a letter of credit) would not be sufficient. This is not necessarily the approach taken in other Member States.

An ISPV must ensure that at all times its assets are equal to or greater than its liabilities. This will require sufficient resources to carry out its activities, including paying employees and for its administration.

An ISPV must include in each of its contracts of reinsurance terms which secure that its aggregate maximum liability at any time under those contracts of reinsurance does not exceed the amount of its assets at that time.

An ISPV must ensure that under the terms of any debt issuance or other financing arrangement used to fund its reinsurance liabilities, the rights of the providers of that debt or other financing are fully subordinated to the claims of creditors under its contracts of reinsurance.

As a result of the provisions of GENPRU and INSPRU, an insurer may not obtain any benefit from the reinsurance arrangement with an ISPV unless it first obtains a waiver to that effect from the FSA. If it obtains a waiver then, depending on the terms of the waiver, it may be able to benefit from the reinsurance by either including it in the solvency margin calculation or treating it as an asset eligible to cover its solvency requirements ('an admissible asset').

Where the ISPV is not a UK ISPV, the FSA will expect to receive confirmation that the ISPV has received an official authorization in accordance with Article 46 of the Reinsurance Directive in the Member State in which it has been established and that it is fully funded (as well as certain other information). No credit may be taken for a contract of reinsurance with an ISPV unless there has been an 'effective transfer' of risk from the insured to the ISPV.

Notwithstanding that the ISPV regime has been established in the UK for over a year, none have been used to set up a securitization. In part this is due to factors other than the rigidity of the regime, including market turmoil, the fact that many ILS do not use reinsurance contracts as the form of risk transfer – particularly in the non-life side where parametric payouts rather than indemnity-based contracts have been more common – as well as difficulties over taxation.

ILS contingent loan structures

Few Member States have specific provisions dealing with how the term 'assets free from foreseeable liabilities' is to be determined – in the context of a contingent loan this would be the money advanced free of the repayment obligation. In the UK, however, the FSA has set out how this will operate in the life sector. A valuation difference will arise where the normal method of valuing an asset or liability is replaced with an assumed basis of valuation in the relevant rules and there is, as a result, a difference between the two. The basic premise in relation to a contingent loan falling within the provisions of INSPRU 1.2.77A-89 is that, while for accounting purposes it would be shown as a liability, if the provisions of INSPRU 1.2.77A-89 are met, it would be ignored as a liability and a valuation difference would therefore exist, resulting in an increase in the actual solvency margin.

While the provisions in INSPRU 1.2.77A-89 are drafted by reference to 'reinsurance', INSPRU 1.2.77A provides that this includes 'analogous non-reinsurance financing agreements, including contingent loans, securitizations and any other arrangements in respect of contracts of insurance that are analogous to contracts of reinsurance in terms of the risks transferred and finance provided'.

To obtain the requisite treatment, certain provisions need to be met. These can be summarized as follows:

- Reinsurance cash outflows that are unambiguously linked to the emergence as surplus of margins included in the valuation of existing contracts of insurance or to the exercise by a reinsurer of its rights under a termination clause need not be valued.
- The 'link' must be such that a contingent liability to pay or repay the amount to the reinsurer could not arise except when, and to the extent that, the margins in the valuation of the existing contracts of insurance emerge as surplus, or the reinsurer exercises its rights under a termination clause in the contract of reinsurance as a result of:
  - ○ fraudulent conduct by the insured under or in relation to the contract of reinsurance;
  - ○ a representation as to the existence, at or before the time the contract of reinsurance is entered into, of a state of affairs which is within the knowledge or control of the insured and which is material to the reinsurer's decision to enter into the contract being discovered to be false;
  - ○ the non-payment of reinsurance premiums by the insured; or
  - ○ a transfer by the insured of the whole or a specified part of its business without the agreement of the reinsurer, except where that agreement has been unreasonably withheld.
- The provisions allow an insured not to value reinsurance cash outflows provided the contingencies in which the reinsurance would require repayment other than out of future surpluses are limited to termination clauses concerning fraud, material misrepresentation, non-payment of reinsurance premiums by the insured or a transfer of business by the insured without the agreement of the reinsurer, except if unreasonably withheld.
- Where the reinsurance cash outflow is payable by a fund or subfund that generates such profits, charges or transfers, the insured need make no provision for such payments provided that repayment to the reinsurer is linked unambiguously to the emergence of future surplus. Where the profits, charges or transfers arising under a block of business are payable by a fund or subfund to another part of the insured, then only where the insured has committed to remit such profits, charges or transfers directly to the reinsurer would it be acceptable for no provision for payments to the reinsurer to be made.

ILS – other structures

Many ILS structures involve neither a contingent loan nor reinsurance. In such cases, depending on the applicable solvency regime, the question will arise as to whether that regime permits the form of risk transfer contract to have the same effect as reinsurance in respect of the risk transferred or allows the contract to be otherwise taken into account to reflect its true value. In the EU this will generally not be the case. Solvency II is intended to put insurance solvency margin requirements onto an economic principles basis and will provide specifically for securitizations, though this is currently not expected to be implemented until 2012.

26.3 SOLVENCY II

This section summarizes the principles applicable to determining the required regulatory capital of insurance and reinsurance undertakings subject to regulation within the EU, based upon the version of the 'Directive of the European Parliament and of the Council on the Taking-up and Pursuit of the Business of Insurance and Reinsurance' (Solvency II) ('the Directive') promulgated by the Council of the EU. The Directive is meant to come into force in each Member State by way of adopting legislation not later than 31 October 2012.

Once enacted, the Directive will be a framework directive which anticipates further implementing action on the part of both the European Commission and the Member States. The reader of this chapter should keep in mind that the Directive may change prior to its final adoption in respects which may be material. In addition, this chapter provides only a summary overview of certain provisions of the Directive. Thus, the reader is referred to the text of the Directive for a more complete description of the regulations discussed in this section.

Once enacted, the Directive will change in material respects the manner in which insurance and reinsurance undertakings determine their regulatory capital. Under the Directive, the market value of an insurance or reinsurance undertaking's assets must equal or exceed the sum of an undertaking's technical provisions and its required regulatory capital, all as described below.

The components of Solvency II regulatory capital requirements for insurance and reinsurance undertakings are represented diagrammatically in Figure 26.2.

In summary, an undertaking's 'technical provisions', will consist of a 'best estimate' equal to its probability-weighted average of future cash flows, and a 'risk margin' sufficient to ensure that the total value of the technical provisions is equivalent to the amount an insurance or reinsurance undertaking would be expected to receive in order to take over and meet the transferring undertaking's insurance and reinsurance obligations. In addition, each undertaking will be required to determine two tiers of regulatory capital. A first tier of regulatory capital will

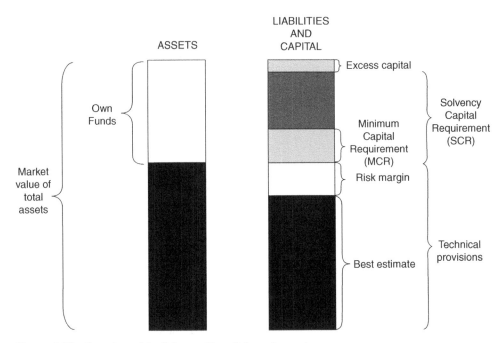

Figure 26.2   Overview of the Solvency II capital requirements

be an undertaking's 'solvency capital requirement', calculated either pursuant to a standard formula or using a supervisor-approved internal model. A second tier of regulatory capital will be an undertaking's MCR, corresponding to an amount of eligible basic own funds below which policyholders and beneficiaries are exposed to an unacceptable level of risk if the undertaking is allowed to continue its operations. An undertaking's MCR is a subset of its solvency capital requirement.

26.3.1 Valuation of assets and liabilities

As mentioned above, insurance and reinsurance undertakings must value their assets and liabilities at market value. Specifically, assets must be valued at the amount for which they could be exchanged between knowledgeable willing parties in an arm's length transaction. Liabilities must be valued at the amount for which they could be transferred, or settled, between knowledgeable willing parties in an arm's length transaction. When valuing liabilities, no adjustment may be made to take account of the own credit standing of the insurance or reinsurance undertaking.

26.3.2 Determination of technical provisions

Each insurance and reinsurance undertaking must establish technical provisions with respect to all of its insurance and reinsurance obligations towards policyholders and beneficiaries of insurance or reinsurance contracts. The total value of technical provisions must equal the current amount an insurance or reinsurance undertaking would have to pay to transfer its obligations immediately to another insurance or reinsurance undertaking. The calculation of technical provisions must make use of and be consistent with generally available financial market information and data on insurance and reinsurance technical risks, and must be calculated in a prudent, reliable and objective manner. When calculating technical provisions, insurance and reinsurance undertakings must segment their insurance and reinsurance obligations into homogeneous risk groups, and at a minimum by lines of business.

The value of an undertaking's technical provisions will equal the sum of a 'best estimate' and a 'risk margin'. The best estimate must equal the probability-weighted average of future cash flows, taking account of the time value of money (expected present value of future cash flows), using a suitable risk-free interest rate. The cash-flow projection used in the calculation of the best estimate must take account of all the cash in- and out-flows required to settle the insurance and reinsurance obligations over their lifetime. The best estimate must be calculated gross, without deduction of the amounts recoverable from reinsurance contracts and special purpose vehicles. Those amounts must be calculated separately, as described below. The risk margin must be sufficient to ensure that, taken together with the best estimate, the value of the technical provisions is equivalent to the amount that an insurance or reinsurance undertaking would be expected to require in order to take over and meet the transferring undertaking's insurance and reinsurance obligations.

The best estimate and the risk margin must normally be determined separately. However, if future cash flows associated with insurance or reinsurance obligations can be replicated using financial instruments for which a reliable market value is observable, the value of technical provisions associated with those future cash flows may be determined on the basis of the market value of those financial instruments and, in such a case, separate calculation of the best estimate and the risk margin is not required. Where the best estimate and the risk margin are determined separately, the risk margin must be calculated by determining the cost of providing an amount of eligible own funds equal to the solvency capital requirement necessary to support the insurance and reinsurance obligations over their lifetime. The rate used in the determination of the cost of providing that amount of eligible own funds (the 'cost-of-capital rate') will equal the margin above the relevant risk-free interest rate that an insurance or reinsurance undertaking holding an amount of eligible own funds equal to the solvency capital requirement would incur to hold those funds.

When calculating amounts recoverable from reinsurance contracts and special purpose vehicles, insurance and reinsurance undertakings must take account of the time difference between recoveries and direct payments. That calculation must then be adjusted to take account of expected losses due to default of the counterparty. That adjustment must be based on an assessment of the probability of default (PD) of the counterparty and the average loss resulting therefrom (loss-given-default or LGD). Both PD and LGD are concepts used throughout the EU Capital Requirements Directive (CRD) implementing the Basel II regulatory capital accord for determining the regulatory capital of financial institutions.

In implementing the Directive, the Commission is required to adopt implementing measures establishing, amongst other things, (a) the actuarial and statistical methodologies required to be used to calculate an undertaking's 'best estimate' referred to above; (b) the relevant risk-free interest rate; (c) the circumstances in which technical provisions must be calculated as a whole, or as a sum of a best estimate and a risk margin, and the methods to be used in the case where technical provisions are calculated as a whole; (d) the methods and assumptions to be used in the calculation of the risk margin including the determination of the amount of eligible own funds necessary to support the insurance and reinsurance obligations and the calibration of the cost-of-capital rate; (e) the lines of business on the basis of which insurance and reinsurance obligations are to be segmented in order to calculate technical provisions; (f) the standards to be met with respect to ensuring the appropriateness, completeness and accuracy of the data used in the calculation of technical provisions, and the specific circumstances in which it would be appropriate to use approximations; and (g) the methodologies to be used when calculating the relevant counterparty default adjustment.

26.3.3 Solvency capital requirement

Each insurance and reinsurance undertaking must hold sufficient eligible own funds to cover its most recently reported solvency capital requirement. Essentially, the solvency capital requirement should equal the amount of economic capital that an insurance or reinsurance undertaking needs to hold in order to ensure that such undertaking will be able, with a probability of at least 99.5%, to meet its obligations to policyholders and beneficiaries over the forthcoming 12 months (or, in other words, that insolvency will occur no more often than once in every 200 cases).

The solvency capital requirement is to be calculated either in accordance with the 'standard formula' or using an 'internal model', all as described below. The solvency capital requirement will, in each case, be calculated on the basis that the undertaking will carry on its business as a going concern. The solvency capital requirement must be calculated at least once a year and reported to the supervisory authorities.

The solvency capital requirement must be calibrated to ensure that all quantifiable risks to which an insurance or reinsurance undertaking is exposed are taken into account. It must cover existing business, as well as the new business expected to be written over the twelve months following each determination. With respect to existing businesses, it will cover unexpected losses only. The solvency capital requirement must cover at least non-life underwriting risk, life underwriting risk, health underwriting risk, market risk, credit risk and operational risk. Operational risk includes legal risks, and excludes risks arising from strategic decisions, as well as reputation risks.

When calculating the solvency capital requirement, insurance and reinsurance undertakings may take account of the effect of risk mitigation techniques, provided that credit risk and other risks arising from the use of such techniques are properly reflected. Thus, diverse risk mitigation techniques such as reinsurance, securitization and derivatives should all get equal treatment under the Directive to the extent that they are commercially equivalent.

Insurance and reinsurance undertakings must monitor the amount of eligible own funds and the solvency capital requirement on an ongoing basis. If the risk profile of an undertaking deviates significantly from the assumptions underlying the last reported solvency capital requirement, the undertaking must recalculate the solvency capital requirement without delay and report it to the relevant supervisory authorities. In addition, where there is evidence to suggest that the risk profile of an insurance or reinsurance undertaking has altered significantly since the date on which its solvency capital requirement was last reported, supervisory authorities may require the undertaking to recalculate the solvency capital requirement.

Standard formula

The solvency capital requirement calculated in accordance with the standard formula will equal the sum of the basic solvency capital requirement, the capital requirement for operational risk and the adjustment for the loss-absorbing capacity of technical provisions and deferred taxes, all as described below. The standard formula is reproduced in the appendix to this chapter.

The basic solvency capital requirement will consist of individual risk modules that are aggregated as described below. The modules will consist at least of non-life underwriting risk; life underwriting risk; health underwriting risk; market risk; and counterparty default risk. Insurance or reinsurance operations must be allocated to the underwriting risk module that best reflects the technical nature of the underlying risks. Subject to approval by the supervisory authorities, insurance and reinsurance undertakings may, within the design of the standard formula, replace a subset of its parameters by parameters specific to the undertaking concerned when calculating the life, non-life and health underwriting risk modules. Such parameters must be calibrated on the basis of the internal data of the undertaking concerned, or of data which are directly relevant for the operations of that undertaking using standardized methods. When granting supervisory approval, supervisory authorities must verify the completeness, accuracy and appropriateness of the data used. The correlation coefficients for the aggregation of the risk modules, as well as the calibration of the capital requirements for each risk module, must result in an overall solvency capital requirement that achieves a confidence level of 99.5% over a one-year period.

The capital requirement for operational risk must reflect operational risks to the extent that they are not already reflected in the risk modules referred to above, and must also achieve a confidence level of 99.5% over a one-year period.

The adjustment referred to above for the loss-absorbing capacity of technical provisions and deferred taxes must reflect potential compensation of unexpected losses through a simultaneous decrease in technical provisions or deferred taxes or a combination of both. That adjustment may take account of the risk-mitigating effect provided by future discretionary benefits of insurance contracts, to the extent that insurance and reinsurance undertakings can establish that a reduction in such benefits may be used to cover unexpected losses when they arise. The risk-mitigating effect provided by future discretionary benefits must be no higher than the sum of technical provisions and deferred taxes relating to these future discretionary benefits.

An undertaking may use a simplified calculation for a specific risk module where the nature, scale and complexity of the risks it faces justify it and where it would be disproportionate to require it to apply the standardized calculation. In addition, if it would be inappropriate for an undertaking to calculate the solvency capital requirement in accordance with the standard formula because its risk profile deviates significantly from the assumptions underlying the standard formula, the supervisory authorities may, by a decision stating the reasons, require the undertaking concerned to replace a subset of the parameters used in the standard formula calculation by parameters specific to that undertaking.

The Commission must adopt implementing measures establishing, amongst other things, the standard formula; the methods, assumptions and standard parameters to be used when calculating each of the risk modules; the correlation parameters; where insurance and reinsurance undertakings use risk mitigation techniques, the methods and assumptions to be used to assess the changes in the risk profile of the undertaking concerned and adjust the calculation of the solvency capital requirement accordingly, and the qualitative criteria that such risk mitigation techniques must meet; the methods and parameters to be used when assessing the capital requirement for operational risk; and the method to be used when calculating the adjustment for the loss-absorbing capacity of technical provisions.

Principles on the recognition of risk mitigation tools

In order to achieve recognition in the standard formula calculation described above, a financial risk mitigation technique must comply with the following principles:[12]

1. **Economic effect over legal form.** Financial risk mitigation techniques should be recognized and treated equally, regardless of their legal form or accounting treatment. New risks acquired as a by-product of mitigation techniques should also be recognized.
2. **Legal certainty, effectiveness and enforceability.** Such techniques should be legally effective and enforceable in all relevant jurisdictions. The undertaking in question should take all appropriate steps, including a legal review, to ensure and confirm the effectiveness and continuing enforceability of the mitigation technique. In addition, for collateralized transactions, the legal mechanism by which collateral is pledged or transferred must ensure that the insurer has the right to liquidate or take legal possession of it in a timely manner.
3. **Liquidity, ascertainability and stability of value.** The mitigation instruments should have a value over time sufficiently reliable and stable to provide appropriate certainty, with no double-counting.
4. **Credit quality of the provider of the risk mitigation instrument.** Providers of mitigation should have an adequate credit quality to guarantee the relevant benefits with almost certainty. In the case of financial institutions, they will only be considered for the purposes of the formula if rated BBB or better, and the degree of correlation between the value of the instrument and the credit quality of their provider should be positive. The mitigation instrument should be capable of being retained, or liquidated, in a timely manner.

---

[12] Annex B to the QIS3 Technical Specifications published by CEIOPS.

5. **Direct, explicit, irrevocable and unconditional features.** These mirror the equivalent provisions under the CRD regime. The mitigation instruments must provide a direct claim against the protection provider, and contain explicit reference to specific exposures or pools of exposure; they must not contain any clause that would allow the provider unilaterally to cancel, or that would increase the effective cost of the cover as a result of certain developments in the hedged cover, nor must they contain any clause outside the direct control of the insurer that could prevent the protection provider from being obliged to pay out.

There are special requirements for mitigation techniques involving credit derivatives, which are similar to equivalent requirements under the CRD regime and which specify the minimum key events (non-payment, insolvency and restructuring) that must be covered by the defined credit events thereunder.

Full and partial internal models

One of the major advances represented by the Directive is the determination of regulatory capital on the basis of internal models. The Directive provides for greater flexibility in the choice and operation of internal models than the CRD does for financial institutions. A partial model may be used to determine any of the risk modules of the basic solvency capital requirement; the capital requirement for operational risk; and the adjustment for the loss-absorbing capacity of technical provisions. Partial modelling may be applied to the whole business of an insurance and reinsurance undertaking, or only to one or more major business units.

The use of an internal model, whether full or partial, by any insurance or reinsurance undertaking is subject to prior approval by the relevant supervisory authority. As part of the initial process of approving an internal model, the supervisory authorities will approve the policy for changing that model, and that undertaking may only make major changes to its internal model in accordance with that policy. Minor changes to an undertaking's internal model may be exempt from prior supervisory approval only if they are permitted by such undertaking's approved policy.

After having received approval to use an internal model, an insurance or reinsurance undertaking may generally not revert to calculating the whole or any part of its solvency capital requirement in accordance with the standard formula except with the approval of the supervisory authorities. However, if, after having received approval from the supervisory authorities to use an internal model, an undertaking ceases to comply with the requirements for the model, it must, without delay, either present to the supervisory authorities a plan to restore compliance within a reasonable period of time or demonstrate that the effect of noncompliance is immaterial. In the event that the undertaking fails to implement the compliance plan, the supervisory authorities may require the undertaking to revert to calculating its solvency capital requirement in accordance with the standard formula.

No internal model may be approved unless it is widely used in, and plays an important role in, an undertaking's systems of governance, risk management and economic and solvency capital assessment and allocation processes. In addition, an undertaking must demonstrate that the frequency of calculation of its solvency capital requirement using the internal model is consistent with the frequency with which it uses its internal model for such purposes.

An internal model must cover all of the material risks to which an undertaking is exposed. As a minimum, an internal model must cover the risks addressed by the standard formula. As regards diversification effects, an undertaking may take account in its internal model of dependencies within risk categories, as well as across risk categories, provided that supervisory authorities are satisfied that the system used for measuring those diversification effects is adequate. In addition, an undertaking may take full account of the effect of risk mitigation techniques in its internal model, as long as credit risk and other risks arising from the use of risk mitigation techniques are properly reflected in the model.

An undertaking must, if practicable, derive its solvency capital requirement directly from the probability distribution forecast generated by its internal model, using the value-at-risk measure described above. Where an undertaking cannot derive its solvency capital requirement directly from the probability distribution forecast generated by the internal model, the supervisory authorities may allow approximations to be used in the process to calculate the solvency capital requirement, as long as the undertaking can demonstrate to the supervisory authorities that policyholders are provided with a level of protection to a confidence level of 99.5% over a one-year period.

Supervisory authorities may require an insurance or reinsurance undertaking to run its internal model on relevant benchmark portfolios and using assumptions based on external rather than internal data in order to verify the calibration of the internal model and to check that its specification is in line with generally accepted market practice.

Each insurance and reinsurance undertaking determining its solvency capital requirement pursuant to an internal model must review, at least annually, the causes and sources of profits and losses for each major business unit, and demonstrate how the categorization of risk chosen in its internal model explains the causes and sources of profits and losses. The categorization of risk and attribution of profits and losses must reflect the risk profile of the undertakings.

Each insurance and reinsurance undertaking must establish a regular cycle of model validation which includes monitoring the performance of its internal model, reviewing the ongoing appropriateness of its specification, and testing its results against experience. That process must include an effective statistical process for validating the internal model which enables the undertaking to demonstrate to its supervisory authorities that the resulting capital requirements are appropriate. The statistical methods applied must not only test the appropriateness of the probability distribution forecast compared to loss experience, but also to all material new data and information relating thereto. The model validation process will also include an analysis of the stability of the internal model and in particular the testing of the sensitivity of the results of the internal model to changes in key underlying assumptions. It must also include an assessment of the accuracy, completeness and appropriateness of the data used by the internal model.

26.3.4 Minimum capital requirement

Each insurance and reinsurance undertaking must hold sufficient eligible own funds to cover its most recently reported MCR. Essentially, the MCR must equal an amount of eligible basic own funds below which policyholders and beneficiaries would be exposed to an unacceptable level of risk if an insurance or reinsurance undertaking were allowed to continue its operations. Insurance and reinsurance undertakings must calculate the MCR at least quarterly and report the results of that calculation to supervisory authorities.

The MCR will be calibrated to the value-at-risk of the basic own funds of an insurance or reinsurance undertaking subject to a confidence level of 85% over a one-year period and will have an absolute floor of €2 200 000 for non-life insurance undertakings, including captive insurance undertakings (or a higher amount of €3 200 000 if the undertaking engages in certain specified risks); or €3 200 000 for life insurance undertakings, including captive insurance undertakings; or €3 200 000 for reinsurance undertakings, except in the case of captive reinsurance undertakings in which case the MCR must not be less than €1 000 000. The MCR must be calculated as a linear function of a set or subset of the undertaking's technical provisions, written premiums, capital-at-risk, deferred tax and administrative expenses. The variables used must be measured net of reinsurance.

Without prejudice to the foregoing, an undertaking's MCR may not fall below 20%, nor exceed 50%, of the undertaking's solvency capital requirement, including any capital add-on. Certain transitional arrangements for MCR will be enacted as part of the Directive.

26.3.5   Own funds

An undertaking's 'own funds' will consist of the sum of its 'basic own funds' and its 'ancillary own funds', both as described below.

Basic own funds will consist of the excess of assets over liabilities, valued as described in Section 26.1, and subordinated liabilities. The excess of assets over liabilities must be reduced, if relevant, by the amount of its own shares held by an insurance or reinsurance undertaking.

Ancillary own funds will consist of items other than basic own funds which can be called upon to absorb losses. Thus, ancillary own funds may consist of unpaid share capital or initial funds that have not been called up; letters of credit and guarantees; or any other legally binding commitments held by the relevant undertaking. In the case of a mutual or mutual-type association with variable contributions, ancillary own funds may also consist of any future claims which that association may have against its members by way of a call for supplementary contribution within the forthcoming twelve months. Where an ancillary own fund item has been paid in or called up, it will be treated as an asset and will cease to form part of ancillary own fund items.

The amounts of ancillary own funds items to be taken into account when determining own funds is subject to prior supervisory approval. The amount of each ancillary own funds item must reflect its loss absorbency and must be based upon prudent and realistic assumptions. Supervisory authorities must approve either a monetary amount for each ancillary own funds item or a method to determine the amount of each ancillary own funds item. Where a method of determination is approved, supervisory approval of the amount determined in accordance with that method must be granted for a specified period of time. When determining the amount of ancillary own funds items, supervisory authorities will assess, amongst other things, the status of the counterparties in relation to their ability and willingness to pay; the recoverability of the funds, taking account of the legal form of the item, as well as any conditions which would prevent the item from being successfully paid in or called up; and any information regarding the outcome of past calls to the extent that information can be reliably used to assess the expected outcome of future calls.

Own funds items will be classified into three tiers. The classification of own funds items will depend upon whether they are basic own funds items or ancillary own funds items and the extent to which the item has 'permanent availability' and 'subordination'. Permanent availability exists to the extent that the item is available, or can be called upon, to fully absorb losses on a going-concern basis, including in the case of winding-up. Subordination exists to the extent that the total amount of the item, in the case of winding-up, is available to absorb losses and the repayment of the item is refused to its holder until all other obligations, including insurance and reinsurance obligations towards policyholders and beneficiaries of insurance and reinsurance contracts, have been met. When assessing the extent to which own funds items possess the two characteristics described above, currently and in the future, due consideration will be given to the duration of the item, in particular whether or not the item is dated. Where an own funds item is dated, the relative duration of the item as compared to the duration of the insurance and reinsurance obligations of the undertaking will be relevant. In addition, the supervisor will consider features such as whether the item is free from requirements or incentives to redeem the nominal sum; whether the item is free from mandatory fixed charges; and whether the item is free from encumbrances.

Basic own funds items will be classified in Tier 1 if they substantially demonstrate both permanent availability and subordination. Basic own funds items will be classified in Tier 2 where they substantially demonstrate only subordination. Ancillary own funds items will be classified in Tier 2 where they substantially demonstrate both permanent availability and subordination. Any other basic or ancillary own funds item will be classified in Tier 3. Without limiting the generality of the foregoing, surplus funds will be classified in Tier 1, and letters of credit and guarantees which are held in trust for the benefit of insurance creditors by an independent trustee and provided by EU credit institutions will be classified in Tier 2.

As far as compliance with the solvency capital requirement is concerned, the amounts of Tier 2 and Tier 3 items will be subject to limits. The eligible amount of Tier 2 together with the eligible amount of Tier 3 will be limited to twice the total amount of Tier 1 items. In addition, the eligible amount of Tier 3 will be limited to half the sum of the amount of Tier 1 and the amount of eligible Tier 2. As far as the compliance with the MCR is concerned, the amount of basic own funds items eligible to cover the MCR which are classified in Tier 2 must be limited to the total amount of Tier 1 items.

26.3.6 Investments

All insurance and reinsurance undertakings must invest all their assets in accordance with the 'prudent person' principle. With respect to the whole portfolio of assets, insurance and reinsurance undertakings may only invest in assets and instruments whose risks the undertaking concerned can properly monitor, manage and control, and appropriately take into account in the assessment of its overall solvency needs. All assets, in particular those covering the MCR and the solvency capital requirement, must be invested in such a manner as to ensure the security, quality, liquidity and profitability of the portfolio as a whole. In addition, the localization of those assets must be such as to ensure their availability. Assets held to cover the technical provisions must also be invested in a manner appropriate to the nature and duration of the insurance and reinsurance liabilities. Those assets must be invested in the best interest of policyholders and beneficiaries.

The use of derivative instruments is permitted insofar as they contribute to a reduction of risks or facilitate efficient portfolio management. Investments and assets which are not admitted to trading on a regulated financial market must be kept to prudent levels. Assets must be properly diversified in such a way as to avoid excessive reliance on any particular asset, issuer or group of undertakings, or geographical area and excessive accumulation of risk in the portfolio as a whole. Investments in assets issued by the same issuer, or by issuers belonging to the same group, must not expose the insurance undertakings to excessive risk concentration.

Member States may not require insurance and reinsurance undertakings to invest in particular categories of assets. Member States may also not subject the investment decisions of an insurance or reinsurance undertaking or its investment manager to any kind of prior approval or systemic notification requirements.

APPENDIX A: STANDARD FORMULA SOLVENCY CAPITAL REQUIREMENT (SCR)

A.1   Calculation of the basic solvency capital requirement

The basic solvency capital requirement equals:

$$Basic\ SCR = \sqrt{\sum_{i,j} \sum Corr_{i,j} \times SCR_i \times SCR_j}$$

where SCR_i denotes the risk module i and SCR_j denotes the risk module j, and where 'i,j' means that the sum of the different terms should cover all possible combinations of i and j. In the calculation, SCR_i and SCR_j are replaced by the following:

$SCR_{non\text{-}life}$ denotes the non-life underwriting risk module;
SCR_{life} denotes the life underwriting risk module;
$SCR_{special\ health}$ denotes the special health underwriting risk module;
SCR_{market} denotes the market risk module;
$SCR_{default}$ denotes the counterparty default risk module.

The factor $Corr_{i,j}$ denotes the item set out in row i and in column j of the following correlation matrix:

Table A.1   Correlation matrix

i \ j	Market	Default	Life	Special health	Non-life
Market	1	0.25	0.25	0.25	0.25
Default	0.25	1	0.25	0.25	0.5
Life	0.25	0.25	1	0.25	0
Special health	0.25	0.25	0.25	1	0
Non-life	0.25	0.5	0	0	1

A.2   Calculation of the non-life underwriting risk module

The non-life underwriting risk module equals:

$$SCR_{non\text{-}life} = \sqrt{\sum_{i,j} Corr_{i,j} \times SCR_i \times SCR_j}$$

where SCR_i denotes the submodule i and SCR_j denotes the submodule j, and where 'i,j' means that the sum of the different terms should cover all possible combinations of i and j. In the calculation, SCR_i and SCR_j are replaced by the following:

$SCR_{nl\ premium\ and\ reserve}$ denotes the non-life premium and reserve risk submodule;

$SCR_{nl\ catastrophe}$ denotes the non-life catastrophe risk submodule.

A.3 Calculation of the life underwriting risk module

The life underwriting risk module equals:

$$SCR_{life} = \sqrt{\sum_{i,j} Corr_{i,j} \times SCR_i \times SCR_j}$$

where SCR_i denotes the submodule i and SCR_j denotes the submodule j, and where 'i,j' means that the sum of the different terms should cover all possible combinations of i and j. In the calculation, SCR_i and SCR_j are replaced by the following:

$SCR_{mortality}$ denotes the mortality risk submodule;

$SCR_{longevity}$ denotes the longevity risk submodule;

$SCR_{disability}$ denotes the disability – morbidity risk submodule;

$SCR_{life\ expense}$ denotes the life expense risk submodule;

$SCR_{revision}$ denotes the revision risk submodule;

SCR_{lapse} denotes the lapse risk submodule;

$SCR_{life\ catastrophe}$ denotes the life catastrophe risk submodule.

A.4 Calculation of the market risk module

The market risk module equals:

$$SCR_{market} = \sqrt{\sum_{i,j} Corr_{i,j} \times SCR_i \times SCR_j}$$

where SCR_i denotes the submodule i and SCR_j denotes the submodule j, and where 'i,j' means that the sum of the different terms should cover all possible combinations of i and j. In the calculation, SCR_i and SCR_j are replaced by the following:

$SCR_{interest\ rate}$ denotes the interest rate risk submodule;

SCR_{equity} denotes the equity risk submodule;

$SCR_{property}$ denotes the property risk submodule;

SCR_{spread} denotes the spread risk submodule;

$SCR_{concentration}$ denotes the market risk concentrations submodule;

$SCR_{currency}$ denotes the currency risk submodule.

Index

Abbey 219
Act of God bond 9
actuarial advisers 2, 180
adverse selection issues 24
AEGON 203, 211, 227
AEGON Scottish Equitable 219, 221, 222, 226
aggregate exceedance probability (AEP) 72, 73
AIG 121, 235
AIR Worldwide Corp. 70, 131
aleatory uncertainty 54
all or nothing payment 57
Allianz Blue Wings program 25
Allianz Global Corporate & Specialty 25
Allianz Re 21–7
Allianz Risk Transfer 12, 25
Ambac Assurance Corporation (Ambac) 223,
      296
AmerUS 219
amortization 227
arrangers 2
Atlas *see* SCOR
AURA RE 32–3
aviation risk 12, 118
Aviva 219
Avondale 219, 221, 222, 227, 295–8
AXA 29, 283–91
AXA Cessions 286
AXXX securitization 191

Bank of America case 334–5
Bank of Ireland (BoI) 296, 297
   Equity Core Tier I capital 295
Bank of Ireland Group 295
Bank of Ireland Life (BoI Life) 295, 298
Barclays 203
Barclays Life Assurance Company 252
Basel I 220

Basel II 220, 227
basis risk 16–17, 23, 24, 33, 36, 38, 49–63, 85,
      87, 88, 89, 90–3
   cat model error/shortcomings 55–6
   cat model input 63
   in catastrophic risk modelling 85, 87, 88, 89,
      90–3
   choice of index 62
   defining 56–7
   digital hedges 59
   dynamic 56
   key drivers 92–3
   minimizing 60–3
   modelled 90–2
   modelled index loss vs modelled company
      loss 56
   non-modelled 90
   one-tailed measures 60
   over-hedging 60–2
   positive 59–60
   pro rata hedges 58–9
   quantifying 58–60
   reset clauses 62–3
      changes in industry exposure database 62–3
      changes in model mechanics 63
   in SCOR 158–9
   sources of 55–6
   in Standard & Poor 76–82
   two-tailed measures 60
Bay Haven 57, 136
Bermudian insurers 21
binary hedges 57
Blue Coast Ltd 12, 25
Blue Fin Ltd 24–7
BNP 254
BNP Paribas 252, 269
bond terms 13

The Handbook of Insurance-Linked Securities   Edited by P. Barrieu and L. Albertini
© 2009 John Wiley & Sons, Ltd

Index compiled by Annette Musker

Printed and bound by CPI Group (UK) Ltd, Croydon, CR0 4YY

23/04/2025

14660970-0003